12-11-73

LOUISE HOMER
and
the Golden Age of Opera

LOUISE HOMER
and
the Golden Age
of Opera

by Anne Homer

William Morrow & Company, Inc.

New York   1974

BOOK DESIGN BY HELEN ROBERTS

PRINTED IN THE UNITED STATES OF AMERICA

1 2 3 4 5   78 77 76 75 74

Library of Congress Cataloging in Publication Data

Homer, Anne.
  Louise Homer and the golden age of opera.

  Bibliography: p.
  1. Homer, Louise Dilworth (Beatty) 1871-1947.
I. Title.
ML420.H6H6   782.1′092′4 [B]   73-11250
ISBN 0-688-00208-8

To my Mother and Father

LOUISE HOMER
and
the Golden Age of Opera

Chapter I

In Shadyside the seamstress, Maggie Johns, moved from one household to another in the community, doing the "sewing up." She was a small woman, with wispy hair and big dark eyes, and in her field she was an expert, for she could alter dresses so intricately designed, with bustles and stays, tucks, and bindings of ribbon or velvet, that any alteration must be considered a work of art. Most of the families she worked for were prosperous. There was usually a coachman and more than one carriage in the carriage house, the kitchens were lively with kitchen help and redolent with good food, and she could be sure she would cut only the best quality of serge and sew the finest taffeta.

When she worked for the minister's family one of the ladies of the parish paid her small wages. And she was in the Beatty home a good deal during the winter of 1870, making window drapes and upholstery for the new parsonage, and sewing a layette for the baby that was expected in the spring. It seemed to everyone a happy arrangement that the family would be settled in their new home some months before the baby's birth. But in December the brick parsonage, which was just being completed, mysteriously caught fire, and the damage was so severe that it couldn't be built up again until summer. Then, in the middle of that disastrous winter, there was an onset of illness, a kind of fever and quinsy sore throat that went right through the Beatty family.

Allie, a sturdy little girl of ten, had it first. Then eight-year-old Willie caught the fever, and a few weeks later Bessie, who was six that winter. The older children had all recovered when Mary, the youngest, came down with it. She was just four years old, a frail, appealing child who'd been guarded by her mother with such passionate anxiety that it had seemed, for a time, that she might escape the epidemic. But in March, Mary Beatty died, and for a time the mother was so frantic with grief that no one could reach her. Obscurely she blamed herself for the child's death, while at the same time believing it the will of God—for this was a contradiction, bleak and tormenting, that she lived with always. "It's His will," she would say, "He's taken her to be with Him. But if only I'd wrapped her more warmly when she went out to play!"

A few weeks later, on April 30, 1871, the new baby was born, and then her anxious friends could say, to comfort her, "Another little girl!" But the grieving mother could not accept such a facile substitution. And though she named the new baby daughter for her dear friend Louise Dilworth, nursed her and gave her the proper maternal care, there was a passiveness that was not, in the true sense, rejection, but which created, nevertheless, a kind of detachment. And so, when Maggie Johns came to the Beatty home, this new little one would seem, more than any of the others, a family child. Sometimes Allie and Bessie would have her out in the yard in her carriage, a willing accomplice in their games of make-believe. Occasionally her father would take her to his study while he wrote his sermons. And often she would be in the kitchen, tied into a big chair so she could safely watch the work and bustle. She seemed to belong to everyone, yet not quite to anyone, a situation so like Maggie Johns' own status that she understood it well, and whenever she came to the house she would say, at once, "Where's my pet?" then carry Louise off to the sewing room, to play with the empty spools and the darning egg.

Two years later another baby girl was born. Since, by this time, the poignant grief was in the past, it was Ella who became, like Mary, very close to their mother. Then, a year or so after that, there was a baby boy, Howard—doubly welcome because he was a second son. In the family circle, Louise was tucked into an

unremarkable slot—a middle child, loved by everyone but so
often overlooked that Maggie Johns felt for her something she
wasn't accustomed to—she felt needed. All the children in the
homes she worked for were fond of her, but this one really
needed her. And when she came to the Beatty house Louise
would fly into her arms with a look of confiding, adoring love
that she couldn't get over.

Much of the time they would spend together in the sewing
room on the third floor, where the little girl could play with her
toys or blocks in a cleared space under the dormer window,
while Maggie Johns sat in a small, green-tufted rocking chair,
threading a needle with lightning speed, then tucking another
into a pincushion shaped like a strawberry that she kept fastened to the bib of her black apron. Many times she told stories
of the past, creating for this child a kind of remembered radiance. But she also listened. Even in a big family—perhaps especially in a big family—a little girl needs someone who is never
too busy to stop and listen, and Maggie Johns could tell from a
child's voice if something important had happened. When she
heard Louise pounding up the stairs, and heard that portentous
note in her voice, "Look! Look what Papa gave me!" she didn't
just glance up from the cutting table. Instead, she would lay
down the scissors, put aside the cloth, and go to the window so
she could see better. One time the child had a most unusual
treasure—three pieces of silver-colored metal, shaped into a triangle. And when, after holding up the mysterious contraption,
she exclaimed dramatically, "Listen!" then hit the metal pieces
with a small wooden wand, the musical notes that vibrated
through the sewing room were high and resonant, like chimes.

That evening Maggie Johns was having a cup of tea in the
kitchen when she heard the clamor and jangle of music drift
through the house. She'd grown accustomed to this form of family
entertainment. ("There!" she'd exclaim to herself. "The Beattys
are at it again!") But this time she found an excuse to wander
into the front hall so she could have a clear view of the doings
in the parlor.

Dr. Beatty was playing the flute, and she thought he looked
very grand, with his beard and his somber clothes. His head was

slightly tilted and he had an air of great contentment; during the day he seemed such a driven man, with too many souls to save, and too many burdens, but the music seemed to rest him. Allie was at the piano, and Maggie Johns couldn't help admiring the ripples and chords and the firm way she held them to the tune. Allie, at fifteen, was so accomplished that she could even play the hymns for the Wednesday evening prayer service.

As usual Willie was clowning, manipulating the drums and cymbals with an exaggerated flourish. She was amused by Willie and impressed with Bessie, who played the recorder so nicely. But all the time she was watching Louise, who was sitting on a small stool in the center of the group, holding her triangle in one hand, her wand in the other, her eyes riveted on her father, waiting for a signal. She seemed to be frozen there, the concentration so total that Maggie Johns felt as though she were watching a small, attentive statue. They were all enjoying themselves, the music a cheerful, discordant din. But finally the proper signal was given, and then the little statue came vividly to life, to make the musical chimes vibrate, clear and bell-like, through the room. And though Maggie Johns had no brothers or sisters, no children of her own, she understood perfectly the breathless quality of that moment—the grave responsibility, the beating heart and finally the heady triumph at the end.

Often, after that, when she was staying with the Beattys, she would have a peek into the parlor so she could share that suspenseful interlude, waiting for a signal. But sometimes the wait seemed very long, and after a time she began to wonder if the triangle weren't too sweet and pallid an instrument, and the role too passive for such a buoyant temperament. Though Louise never seemed to tire of her triangle, Maggie Johns was glad, the next summer, when her father bought her a tambourine. One of the parishioners had given Willie some "bones," a contraption of wood and wire often used in minstrel shows. So now, while Willie manipulated his bones, and Allie pounded the piano, little Louise would prance about, jangling and thumping her tambourine. Around and around she'd whirl, her pinafore swirling above the tops of her shoes—wilder and wilder, more and more jubilant, around and around, her eyes brilliant with excitement, and no one minding the wild shaking and jangling of the tambourine, for they were all making their own share of noise.

Maggie Johns was enchanted, for she hadn't another family as changeable as this one—so pious and decorous on Sunday, but during the week so noisy, with all the children in the neighborhood racing in and out. It was a puzzle that added color to her life, for Maggie Johns was pious, too. She was an orphan, and when she spoke of "Our Dear Father" there was real love in her voice, but she had an inner sparkle that longed for expression. She had grown up, served her apprenticeship and learned her trade in the big quiet homes in Pittsburgh. Then the families she worked for—the Aikens, the Dilworths, the Negleys, the Renshaws, the Spencers—had moved out into the country to spare their children the temptations and crowding of city life. They'd built substantial homes and called their community Shadyside, but at first it had been lonesome, with the woods and fields and even cows, and only narrow dirt roads. It took a full hour to go to the center of Pittsburgh by carriage or horsecar, and that was a lot of traveling for church on Sunday morning.

They were all God-fearing families and well-to-do—mill owners and bankers and the like—and finally they'd decided to start a Presbyterian parish of their own. They already had a Sunday School for the littlest ones, and they'd begun holding services in the railroad station, with the Presbytery supplying a different minister each week. One who came was the Reverend William Trimble Beatty, pastor of a church in New Brunswick, New Jersey—a big man, tall and striking in appearance, but very simple in the words he spoke, easier to understand than any of the others.[1] In 1867 they'd issued a call and the Beattys had come to Shadyside and moved into an apartment over Schiller's drugstore. Maggie Johns had gone there to help them settle in (Mary had been just an infant, then, and Mrs. Beatty, though still in her twenties, had had four young ones to care for), and right away it seemed as though the whole community had come to life and drawn together in some way. There were only twenty-nine members in the congregation at first, but within a year there were

Dr. Beatty when he first
came to preach at the
Shadyside church.

Sarah Fulton Beatty—a
photograph taken at the time
of her marriage, in 1860.

over a hundred, and Maggie Johns had seen it all happen—the meetings at the Aikens' or the Dilworths', the fund-raising committees, the electing of Elders and Trustees.

First they'd built a small wooden church building on Westminster Place, and the very next year Dr. Beatty had wanted to start a college for young women. He was an educator and he thought the need was urgent, so they'd petitioned the Presbytery for a charter and built the Pennsylvania Female College up on the hill.[2] The year after that they'd built the parsonage, a pretty house, with a half porch in front, a big yard in back and a finished attic where Maggie Johns had her sewing room.

It almost seemed as though once they'd begun they couldn't stop, for Will Beatty had brought a kind of drama into their lives. Already people were coming from miles around to hear him preach, and the little church had become so crowded that even the private pews had to be freed. And so the members of the congregation had begun saying among themselves that the little wooden church building wasn't worthy of their distinguished pastor. Instead, they said, he should have a big stone church for his inspiring sermons, a fine tall edifice with a domed ceiling, a slate spire and a handsome illuminated organ.

And so it had started all over again—the carriages driving back and forth, the meetings in this or that house, the fund-raising committees. It hadn't been easy, for in 1873 there'd been a depression and many of the pledges couldn't be honored. But they'd managed, and on December 12, 1875, they'd had a dedication service—a beautiful, solemn occasion, with many prominent people attending.

The new Shadyside Presbyterian Church was made of a light-colored, pinkish-cream stone that had been quarried at a distance, and it had everything anyone could ask for—Sunday School rooms, offices, heavy oak stalls for the choir. Besides all this, in the north wing, under the organ loft, there was a fine big study for their pastor.

The minister was proud of the beautiful church they'd built so soon after the parish was founded. But Will Beatty was a complicated man, and one Sunday he'd preached them a somber sermon. The text was from Mark 11:13: "And seeing a fig tree from afar off having leaves, He came if haply He might find anything thereon; and when He came to it He found nothing but leaves." It was a curious text, not easy to understand, but as soon as he started speaking she'd had a kind of sinking feeling, for he'd spoken with an effort, that day, and told them that he'd been troubled by grave doubts. It was true, he said, that they'd built a fine edifice to honor their Heavenly Father, but had that been wholly their purpose? And did they worship in their proud new building with as much fervor and humility as they had in the crowded plainness of the first little church? Or were they distracted from true repentance by the maroon carpets, the scarlet velvet cushions and other fine adornments? His voice had become so quiet, then, that he'd seemed to be speaking to each one personally. They must be on guard, he'd told them soberly, they must take care, or their prayers would be lost among the handsome walnut rafters and would fade away into the pale blue tinting of the vaulted ceiling, for the leaves were not the fruit of the tree and hadn't Jesus said, "And no man eat fruit of thee hereafter"?

Usually, as soon as the benediction had been given, there would be a rustling and hum of conversation, the ladies, in their silk dresses and flowered or feathered hats, the men in their dark suits and high stiff collars, conversing discreetly among themselves. As a rule there was a kind of quiet animation after the long service was over, but that Sunday they'd filed out of the church almost in silence.

And was it true? Were they overly satisfied with all they had accomplished? In the last church report they'd written proudly of the "tender shoot" that had grown into a "sturdy sapling" and gave promise of becoming a "mighty tree." But though the congregation was growing in size, and the college had more students every year, Dr. Beatty seemed to feel responsible for all their spiritual needs, and that could be a heavy burden.

But fortunately Will Beatty had many sides to his nature, and anyone could see he was a contented man in his garden, tending his flowers, and exhilarated by the expeditions when he went off into the mountains with Mr. Dilworth, or his friend Dr. Gillespie, hunting game. And when he played the flute he was someone else altogether. It was astonishing, the transformation then, almost like a drama. No one she knew in Shadyside had ever seen a drama, for it was sinful to go to the theater and in most homes actresses, opera singers and other stage people weren't talked about openly. But Maggie Johns had her own dramatic flair (the very thing that made the stories she told the children in her families so enthralling), and she could imagine what it must be like when the curtain rose and you were suddenly surprised by a different world. And that's the way it was with Will Beatty when he played the flute, and with little Louise, too, whirling about, pounding her tambourine, her pinafore awry, her eyes blazing with contentment, as though the two of them shared some secret and the parlor at the parsonage had faded right away, revealing another, perhaps wilder, perhaps dreamier landscape, that no one else knew was there.

Chapter II

Louise was standing, as she often did, leaning against the piano while Allie and Bessie played duets. Both her sisters were taking lessons, and she wasn't supposed to interrupt when they were practicing, but Maggie Johns, glancing in at that moment, thought that the child looked ready to burst with longing. "Why don't you show her how, Allie?" she coaxed. "Go ahead, give Louise a lesson." So finally she sat on a piano bench and started to learn.

It seemed to Maggie Johns then that a kind of stillness settled over the child, an intentness, an isolation, though on the whole she appeared placid enough, for the deep reservoir of excitement didn't show. But it was there—her fingers on the keys, making a sequence, almost a tune, and something deep inside finally settling down, and something else soaring higher and still higher . . . "Papa, Allie is teaching me to play the piano!" She'd heard the front door slam, and his heavy tread in the hall, and ran at once to tell him what was happening. But he didn't seem to hear, though his fingers, restless and feverish, brushed the top of her head, making a wisp of feeling that shot right down into her toes. He was carrying the Pastor's Registry, a maroon-colored book with brown leather corners that he usually kept in his study —why was he bringing it home? And when he climbed the stairs, holding on to the rail, his head bent so that his beard seemed to lie heavy on his chest, what frightened her even more than the waxen color of his face was something no one else seemed to see—a going-away look, almost a peaceful look.

It wasn't the first time he'd been ill that winter, and after the doctor had gone, she tiptoed up to her mother's room and peeked in the door. And she wasn't surprised to find her mother kneeling in prayer beside the big bed. It was a familiar sight, the worn Bible close to the folded hands and the pretty head bent, the curly brown hair nicely arranged with combs and tortoise-shell pins, and shot through with strands of silver. This was the way it always was with her mother, the dark and the light, the laughter, spontaneous and silver-clear, like a young girl's, and the heaviness, brooding and resigned because all suffering was the reward of sin.

She turned finally to tiptoe away, not wanting to intrude, but her mother sensed her presence and called to her. Together they stood looking down at the new baby, Fulton, asleep in his cradle. When her father was ill he used a different room so as not to be disturbed by the baby, and now her mother rocked the cradle just a little. Then she answered the unasked question: "The doctor says your father has another fever, Louise, a touch of pleurisy, he calls it. But it's not too serious; he'll soon be well again."

Her mother's smile was so serene that it almost seemed that it was really God who'd told her that he'd soon be well again. But the next day, going to school, she still had a tight, funny feeling in her chest. With Ella she ran across the yard behind the church. On the left, as they ran, was the big fifty-foot shed where the congregation kept their horses and carriages during the church services; on the right was the back of the church itself, and the north wing where her father had his study. Many times she had seen him come through the deep, carved archway, carrying his silver-headed cane, his books for the courses at the college and often his Bible, a rusty black with gold-tipped pages. And soon he would be well again, but at school, when Miss Earnest taught them songs and asked her to sing a verse by herself, her voice wavered and petered off, and Miss Earnest said sharply: "Louise, are you paying attention?"

Louise Beatty in Shadyside, about four years old.

At the end of the day Miss Young gave her a small card with a gold star. All week she'd been working hard to win it, but now she didn't seem to care, and that was surprising, for the cards were important. When you had earned twelve little cards you were given a big card. And when you had three big cards you won a prize—a little book. There were two teachers in the school, and last year when she'd won a book they'd had a ceremony, and she'd marched up on the platform with the other lucky ones. But today she had this funny, gray feeling, as though it didn't really matter.

In the afternoon Bessie helped her, and they took four honey boxes with glass tops and arranged them in the garden behind the house. Under the honey boxes they planted seeds, deep in the ground. The long glass hotbeds that her father tended so carefully had row after row of small green shoots, and now she and Bessie had four miniature hotbeds of their own. It was such an interesting occupation that she began to feel a little better, and then she went into the house and discovered all that happiness. "Your father has received a very great honor," Maggie Johns said. She was having a cup of tea in the kitchen, the cook was stirring something on the stove and they both had a mysterious, eventful air: the kitchen shimmered with it, and so did the rest of the house. In the parlor there was company. Louise caught a glimpse of the black suits, the beards, the drift of tobacco smoke. Mr. Dilworth and Mr. Aiken and Mr. Spencer and Mr. Renshaw—she couldn't see them all, but she knew they were Elders and Members of the Board.

Willie was on the stairs, hanging about. "Papa has been elected a Delegate to the Presbyterian Council," he whispered. "It's an honor, and it means he'll go to Scotland in June. Then, after he's attended the meetings in Edinburgh and given a speech, he'll make a grand tour of Europe. The ocean voyage and the change of air will make him well," Willie said soberly. "When he comes home he'll never be sick again."

Willie was thirteen, a tall boy, witty and serious, and she believed him, because she always had. But her own brief joy soon shriveled into sadness, for she'd known last night that Papa was going away. She'd seen it in his face—that peaceful look, as though he'd already covered a great distance, leaving them behind.

For the parishioners of the Shadyside church their pastor's illness was something more than a recurrent anxiety, for he filled, now, a unique place in their lives. When he'd come to Shadyside, over ten years ago, they'd described Will Beatty, in their *Historical Sketch*, as "a towering man of unusual height, well over six feet, with an athlete's physique and bearing." He'd been in his early thirties then, vigorous, almost tireless, and so rugged that he'd never known a day of ill health. But though they'd done everything they could to care for him and his family, it was here in Shadyside that that rugged strength had seemed to wane, and they'd begun to see, in their pastor's face, a strange new pallor, an almost spiritual look of frail endurance.

But now, throughout the parish, there was an air of confidence, for it was well known that the most effective treatment for almost any kind of illness was a change of climate. To achieve such miracles seriously ill people traveled constantly—to Atlantic City and Saratoga, to the Adirondacks, to Michigan or Wisconsin, so that some magical properties, in the air, and perhaps in the water as well, could restore their health. A sojourn in

Scotland and a grand tour of Europe were certain to top all these as a cure for the months of illness. So they gave him many travel gifts—fine luggage, even one of the new cameras—and he sailed on June 22, 1877, on the S.S. *Devonia.* In the Pastor's Registry he noted that he preached a sermon on board ship July 1st. "The ship was rolling," he wrote, and the wind was "very high," which meant that he had to hold fast to the lectern, a tall, gaunt man, his beard blowing in the wind, his resonant, deep voice carrying even above the pounding of the waves. The text of his sermon that day was from John 14:19: "Then said Jesus unto them, yet a little while I am with you, and then I go unto Him that sent me."

Meanwhile, in Shadyside, the same devoted parishioners were hovering over the family he'd left behind, helping them prepare for the summer in Chester Valley. Every year they went for a month or more to stay with Sarah Beatty's relatives, Uncle and Auntie Fulton.[3] And this year, in Chester Valley, the letters from Europe were an important part of the summer. All day long they played in the fields and the barn, and then, in the evening, their mother would read to them about a journey down the Rhine, or a sermon their father had preached at Bellagio on Lake Como, or about the Jungfrau in Switzerland, or "shopping for bric-a-brac" in Paris. The lilt of the adventures was almost like a promise, and seemed to Louise part of the long summer days, when she could run through the fields, her skirts pinned up to give her more freedom, picking daisies and buttercups, and sometimes raspberries or huckleberries, for Auntie Fulton's cook to bake into pies.

She had always thought of Auntie and Uncle Fulton as grandparents, but with a difference, for they had taken Mama and her three brothers to live with them when their own parents had died in an epidemic. Uncle Fulton was pastor of the Chester Valley Presbyterian Church, and in the morning he and Auntie would sit at one end of the wide front porch, reading aloud from the Bible or one of their many religious tracts. They would all have their dinner at noon, at a table in front of the porch windows, and Auntie Fulton would keep a long-handled whisk beside her chair to brush away the flies that settled on the food.

The whisk had strands of different-colored paper, and all during dinner she would wave it gracefully, back and forth, back and forth, putting such elegance and dignity into each gesture that Louise would be hypnotized watching, for she thought Auntie Fulton looked very grand sitting at the foot of the long table, a lace cap pinned to her gray hair, a watch with a gold bow pinned to her dress, and in her hand the beautiful many-colored whisk.

Meanwhile, during dinner, Uncle Fulton would tell them lively stories about Jonah or the Ark or the Red Sea opening up. He knew how to turn a phrase, and had a quiet, puckish wit—sometimes, in this vein, he wrote small pamphlets or articles for the *Presbyterian Banner* on subjects like "Maternal Influence," "Faith in the Home," or "The Evils of Card Playing." His long, sparse beard straggled almost to his waist, he never went outside without his tall, rusty-brown silk hat, and with each of the children he shared a special private joke that he repeated many times during the summer.

The goldenrod was in the fields when Will Beatty came home. He preached twice in Uncle Fulton's church and then they all returned to Shadyside, where the congregation gave him a "welcome home" reception.⁴ For the first Sunday service the church was crowded, and as usual, as soon as they were settled in their pew, Louise looked quickly to see if the number of her favorite hymn, "Come Thou Almighty King," was in a plaque on the wall. She always did this, for when it was, and she knew she was going to hear her father sing those great descending arpeggios, the whole church service would become like a drama, wending its way toward a climax. All through the long prayers and the reading of the Scriptures she would be almost holding her breath waiting for the moment to come when she would hear his powerful deep voice go down, down, down, in such harmonious, measured tones that she would experience each time a familiar, almost overwhelming bliss.

Today the hymn was there and the sun streamed in cascades of color through the stained-glass windows, and when he stood, tall and bearded, in the front of the church to lead the singing, the vibrant tones, soaring above the congregation, were so reso-

The Shadyside Presbyterian Church in 1876. At the right is the first church building, and at the left, the parsonage where the Beattys lived.

A meeting of the Presbyterian General Assembly in Saratoga, in 1879. Will Beatty is seated at right.

nant, so dark and beautiful, that she shivered. The sermon followed, with a text from John 1:7: "And the light shineth in darkness; and the darkness comprehendeth it not." But suddenly, in the middle of the sermon, there was a break in his voice, and a moment later he put his hand to his throat, and announced, in a fading whisper, the final hymn.

After that everyone was very quiet, filing out of the church, and at home Louise heard her father say, sounding weak and tired, "My throat failed me." Feeling somewhat disoriented, she climbed the stairs to the sewing room. Maggie Johns wouldn't be sewing on the Sabbath, but she had come, as soon as they returned from Chester Valley, to get them ready for school, and now she was sitting in the green-tufted rocking chair with her Bible in her lap.

There was a new dress form in one corner of the room, recently made for Allie, and there were interesting things hanging about on pegs—nets and wools and lengths of colored ribbon. She didn't want to talk about what had happened in church; she just wanted to be there. But Maggie Johns started in at once. "You know, Pet," she said, in a strong, bright voice, "it isn't in the nature of a man like your father to have a restful time traveling around Europe. He'd want to see places and people and not miss a thing, and I imagine he just wore himself out. But as soon as he's had a bit of rest he'll be himself again."

She sounded so sure that the room brightened, and Maggie Johns was right, for in a few days he was well enough to return to his duties—teaching at the college, preaching in church, even holding an eloquent Week of Prayer. Nevertheless, there was a feeling of concern among the parishioners that heightened the excitement for the children at Thanksgiving, and many times during the week Louise watched from an upstairs window, with Ella and little Howard, while the carriages came and went and a great assortment of crates and boxes and packages was presented at their door. You weren't supposed to appear too eager, but almost enough provisions for half the winter were given them at Thanksgiving—sugar and tea, big bags of flour and corn meal, tubs of lard, barrels of apples, sacks of potatoes, sides of beef and, best of all, a wonderful variety of cakes and sweets and tins of biscuits. Suddenly the kitchen and larder were full of provisions, and when they bowed their heads at the table their father would thank the good Lord for the many blessings bestowed on them by a generous people.

That's the way it often was, when you were a parsonage child. There were contrasts, and even mysteries, like the one this year on Christmas morning, when her father took her to look behind the big chair in the corner . . . but really the mystery had started three days before that, when they'd all gone by horsecar to the center of Pittsburgh, to see the shops and the decorations. As usual, each of the older children had had a younger one to look out for, and she had been put in Willie's charge, an arrangement that suited them both, for there was a rapport between them, and they were exhilarated, wandering up Fifth Avenue, with all about the sleigh bells jingling, the women wrapped in furs, and the shop windows decorated with holly and pine.

But in the middle of the expedition she had discovered an object in the window of a luggage shop, a creation so unexpected and so fascinating that she fell into a trance, and Willie couldn't lure her away. It wasn't that she coveted the magical little thing, it was just that she wanted to keep on looking and looking, so absorbed and so hypnotized that anyone inside the luggage shop at that moment, a parishioner, perhaps, or a friend of her father's, might well have noticed, for she was a beguiling little figure in the bright red scarf and cap Auntie Fulton had knitted, her cheeks rosy from the snow and her hazel eyes brilliant with excitement and longing and fascination.

What Louise had discovered wasn't a toy, and it wasn't even for sale. But it was a beautifully contrived little thing, a miniature Saratoga trunk, made for display purposes—trimmed with real leather, studded with tiny brass nails and fitted inside with an array of trays and drawers. A little girl with many brothers and sisters might well dream about what it would be like to slide out the little drawers, all lined with tufted satin, and store away her treasures. . . .

So then it was Christmas, all the presents around the tree had been given out and her father was taking her to a big chair at the far end of the room. And when he pulled the chair aside it was like staring and staring at a rainbow, and suddenly discovering it in the grass at your feet—all the shifting colors, close enough to touch, right there in your own backyard. She was too stunned to move, so her father unbuckled the slender leather straps, then turned the tiny key in the lock. And inside one of the satin drawers he found a card that said: "To the little girl who looked in the window."

After that it was hard to believe that everything could go on just the same. In church the choir sang hymns quite calmly, "Adeste Fidelis," they sang, while outside the horses were covered with blankets and stamping their feet in the snow. And all during the service she kept returning in her thoughts to what had happened, for it wasn't only the miracle of the surprise—most of all it was the mysterious pleasure of being singled out from all the others in such an unusual way.

Who had given her the little trunk? She didn't know and often wondered, and then it was spring and all the hotbeds were planted with seedlings and her father bought a cow; with so many children, he said, it would be cheaper in the end. The cow was to be kept in the big shed behind the church, and the first morning, soon after dawn, she heard a rumpus in back of the house—the hoarse shouts of men, a scuffling and confusion. Quickly she dressed and ran outside, and what she saw astonished her, for the little farm boy who had come to take the cow to pasture wasn't wearing any shoes. His feet were bare in the dusty road and the dewy grass, and the rest of the scene was enchanting, too, for the cow didn't want to leave their yard. The boy tugged at her rope, and two men pushed from behind, but the stubborn cow refused to move and bellowed defiance, and seeing all this, she felt a most exhilarating enjoyment, but at the same time passionate envy, for never in her life had she been allowed outside without shoes. She had never even thought of such a thing, but she could imagine just how it would feel, how delicious, how desirable, to rub your toes through the cool, damp dirt and feel the wet grass against the soles of your feet.

Almost every morning after that she got up early and dressed as quickly as she could in the petticoats and thick stockings, the gown and over it the pinafore, pulling on, last of all, the thick-soled shoes. Then she would run outside to watch the cow being taken to pasture, noting each time, with awe and twinges of jealousy, the swaggering freedom of the farmer's boy. Though he wasn't much older than she was, every morning he could walk off down the road, whistling to himself and holding in his hand a leafy switch to brush away the flies.

The backyard was different so early in the morning, with the sun just touching the church spire, and one day, when he came to fetch the cow, the farm boy brought her a present—a big, very big armful of lilacs, almost more than she could hold, newly picked, fresh with dew and delicately fragrant. She was so delighted with the gift that often after that he would bring her a bouquet of lilacs, and after he had left she would stand for a while under the apple tree beside the swings. With the lilacs in her arms, encased in the familiar trappings of the proper parsonage child, the petticoats, the bodice, the thick, scratchy stockings, she would imagine what it would be like to run, barefoot and lightly clad, through the fields and into the woods—and perhaps all over the world! These startling thoughts had to be kept very secret, for she lived in a family where it was difficult to have any private thoughts at all—a gregarious family, good-natured, lively, talkative, witty, teasing, prying, and usually she loved the big gatherings and didn't mind the teasing and laughed harder than anyone at the jokes. But there were times when she shrank from the sociability, afraid to have them guess at the odd feelings she had, jubilant feelings, exhilarating but painfully secret, the way she felt now, holding the lilacs, with the sun just coming up, the clouds lacy and pink-colored, and everything so quiet.

Now that Louise was older her father had decided that the little Shadyside School on Westminster Place, with the two teachers, Miss Young and Miss Earnest, wasn't hard enough. So she was going, instead, to the public school in East Liberty, and every morning, instead of running behind the church, the way she used to, she walked a mile or so, carrying her lunch. In this bigger school she could hardly wait for classes to begin, for the day started off with a music drama which, though she could hardly have known it then, had many of the most stirring elements of opera—ritual, repetition, crescendo, climax—and a musical theme that set her heart to racing every time. The jubilant chord that the teacher played so dramatically on the piano was the overture, and at once they would all take their places and line up in the hall, the stamp, stamp of their feet keeping time to the music, like the clarion calls of the bugles in *Aida,* trumpeting the grandeur of the action to come. Then they would be off, winging their way to the rhythm of the music, through the halls and the classroom doors and down the proper aisles, all the high-buttoned shoes and swinging pinafores, the long black stockings, the knickers—stamp, stamp, marking time while they stood at their desks and the martial music soared to a crescendo. Then, with a crashing chord, they would all sit down.

Here in East Liberty, when they had assembly, two hundred voices would be singing in unison, soaring higher and higher and louder and louder, straight up to the rafters. And the way that made her feel was almost too blissful to comprehend.

One of the parishioners had promised to send Willie to college, for it was evident he had a brilliant mind. Indeed, it might seem that the Beatty family had an ideal situation, for they were loved and honored by the community, and the comfortable parsonage had become a kind of magnet for friends of all ages, a sunny, reassuring place for a child to grow up. But there was a shadow that darkened year by year—the increasing severity of their father's illness. In the Pastor's Registry he recorded the attacks as "malarial fever," "ague" or "pleurisy," though never by the true name, tuberculosis, and as soon as he'd recovered, he'd return to his duties—the preaching, the many meetings, the teaching at the college.

Meanwhile his devoted friends took him on invigorating trips to restore his failing health. There were expeditions to the Catskills, the Adirondacks and northern Minnesota. But though the trips were exhilarating, almost always they would be followed by another attack of illness, and there was some thought, now, that the study in the church might have played a part in the onset of this persistent malady. Through some whim of the architect's, it had been placed under the organ loft in the north wing, so that no sun came through the leaded windows to warm the double thickness of brick and stone. And it was during the winter months following the dedication of their fine new church that he'd first been troubled by the heavy colds, the lingering coughs and the mysterious attacks of fever.

He now no longer used the pastor's study in the winter, but the illnesses persisted. To his anxious friends it was evident that he needed a longer stay in a bracing climate, and finally they devised what seemed a most promising arrangement. It had been learned that Dr. Breed, pastor of the House of Hope Church in St. Paul, Minnesota, was taking a six months' leave of absence to travel abroad, and the plan was for Dr. Beatty to supply the pulpit in Dr. Breed's absence, then return to his own parish in the fall. This seemed to everyone an ideal solution, for the people of Shadyside didn't want to lose their pastor, and Will Beatty didn't want to lose his church, his home and the community of which he had become so much a part. This way there would be a brief separation—a suspension—six invigorating months in Minnesota. Then they would all be reunited again.

He left alone, at the end of April, to take over his new parish and find a home for his family, who would follow in June, when the children had finished school. But the trip was exhausting, and when he reached St. Paul, as he noted in the Registry, he was "feeling very badly—sick, chill, fever, miserable, miserable." The next day he preached for the first time in the House of Hope Church in St. Paul. And later the people of St. Paul would say of him, "In his ministrations he at once attracted attention by his noble presence and resonant sweet voice. He preached the whole gospel of Jesus Christ with earnest fervor and made, we believe, a lasting impression upon our hearts, our consciences and our lives. Daily associations revealed the beauty and simplicity of his life, and, in common with all who loved him, we felt we beheld in him the 'Perfect and upright man.' " [5]

Chapter III

In Shadyside they prepared, in June, for the trip to Minnesota, where their father had found a place for them on the outskirts of St. Paul. The house he had rented was Senator McClelland's summer home, and since it was intended for vacation use only, there was no indoor plumbing and no central heating. But it would do for a few months, and in the fall they'd be coming home again.

That was the theme of all the good-byes. We'll be back before school starts, they'd say, we'll be back in a few months. But when Louise climbed the stairs to the sewing room, where she'd spent so many important hours of her life, she varied this and said, "Maggie Johns, please come with us." And Maggie Johns, glancing up from her sewing, saw that the afternoon light was full on the child's face, and for a moment was silent, studying, and perhaps memorizing, the uniqueness of that young face—the serious brow, the saucy nose, the chin bravely lifted, the hazel eyes wide-spaced and troubled now, and all so harmoniously contrived that she felt a sudden tangle of loss and reassurance. "I can't go with you, Pet," she said. "But I'll be waiting. I'll be here when you come home."

They took with them many baskets of provisions, provided by the generous and troubled friends they were leaving behind. And at first it was a lively trip, with a change of trains and stations in Chicago, and a glimpse of the big steamers on the lake. But the rains were so heavy that the Mississippi overflowed its banks, and some miles beyond La Crosse they were caught in a flood. For three days the train was stranded and couldn't move.

The first day of the flood their mother had a few provisions left, which she doled out very carefully. But the next day they had nothing to eat at all, and then it became a weary time, with the hungry hours inching by, and the rain streaming in great gusts against the windows. When finally it began to get dark, Louise made an interesting discovery, for it seemed that when you were empty inside, you had such a light, busy feeling in your head that you couldn't go to sleep. Then suddenly there was a bustle at the end of the car, and a very tall man appeared, with a large box in his arms. The box was full of soda crackers and hunks of American cheese—crackers that were big and square and crisp, with a flat, plain taste, and cheese that had a deep rich tang. Her mother said she could have all she wanted, and nothing had ever tasted so good.

They were three days late arriving in St. Paul, and the ladies of the parish helped them settle in their new home. So now they had a temporary affiliation with a church, a rented house and hopes of a cure. But in spite of the bracing climate, the illness seemed no better, and in October Will Beatty recorded in the Registry, "Not able to preach for the present, very weak, no appetite, high pulse. Dr. Rough pronounced the right lung one half congested."

His Shadyside friends were so concerned that Mr. Dilworth came west and took him on a trip to Yellowstone Park, hoping he would benefit from that magical climate. And this time, at last, there was a change for the better. "Began to improve at once," he noted in the Registry; and a week later, "stronger every day . . . returned home October 24th vastly better and continued to improve."

Throughout November he preached at various churches in Minneapolis, and reported, on successive Sundays: "Feeling much better . . . better still . . . health still improving." But then there was a setback that was all but disregarded in the Registry, with just two small words: "so-so."

By this time it was December, and the time had come to take

stock. But the outlook wasn't promising, for the thermometer stood near zero, the house wasn't adequate for such weather and another baby would be born in the spring. However, the doctors said a return East was out of the question, so on December 23, 1880, just two days before Christmas, Will Beatty sat at his desk writing a letter of resignation to the congregation of the Shadyside Presbyterian Church:

> Through all the weary months of my sickness, I have been comforted with the assurance that those whom I have been proud to call "My own dear people" have been praying for me. . . . It may be that my work is substantially done. It should be thought no strange thing if a stewardship should be thus early brought to a close. . . . Once more it is my privilege to sign myself as I have been so proud of doing all these years, Very sincerely and affectionately, your pastor, William T. Beatty.

In Shadyside the letter was read aloud to the congregation at the morning service, and after a meeting of the Elders, a resolution was agreed on. Because there was no alternative, they would accept their pastor's resignation, but they would continue to pay him his salary of three thousand dollars a year.

This unusual gesture affected Will Beatty deeply, and on January 27, 1881, he wrote another letter to the congregation of the Shadyside church, expressing a restrained but pervasive sense of personal loss:

> I need not tell you how deeply I feel the bond that has bound us together. Much as I have thought of the possibility of having to give up my work and home in Shadyside, I failed utterly to anticipate the feeling of final and entire separation. After twenty years of experience in the pastoral office, I am lost without a church and people I can call my own. . . . With love and gratitude, yours, in the bonds of Christian Fellowship, William T. Beatty.

In this signature he had, of necessity, omitted the no longer applicable words: "your pastor." But within a week or two that office would be restored to him, and he would be spared the disorientation that had made him feel, when cut adrift from a pastorate, so unnatural and bereft.

Will Beatty's association with the Plymouth Congregational Church of Minneapolis had an element of the mystical. The parish had been without a permanent pastor for some time, when, by chance, on December 5th, he supplied the pulpit as guest speaker. The theme of the sermon, "Someone has been thinking of us," had struck a responsive chord and decades later the people of Minneapolis would be talking and writing of Dr. Beatty's first sermon at the Plymouth church.

In January they asked him to become their pastor, and he began commuting to Minneapolis for two services each Sunday. But the weather was bitterly cold (the coldest in the memory of many old-timers), and Senator McClelland's summer home was chill and uncomfortable. Nevertheless the family was stranded there, and for the younger ones it was exhilarating. Because the house was so uncomfortable, their mother kept them outdoors much of the time, carefully bundled against the cold. Afterward Louise would remember, of that first Minnesota winter, the snow men, the snow forts, the coasting, the skating, all within a cozy cocoon, a shelter so ingeniously devised from jackets and caps and scarves and woolen shawls that nothing would be showing but her eyes, and when she ran up the path toward home, in the vivid, sparkling air, the snow would be piled so high on either side that she couldn't even see over the top.

Auntie and Uncle Fulton came to live with them that winter. Because they felt they were needed, Uncle Fulton resigned from the Chester Valley church, and this gentle, elderly couple left their comfortable home, their community, their friends and all their other relatives, and made the long journey to St. Paul. Auntie Fulton always had come to stay when a new baby was expected, and now, more than ever, they didn't want to be too far away.

Will Beatty knew he hadn't long to live, and he wanted his family settled in their own home before he died. So he looked for a house to buy in Minneapolis, and was helped in this project by his good friend and lawyer, Mr. Charles Woods. Together they drove about in a gig, until he found a place he liked, in a residential area of the city. The house he chose, at 318 South Ninth

Street, had a comfortable front porch and intricate scrollwork on the overhang of the roof. He then sent to Shadyside for all their furniture and possessions, and on April 4th noted in the Registry: "Began to move." Three days later there was another brief notation in the Pastor's Registry: "Baby daughter born April 7th."

Meanwhile, under his pastorate the Plymouth church was experiencing a revival. There were scores of new communicants, and many from all over the city were flocking to hear him preach. The church that had, for so long, been without a minister, had suddenly come alive, and at the services there would be an atmosphere of rapt attentiveness, as though the people felt that they had, in some mysterious way, been singled out, and accorded what they would later call "the rare privilege" of experiencing "the final ministry of one who walked the borderline of Heaven."

He preached twice every Sunday, at a morning and evening service. And for the sermon on Sunday evening, June 12, 1881, he used a text from John 14:3: "In my Father's house are many mansions. . . . And if I go to prepare a place for you, I will come again and receive you unto myself; that where I am there ye may be also." This was the last sermon he would preach, and the recording of it is the final entry in the Pastor's Registry.

He didn't know it at the time, and after noting "five infants baptized" at the morning service, recorded his health that day as "so-so." But the next week he wasn't well enough to continue with his work, and after that there was a progressive decline.

By the middle of summer he was confined to his room, and his parishioners bought him an invalid chair, with a back that let down and a footrest that could be raised. Hour after hour he would sit by the window in his invalid chair, and sometimes when he was very tired he would say, "Where's my little Petty today?" And then Louise would come and very gently pat and smooth his hair and brow, to soothe away the great fatigue. He liked to have her there, for ten is an uncomplicated age, and comfortable to have around. But often she would become weary, for it wasn't easy for a ten-year-old to stand still for very long; such a subdued and monotonous task can be quite tiring, and it would be a great relief when he would finally say, "That's enough, you'd better run and play now." But the next day she'd be back again, and sometimes when she was standing by his invalid chair, fluttering her fingers so gently, he would open his eyes and see her face bent over his, see the dazzling health in the dark hazel eyes, the sweet natural way the hair sprang back from the brow, and think, "What is going to happen to my children when I am gone?"

Then it was winter, and the snow was swirling in gusts among the bare branches of the trees. One bitter cold day, when she was standing beside her father's invalid chair, gently stroking his brow, one of the parishioners came in—a very pretty lady, wrapped in furs. People were always bringing unusual things to tempt his failing appetite, and this lady had a mysterious covered dish, which she placed on a nearby table. Then she removed her gloves and shook hands, exclaiming, "Cold hands but a warm heart, Dr. Beatty!" And for Louise that moment was caught up into a kind of crystal web. "Cold hands but a warm heart"— what an interesting thing to say! What did it mean? And what was in the covered dish?

They all had a taste of the mysterious dish that evening for supper, and it turned out to be cold and sour and rather strange, but at the same time tantalizing and very good. It was called "potato salad," and they'd never had anything like it before. But her father was too tired to enjoy all the interesting things brought to tempt his appetite, and soon he wasn't even able to use the invalid chair. For some weeks he was in bed all the time, and the doctor was there a great deal, and the snow was melting and the birds were coming back. Then it was spring, and it seemed there were a great many people coming and going. But the end was very peaceful. "So quiet was his passage through death," it was said afterward, "that those who watched thought him dead when sleeping, and sleeping when he died." On Easter morning Auntie Fulton told the children, in her firm, gentle voice, "Your father is with his Heavenly Father—on this day of all days!"

Her mother wore a widow's veil, cascades of black chiffon framing sorrowful dark eyes and soft curling hair that had become suddenly dove-white in color. The contrast was sober but dramatic, and it had a certain effect on the wondering child. In just one winter her mother's hair had changed from the silver-dark she remembered, and she associated this transformation with her father's death. Her imagination was stirred, and though she could feel the sadness, she was not quite eleven, too young to fully understand the loss. Many people said, in awed voices, "On Easter morning! Just as the sun was rising!" which seemed to have a comforting sound, and so she listened, and wondered, and her first awareness of death had an element of lyric mysticism.

In the weeks that followed, her mother put her trust in the Lord and visited with Him in her prayers many times each day. But in spite of this, there was a growing undercurrent of uneasiness in the house, a feeling of crisis. How were they going to live? Where was the money coming from? What would happen to them now?

Mr. Woods and others of her father's friends came often to the house. There were long sober talks in the parlor and somewhat disjointed ones at the dinner table, and all this she thought of as a confusing scramble to find more money and spend less. Uncle Fulton had a pension; he and Auntie could pay fifteen dollars a week board, and her mother referred to this as a "blessing." There was also the life insurance, which was fifteen thousand dollars. But Mr. Woods warned that if they used what he called their "capital," they would soon be penniless. They had nothing else to look forward to, he said, so they must invest it in mortgages, and have at least an income of one thousand dollars a year, for there were many years ahead, and many young children to care for.

But that wasn't enough to live on, and now Louise was finding it uncomfortable being a middle child, for it seemed she could understand too much, or else not enough. The younger ones were unconcerned. The two little boys slid down the banisters, or wrestled in the yard, and were never still. The baby slept and played in her crib or her carriage on the porch, and even Ella was too young to worry. Meanwhile the older ones could take part in the solemn discussions. They advised and planned right along with the grown-ups, and one plan they had was for Allie to teach school. She was twenty-one now, and she'd had two years at the Pennsylvania Female College. But when she applied to the Board for a teaching position, she discovered that she was too late and the lists were already filled.

The disappointment when Allie learned there were no openings seemed to bring all the dismal worries into focus. Suddenly there was a feeling of alarm in the household, and when they sat at the dinner table she could see, in the faces of the grown-ups, a tangible feeling of dread.

However, it didn't last long. The very next week Willie got a job in a wholesale hardware company, and a few days later Allie was told that she could serve as a substitute in the schools and make at least a few dollars now and then. These developments might not bring in much money, but they were hopeful and they changed the outlook. At once there was a general feeling of relief and everything seemed to settle down.

The sunny corner of the porch was reserved for Auntie and Uncle Fulton, and as usual they were there every morning, reading aloud to each other—Uncle never without his tall, rusty-brown silk hat, Auntie in her bonnet and shawls. One of the parishioners offered to send Bessie to Miss Bennett's private school. And during the summer vacation Mrs. Gale invited Louise to visit for a month at Lake Minnetonka.

Marion Gale was a school friend, in the summer the Gales had a home right on the lake, and while Louise was visiting them she learned how to row a boat. She'd never had a chance before and at first she was very clumsy with the oars. But eleven is an age for working hard at skills, and gradually she improved until she could practically skim over the water, swift and light and easy, around and around and back and forth, hour after hour after hour. Mrs. Gale made rules, and she couldn't go out too far. But whenever a big steamer passed, moving slowly up the lake, she'd row out as far as she was allowed and wait for the waves to come in. Sometimes the people would wave from the decks, the gentlemen in their straw hats, the ladies with their many veils, and there she'd be, bobbing about in her own little boat, her braids looped up and tied with ribbons, the sailor collar of her dress awry and everything blissfully damp.

When she returned to Minneapolis, late in August, she was surprised to find huge piles of dirt heaped up in parallel rows on both sides of the road in front of their house. It seemed the city was installing water mains on Ninth Street, and Uncle complained about the inconvenience when he took his daily walk. But for the children on the block it was a bonanza, and they invented a whole series of games. During the fall months they made long tunnels in the towering mounds of mud and sand, then rolled marbles and small rubber balls through the winding tunnels and miniature roads. In the winter, when ice formed in the wide ditches, they skated right up the street. And in the spring, after the ice had melted and everything had turned to a sea of slush, they could make mud pies and cakes and even small castles, and bake them in the sun.

Many of the workmen were foreign, with heavy moustaches and guttural voices. They worked slowly, with pick and shovel, and the older people complained. But for the younger ones it was a novelty. And in New York, that same year, other workmen, skilled artisans, were completing the interior of an opera house, fashioning marble cupids for the drinking fountains, and graceful adornments for the proscenium arch. In May the sponsors of the new opera house drew lots for their private boxes, while in the eighth grade of the Minneapolis school the girls were playing skip-rope—holding up their skirts and jumping, jumping, while the rope flicked over their heads and under their feet, in a breath-less, rhythmic pattern.

Louise started high school the year she was thirteen, and since Minneapolis was a thriving, expanding city, the school was big and new, with over three hundred students thronging the halls, and classes in philosophy, botany, astronomy and many other un-familiar subjects. But for a while she was distracted by another milestone, for she was preparing now to join the church. She had long ago completed the study requirements, and could recite by heart the books of the Bible, the kings of Judah and Israel, the Shorter Catechism, the Fifty-Two Golden Texts and many chap-ters from the Old and the New Testament. But before she could be confirmed she must meet with the Elders and prove to them that she had had a "true conversion." For one who responded most naturally to feelings and instinct, and seldom thought to think about herself, this was a difficult assignment. But though it was confusing, she tried to comply, and every day spent some time in earnest "contemplation"—"searching her heart," ponder-

Louise in Minneapolis when she was thirteen.

ing her beliefs and trying to evaluate her "spiritual readiness."

Her mother took her to the church to meet with the Elders, and for this important occasion Louise had a new dress, her first really grown-up gown, cut down from one of Bessie's and made of dark red wool and matching satin trim, with a tight bodice, a slight bustle effect and an ankle-length skirt that looped gracefully in front, in pretty, natural folds. Her brown hair she wore in a fringe across her forehead and two tight braids that fell to her waist in back.

The Elders of the church were the business leaders of Minneapolis—tall, bearded men, impressively attired in somber black. She had to meet with them alone, and answer their questions in an atmosphere of dignified restraint. Afterward, when it was all over, the minister took her back to her mother, who was waiting at the front of the church, and said solemnly, "You would have been proud of your daughter, Mrs. Beatty." To this her mother replied at once, in her soft, bright voice, "I know, Louise is the most conscientious of all my children." And that was a tantalizing moment, one she would always remember—for what did "conscientious" mean? Already her mother and the minister were talking on and on about other things, and so the word had to stay there, poised in her thoughts, like a surprise, a gift, an interesting promise. In what way did she excel? Why was her mother proud? When they were finally walking home she asked as quickly as she could, "Mama, what does 'conscientious' mean?"

But even then she didn't really know, for the explanation was involved and so confusing that in the end it seemed to mean many different things. Which meant that when she thought about it afterward, as she often did, daydreaming and wondering about the future, she would remember, with a feeling of surprise, that in some mysterious way she was like her father.

As soon as she had joined the church she was allowed to go with the others to the Wednesday Evening Prayer Meetings. Always before she had had to stay behind while her sisters prepared for this weekly event—carefully firming the tortoise-shell pins in their pompadours, adding a bit of veiling or a new ribbon, smoothing on their gloves. It was a privilege to be allowed to go, too, and share in the activities, for on Wednesday evenings there would be a different feeling in the church, a kind of intimacy. The young men would notice the touches of finery, and at the end of the meeting might escort this or that young lady home. During the hymns and prayers glances would be exchanged, companionships deepened, flirtations begun. So this church service was not quite like any other, the flickering oil lamps, the furs and feathers and velvet flowers, the mingled voices, the complicated strands of communication making an eventful, crisscross pattern, so that the older people would look forward to the solemnity and quiet, while the younger ones could hardly wait for the festivities to begin.

Louise sang in the choir at the Prayer Meetings, and sometimes she sang duets with Bessie. But their voices didn't blend as naturally as they should, for while Bessie's rose easily to the high notes, hers would boom out too loud and heavy in the low tones, then fade away in the upper ones. It seemed that she had a clumsy voice, with a break in the middle and a downward drag, a peculiar voice, too big at times, and very hard to handle. But one evening Bessie suggested she sing the alto part, and when she did that her voice was under better control. She especially liked the harmonizing, and the lower range seemed more comfortable. Now, while Bessie's soprano carried the tune, her alto would accompany it, adding a new dimension, a kind of depth, like the haunting echo of a chord.

That spring of 1885, when she would soon be fourteen, the Ninth Street house was put up for sale. They'd always known that some day they'd return to Pennsylvania. But after their father's death their mother hadn't been able to face the great effort of such an undertaking, and so they'd stayed on, from year to year, going to school and growing up. But all their relatives were in the East, all their old friends. And there were those in the family, Auntie and Uncle Fulton especially, who were homesick.

Meanwhile the city of Minneapolis had engaged the great conductor and impresario, Theodore Thomas, to come in the spring for a music festival. This would be the community's first big cultural event, and at the moment Minneapolis had no hall big enough. But that was no problem for they were hastily building one, running up, almost overnight, a mammoth, barnlike structure, to be called Exposition Hall, with a decorative tower, a massive skylight and steep tiers of seats behind the stage for the thousand children in the chorus.

Louise was to be one of the children in that youthful chorus, and day after day they practiced their songs in school. Often they rehearsed more than they studied, so that they would be letter-perfect when the great man came, with his orchestra and soloists, to create, from the various amateur and professional groups, a festival of music. And the city fathers had chosen well, for Theodore Thomas was a potent force in the musical life of the country. A small man in stature, but dynamic, for some years he had been traveling about, strewing his pearls of music here and there over the barren countryside. A child prodigy, making his debut as a violinist at the age of five, Theodore Thomas had become a gifted conductor and a distinguished impresario. In the summers he would travel abroad, and usually engage one or two of the most celebrated opera singers to appear as his soloists. This year he had with him, in addition to a competent orchestra, the wonderful Hungarian soprano, Etelka Gerster.

At the music festival the morning rehearsal was almost as eventful as the performance, with many people attending to watch the thousand children, packed into the steep backless seats behind the stage, and the small, forceful man who would weld together the various groups into a finished whole. The weather was lowering that day, but the children were well scrubbed and well behaved. And later, at the performance that night, the girls in the chorus were all dressed in white, many with white hair ribbons, neatly arranged, usually at the back of the head, to fasten the looped coils or braids. The thick, menacing weather had exploded, by that time, into a violent storm, but everyone was so caught up in the excitement of the occasion that they hardly noticed the heavy rain drumming on the skylight, or the flashes of lightning and long rolling peals of thunder.

Exposition Hall was packed that night, for violent storms were frequent in Minnesota, and very few had thought of staying home. The atmosphere was festive, and even the heavy rain on the skylight couldn't drown out the eloquent strains of the orchestra, the birdlike trills of the lovely soprano and the high, caroling voices of the children when they sang their pretty tunes. They were singing, when it happened, one of their prettiest songs. Eagerly they were following the rise and fall of the baton, proud of their situation, overlooking all the thousands and thousands of people packed into the great hall, and on the stage the stately Swedish singer, her luxurious golden hair piled high and trimmed with jewels. They were singing one of their prettiest songs, and then suddenly they were in the midst of a great black bubble, with shards of glass raining down all around them, and everyone screaming, screaming, screaming.

The hideous black nightmare was so violent and so total that they could have no knowledge of what had happened—the decorative tower struck by lightning, the skylight shattered, and in that same instant a huge blast and suction of air, extinguishing all the gas lamps and plunging the huge hall into darkness. It was a nightmare they were trapped in, and they wouldn't know till later that the superintendent, trying to scale the roof to remove the burning timbers and prevent a fire, had been killed. But meanwhile their situation was perilous, for no one had thought of providing a safe way for the thousand children in the chorus to leave their seats. If they were to escape they would have to climb steep, narrow steps to the very top, squeeze through a narrow hall, and descend even narrower steps to the ground. The whole arrangement was so cramped that in the confusion many of the children panicked and jumped, trying frantically to find their parents. Others fought their way upward in a suffocating maze, then tumbled and trampled and pushed, arms and legs flailing, down those makeshift stairs to the ground.

Louise was one of those carried upward, in a stampede of screaming, clawing pandemonium. And eventually she escaped, her white dress and ribbon torn and streaked, the terror making a shaking and quivering that wouldn't seem to stop. But she tried to bottle it up—the panic of that great black bubble, with the lightning streaming in long flashes through the shattered hall, and the thunder rolling and blasting all around them while they fought and scrambled to escape.

And since it was bottled up and unexpressed, the next day the shock and terror popped out all over her body in bright red spots.

The doctor called this mysterious ailment a "nervous rash," and at home she was put to bed, petted and made much of. This was a rare experience, becoming, for a while, the center of attention in the family, and she was very proud of her "nervous rash," and all the comfort and concern.

But though the enjoyable rash soon went away, a suffocating fear of storms never did, and after that she all but lived in terror of an impending storm—watching the sky, hour after hour, day after day, for even the smallest cloud, unable to control the fear and apprehension. She'd heard people say that the mountains of the northwest attracted violent thunder storms, that this was "storm country," and she began to long for the time when they would go East again. She hadn't been sure before that she wanted to leave her friends and her school, but now this new tormenting dread overshadowed everything else.

In May they had an offer Mr. Woods approved of, and sold the house, and all the furniture. They planned to go first to Philadelphia to visit their mother's sister, Aunt Lizzie Steen—all but Willie, who would go halfway, then stay behind in Chicago. So it seemed that they were now in the midst of a great change. But Louise was still watching the sky for those threatening clouds; and when they finally boarded the train, she was secretly very relieved.

Chapter IV

The baby was four years old now. She'd been christened Marguerite, but she was always called Daisy, and in Philadelphia she was cuddled and admired by all the relatives who came for family visits. Uncle Samuel Fulton and his wife, Sarah, lived only a few blocks away, and they came often. Uncle Robert Fulton came from Bloomington with his wife, Lizzie, and Uncle Elisha Fulton, and his wife, Aunt Sarah-Elisha, came from New York, where they lived on Gramercy Park. Daisy was always dressed in white, Sarah Beatty wore only black; the two were seldom apart, and everyone made a great fuss over the little one who'd been born in the West.

They stayed in Aunt Lizzie Steen's house on Thirty-third Street, though there was hardly room enough, for it was just a slice of a house, made of brick and stone, with a high stoop and iron rails. Aunt Lizzie was their mother's only sister, and after such a long separation the talk was like a river of sound, bright and constant. Uncle Robert had a daughter, Roberta, who was Bessie's age and engaged to be married, and Uncle Samuel had a daughter, Lizzie, who was Allie's age. There were younger cousins, too, but the relative Louise watched for most eagerly was her Uncle Elisha Fulton.

He was her mother's oldest brother, president of something called the Cordage Trust. And though she rarely spoke to him,

from a distance she noticed everything—his great height, his
slight stoop, the drooping moustaches, the small cape he wore
attached to his greatcoat and, most of all, his courtly manners,
a certain wry gentleness that she found most fascinating. When
all the relatives were assembled it was Uncle Elisha she listened
to—respectfully, attentively, almost with a feeling of awe. He
had an aristocratic air, a certain patrician serenity that in her
imagination she associated with the mysterious future, with distant times and distant places, though she couldn't have known
then that when many years had passed, and he'd lost all his
wealth and was living out his life, with his ailing wife, in a house
so small that he had to stoop to enter his own front door, that
when all that had happened and he'd become very old, she'd
go often to see him, during a season of opera, and listen, just as
she did now—respectfully, attentively, still in awe of her Uncle
Elisha.

The heat was intense that summer. Just as their first winter in
Minnesota had been the coldest anyone had known, now people
were telling them that this was the hottest summer they'd ever
had in Philadelphia. Most of the children didn't mind the heat.
The two boys raced through the house and were as lively as ever
at the dinner table; and Allie was having reunions with her old
friends from Shadyside—hilarious visits back and forth. But for
their mother, who was trying to make order out of chaos, and
keep the young ones quiet so the older ones could have some
peace, the noise and heat and crowding were increasingly
oppressive.

She hadn't foreseen the difficulties of becoming a visiting
mother with such a big family of children. She had imagined
that she would take her time about deciding on a permanent
place to live, and meanwhile enjoy the hospitality of her relatives.
But now she longed for a place that would be cool and quiet,
with the children properly housed in their own home. And one
morning, when the heat was stifling, and the confusion at breakfast even worse than usual, she simply put on her hat and took a
trolley to the railway station.

She hadn't given much thought to a destination, but on the
trolley she decided to try Chester County. And at the station,

when the ticket agent inquired, "Where to?" she replied quickly and firmly, "To the end of the line," for it had occurred to her, in a moment of inspiration, that the farther she went from the city, the cooler and quieter it would become. The trip took an hour, the name of the town was West Chester, and as soon as she had alighted from the train she realized, gratefully, that she had been quite right in her surmise, for it was, indeed, unusually cool and quiet. There seemed to be many tall trees in the stately old town, casting deep shadows on the brick sidewalks, but hardly any people, and the quiet was so dense as to be almost dreamlike. Hopefully she inquired of the stationmaster, who found her an agent. And the agent found her a most desirable house at 411 South Walnut Street—a roomy, comfortable place, red brick with dark green trim, an ample porch in front and an ideal bed-sitting room for Auntie and Uncle Fulton—all for only half what she'd thought she'd have to pay, so she bought it.

This adventure astonished her family when she returned that evening, triumphant, to tell them that she had just bought a house with plenty of room for everyone. But when she described West Chester as such a cool, quiet, peaceful place, though Auntie Fulton nodded approvingly, the younger ones were somewhat doubtful, for they weren't the least bit interested in peace and quiet. What were the people like? they wanted to know. What was there to do? But what they were really asking about was the future. Would there be young men to escort them home from the Wednesday Evening Prayer Meetings, eligible young men to marry? Would there be playmates for the younger children, work for the boys when they were older, activities and opportunities? However, their mother had no ready answers, for she hadn't thought to inquire.

They moved early in September, to be ready for the start of school, and their arrival caused something of a stir. Indeed, the sudden descent of this large and varied family, more or less out of the blue, was in the nature of a seven-day-wonder in town, for they were the first new family to move into West Chester for more than a generation. People moved away, at times, and now and then they died, and then one of the big old houses would be boarded up and stand empty year after year. But no one ever moved in, for there was nothing to bring them. This accounted for the very low price their mother had had to pay for the comfortable home she'd bought for them on South Walnut Street.

However, it hadn't always been like that, for this was an historic old town. At one time there had been industry and a wealth of activity, and as a legacy from those early days there were now many big old homes, some three or even four stories high, gracing the quiet cobbled streets. Some had cupolas or towers, others ornate pillared doorways, and most of the houses were set well back on dense, dappled lawns, under immense old shade trees. Quite a few of these spacious homes were occupied by an elderly spinster, perhaps with an old bachelor brother, for it seemed people didn't marry very often in West Chester. A good many were Quakers, and their lives were orderly and muted—as quiet and subdued as the town itself.

After the lively bustle of Minneapolis, and the enjoyable confusion of Philadelphia, what Louise noticed first about her new hometown was the scarcity of children, though she thought of it the other way around, as "so many old people!" When her mother sent her on an errand to the store she would pass them on the street, strolling slowly and with dignity under the towering shade trees. A good many of them wore strange costumes, the men, long black coats and very tall black hats, the women, flowing dark skirts and black bonnets with wide stiff brims shaped into an oval by wide black satin ribbons that tied under the chin, making a long black tunnel out of which their faces peered. They talked in a strange way, too, using "thee" and "thou," their voices gentle and serene.

The Quaker costumes made the town seem like a foreign place, or perhaps a stage set. The streets were cobbled, the sidewalks brick, the trees immense. The houses seemed, to her, very big, too, and still and lifeless. While she hurried on her way to the store, her braids, tied with colored ribbons, bouncing on her shoulders, she would stare at the empty yards—where were the children?—and at the cobbled streets—only one buggy as far as she could see!

The high school was a disappointment at first, it was so small. In Minneapolis they'd had a big new building, with hundreds of young people thronging the halls and the auditorium. But here in West Chester the school wasn't much bigger than an ordinary house, and there were exactly fourteen students in her class, six boys and eight girls, including herself. And that wasn't easy to get used to—so few of them, sitting quietly at their desks, doing their lessons. But they had to work hard, for this was a Friends school, and the standards were high.

Competition was encouraged at the West Chester school. And each month they were given report cards beautifully printed on glossy squares of cream-colored cardboard, with decorations of neatly drawn scrolls. On the front of the report cards they received two marks for each subject, one in "scholarship," and one in "conduct." Demerits, failures and extra credits were also listed, and at the bottom the month's average was carefully computed. But the real leverage of the report cards was on the back, where the name of each student was listed, class by class, according to his scholastic standing. If you were at the top, everyone knew it, and if you were at the bottom, they knew that, too.

The people were friendly in West Chester; everywhere the Beattys received a warm and kindly welcome. And for the minister of the Presbyterian church their coming was a bonanza, for in one way or another they were all irresistibly involved—singing in the choir, helping out in the Sunday School, taking part in the entertainments and contributing to the Missionary Fund.

Louise sang alto in the choir, just as she had in Minneapolis. And in the fall of her junior year, when she was fifteen, Mr. Hermann Wyers, their music director, asked her if she would sing the title role in the cantata *Ruth the Moabitess*. And that was a dazzling surprise, for the cantata was an important annual event, with all the participants much older. Mr. Walter Brooke, a prominent lawyer, was singing Boaz; Bessie had the part of Naomi; Mrs. Hill was to be Orpah; Mr. Chalfant the First Reaper. She wasn't sure her mother would let her take part in such a grown-up event, but when Mr. Wyers made a formal request, her mother said she could if she wanted to, and of course she did.

They had rehearsals, and while she was studying at home, because she didn't like to interrupt the drama, she learned the whole cantata by heart. First she'd sing Ruth's song, "Why have I found grace?" then drop her voice for Boaz' melodious reply, "It hath been fully shown me." This was the first dramatic score she'd ever had, and she wasn't going to miss any of it.

But when she went with her mother to the church for the performance, they discovered that all the preparation and rehearsing had been wasted. A pall of disappointment hung about the place, some of the audience were already starting to leave and Mr. Wyers hurried to tell them what had happened. Mr. Walter Brooke, their Boaz, had gone to Harrisburg on legal business, he said, and missed the last train home. They'd just received a telegram, and without Boaz it would be impossible to give the cantata, which of course was foolish, since Louise could sing his part too, which she explained blithely and innocently, not realizing that it might seem odd to have a girl singing a man's role.

Though the music director was astonished, and quite doubtful, because there was no alternative that was the way it was done. Louise sang both parts; Boaz answered Ruth's questions in the same voice with which they had been sung. And Mr. Wyers, listening with some apprehension, was startled by the rich, vibrant music that flooded the hall. The powerful, soaring tones were badly handled, and sometimes off-key, but they had a resonance that tingled, and in the Boaz lines there was a plunging depth, a strange stirring quality that he'd never heard in any voice before. Unfortunately the singing was very imperfect. All through the cantata the child swooped and flatted, quavering perilously between the octaves. But he sympathized, for he understood the reason. Clearly this was an instrument too powerful for an untrained singer, heavy, clumsy, badly placed, but marvelous just the same.

The next day Mr. Hermann Wyers paid a formal call on Mrs. Beatty to urge that Louise have singing lessons as soon as it could be arranged. And since she happened to be there when they were talking, she heard the things he said. He called her voice beautiful, unusual and, especially, "very difficult." He said she had a voice that "badly needed training," and that was a profound relief, for she'd known all along that something was wrong. Too often, it seemed, her voice would take off on its own, booming out when she was striving for a quiet tone, soaring when it wasn't supposed to and acting up like a skittish horse that breaks into a gallop instead of an elegant walk, and won't obey the reins. But though she'd known something was wrong, she hadn't known before what she was going to do.

Her mother was only mildly impressed by the talk with Mr. Wyers, for her children were all talented, and she'd become so accustomed to these compliments that she'd evolved a series of phrases to counter them with, such as "pretty is as pretty does." However, that didn't matter, for Louise knew her mother couldn't afford to pay for singing lessons. Meanwhile that talk with Mr. Wyers was important, a kind of milestone, the start of a plan and a future for she knew now what she was going to do when she had finished high school. She was going to earn money and become independent. Then she would save enough so she could take singing lessons, and learn how to sing.

She had a best friend to share these momentous plans with— Sally Jefferis, whose father was their doctor in West Chester. With Sally there were long, absorbing discussions about various philo- sophical problems, such as whether it was proper to have a picnic on the Sabbath (Sally thought it was), or what you should do after the Wednesday Evening Prayer Meeting if two boys stepped up into the lamplight outside the church to request the privilege of escorting you home—should you accept the one who spoke first, or the one you liked best?

The two girls were inseparable, and during their junior year in high school they founded a club. Sally was president, Louise was secretary, and they had four "charter members." They called their club The Young Ladies Sorosis of West Chester, and the talented local printer devised, for their "constitution," a tiny booklet, just two inches square, tied with a yellow bow. In those miniature pages the rules of the club were set forth with business- like decorum. The meetings, it was recorded, were to be devoted "half to the standard authors, half to social intercourse," the dues were to be "five cents a time" and the refreshments "two in number."

Louise kept the constitution in the Saratoga trunk that had been given her all those years ago in Shadyside. Ever since then the little trunk, with its satin-lined drawers and compartments,

had protected, in a most satisfying way, all her personal treasures
and mementos—the fancy table napkins, autographed by friends,
the programs and invitations. Many of the invitations that she
saved had been prettily decorated, with ribbons or tiny bouquets
of imitation flowers, and one was handsomely engraved in gold.
This was for "The Annual Gathering of the Young Women's
Christian Temperance Association," that was held in the "G.A.R.
Rooms," and the thick creamy paper was embossed with purple
violets and tied with long streamers of white satin ribbons. She
kept her letters in the trunk, and her report cards and the auto-
graph book Mrs. Chesebro had given her in Minneapolis—a
beautiful little book, brown leather with gold trim. All her
Minneapolis friends had written in it, and on the first page, the
one with the most elaborate scrolls, her mother had inscribed two
verses from the Bible: " 'Thanks be unto God for his unspeakable
gift,'—'I gave my life for thee; what hast thou given for me?'
Mama."

In the spring Miss Spicer, the principal of the high school,
asked her if she would sing a solo at the Commencement exercises that year. But there was a problem, for she had no alto
songs except those devised for *Ruth the Moabitess*. So one Saturday afternoon they went together to Philadelphia to see if they
could find one at Bonar's music shop.

Bonar's was the biggest music store in the city—a firm that
published music as well as selling it—Louise had been there before with her sisters, and it was a fascinating place. The shop itself was dark and narrow, with long polished oak counters
extending far back into a mysterious interior. Many of the
instruments were hung on the walls—violins, violas, flutes. And
since the upper floors were rented out as teaching studios, often
you could hear faint echoes of music drifting about.

The sheet music was on the shelves behind the counters, and
when Miss Spicer asked for "low songs," the clerk brought a
collection of songs written for the deepest men's voices—baritone
and bass. But neither Miss Spicer nor her pupil knew the difference, so they leafed them through, then picked out three. And
at home, when she had studied them all, she chose the most dramatic for her solo—a song called "The Diver," with a tragic

story and such a stirring finale that when the poor diver drowned at the bottom of the sea her voice would descend down, down, down, almost to her toes.

She'd just had her sixteenth birthday, which meant that she could wear her hair up for the Commencement exercises. Her sisters helped with this transformation, and in part because of it she felt rather odd, sitting on the platform with Miss Spicer, watching the audience assemble—Mr. Wyers, Sally Jefferis, Auntie and Uncle Fulton, so many that she knew. But when her turn came on the program she poured her deepest feelings into her solo, stressing the drama, and singing with a voice almost too powerful for Horticultural Hall, a searing, weighted, doom-laden voice that startled her audience of parents and children. How pretty she looked, they said, but what a pity the poor diver had to suffer such pangs in his plunge to the bottom of the sea!

Bessie was married that summer to Joe Barrows, a young man from Massachusetts. They made their home in Arlington, just outside of Boston, but there was no real feeling of separation, for Bessie had her family in relays to visit, and came often to West Chester. Willie, however, was still in Chicago working for a firm called Goulds and Austin. He wasn't making much money, but he wrote long, witty letters home on company letter paper that was reassuringly impressive, with, at the top of the page, a lavish flower design, gracefully encircling pictures of the Seneca Falls factory and the Chicago office building, and all down the side a list of the goods they sold: "road graders, scrapers, wheel barrows, twine, corn shellers" and other important commodities. And from Minneapolis Mr. Woods sent a picture of the stained-glass window the congregation of the Plymouth Church had dedicated to Will Beatty. "The figure of the prophet is taken from an old painting by Perugino," he wrote, "and I think you will be able to imagine the beauty of the lilies which so fittingly commemorate his Easter-morning entrance to the Beautiful Land."

In September Sally Jefferis moved away, and senior year in high school is perhaps the worst time to lose your closest friend. Sally understood how she felt about the future, but almost everyone else took it for granted that when she had graduated, she would start teaching school. Her mother's friends, Auntie Fulton's, the parishioners in church, again and again they would ask, "When you are through high school, Louise, are you going to be a teacher?" She didn't know how to explain her strong resistance to this disposition of her life—to the plainness, the sameness, the careful constraint. She couldn't explain either, how she felt about her voice, for it was a complicated feeling, like, perhaps, someone with a flawed but valued possession, who longs to have it mended. So her plan was to make money, but in some more interesting and unusual way. Then she would take singing lessons, and all those mysterious troubles with her voice would disappear.

Meanwhile she had managed, all year, to stay at the top of the list on the report cards, and in the spring was named valedictorian of her class. That meant she would make a speech at Commencement, and also sing a solo, and since this was the first chance she had ever had to send out personal invitations, she sent them far and wide, and saved the interesting replies in her Saratoga trunk. Marion Gale wrote from Minneapolis about their high school, which had "grown so you'd hardly know it!" And Miss Harriett Dawson wrote from Shadyside, describing the vital flaws that had been discovered in the Presbyterian church. This news was so strange and unexpected that it almost seemed Will Beatty might have had a premonition when he'd preached his somber sermon, warning that "the leaves are not the fruit of the tree . . . ," though he couldn't have known, then, that the chill and damp in the pastor's study would lead, finally, to his death, or that the church itself would crumble within fifteen years, the victim of a builder who had cheated. "I suppose you know the fate of our beautiful church!" Miss Dawson wrote. "Not one stone to be left upon another. Cause, bad mortar. The vine, which has grown now to the top, looks so lovely that it seems almost wrong to take it down." [6]

As a subject for her Commencement address, Miss Spicer chose Mnemosyne—a topic so obscure that for weeks she wrote page after page, only to tear them all up in a rising fever of frustration. "I suppose," Willie wrote from Chicago, "that West Chester will become well acquainted with Mnemosyne before long, as I imagine he has been something of a stranger to them all these years." Willie thought Mnemosyne was a "he," but really it was a "she," the Goddess of Memory, Mother of the Muses by Zeus, a figure so nebulous that she kept floating right away, and the misery of trying to turn her into a speech all but ruined the spring.

But finally it was over, and there she was, through school and still with no idea what she was going to do next, and not too worried about it, either, for she was barely seventeen, with picnics and other diversions to occupy her time. Then, too, she still imagined, in a somewhat heedless fashion, that something would turn up—some interesting and enjoyable way of making a lot of money.

Quite often, in the summer, her mother would go to Indian Deep, taking a few of the children along, to stay in a comfortable farm boardinghouse near the Brandywine River. But Louise might not have been included this year if one of Allie's friends hadn't dropped out at the last moment. Allie was keeping company with a young man named Will Husted, a clerk at the bank, and it was with the thought of furthering their romance that she'd planned a small house party at Indian Deep, with her mother as chaperone. But just before they were to leave one of her guests couldn't go, so she'd said, "Why don't we take Louise instead?" and suddenly there she was, swimming, boating and riding bareback on the big farm horses.

Meanwhile her mother, as usual, was becoming acquainted with the other boarders, including, this summer, a young lady from Philadelphia who was spending her vacation at Indian Deep. And one day, after their noonday dinner, Louise just happened to be sitting idly on the steps, wondering what to do next, while her mother was talking on the porch to the visitor from Philadelphia. And that was how she happened to overhear a most unusual story.

Her mother had a way of making new friends and drawing people out. She might ask a few interested questions, in her soft, musical voice, but most of the time she would listen, with, occasionally, a flashing glance of sympathy and communication that could lead, at times, to the story of a life. Now, responding to such an attentive audience, the pretty visitor was describing her occupation. She worked in an office in Philadelphia, she said, as a "lady typewriter," and she made nine dollars a week.

It was that nine dollars, so lightly mentioned, that riveted the attention of the one sitting idly on the porch steps. Now she was no longer wondering what to do next, for it seemed that suddenly, in the midst of the humming of bees and insects, and the squeaky metronome of the rocking chairs, she was discovering a most unusual way of making money. But what was a lady typewriter?

Quite casually her mother's charming new friend told them all about it. She'd gone to the Lingle College of Shorthand and Typewriting in Philadelphia, she said. The course took three months, the charge was fifteen dollars a month, and the college taught their students to write on the new typewriting machines and take dictation using a method called "shorthand." The students must be able to write in this shorthand at a speed of not less than a hundred and twenty-five words a minute, and afterward the Lingle College awarded a Certificate of Commendation, and sometimes found positions for their graduates.

So there it was, in the midst of a lazy summer afternoon at Indian Deep—the occupation and the alternative she'd been hoping for. There was her future, all neatly laid out—complete and possible.

Chapter V

Now that she had a plan, she was anxious to get started, and early in September she went to stay with her Aunt Lizzie Steen in Philadelphia. If the college was really the way the young lady in Indian Deep had described it, her mother was going to pay the tuition. But she wanted to be earning something while she was studying, and a church choir seemed the most likely way. So early the next morning she started out from Aunt Lizzie's to walk across the city and inquire about a choir position.

She was going for advice to Bonar's music shop, since it was the only place she knew. She was wearing her Sunday suit for this important interview, her Sunday shoes and a few adornments to stress maturity—her gloves, of course, a silk scarf and new satin flowers on her hat. At Bonar's she told the clerk that she would like to speak to Mr. Bonar. And when, looking somewhat doubtful, he had disappeared into the back of the shop, she waited near the front, where the instruments were hung on walls and the music piled, so tantalizingly, on shelves. But it seemed a long wait, with the sun drifting through the windows onto the dim shapes of the spinet pianos, under their coverings of green felt.

Mr. W. H. Bonar, at work in his office, was surprised when his clerk told him that a young lady wished to speak to him, for he rarely waited on customers. His firm was the most important of its kind in the city, and he devoted most of his time to the publishing of music. He was a youngish man, a bachelor in his middle thirties, and for some years had served as organist and choir director for the Spruce Street Presbyterian Church.

Though he didn't like being disturbed, finally, with some reluctance, he went to the front of the store. And there, the young lady who had been waiting for him explained her errand. She spoke too hurriedly, though with an air of confidence, and it was apparent that she had rehearsed her little speech many times. Her name was Miss Beatty, she said, she had an alto voice and had been singing in the West Chester choir. Now she was planning to study in the city, and was hoping he would direct her to a choir position.

Mr. Bonar was surprised. Such a request from a stranger was most unusual, and the way she was looking at him, so seriously and so confidently, was enough to make any man uneasy. Unfortunately, it seemed she knew nothing about such matters, so he had to explain regretfully that in Philadelphia contracts for choir positions were made in the spring. Since it was now September, it would be too late to apply this year, for all the places would be filled.

"Oh, I never thought of that!"

It seemed to Mr. Bonar, caught up unexpectedly in this dilemma, that the visible fading of such confidence, indeed, such radiance, altered even the familiar contours of his shop. Did the sun still filter through the windows, brightening the instruments that adorned the walls? Was there any brightness at all when a man was confronted with such dismay? Perhaps she was too young to dissemble, or perhaps she had been, at first, too naïvely confident, for now the gray eyes seemed suddenly darker, the expression, the beautiful mouth, especially, quite sorrowful and the pretty adornments she wore, the silk scarf and satin flowers, a kind of mockery. In fact the contrast was so unendurable that he heard himself say hurriedly that he was, himself, organist for the Spruce Street Presbyterian Church, and if she cared to she could sing for them next Sunday on trial, though they had no permanent pastor, and of course no commitments were possible . . .

The radiance, returned, was even more dazzling than before. Warmly she thanked him for the opportunity, promised to come promptly on Friday for the rehearsal, then sailed out of the shop, evidently intent on some other errand. She had a pretty way of walking, light and airy. There was an exhilarating grace in the way she walked, and it was only after she had left that he remembered that he had forgotten to ask her to sing.

From the music shop she walked another mile to the Lingle College of Shorthand and Typewriting. There she was immensely relieved to find that everything was just as the young lady in Indian Deep had described it. The tuition was fifteen dollars a month, they told her, the course took three months and she could start the next day.

Then she walked back across the city to Aunt Lizzie's, this time all but wafted on her way, to write her mother to send the money for the tuition, and to start a new life.

The Lingle College had been established to meet the demands of the new typewriting machines, for these innovations had only recently been perfected to the point where they could write faster than the pen. But though the college was new and still experimental, the building was old—an abandoned, fading mansion, with dark walls, flickering gaslight and a good deal of stained glass. Here the incipient Kitty Foyles labored to master their craft. With their ink-stained fingers, their pretty pompadours and stiffly starched shirtwaists, they didn't think of themselves as pioneers—but they were. The new writing machines had created a demand for young ladies in the field of business, and those who responded had an adventurous spirit. For one reason or another they were seeking independence, armed with a notebook filled with loops and squiggles known as "shorthand," and a puzzling technique called "the touch system." Instruction at the college was on an individual basis, the hours were long, and afterward you took your notebook home and worked more hours memorizing those baffling symbols. Aunt Lizzie didn't know what to make of it, and neither did Uncle John Steen. But Louise worked so ardently that soon she had enlisted their help and they were giving dictation, and even timing it.

On Sunday she sang in the Spruce Street church, and Mr.

Bonar, at the organ, heard the organlike tones of a new voice.
He had never heard a voice like it, and that evening he wrote a
letter to Miss Beatty, composing it carefully and hedging it about
with escape clauses, so she wouldn't be too hopeful, and he
wouldn't be too committed. However, this precaution was useless,
for at Aunt Lizzie's the letter was joyfully received, and all the
hedges faded away in a dazzling mist of dollar signs—three in a
row . . .

> Miss Beatty, If you care to enter into an engagement for the
> remaining Sundays of the month I will be glad to have you
> sing for us, and it may result in your securing a permanent
> position with us. Still I am not fully authorized to hold out
> a permanent inducement to you, for the reason that there
> can be nothing of a decisive character until a minister has
> been secured. We can offer you "three dollars" for each
> Sunday of this month, two services a day. Please let me
> know by return post if you wish to engage on these terms.
> Yours truly, W. H. Bonar.

The Spruce Street Presbyterian Church was one of the oldest
in the city, a dignified house of worship, touched with the patina
of age and friendliness. For years members of the same families
had been attending, and they were comfortable with the simplicity, and the familiar routine of the services. Music was important in all the churches of the city, and choir singers usually
received salaries and contracts—for this was almost the only
music many people heard.

They had their rehearsals on Friday evenings, and when she
was trying to scale her voice down to the quiet legato singing,
she would think hopefully of the singing lessons she would have
as soon as she could afford them. Her peculiar voice made choir
singing difficult, for in a sense it was like trying to play a piano
with only a forte tone, or perhaps one with a pedal permanently
stuck, so that the lyric definitions would be blurred by the strange
resonance. But now, when she stood in the choir stalls on Sunday,
trying to stem the too powerful and vibrant tones that rolled out
unwittingly, to cloud the mood and intent of the anthems, she
would think of the singing lessons and the control she would have

then, all the troubles finally ended with her flawed and difficult voice.

Meanwhile she was working hard at the Lingle College, and at the end of the three months received a certificate, dated December 19, 1888, stating that, "The Bearer, Louise Beatty, has completed a thorough course of instruction in this Institution, and in the judgment of the Principal, is qualified for ordinary office work as a Shorthand and Typewriter Operator." Under his signature the principal of the college, Mr. J. M. Pringle, had added a note of "special mention." "Miss B.," he wrote, "takes shorthand at a speed of about 125 words a minute and is a neat and accurate operator on the typewriter. The bearer is exceptionally quick and particularly well fitted for the duties of a correspondent."

Soon after Christmas Louise found a position in West Chester with a lawyer, Mr. Talbot, at a salary of three dollars a week, and commuted to Philadelphia to sing in the Spruce Street choir. And since she was finally earning money, she tried to keep track of every penny. "On hand," she would write in a small red leather notebook, "$1.63—carfare .10, carfare .05—on hand $1.48— ring .40—on hand, $1.08—stamps .04, candy .10, Missionary Soc., .30—on hand .64—hack .10, Mr. Talbot $3.00—on hand $3.54."

In March her employer raised her salary to four dollars. But she wanted to earn as much money as she could, and when she heard of a position in Philadelphia that paid twice as much, she applied and was accepted. Mr. Talbot was then most understanding, and gave her a farewell bonus of five dollars.

The firm in Philadelphia dealt in steel and steel products, and Louise worked for one of the executives, a Mr. Smith. There were a number of lady employees, and when they sat at their desks they wore quite elegant hats, trimmed with feathers, bits of veiling, glittering aigrettes or silk and satin flowers. So that she would feel more at home in her new surroundings she bought an "office hat, $2.62," but she was also saving for a summer vacation and in August was able to pay, out of her own pocket, thirteen dollars for two weeks in Indian Deep.

So once again she was back on the Brandywine, embracing

Louise Beatty beside the Brandywine.

the summer—riding bareback on the big farm horses, and with the others laughing wildly as they galloped across the fields. But this summer there was a difference, for now she was eighteen, and had a most satisfying profession.

In October Mr. Smith raised her salary to twelve dollars, and she was able to pay her mother five dollars a week board. But the commuting was so difficult, once the snows had started, that she realized that if she was to continue, she would have to move to Philadelphia. It was Aunt Lizzie who found an ideal solution and a perfect chaperone—her good friend Mrs. Marshall, who lived with her husband and daughter in a comfortable boarding-house at 1314 Arch Street. The charge at the boardinghouse was eight dollars a week for room, board and "evening entertain-ment"; the location was near both the firm where she worked and the Spruce Street church, and Mrs. Marshall would be her chaperone.

After moving in she rented a piano for fifteen dollars, and bought a muff for four dollars (leaving an "on hand" balance

of $7.54). Next she went to Bonar's and asked Mr. Bonar if he
would recommend a singing teacher—one who could give her
lessons on Saturday afternoon. And what happened then was like
a drama spiraling so soon to a climax that you are left breathless
with the wonder of it. "Why, Miss Beatty," Mr. Bonar exclaimed,
"I know the very one! Miss Abbie Whinnery has her studio right
in this building, and she's the finest teacher in Philadelphia!"
Then, almost before she knew what was happening, she was
being wafted upstairs, to meet a woman with a kind, generous
voice and a wonderfully warm personality—a teacher so inspiring that she fell in love with her at that first meeting, and remained devoted to her all her life.

Perhaps she had been made unusually susceptible because
she'd been working alone so many years, first at the piano, then
at the singing, with no one to tell her what to do. Now she was
passionately anxious to listen and to learn, and Miss Whinnery
had an air of firmness and authority that inspired confidence. She
told her new pupil that her voice was beautiful, and she had only
to master the basic techniques of breath control, placement and
projection. Then she gave her a few exercises to start with, and
they arranged for a lesson every Saturday afternoon. Mr. Bonar
was delighted. And a few months later, when Sally Jefferis came
from Chester for a visit, Louise could show her old school friend
the exercises she had already learned—sitting at the piano and
running through the scales and arpeggios for an admiring audience. Sally had always been sympathetic about this trouble with
her voice, and she could show her, too, how she was supposed to
stand, breathing with a proper rhythm, deep and slow. There
hadn't been any miracles yet, she had to confess, but Miss Whinnery said that was because her voice was too heavy and pitched
too low, and progress was bound to be slow. Miss Whinnery,
Miss Whinnery—the hours were long at the office, and there were
many letters and reports to type, but at the end of every week
there was Saturday afternoon.

On many weekends, and always in the summer, she returned
to West Chester. Allie was married to Will Husted now, and they
were living in a house just a few blocks from 411 South Walnut
Street. And in the spring Uncle Fulton died. But his death had

been expected, and for Auntie it was only a temporary parting; surrounded by their familiar treasures, comforted by memories, she carefully preserved his letters, his writings and all the books they'd read aloud together over the years.

There was a cadence to life in West Chester, and a certain cadence to life in Philadelphia, too. But then one February, when Louise was nineteen and had been working almost two years for Mr. Smith, there was an unexpected development that started with a mysterious letter from her cousin Nellie Fulton. Nellie was a good deal older, and they'd never corresponded, so when she carried the letter into the parlor, where the boardinghouse ladies were sitting about, waiting for supper to be served, and exclaimed, mystified, "What can Nellie want!" she was including them all in a certain interlude of suspense, and it was this that so endeared her to the other boarders. Many of them were former schoolteachers, elderly spinsters or widows, living alone in retirement. Since she so naturally and artlessly shared her life with them, she had, at the Arch Street boardinghouse, half a dozen or more attentive chaperones.

Now it was a mystifying letter, and they were all wondering what it could be. But when she tore open the envelope she found inside—a blank sheet of paper! But not quite, for pinned to the top, with a black-headed pin, was a tiny newspaper clipping. How like Nellie! Not a line of greeting or explanation! But Nellie was a great newspaper reader, even to the smallest classified advertisements, and that's what this was—a "help-wanted" advertisement, which she read aloud in a voice that rose and fell with astonishment, conveying nothing so much as total disbelief. "Wanted," she read, "a secretary for a fine private school; two months vacation; hours 8:30 to 2 o'clock; salary $800. a year. Apply to Mr. Richard Jones, William Penn Charter School."

The implications contained in that small paragraph were dazzling, yet there it all was, plainly stated—a fine salary, much more than she was making now, a long summer vacation and, most astonishing of all, those extraordinary hours: "8:30 to 2 o'clock." Of course it was a position every secretary would covet, which was why Nellie had sent it to her. Nevertheless, Louise started composing a letter at once, with the help of many willing advisers, and while they worked the boardinghouse parlor, with the fringed lamps and dark table covers, the careful grouping of rocking chairs and sofas—all the familiar furnishings—became part of a conspiracy, for who ever heard of a secretary who could leave the office at two in the afternoon, free to visit friends, stroll through the streets, shop in the stores, practice her music, do as she pleased? It was, indeed, an impossible opportunity, but she posted the letter that evening, then waited, without much hope, for a reply; and finally it came, a long questionnaire to fill out, listing her experience and her qualifications. When that was done the suspense deepened, for now there was a measure of hope, perhaps too much, as well as apprehension, but one evening, when she returned from work, there was a note asking her to call for an interview, and after the interview she was accepted.

Throughout all this she had consulted with her employer, Mr. Smith, and he had responded with a generous letter of recommendation, addressed to Mr. Richard M. Jones, Philadelphia, Penn., stating that:

> Miss Beatty has been with us nearly two years, and we can testify heartily to her thorough competency, ability, willingness and general usefulness—in addition to her excellent ability as stenographer and type-writer. We are exceedingly sorry to lose her and we feel it will be almost impossible to fill her place.
>
> Were it but a question of money, we would gladly make that up to her, but you can readily understand, in our business, that it is impossible for us to compete with you, both in the daily hours and in the two months' summer vacation. It is on this account that we have advised her accepting your offer, and in securing her, we feel you have secured a prize.

The Penn Charter School was one of the oldest private schools in the country, and therefore it could indulge, complacently, in the usual plain decor of such establishments—the scuffed floors, fading walls and spartan aspects of an institution with a distinguished reputation, where only the most select young men were accepted. Louise had her desk in a small room adjoining the main hall so that she could more easily attend to one of her duties, which was to "preside"—show new parents through the school, greet relatives when they came to visit, help the new boys settle in. While she worked, typing letters or making out bills, she would hear, at the end of each period, the thunderous echo of many feet tramping through the halls, and sometimes she would hear her name and look up to see a young man waiting to ask a question.

Then she would listen, with an air of great composure, while he asked if he might go to the basement, and after consulting a chart, would either grant permission or withhold it, maintaining all the while an attitude of demure efficiency, and repressing, with the skill of an actress, the smiles, the blushes, or even a tantalizing impulse to laugh. Nevertheless this aspect of her duties seemed to her most comical, for many of the students were older than she was, grown-up young men, quite worldly in appearance, yet all day long they must come to her for permission to go to the washroom in the basement, where only one student was allowed at a time.

When Mr. Jones, the headmaster, wanted to dictate a letter or transact some business, he would send for her to come to his office. He was a heavyset man, bearded, pompous, perhaps a bit vain, and his office, designed to impress parents and depress boys, was a spacious, ponderously furnished room, with paneled walls and dark shelves filled with books. Here she would sit, notebook in hand, taking dictation and attending to various assignments. One of her duties was to keep the school accounts and balance the checkbooks, and at the end of the morning she would send the janitor, a tall, gray-haired, colored gentleman, to the bank with the day's receipts. All this gave her a pleasant feeling of responsibility, but one day, when the janitor returned with seven cents, saying the figures had been wrong, and Mr. Jones assumed that she had juggled the books to make them agree, she was incensed and vividly angry. The fact that he had so readily assigned to her the role of a cheat was intolerable, and in a fury she slammed on her hat, flew to the bank, talked to an astonished vice-president, discovered that they had mistaken a three-cent piece for a ten-cent piece, then returned to the school, vindicated. Mr. Jones was so amused by this little episode that for several days afterward he would laugh, in a soundless, chuckling way he had, every time he passed through her office. And though he made no apologies, he said that it was the first time he'd ever known the bank to be caught in a mistake.

There were many things Louise enjoyed about her new situation. Every day, at noon, a delicious lunch was brought to her desk—an attention which seemed most luxurious; and she liked the variety of the tasks, the friendships with the young teachers, the youthful atmosphere. But best of all she liked the hour when she could leave, and when that moment came she would be poised, like a sprinter waiting for the signal, ready, at the proper instant, to snatch up her muff and sail out the door.

When she'd worked for the steel company it had been dark before she could finally return home. Now it was the early afternoon, but though she had many free hours to devote to her singing, her voice didn't seem to have improved, and that was a great disappointment. She had been confident that as soon as she started lessons, the troubles would begin to go away. But though she still loved Miss Whinnery as she had from the first, all the exercises and instruction were only making matters worse.

This was a great puzzle, and lately there had been unhappy discussions with Mr. Bonar and Miss Whinnery. Should she consider a change? Recently a singing teacher had returned to Philadelphia after a year of study in Paris. Would the French Method be better for her voice? Mr. Bonar thought it might, and so did Miss Whinnery, for she was just as discouraged as her pupil by the futility of her teaching methods. Never, in all her years of experience, had she had a pupil who worked so hard and accomplished so little. And so the lessons had become, for Miss Whinnery, an ordeal, for it was painful to watch such an ardent, hopeful student stand there at the piano—so enchanting to look at, so serious, so attentive—and try in vain to master a simple, routine exercise that was quite easy for everyone else. After more than a year of study this conscientious student couldn't even sing a simple arpeggio the way it was supposed to be sung—expanding to a crescendo, then contracting harmoniously to a diminuendo. For some unaccountable reason, her voice didn't respond as it should, yet again and again a single note would fill the studio with such radiance and power that it was hard to believe such a beautiful instrument could be so faulty.

Miss Whinnery, unhappy with the situation, urged her pupil to try the French Method. Mr. Bonar agreed, and in April she started lessons with Miss Anna Groff, who had a studio just a few blocks from the Arch Street boardinghouse.

Mr. Jones seemed more than satisfied with her work, and at the end of the year gave her another contract, with a raise in salary to nine hundred dollars a year, while the Spruce Street church gave her a choir contract for three hundred dollars a year. So after an enjoyable vacation in West Chester and Indian Deep, she could return to quite comfortable circumstances in Philadelphia. And in October, that year when she was twenty, she received an invitation to a football game from John Waddell, a young man she knew only slightly, who was now in his final year at the Princeton Theological Seminary, though it was a somewhat confusing letter, for it seemed that he was inviting her to go to the game with someone else.

And that was indeed the case, which meant that Mr. Waddell had had to compose his surprising letter with considerable ingenuity, for he was, himself, promised to another young lady, but he had met Miss Beatty while visiting in West Chester, and had concluded that she would be an ideal companion for his roommate, John Calhoun. And this hadn't been a hasty deducton, either, for from within the sanctum of the Princeton Seminary he had done a bit of computing, before the days of computers, and come up with a neat equation. His roommate had a wonderful singing voice, the finest in the Seminary, and often sang solos with their choral groups; he was strikingly good-looking, the tallest of all the young men in the Seminary; he was dedicated to the church and the ministry. On the other side of the equation he could readily imagine a young lady he recalled as very charming, with a brightness, a bewitching air, sweet, serious and somewhat flighty, that was all but irresistible. Miss Beatty also had a beautiful singing voice; her father had been a minister; and she was dedicated to the church.

With all this in mind Mr. Waddell had embarked on a delicate social maneuver, for it isn't easy to invite a young lady you scarcely know to go to a football game with someone else. His letter had had to be carefully composed, bolstered with flowery phrases and neat bits of camouflage, so he wrote:

> On the 7th of November, which same is Saturday, there will be played at Germantown a game of "football" between the University of Pennsylvania and Princeton. "Me and my roommate" count on being present. Now I would like very much to see you, and as this "roommate" is rather young and inexperienced to be left alone in a great city like Philadelphia, I see no other way than to consolidate all forces, and invite you, conjointly, to accompany us to the game. His name is Calhoun. "Miss Beatty, I have the honor of presenting Mr. Calhoun. . . ."

He also managed to suggest delicately that it might not be amiss if she would bring along another young lady for him.

On Saturdays Louise finished her work at the Penn Charter School at noon. She would be free, and wrote Mr. Waddell accepting, then asked Lizzie Marshall, whose mother was her official chaperone, to come with them. The Princeton letter had been discussed at length at the dinner table, and the boarding-house ladies, finding the whole venture quite romantic, suggested a variety of long veils. Franklin Field was sure to be windy, they said, you couldn't have too many veils. And when the two young men arrived they approved at once of Mr. Calhoun, who was very tall, indeed, a towering young man, blue-eyed and with the most gracious manners, for it seemed he came from a distinguished Southern family.

Although he had been described as "young and inexperienced," John Calhoun was actually twenty-eight years old. After graduating from Princeton he had spent three years in business before returning to the Seminary, and this varied experience gave him, in Louise's eyes, a certain distinction, for he was, in fact, not like anyone she'd ever met before—in West Chester, or Indian Deep, or Philadelphia. And so, throughout that long, vivid day, while the wind blew the veils about, and the burly young men, in their orange and black and red and blue, raced and pushed and pummeled each other up and down the field, it became increasingly apparent to John Waddell that Miss Beatty and his roommate had together, just as he had surmised, that subtle electric aura of two who are discovering each other. And in the months that followed he watched, with sympathetic interest, the deepening friendship—the many letters back and forth, and all those weekend trips to Philadelphia.

When John Calhoun came on his romantic visits, Louise would take him to visit her new friends, Dr. and Mrs. Paxton, for it was there that she now felt most at home, and where, in an atmosphere of tact and kindness, of books and music and lively conversation, they could most naturally and simply be themselves. Dr. Paxton was the new minister for the Spruce Street church. He had taken up his duties some months before, when, to Mr. Bonar's great delight, the congregation had finally settled on a permanent pastor. And they had chosen well, for Dr. James Paxton, a youngish man in his early thirties, was an inspired preacher, with a distinguished background of education and travel, while his wife, Helen Paxton, a slender, dark-eyed young woman, had unusual grace and charm.

Between them the Paxtons had brought the somnolent old church to life, and for Louise their coming had meant a new horizon. In their home she had found a way of life and a setting —the English antiques, the oriental rugs, the glow of polished mahogany—that was quite unlike the plush and fringe and round oak tables she was accustomed to. Here the colors and fabrics were subtle and understated, and the rooms were full of books and flowers and sunshine. She was impressionable, and the simplicity appealed to her. But it wasn't only the decorations and the homelike atmosphere, for Dr. and Mrs. Paxton had given her a feeling that was delicate and most tantalizing, almost a new feeling of identity. They were interested in her voice, her studies, in everything about her life, and soon were inviting her back after Sunday School and the Sunday Evening Prayer Services, for a "late supper" and to spend the night. They had traveled a good deal, and her own experience was so limited that much of this sophistication was quite new—the "late suppers," the books, the conversation, the style in which they lived. Inevitably, when Mr. Calhoun came from Princeton, she would take him to

A picture taken of Louise when she was living in Philadelphia at the Arch Street boardinghouse.

the Paxtons'. He was an aristocratic young man, tall, sensitive, fine-looking. And though he had won the hearts of all the boardinghouse ladies, it was at the Paxtons' that he seemed most at home, talking to Dr. Paxton about the ministry, about his studies and where his first "call" might be.

In the spring, when the Paxtons had first come to Philadelphia, Louise had often wondered why they bothered with her, why this sophisticated older couple were so kind and attentive to a girl only twenty, whose experience was so limited. But in fact the benefits were mutual, for the Paxtons, a childless couple, had been immediately drawn to the young alto in the church choir who was living alone in a boardinghouse, and making her own way as a secretary. This had seemed to them a most unusual arrangement, and they had been touched by her responsiveness, by that artless way she had, so guileless and so appealing. And, perhaps more than any others in the congregation, they were moved by the quality of her voice, by those so powerful and lyric tones that soared, each Sunday, in a velvet cloud, out into the pews and stalls of the old Spruce Street Presbyterian Church.

But Louise was, herself, unhappy with her singing, for it had become apparent that the lessons with Miss Anna Groff weren't helping her voice very much. The French Method was more relaxed, and the lessons with Miss Groff not as tense and strained as the ones with Miss Whinnery had been. But all the old troubles were still there—the low, uncertain pitch, the downward drag and, especially, the unwieldy timbre and resonance that she seemed unable to control.

As usual, Mr. Bonar was sympathetic. All voices responded differently, he said, and in New York there were a number of Italian singing teachers. Could the Italian Method be the answer? Lizzie Marshall, her friend at the boardinghouse, was the one who had the brilliant inspiration. Lizzie's father worked for the Pennsylvania Railroad. He had a pass on the train to New York, and Lizzie suggested that they use his pass and go together to the city to see the Italian teachers. Then, if arrangements could be made, Louise could have her singing lessons in New York on Saturday afternoons.

This was an exhilarating prospect, and now that she had more money it would be possible. Recently the Spruce Street church had raised her contract to three hundred and fifty dollars a year, and Dr. Paxton had asked her to take down his sermons in shorthand and transcribe them onto the typewriter. Since he used only notes, such a record was valuable, and he was paying her seven dollars a week.

So she would have enough money, and they made a lark out of the expedition. On Saturdays she was free to leave the school at noon, and this time she watched the clock like a sprinter at the Olympics, departing actually a few minutes early, snatching up her muff, pinning on her hat, meeting Lizzie at the door, taking a trolley to the station and catching the train with barely a second to spare—both of them dissolving, then, into the unrestrained giggles of two young ladies, barely out of their teens, all set for an adventure in New York.

She had made appointments with two Italian teachers, Signor Aggramonte and Signor Arani, and the magic day proceeded in cloudlike fashion, for both these distinguished gentlemen praised her voice and offered to give her singing lessons at greatly reduced rates, any hour she wished on Saturday afternoon. After the interviews, they returned to the railroad station in high spirits, their skirts jauntily sweeping the ground, their newly trimmed hats almost dashing enough for New York, their adventure an unqualified success.

She had arranged to have her lessons with Signor Arani, and meanwhile must endure a week of wondering about the Italian Method, and more hours of prickling suspense during the return trip to New York. But finally she was standing beside the piano, at Signor Arani's elbow, while he rippled the keys and played a succession of beautiful chords. Then, quietly and patiently, he explained the first exercise, which he called "the cornerstone" of his technique. And it had all gone so smoothly and easily, that it was hard to believe that she had finally embarked on the blissful road of learning how to sing.

The exercise, when Signor Arani showed it to her, didn't seem too unusual, for he simply "attacked" a single note, pianissimo, then expanded gradually to a forte tone and very gradually contracted again, slowly, slowly, to a beautiful, almost inaudible pianissimo, all on the same note. Several times he did this for her, his voice expanding and contracting with exquisite ease. Then it was her turn, and she took a deep breath and "attacked" her note. But her voice tended to rise on the forte and descend on the pianissimo; for some reason she couldn't seem to stay on the same note. To help her, her new teacher did it for her again, his rich tone expanding and contracting with such effortless precision that it might almost have been a single string of a violin.

Signor Arani was dramatic in appearance, and his manners were expressive. He used his hands when he talked, a shrug, an upward glance of vexation and despair. After she had wobbled and wavered again and again, he asked her sternly, what was the matter with her voice that she couldn't do even the simplest exercise?

She tried, then, to probe the mystery of this thing he wanted her to do, and asked him to tell her *how* to keep her tone on one note. But it seemed he couldn't tell her *how*, he could only show her, again and again and again, how supremely easy it was. And each time she would try once more, and fail once more, until finally she was in despair, fiery hot all over, close to tears, wretched and ashamed. So at the very outset they had reached a frantic impasse, for since this exercise was "the cornerstone" of his technique, if she couldn't master it, he told her, with an eloquent shrug, a gesture of utter futility—if she couldn't master it, he couldn't help her.

She returned the next week for a session even more desperate than the first one had been—her own misery deeper, his excited insistence fiercer. Then she gave up the Italian Method, went back to Miss Groff and continued as before.

She had more responsibility at the school now, and sometimes, when a shipment of supplies had arrived, or a new boy was expected, Mr. Jones would send for her to come to his office before she started her day's work. Therefore the note delivered by messenger one evening in February didn't come as a surprise: "Miss Beatty, Could you call for a moment on your way down tomorrow. Before nine would suit me better than after. Yours truly, R. M. Jones."

If it was supplies, she'd catalogue them, if it was a new boy she'd help him find his way around the school. All this she'd done before, for she served as his assistant, her time from eight thirty till two o'clock belonged to the school and she had, she believed, a most desirable situation. It was, in fact, her livelihood, and she'd given very little thought to Mr. Jones himself. She hadn't noticed that often the young lady teachers, in their starched and ruffled shirtwaists, would be grouped around him, tittering at his jokes or listening to some story he'd told a dozen times before. It hadn't occurred to her that he might appreciate a bit of flattery, or that when he saw her at her desk, so intent on her work, and saw the picture she made there, a convenient pencil jabbed into the dense dark hair, a stray curl escaping now and then from the restraining combs and ribbons—that at such times he might not be pleased when, after he had spoken to her, she treated him like a stick of wood, "Yes, Mr. Jones?" polite and respectful, but without the pretty, artful airs that are so becoming in a young lady.

She didn't know that this was not an attitude designed to please a vain and aging man, but Mr. Jones had seen the way she put on her hat on the very dot of two, often with an impatient, adventurous look, as though her own day was about to begin. And obscurely he was jealous of the rest of that day, believing her deficient in "loyalty to the school." To have such casual radiance blow in and then out again, week after week, can be intolerable to the one who is excluded, and the headmaster expected, from his employees, nothing less than total dedication. For some months there had been a nucleus of dissatisfaction, which had finally come to a head when he'd discovered, on his staff, a new young teacher who was both properly dedicated and properly appreciative. So he'd sent a note by messenger, and the next day waited in his office, and when she came promptly, and said respectfully, "Yes, Mr. Jones?" he savored the heady moment, then asked for her resignation.

On that unguarded face the look of shock and dismay would have satisfied any man intent on wounding. This was followed, as was to be expected, by an outburst of hurt disbelief. But she was still only twenty, the age of some of his students, and Mr. Jones knew how to deal with young people—the gruff, clipped phrases, the overbearing manner. To the outraged question, "Why?," he gave a perfunctory reply. She had omitted the "Jr." on two addresses, and her handwriting on another had been careless. Since she'd often been complimented on her neat, clear script, the injustice of this rankled painfully. But she countered with a protest about her contract—she had signed in good faith, hadn't he signed in good faith? However, he cut her short, for he was adept at the curt dismissal, and so she fled to her boarding-house, stunned and deeply shaken.

When news of what had happened filtered through the school there was a stirring of rebellion among her fellow workers not unlike the protests and demonstrations of later years. During the lunch hour a hasty meeting was called, a letter drafted, signatures obtained and a delegation appointed, to go, after classes, to the Arch Street boardinghouse. Many of the teachers were vulnerable themselves, relying for their livelihood on their positions in the school. But this summary dismissal, without due cause, outraged a sense of justice that can run like a reservoir beneath the seeming compliance of those most dependent upon an employer's goodwill.

The three who came to the boardinghouse in the afternoon sought first to remove any trace of self-condemnation. It wasn't the "Jr." on the envelopes, they told her, and it wasn't the handwriting. In fact, Mr. Jones was jealous of her music. He didn't like his staff to have any interests outside the school, and was planning to put in her place a new young "favorite." This explanation eased the hurt a little, and so did their great concern, for the committee told her vehemently that they were planning to complete a letter of protest, which would have many signatures, and present it that evening to Mr. Jones. Then they begged her, tearfully, not to resign, for they were sure she would be retained.

It was an emotional meeting, for all the young ladies felt anxious and threatened. But she tried, while they were there, to maintain a certain composure, and cling to the remaining vestiges of pride and dignity. Her sense of justice had been badly shaken, for she believed, with the passionate naïveté of youth, that if you had an obligation, you met it, if you gave your word, you kept it, and she was shocked that this shouldn't apply, as well, to the principal of a school. But she didn't want to endanger the positions of her friends; her pride, though at the moment in tatters, must somehow be preserved. And so she told them that they mustn't plead her cause, for she wouldn't want to work where she wasn't wanted.

However, as soon as the committee had left, this flimsy armor melted right away, and she was again assailed by the shock of what had happened. She had been dismissed from her position, and her situation was precarious, for in the "on hand" column in her account book there was just sixteen dollars, and soon she would owe twenty dollars for singing lessons, five dollars for piano rental, as well as the weekly payment at the Arch Street boardinghouse. It was all more than she could contemplate alone, and finally, in a state of great agitation, she took a trolley across the city to Aunt Lizzie's on Thirty-third Street, and poured out the whole story to Uncle John Steen.

Uncle John had been retired for some years. He was a tall man, dignified, thoughtful, with a beard that flowed from both cheeks but not from his chin, and what he did for her now was listen, quietly, calmly, to the whole disjointed, agitated story. Louise was by this time weeping, outraged, trying to unburden a tangle of distraught emotions, and in his eyes she was very, very young. He had never really approved of this niece of his living alone in Philadelphia, dealing with employers, and using that new machine called a typewriter. She came from a sheltered, religious home; he felt that that was where she belonged, and now he advised her firmly that her mother would have to be told. But that threw her into a panic, for she didn't want them to know at home that she had lost her fine position with the Penn Charter School. Fervently she begged Uncle John not to tell anyone until she had found some other work. And it was this prospect of the reaction at home that dried her tears and calmed her agitation.

As soon as possible she must find another position, and the next day she went to see her uncle Samuel Fulton in his office in the new Bullitt Building on Fourth Street. There she again poured out her story, and Uncle Samuel, a businessman, much younger than Uncle John, was also more incensed by the story of the broken contract. He thought she had been shabbily treated and was quite ready to have it out with Mr. Jones. But since she didn't want that, he tried to think of an alternative, and soon came up with an interesting idea. It might be possible, he said, for her to have a desk in his office, and become a Public Stenographer. The location, in the heart of the business district, would be favorable, and the new typewriting machines had become so popular that the demand for Public Stenographers was increasing every day.

Uncle Samuel's idea sounded like a most buoyant reprieve, and she set about at once making the arrangements. She ordered cards and letter paper with her new business address, rented a typewriter for ten dollars a month, bought a supply of notebooks and pencils and had her name inscribed on the door in neat gold letters: MISS BEATTY, STENOGRAPHER AND TYPEWRITER. She was then able to write her mother that though she had lost her position with the Penn Charter School, she had already found something else that might be even better.

The Bullitt Building was the newest and largest office building in Philadelphia. In a recent book about the city it had been described as "an imposing building, built of brick, with heavy stone columns and massive brown stone trim. . . ." The writer had also noted that "the walls of this enormous structure rise to a height of eight stories and are surmounted by conspicuous towers on the Fourth Street Front. The building contains the Fourth National Bank, the offices of several private bankers and numerous other offices, with a popular restaurant on its upper floor." As Uncle Samuel had said, it was an ideal location, for the neighborhood was active, with messengers hurrying through the streets and corridors, bringing work to the stenographers, or stenographers to the offices to take dictation. And within a month there was vindication of a sort, for it seemed the new young "favorite" Mr. Jones had put in her place couldn't handle all the work. Soon they began bringing some of it to her, and she could add to her growing list of accounts "The Penn Charter School."

Meanwhile, throughout the spring, while the streets with the names of trees were blossoming into a delicate greenery, John Calhoun was coming, more and more often, to Philadelphia. And when he came he stepped right into a frame that had been in the making for years. And so there was an almost dreamlike feeling of inevitability, stretching way back to those childhood years when she had watched her father lead the hymns and prayers in the Shadyside church. She was impressionable, and almost all the color, the drama, the music in her life she associated with the church. She was emotional, and the vague longings, the uplifted feelings, the deep commitments—these, too, she'd experienced most often in church. Even now she was singing in the choir, teaching in the Sunday School and devoting much of her time to the work of the church. And all this she could share with John Calhoun, who was earnest, dedicated, on the threshold of his career.

At the Arch Street boardinghouse there was the cadence of romance, and many of the ladies were sure they had guessed, from the look on both young faces, the day they became engaged. It had to be a secret engagement, for he hadn't yet met her mother, and she hadn't met his. But still they could make plans, and they did. In April John Calhoun was ordained; in the fall he would begin his duties as an assistant pastor in a parish on the outskirts of Philadelphia. They decided to be married in the late summer, and to that end she blithely burned all her bridges. Usually she spent the summer months in West Chester, in any case, and now she would be sewing her trousseau and preparing for her wedding. So she moved everything she owned out of the Arch Street boardinghouse. She resigned her choir position at the Spruce Street church, and closed her office in the Bullitt Building —returning the typewriter and cleaning out her desk, all in a delicious whirlwind of finality.

Although the engagement hadn't yet been made official, a great many people knew. In West Chester her mother, believing the marriage "made in Heaven," was thankful that this young daughter, who had seemed the most unpredictable and impulsive of her children, was to marry a fine young man from the Princeton Theological Seminary. And in Philadelphia almost everyone knew—the boardinghouse ladies, of course, and the parishioners of the Spruce Street church, for many of them had seen Mr. Calhoun at the services, and shared vicariously in the romance. The Paxtons knew, and Mr. Bonar and Miss Groff and Uncle Samuel, and her friends from the school, her friends all over, and there were many quite touching farewells.

In August she went with John Calhoun to his home in southern New Jersey to meet his widowed mother. Because at first there was a pretense, an air of graciousness, a veneer of hospitality, she didn't understand that she had been plunged unwittingly into an untenable situation. But in fact this was a classic confrontation: the bitter winds of the Civil War, the years of aristocratic tradition, the loyalty a son owes his mother, all seeking to divide two who were in love.

John Calhoun was bearer of a famous name, a descendant of one of the most aristocratic families in the South, and his mother had always considered it inevitable that someday he would marry into a distinguished Southern family. So in a sense this was more than a social impasse, for the devastation and humiliation of defeat were still not far distant, and to counter this there was the heritage of pride.

Throughout the courtship John Calhoun had imagined that once his mother had met Miss Beatty she would be won over. But he had misjudged, for to his mother it was unthinkable that her son should forsake the heritage to which he was entitled. If he should marry a girl with a Northern background, that would be the final defeat.

During the visit, bit by bit the veneer of hospitality dissolved into an interval of deepening misery. And this was an uneven confrontation, for Louise had come expecting to be warmly received, and she was too proud, too sensitive and too inexperienced to withstand the crosscurrents of disapproval and ill will, the numbing scenes and veiled conflicts. She didn't understand the subtleties of the situation, but to sustain her there was that proud, inarticulate feeling she'd always had that she mustn't be where she wasn't wanted. So finally, at the end of a confused and desperate week, she broke her engagement and fled to the only refuge she had left—Bessie's home in Arlington, Massachusetts.

From there she wrote her mother about the broken engagement without revealing the true circumstances, and as a result, the reply was barbed and wounding. With some ambivalence her mother wrote:

> I received your letter and was rather surprised. Sad, glad in turn. Sad because I am sorry you did not love Mr. Calhoun, as from what I had heard of him, he would have made you a good husband. And also, in that sphere (a minister's wife) you would have had a large door open to you for usefulness. This was my selfish feeling. Then a gladness because you might have had to go far from home. It must be all right as you have decided it, *we* had left it all to the guidance of our Heavenly Father. I am sorry, very sorry for Mr. Calhoun. I trust he may find some other love, but I think he will not soon come across such an one. I do

think you would have made him a splendid wife. Poor Mr.
Waddell will have to try again!

She also wrote the Paxtons, touching especially on the painful
situation in Philadelphia. And in his reply, Dr. Paxton tried to be
tactful and reassuring. "Dear Miss Beatty," he wrote,

> We are so sorry you are unhappy, and yet I suppose we
> should be glad that a greater evil has been avoided. The
> news has spread rapidly and I do not think you will be an-
> noyed. You will forgive us all if with our sympathy for you
> there is mixed a good deal of selfish satisfaction that you are
> to remain with us. Mr. Bonar is even jubilant. You must
> come and see us when you can, and tell us about it if you
> choose. I am satisfied, however, without hearing anything,
> that you have done right.

Nevertheless, she stayed on in Arlington, clinging to her temporary refuge, saddened, disoriented, afraid to face the future.
Her friends in Philadelphia understood her reluctance, and after
a time Mrs. Paxton sent another letter, designed to pave the way:

> My dear Miss Beatty, I want to ask a great favor of you, and
> that is that you will come and make us a visit while you are
> still unsettled about your plans for the winter. You know
> we are very selfish creatures and we cannot help feeling very
> glad ourselves that we are not to lose you this winter. You
> have so many warm friends in the old church and we will all
> be so glad to see your bright face and hear again the lovely
> voice that has been so sadly missed these last few Sabbaths.
> May I not expect you this week? Very lovingly yours, Helen
> Paxton.

This kind, perceptive letter gave her just enough courage, and
late in September she boarded the train for Philadelphia.

Chapter VI

She had imagined that in West Chester all the talk was revolving about her and her lost love—all the witty remarks and neatly turned phrases, when they sat about on the porch, comfortable and convivial, speculating about this latest mishap in the family. But, in fact, there was a much more pressing issue in West Chester this year, one that was causing a good deal of anxious concern, and that, quite simply stated, was—what to do with Howard, now that he was through school?

Her brother Howard was seventeen. He had graduated from high school at the top of his class, and was a tall, vigorous young man, and very handsome, with lively, snapping black eyes, and a volatile, inquiring mind. But in West Chester his prospects were less than zero.

Years ago, in Minnesota, their mother, foreseeing this dilemma, had invested in an "Education Endowment Fund" for Howard and Fulton, so that when the time came both boys could go to college. But the Fund had proved to be a fraud, all the money had been lost and now she had turned for advice to Mr. Woods, who was still handling her affairs from his office in Minneapolis. But the old lawyer, reluctant to have her use any more of her dwindling capital, wrote cautiously:

As to the wisdom of the sacrifice on your part of assisting

Howard, I have heard it said that the best thing that can happen to some boys is to be thrown out on their own resources. Furthermore, there is the question of your being able to live comfortably with this reduction in your capital. Then again, how will it affect his self-reliance if you assume the burden of his expenses? I have intimated the lines along which I think your thoughts should run, and that, I fear, is the most I can do.

However, with the depression of 1893 in the making, business was very slow, and throwing Howard on his own resources hadn't been much of a solution. Here was an anxious, intelligent boy with nothing to do, and in this difficult situation Louise was able to come to the rescue. She could, she told them, take Howard to live with her, in Philadelphia, at the Arch Street boardinghouse. There she would pay his board, give him a small allowance and he would have the advantages of city life, with more opportunities.

To make this plan feasible she shared a room with another boarder, Miss Marion Cock, and rented a small one for Howard. Miss Cock was a spinster in her early thirties—an outspoken, most companionable roommate. The new responsibilities and arrangements proved a welcome distraction, and the winter turned into a busy one, with singing lessons, choir rehearsals, and occasional diversions—one of the most memorable a recital at the Academy of Music given by the Polish pianist, Ignaz Paderewski, who had come to the country this year on his first American tour.

In spite of the depression, her own business was thriving, and at the Bullitt Building she worked long hours typing up letters, taking dictation and acquiring new clients. Most of the work was routine, but now and then there would be an adventure, and one morning a messenger dashed in, in a fever of excitement, urging her to hurry to the office of a lawyer, Mr. Cloud. Hastily, she complied, and when they reached the office, she was surprised to find a motley gathering of rough-looking sailors and longshoremen, huge, dark-browed men, angry and sullen, lounging about on the handsome furniture.

The atmosphere was one of great tension, and quickly she took her place beside the desk. But before they could begin, Mr. Cloud, a distinguished, silver-haired gentleman, turned to her and asked, "You are a court stenographer, Miss Beatty?" To which she replied, blithely, "No, sir, but I can do it," a response that occasioned a startling interruption while Mr. Cloud laughed and laughed, and then told a story about an old man who, when someone asked if he could play the violin, replied, "No, but if you'll show me one, I'll play it." He then laughed some more, but finally turned to the business at hand, and the testimony began—an avalanche of angry voices shouting back and forth. It seemed there had been trouble on the docks, between longshoremen and sailors. Now fierce arguments swirled about the room, and caught up in the excitement Louise worked at a furious pace, taking down at lightning speed the brittle, rapid-fire confrontations.

Later she transcribed the testimony onto the typewriter, and Mr. Cloud was so satisfied with her work that he made her one of his most trusted stenographers. Regularly she worked for him on briefs and letters. In the spring, when he broke his leg and was confined to his home in New Jersey, he sent for her and she rode back and forth on the ferry to Camden, carrying his correspondence and handling his affairs. She also traveled to Washington with the Hon. Wayne MacVeagh, a prominent Philadelphia lawyer who had been Attorney General under President Garfield. Mr. McVeagh occasionally had business in the capital and he liked to have her there, for she had become an expert now, one of those pioneers, those distaff innovators, who were making, out of the loops and squiggles and the new typewriting machines, a profitable career.

All this meant a steady rise in income, and this year she was earning as much as two hundred dollars a month, a most unusual sum for a young lady not yet twenty-two. In West Chester they teased her about becoming so "wealthy," but they were pleased with her new prosperity, and she was able to help them a good deal—a twenty-five-dollar birthday present for her mother, and her mother's bill paid at John Wanamaker's, Howard's board in Philadelphia, a trip to Atlantic City for

Ella. She could also spend more on herself, and in the spring bought a "silk gown, $12.60," a "cloth gown, $9.80," and from Richmonds & Co. "lace shoes, $6.00," which was something of an innovation, for shoes with laces were quite new and considered much more stylish than the usual buttoned kind.

At the Arch Street boardinghouse "evening entertainment" was included in the fee, which meant, twice a week or so, parlor games, amateur musicians, or perhaps a lady lecturer. And this year many of the entertainments dealt with the Columbian Exposition that was being built in Chicago. It was to be a huge affair with many exotic exhibits, and the lady lecturers could describe vividly the strange habits of the real live natives, from the South Seas and other faraway places, who, it was said, would actually be visible in person at the Exposition.

For months fantastic rumors had been circulating; the Columbian Exposition was more talked about than anything that had happened in years. And when the great day finally came, and President Cleveland pressed a button in Machinery Hall that started all the tall fountains in the beautiful lagoons, it seemed as though the sparkling drops of water enriched the entire country. Soon afterward Louise had a letter from her brother Will, inviting her to visit him and see the Exposition. But though she had enough money saved, she felt that it would be flighty and irresponsible to close her office, use up half her savings and travel such a distance. The whole idea was so improbable that, reluctantly but firmly, she refused.

Will was married now, to a schoolteacher friend of Allie's called Vallie. They had a home in Norwood Park, near Chicago, and she was tempted to accept, but she resisted until she discovered that her roommate, Marion Cock, was going, as well as many other people she knew, and then the prospect became so irresistible that she changed her mind. Since that meant she'd be closing her office anyhow, she also accepted an invitation to visit the Paxtons in their summer home on Lake George. Then she settled down to earn as much money as she could for this unexpected and most desirable vacation.

With so much to look forward to, it was no hardship to work long hours. But one evening, when Louise was at her desk in the Bullitt Building, a curious thing began to happen, a kind of discouragement invading her thoughts, an unbidden and too bland perspective, so that she could almost see herself, day after day, traveling a too familiar path, from the Arch Street board-inghouse to the Spruce Street church, to Miss Groff's studio, to the Bullitt Building.

It was a hot summer evening and quite late. Since every-one else had gone home, she was a solitary figure in one corner of the room, the gaslight shining on her work, only the rhythm of the keys breaking the mournful silence. And it was while she was typing that the discouragement turned into a question. What am I doing here? Where am I going? She had come to Philadelphia to learn how to sing, but though she had worked hard at her music, she was making no progress with her voice. All the old limitations were still there, as well as those moments of unusual beauty that made her feel that she had in her keep-ing a flawed yet cherished gift, one that was not hers to throw away while she saved money and bought dresses and lace shoes and went on vacation trips. . . . It was a curious mood that assailed her, part discouragement, part elation. Had she, with-out realizing it, drifted into aimlessness, into pointlessness? She had wanted to learn how to sing, but with her troublesome voice she had failed. And now just acknowledging that failure brought an unexpected lightening of the spirit, as though all these thoughts had been lying dormant, ready to form themselves into a plan, a determination, a future with some hope.

By the time she had finished her assignment at the typewriter she knew what she was going to do. Before starting her vacation she'd close up her office in the Bullitt Building, resign from the Spruce Street church and move out of the Arch Street boarding-house. Then, when her vacation was over, she'd go someplace else—to Chicago, perhaps, or Boston—find a teacher who could really help her and learn how to sing.

At home, when she told them of her plans, there was more opposition than she'd expected. Her family had always said she was impulsive, and now they were sure of it, for they found it hard to believe that she'd abandon such a successful career for some vague, quite nebulous future arrangement. However, she felt easier in her mind about her family, for Howard was planning to live next winter with Will in Chicago, where there would be more opportunity for employment. And her mother now had Aunt Kate and Uncle Martin, who had come to live with her. Aunt Kate was Auntie Fulton's sister, and a year ago, when her husband, the Reverend Martin Schoonmaker, had retired from his church in Walden, New York, they had come to West Chester for a visit, and had been so content that they'd wanted to live there always. Since there wasn't room for this arrangement in the Walnut Street house, they'd built a new home for her mother at 313 South High Street. There they planned to live out their lives, leaving her the house in a will. If it hadn't been for Aunt Kate and Uncle Martin she wouldn't have felt free to give up her work and the earnings that might be needed at home. But now, with Uncle Martin's pension, the situation in West Chester was much brighter. Nevertheless, she felt a certain responsibility, and after paying for her railroad tickets, and keeping out twenty dollars for the Exposition and ten dollars to start a new life, she gave the rest of her savings to her mother.

Her vacation began late in July with a visit to the Paxtons on Lake George. There, on the west shore of the lake, the Paxton clan had several homes built close together by the water. It was a big family, and there were two young cousins, Jay and Don Paxton, to take her swimming and boating. There was also a visitor from New York, a Mr. Scott, who, within a day or two, decided that, after a proper courtship, he would marry her. He was an eligible young man, successful in business, much sought after socially and not prepared, himself, for such a rash commitment. But circumstances conspired against him. When they went canoeing in the evening, and she laughed at something witty that he'd said, her laughter would float out over the silvered lake, and to the one paddling sedately in the stern of the canoe, it seemed to echo, with the quality of music, along the darkened shore. Then, when they rose at dawn to climb Prospect Mountain, there would be that radiance again, in still another guise.

Although she scarcely realized it, by the time Mr. Scott put her on the train in Albany (with Don and Jay Paxton as additional escorts), he had made his winter plans—weekend trips to wherever she was living, luncheons, matinees, letters, flowers, a proper courtship. Meanwhile the big train with its many sleeping cars thundered into the station, and she closed up her red parasol and said a last farewell before starting off on still another adventure.

Will met her in Chicago in a holiday mood. He was taking the day off from work, he said, to show her the Exposition. It was very hot in the city, ninety in the shade, so they went by boat on Lake Michigan to the fairgrounds, and when she saw the immense lagoon, the green grass like velvet, the towering marble arches, the massive white buildings, the huge statues, the fountains so tall that they seemed to be reaching for the sky—when she saw all this she was so astonished that she could only write her mother that "the grandeur far surpasses anything we could ever conceive of."

For a while they sat on the moving sidewalk, and then took a ride in an electric boat. The lagoon was so immense that the ride took three quarters of an hour, while they admired the beautiful islands, which were filled with "strange grasses, bushes, trees and flowers," and a great variety of birds, "ducks, swans, even cranes," and noted all the other boats circling among the tall fountains—"gondolas, electric launches, canoes, and some with sails."

After going rather hastily through the principal buildings of the Exposition—Agricultural Hall, Liberal Arts Hall, Transportation and Machinery Hall—they lingered happily in the Midway Plaisance, and here, she wrote her mother, "I felt as though I was walking in a street on the moon." The Midway had replicas of many strange foreign places, as well as entertainments, and already the most famous was The Street of Cairo, with houses like those in Egypt, and camels and donkeys for the visitors to ride. They had lunch in a Moorish restaurant, and then saw a tiny Sudanese boy dance a native dance, "trying all the while to catch hold of my red parasol." Finally they took a ride all around the fairgrounds in an electric car.

After that she went every day to the Exposition, and listed

all the wonders in a small red leather notebook. But at the same time she was trying to plan for the future, and included the names of two singing teachers, one in Chicago and one in Boston, as well as "Russia, gold piano; Turkey, Bedouin Village; California, enormous fruit." She didn't want to be a burden to anyone, and tried to make this clear in a letter to her mother. "Do ask Bess if she can afford to have me in September," she wrote. "I mean if Joe is going to his mother's it would be cheaper for them, and I could board some place else."

In the Liberal Arts Building there was "an old piano from the sixteenth century, with black keys and white flats"; in the Agricultural Building "free Bakers chocolate and cake"; and in Festival Hall she heard a memorable concert—"a thousand voices and an orchestra of two hundred, performing Handel, Beethoven and Berlioz." Meanwhile she was thinking most seriously about Boston, where she'd been told there were many opportunities—the famous St. Cecilia Chorus, the Symphony Orchestra, the Handel and Haydn Society. In Boston, it was said, there was a classical tradition, a tradition of excellence, and she decided, finally, that that was where she would go.

Chapter VII

In September Louise went to stay with her sister Bess in Arlington. And the next morning, so no time would be wasted, she took a trolley into Boston to inquire about a choir position. She wanted to be earning something while she was studying, and this was especially urgent since Bess was one of those who thought she had been foolish and flighty to abandon so heedlessly such a desirable situation in Philadelphia. Though Bess was generous, and happy to make her welcome, she didn't approve, and was outspoken about saying so. Therefore it was especially urgent that she have some money coming in so she could pay her board and her own expenses, and a choir position seemed the most likely way.

The date was September 13, 1893, she was twenty-two years old and perhaps too preoccupied to realize that there was something familiar about this expedition—that artistic arrangement most often used by composers, in which a theme is repeated with certain variations. Nevertheless it was five years ago, almost to the day, that she'd arrived at Aunt Lizzie's and started across Philadelphia to Bonar's music store, feeling then just as she did now—anxious, hopeful, buoyant, vulnerable—a feeling of heightened sensibility experienced most often by those who present themselves, again and again, with moments of challenging responsibility. A great deal had happened in five years, but she still hadn't learned how to sing, and now she was in a city where the brick and stone buildings veiled certain mysteries that might be called the very essence of music. And so she was experiencing all over again that buoyant, vulnerable feeling when she had found her way to a leading music store in Boston and asked the clerk if she could speak to the manager, Mr. B. F. Wood.

This time she had a letter of introduction from Mr. Bonar to smooth the way, but much else was the same, for once again the ardent aspiration, the earnestness and a certain appealing radiance—all this was like a subtle invasion, altering for a while the quiet formality of the music shop. As before, Mr. Wood had to explain regretfully that in Boston all the contracts for choir positions were made in the spring. But when he saw the buoyant confidence fade into disappointment, he quickly followed this up with many helpful suggestions—a Mr. Davenport she might audition for, and a Mr. Rising, organist of the Park Street Church; singing teachers she might inquire about; an audition he would arrange himself with the Committee of The Cecilia Society. And, not wanting to lose any time, she started that very day making some of the calls.

Mr. Wood hadn't asked her to sing, for he'd been quite willing to rely on the judgment of his old friend in Philadelphia. But later, somewhat bemused by a lingering enchantment, he wondered if he might not do more for his friend's young friend, and sent a letter to Arlington, asking her to return for an audition. On September 16th, she sang for him, and when he heard the subtle textures of that voice, the brilliant overtones, the depths and the unwieldy power, he decided to turn for advice to the one man most qualified to help young musicians. It wasn't easy to arrange, but later in the week he managed to have a word with Mr. George Chadwick, and the promise of an audition on September 30th. Then he cautioned her to do her best, explaining earnestly that Mr. Chadwick's approval could open many doors to a young singer. A distinguished composer, director of music for the First Universalist Church, a teacher at the New England Conservatory of Music and, many people said, soon to be director of the Conservatory, George Chadwick wouldn't be an easy man to sing for, but there wasn't another musician in Boston who was as influential.

Louise listened to all this with some apprehension, for during these past two weeks she'd had an uneasy feeling, as though, here in Boston, she was way out of her depth. Almost every day there'd been auditions. She'd sung for Miss Franklin, Miss Roll-wagon and Miss Munger. She'd sung for Mr. Blake as an appli-cant for his church and been engaged to sing with their choir October 1st, on trial. She'd auditioned for Mr. B. J. Lang, the brilliant director of The Cecilia Society, and he'd asked her to become a member of that famous choral group.

Everything seemed to be going well, but still she was disturbed, for she'd never realized before how unprepared she was, and how very limited. In Philadelphia the lack of a musical education hadn't seemed to matter too much, for most people were in the same situation. But here in Boston she often hardly knew what they were talking about, and it was hard to go about among en-lightened, intelligent musicians, when your own learning and background were so inadequate.

So now she had an aspiration that she hardly knew how to put into words, a yearning, ill-defined but urgent, that she tried to describe to Bess while they were waiting for the trolley to take them to Boston for the audition with Mr. Chadwick. What she wanted, she said, was to learn *all* about music, not just how to sing, but *everything* about music. It was an anxious plea, an impulsive confidence, a need for something undefined which Bess interpreted calmly as "the theory of music." The study was called Harmony, she said, and she knew just the teacher. Mr. Homer had a studio in Boston, but his sister, Mrs. Diman, lived here in Arlington, and was a good friend. Then Bess exclaimed, in some surprise, "Why, there's Mr. Diman now!"

Bess was in the habit of getting things done. She was poised, assured—a young woman with many friends and a busy social life. She had always been generous about sharing her opportuni-ties with her family, and now she took charge, running across the street to speak to a gentleman she'd seen there, then returning, triumphant, to board the trolley car. Mr. Homer's studio was in the Pelham Hotel, she said, at the corner of Boylston and Tremont streets. He was one of the best harmony teachers in Boston, and there would be plenty of time to go there before the audition with Mr. Chadwick.

It had all happened so quickly that Louise had hardly had time to think, but she was convinced that she should wait for the harmony lessons until she had at least found a choir position and was making some money. However, Bess didn't agree. There was no time like the present, she said. And so they went to the Pelham Hotel and Bess led the way down a long corridor to a door with a small sign: MR. SIDNEY HOMER. There, without hesitating a moment, she knocked firmly on the door, and when it was opened by the teacher himself, she explained their errand graciously and with authority—my sister is studying singing, and is interested in taking harmony lessons—then launched, without a break, into an animated conversation about mutual friends in Arlington.

Bess was taking charge, for that was her way—a river of conversation, embracing them all. And as the minutes ticked by it was hard to endure the waiting, for she wanted to ask how much harmony lessons would cost. However, she was helpless, for the talk ran on and on. And so she just sat there, in that hotel studio-room, and everywhere she looked there was music—music on the piano and on the piano rack, and piled about on a long mahogany teaching table. Music on a music stand, music on shelves. And on a blackboard, affixed to one wall, several bars of music had been hastily inscribed, but expertly, as though by someone who could write music as easily as words.

All this music was like a beacon light sweeping back and forth through the darkness, and she knew now that she could hardly wait for her lessons to begin. And she was surprised, for she'd imagined from the way Bess talked that the harmony teacher would be old. But actually he was young, probably not yet thirty, with the look of someone who has lived abroad, and also lived with music. The face was poetic, yet rugged, the forehead thin and sensitive, the white silk tie arranged in a foreign way. Otherwise he was all in black, and very tall and thin, and still the talk ran on and on until finally, in desperation, she interrupted and asked Bess how much harmony lessons would cost. And when Mr. Homer answered, himself, remarking quietly that his charge was three dollars an hour, she turned to Bess, aghast, whispering unhappily that she'd thought they'd be about twenty-five cents. In fact, she hardly knew what she was saying, but when the teacher saw how disappointed she was, he quickly offered forty-minute lessons for two dollars, and she seized on that bargain at once. Airily, without hesitating a moment, she agreed to two dollars, but when she was with Bess she was often like that—too coltish, too impulsive, without the kind of poise she liked to have on these occasions.

Afterward, at the audition for Mr. George Chadwick, she was discomfited, remembering how indiscreet she had been. Here, the studio was big and impressive, and Mr. Chadwick was difficult to audition for—austere, detached, his eyes fixed noncommittally on some distant point in the ceiling. She knew she should be concentrating; Mr. Wood had warned her to do her best. But still she was distracted, for her worst blunder had come at the very end, after they'd said their good-byes and were out in the hall, and she'd turned to Bess, her voice rising and falling in peaks of astonishment, "But Bess, you never told me Mr. Homer was so good-looking!" Had the door been properly shut? Was it possible he had heard? Why couldn't she have waited until she was out on the street! But she hadn't, and now she was provoked with herself, and trying at the same time to sing Handel, and muffle, somehow, the soaring tones so that she could convey, harmoniously, the beautiful legatos. Though really they shouldn't be muffled, they should be modulated, exquisitely, and that was something she'd never been able to do.

The audition was finished, finally, and Mr. Chadwick was still reserved and noncommittal. But he asked her to return in ten days to sing for his Music Committee. And he took an interest in her musical education, consulting with Mr. Wood and arranging for her to register at the New England Conservatory of Music. For her singing lessons he selected Mr. William Whitney, one of the most experienced voice teachers in the country. Meanwhile the Cambridge Baptist Church, where she'd sung on trial, offered her a contract, so she was able to start paying Bess three dollars a week board.

The Conservatory of Music was in a fine stone building, a whole block square, filled with teaching studios, practice rooms,

rehearsal halls—a medley of sounds, pianos and cellos, sopranos
and tenors—the strains of music floating here and there, the very
essence of music, the thing she had been starved for. Her singing
teacher, Mr. Whitney, was the son of a famous bass, Myron
Whitney, who had appeared with the National Opera Company
under Theodore Thomas. He had, himself, a melodious bass
voice, and had studied in Rome with the great master, Vannucini. So it was the Italian Method she was learning now, but not
the tormenting technique of Signor Arani, for Mr. Whitney was
very careful. With such a heavy voice, he said, she must guard
against strain, and usually he transposed her songs to a lower
key.

She sang for Mr. Chadwick and Mr. Whittemore, chairman
of his Music Committee, and the next week Mr. Chadwick asked
her to return for still another audition. This time he requested
sight reading of some difficult anthems, and when she had finished
he said abruptly, "All right, I'll engage you, and pay you six
hundred dollars a year. Come to rehearsal Friday evening." This
precipitated a painful dilemma, for she had already made a promise to the Music Committee of the Cambridge Baptist Church.
Haltingly she tried to explain, but Mr. Chadwick cut her short
with, "You'll come Friday or not at all." And so a most unusual
opportunity was slipping away. She said unhappily that she
would see what she could do, for though it didn't occur to her
to go back on her word, she thought the Cambridge church
might make some adjustment in her contract. For three days she
went about Boston and Cambridge, until finally she found the
chairman, Mr. Blake, and when she'd explained what had happened, she was astonished that he should be, at once, so understanding and so sympathetic, saying that though they would be
sorry to lose her, such an opportunity was too valuable to be
missed; he would release her at once, and she didn't even have to
see the other members of his committee.

The next week she joined Mr. Chadwick's celebrated choir in
the First Universalist Church. She was also then rehearsing, with
the Cecilia Chorus, for a performance of Handel's *Messiah*—a
creation so inspiring that afterward the effect was like waking
from a trance. She had never before been able to devote every
waking hour to music—always it had been only in snatches—

and so the deepening experience, here in Boston, was profoundly moving. Often she rose with the sun to do her harmony exercises —the chords, the progressions, all the notes so carefully traced, and sometimes mistakenly, for it was a difficult subject, and usually she did many more than her teacher had assigned, and they took a long time to correct. But Mr. Homer was very patient, for he knew how little experience she'd had with the intricacies of musical composition. He seemed to understand, better than anyone else, how starved she was for learning, and late in October invited her to join, as a nonpaying guest, his group classes in the Beethoven Symphonies.

There were four or five others in the symphony class, and they each had a score to follow, while their teacher stood at the blackboard, explaining the themes and structures. It was slow work, careful and very concentrated, and yet the atmosphere was often electric, charged with a kind of tension, as though they were sitting there quietly, watching a miracle unfold.

Mr. Homer was interested in her musical education, and also in her voice, and usually, when they'd finished with the harmony exercises, he'd ask her to sing for him, then coach her in certain classical interpretations. He'd always, he said, preferred the contralto range, and he showed her songs by Schumann and Brahms that seemed to suit the deep, heavy cadence of her voice. One day he asked her to sing some songs that he'd composed himself, when he was a student in Germany—difficult songs, to German words, but she thought them beautiful. He felt just as she did about Handel's great work, and liked to attend, whenever he could, rehearsals of The Cecilia Society. And on Sundays he came to church to hear her sing, and afterward escorted her home to Arlington by trolley.

The trip took almost an hour; when there were heavy snows it took much longer, and in December Louise decided that it would be more practical to move to Boston. Fortunately this wasn't too difficult to arrange, for Bess's mother-in-law, Mrs. Barrows, was part-owner of an exclusive boardinghouse at 355 Boylston Street. And though the usual prices were far too high, on the unheated top floor there was a very small room which she could have for eight dollars a week.

It seemed a practical arrangement, for Mrs. Barrows would

be her chaperone, and the boardinghouse was ideally situated—
very close to Boston Common, only three blocks from Mr.
Homer's studio, quite near the Conservatory of Music and not
far from the Universalist Church. She would be able to pay the
board from her church salary and she could walk almost every
place to save carfare.

She moved early in December, and once again a certain theme
was being repeated, for it was just four years ago that she had
gone to live in the Arch Street boardinghouse in Philadelphia.
But again there were variations, for here in Boston the other
boarders were more reserved. Like her kind friends in Philadelphia, many were retired schoolteachers, spinsters and widows.
But in their ways they differed, having, on the whole, a certain
self-sufficiency, aloof and unyielding, even an attitude of disapproval. Quite a few had lived so long at No. 355 that they
had, each one, a set place at the table, a favorite chair in the
parlor. They were accustomed to these well-earned privileges and
didn't look with favor on any break in the routine, and perhaps
Louise was just too pretty so early in the morning. Though she
didn't seem aware of it herself, her presence could be a disturbing
invasion of comeliness at the breakfast table—the flawless complexion, the rich dark hair pinned loosely in a coil, the beautiful
creamy curves of the throat, the laughter floating up the dark
polished stairs. All this was uncomfortably at odds with the character of the establishment, and the intrusion was compounded
when her harmony teacher, Mr. Homer, arranged with Mrs.
Barrows to take his meals at the boardinghouse. He was a bachelor, who had been in the habit of eating around, in this or that
café, often with other musician or artist friends. But, as he explained earnestly to Mrs. Barrows, he didn't believe such irregu-
lar meals were good for his health. So now he came every day,
even for breakfast, and always at the last moment, just as the
dining room doors were about to be closed, arriving in a great
hurry, leaving his hat on the rack, his cane in the umbrella stand,
then stating his preference to the waitress quite casually, as
though he weren't causing all kinds of trouble in the kitchen.

In the evenings, after dinner, the two young people would go
out together, even in the coldest weather, for a walk. They
walked on the Boston Common or in the Public Gardens, leaving

the boardinghouse in a flurry of preparations, of wool shawls and scarves and mittens and rubbers, and returning at a proper hour, looking dazed and cold and marvelously content. And though the gentle, susceptible ladies in Philadelphia might have enjoyed the romantic atmosphere all this created, the boarders at No. 355 didn't approve. Nevertheless, they were in part responsible for the cold, dark, star-studded walks, for when you have so many watchful chaperones, you don't feel altogether comfortable sitting about in the parlor.

In her account book she listed her expenses, and also her engagements, and for a few days in January she noted: "Wednesday. Harmony lesson at 11; Apollo concert with Mr. Homer in evening. Thursday, Cecilia rehearsal with Mr. Homer. Friday, singing lesson at 11; symphony class (Mr. Homer) at 12; symphony at 2:30 (Mr. Homer). Saturday, Harmony lesson at 11; sang *But the Lord* at Conservatory (Mr. Homer there); choir at 4:30; lesson at 6. Sunday, Church with Mr. Homer in evening." At the bottom of this page she noted, "Am I seeing too much of Mr. Homer?" It was an anxious comment, and not a happy one, for in some recess of her thoughts there was a shadow of apprehension.

So far it was only an intimation, easily dismissed, not often dwelled on, but still a source of uneasiness, for in their walks together on the Common they had talked of many things, and often of the most important thing—religion. And Mr. Homer had explained, almost too eloquently, his personal feelings in this matter. He was, he told her, an agnostic, one who didn't know. And since she'd never before known an agnostic, he'd outlined his position in considerable detail, for he was much more articulate than she about such matters, and could point out, with telling phraseology, the validity of his doubts and the honesty of his ambivalent point of view.

But for her these distinctions were confusing and not helpful, for if he was, as he said, a nonbeliever, it was only too apparent that nothing could ever come of their deepening friendship. Yet when she saw him round the corner, that tall, thin figure, the black suit, the cane—when she saw him she felt a most dismaying, a most unaccountable lifting of the spirit, and usually forgot all about the bleak complexities. With Mr. Calhoun it had been the other way around—all the pieces falling neatly into place, the childhood memories, the plans, the hopes. But now the pieces were all awry, so blurred and disjointed that it was better not to think about them, and easier to live heedlessly in the moment, a life so filled with diversity, with classes and rehearsals and engagements, that, in fact, there was very little time to think at all.

Late in January he took her to the theater to see *Charley's Aunt*, a play so rich in comedy that she laughed throughout the evening, in radiant octaves, gasps and giggles. And he watched her almost as much as he watched the stage, for he had never been able to laugh in quite that way. Always he had been something of an observer, content to stand aside, to analyze and keep a safe distance. But now she was drawing him into the distractions of life, the buoyancy, the unqualified enjoyment, and all his defenses were blowing about, like straws in the wind.

Every now and then, that winter, Mr. Scott would come from New York to pursue his determined courtship. He'd come first when she was in Arlington and Bess had been delighted that her unpredictable younger sister had such a suitable admirer. Mr. Scott had all the qualifications to make a most eligible husband, and she had quickly aligned herself with him.

However, this well-meant conspiracy was ineffective, for Louise was too absorbed in her music to notice even a careful courtship, and only recently had discovered something altogether new—the study of opera. In Philadelphia she had associated vocal music almost entirely with the church—with big oratorios and the finest choral singing. But here in Boston opera was taken for granted as a possible goal for a singer. Her teacher Mr. Whitney's father had sung in opera; in November she had gone to a recital given by a great operatic star, Lillian Nordica, who in her youth had studied at the Conservatory. And in January Mr. Homer had invited her to join, as a guest, his class in the *Nibelungen Ring*, so that she could learn something of the dynamics of that form of art.

He thought it would be helpful, too, if she could hear some opera, and in February, when the Metropolitan came to Boston for a two-week engagement in Mechanics Hall, he subscribed to two seats on alternate nights. The seats were in the front row, so nothing would obstruct her view, and to save the price of a hack, they would walk back and forth from the Barrows boardinghouse. He wore, of course, his dress clothes, tails and a high silk hat, which she thought most distinguished. And she wore the silk dress she'd bought at Wanamaker's in Philadelphia, the year before, when she was making money, a new scarf she'd bought in Boston for sixty cents, and new shoes, the cheapest she could find ($3.50). In those pretty new shoes she walked on clouds of snow, down Boylston Street and Huntington Avenue, to Mechanics Hall.

There, they heard Nellie Melba sing Juliette, the lovely bell-like trills so silver-bright, so faultless, that they seemed to float about in the air like separate entities. They saw Jean de Reszke, as Lohengrin, sail away in a swan boat drawn by doves, his voice fading marvelously in that final song, mellow and melancholy, with the texture of spun gold. They saw Emma Eames die pitifully as Marguerite, and Emma Calvé survive exquisitely as Mignon, and through it all she was living in a dream.

Afterward, when they walked home together in the starlight, she would be transported, exclaiming, again and again, how wonderful it would be to sing in opera. And he would watch her the way one watches a child, feeling a certain compassion for the frail illusions. He had always, himself, considered most opera composers inferior musicians, preferring only a few and regarding the others with a certain disdain. But now, from this rarified height, he was looking down on a most touching phenomenon— the innocent joy of discovery.

However, it wasn't an ideal interlude, for increasingly Louise was troubled, and often restless and wakeful in that small, unheated room on the top floor. She had never before been so distracted, and as the weeks passed, and she became more vulnerable, she hardly knew where to turn for guidance. She thought anxiously about her mother's teachings, and painfully about her father. There was one day, especially, that returned to her again and again. It had been in the spring, when she was a very little girl and they were still living in Shadyside, and she and Bessie had planted some seeds under the glass tops of four honey boxes. Some days after that she'd happened to go with her father into the backyard, where they'd found that in his hotbeds all the pale green sprouts were coming up in neat, carefully tended rows, while under her honey boxes there wasn't even a single sprout. She'd been so disappointed that her father had tried to explain. "Down there in the dark your seeds may be opening right now," he'd said, in his deep, compassionate voice. "The most important part of growing, the true flowering of our spiritual natures, is seldom outwardly visible. Only He who is on high knows what takes place in the hearts of men." And when she'd been puzzled, and asked, "Papa, can God see the seeds under the ground?" he'd taken her hand and answered quietly, "Of course he can, little Petty. When you grow in understanding, when you resist temptation, God will know, even though no one else seems to."

Now those words that she'd scarcely understood at the time returned to trouble her. And finally, not knowing where else to turn, she wrote a letter to Dr. Paxton in Philadelphia, asking him what she should do. In the letter she tried to describe Mr. Homer, his life and his personality, as well as his religious views, for she wanted Dr. Paxton to understand all the circumstances. But at the close of the letter she stated firmly that she wasn't yet in love, so he must feel free to tell her exactly what he thought.

However, this reassurance may have lacked conviction, for when Dr. Paxton replied he seemed to have some doubts about the matter and wrote anxiously:

> People usually fall in love first and think afterwards, and in spite of your assertion to the contrary, I cannot help fearing that is what you have done. My first feeling was one of great sadness and before I knew it, I found myself saying "Poor girl, poor girl," though probably you do not feel you are to be pitied. . . . Such a marriage as you suggest would, I think, be unfortunate and to be regretted and should be avoided if possible. But there comes the rub. I am not prepared to say that the separation and the loss might not be more unfortunate still. I have not the horror of the agnostic which some people have. There is considerable of it in my own disposition. . . . I want you to be very sensible and cautious—come home, have a good summer, and next Fall you will be in a better position to judge. . . . In the meantime keep as far away from the principal as you can, and cultivate the calm serenity of

the iceberg. . . . Do not make a martyr of yourself, imaginary martyrdom never pays. Your sincere friend, James D. Paxton.

On the whole she found the letter reassuring, especially his tolerant attitude toward the agnostic. But though she knew the advice was good, it was difficult to follow. How could she keep far away from "the principal" when she was going, several times a week, to his studio for lessons, and seeing him at almost every meal and many times in between? And though it was surely wise to be "sensible and cautious," how do you cultivate "the calm serenity of the iceberg" when it is spring, and the swans on the Charles River are skimming the placid waters, elegant as birds in a dream?

The letter came late in March, and in the weeks that followed she was unusually busy, for she'd been asked by the Mozart Society of Pittsburgh to sing the role of Jezebel in the oratorio *Elijah*. They would pay her fifty dollars and had sent the money in advance so she could buy a suitable costume—an "oratorio gown" of green silk and white lace. Mr. Whitney was coaching her in Jezebel, and meanwhile she was preparing for a complicated trip away. On May 8th she would go with Bess to West Chester, and a few days later on to Pittsburgh. Then she would return to West Chester and sing the alto part in a cantata with the Orion Society. It was a neatly dovetailed plan, and that can be a mistake when the one involved is too otherwise involved.

On her twenty-third birthday, April 30th, Mr. Homer gave her a birthday letter, which she carried to her room to read again and again. "May this new year bring you nothing but joy and happiness," he had written. "I know that your life has just begun, and that you do not yet know yourself and your destiny. Our destinies, I should say, for they may be one. Think of it! The very hope fills my heart with joy. . . . My darling, the truth and nobility of your soul has given life a new meaning for me. I believe in you and I love you. You are to me the truth that I have sought and never found. . . ." There was more, much more, and she read the letter many times. Four days later they became engaged, and in only another four days she had to leave Boston to fulfill her obligations to that neatly dovetailed plan.

Chapter VIII

In West Chester she tried to pretend that nothing had happened —sitting about on the porch, fending off their questions and joining in the lighthearted banter. But in between she would scribble hasty little notes. "They are all out on the piazza awaiting me," she would write him, "and it would never do in the world for me to be caught at this. As yet my secret is my own. . . . It is so good to be home, but I really feel they do not understand me as I have been understood this winter. . . ."

She was fearful of their questions, and of the way they sometimes teased her about her "music teacher from Boston." She felt too emotional and too susceptible to deal with it now, and planned to keep her engagement a secret until she had returned from Pittsburgh. Then she would talk quietly and earnestly with her mother. And so the West Chester visit had become an exercise in restraint—the bright, sunny smile, the casual reply. And she might have managed it to the end if it hadn't been for one of those unpredictable family scenes that happen every now and then, rising suddenly out of nowhere, bending the branches, swirling the leaves, an errant, quixotic disturbance on a tranquil summer day.

At the start she was in her room, preparing for the trip to Pittsburgh. But meanwhile, in the parlor, a bit of byplay was in progress, for Bess, unable to resist, had told Allie about the engagement to Mr. Homer. And Allie, not realizing it was a secret, had said brightly to their mother, "What do you think of this engagement to a Boston music teacher?" From the tone, their mother had assumed that Allie was joking, and when Louise joined them, a moment later, she'd said, teasing, "Don't ever let me hear of you falling in love with one of those Boston musicians!"

Her mother's flippant mood had given Louse her cue, and she had managed to reply, in the same light vein, "Never fear, Mother dear!" But then her mother had continued, still in a bantering tone, "For you know I would *never* give my consent, so you must never ask it!" And suddenly Louise found that she couldn't play the game anymore. All her defenses crumbled, she burst into tears and fled from the room. So there she was at the end of the West Chester visit, on the bed in her room, in her best traveling costume, weeping and disheveled, with her mother coming quickly to say she was sorry, she had never dreamed it was seriously meant, and Allie calling up the stairs that the carriage was waiting at the door.

After this debacle she must make the trip to Pittsburgh, and from there she described, in a letter, that final, devastating scene in West Chester. "I will have a good long talk with Mama just as soon as I get home," she wrote, "but darling, I think it is only right that you should write her just as soon as you can, for we must have her consent before we can be *formally* engaged. . . ."

While she was in Pittsburgh she took a train to a nearby suburb for an overnight visit with John Waddell and his young wife. This was a visit with a purpose, for it was meant to heal the breach that had existed ever since that abruptly ended romance with John Calhoun. "I have just been making Mr. and Mrs. Waddell a little visit," she wrote Sidney. "You remember, he was the young minister who introduced me to Mr. Calhoun. I told them of our engagement, darling, and we talked it all over until after twelve, and also had a long talk about my other imaginary love affair. They never felt free to discuss it before, because they didn't know just how I felt, but last night we talked it all over and they are so happy to think I am engaged. They are bound to secrecy however!"

What she needed now was communication. But when she returned to West Chester there was still an alien atmosphere, and intimations of disapproval. Her mother asked the minister to talk to her seriously about her obligations to the church, and that was an ordeal. "The minister came to see me today," she wrote him. "He called in the morning and stayed so long I got so nervous I could hardly sit still. I feel so lonely sometimes, even if I have crowds of old friends around me. In fact, darling, I am always more lonely when I am in a crowd than when I am alone. . . ."

Meanwhile, in Boston, Sidney was trying to write that letter to her mother, and finding the assignment very difficult. In part it was his pride that rebelled, as well as a certain innate detachment, for he had always more or less envisioned himself as a bachelor, viewing the world from a safe distance. Now suddenly here he was, called upon to write an unknown and apparently quite formidable lady in Pennsylvania some kind of accounting, indeed, a justification of himself. "I have tried all day to write your mother," he wrote Louise anxiously, "but have been continually interrupted. Tonight I saw Joe Barrows and he told me how impressed they were in West Chester with my lack of religious convictions, and it has upset me completely. . . ."

However, the next day he did write the letter, fashioning it deftly into a subtle, proud, unyielding document that could not possibly imperil any man's dignity.

> Dear Madam, It is with a feeling of real embarrassment that I write to ask you to approve of the proposal that I have made for your daughter's hand, knowing as I do that you have been entirely unprepared for anything of this kind.
>
> I sincerely trust that you will not gain the impression that the attachment that has grown up between Louise and myself is in any way hasty or ill-considered. Our friendship has been of an unusually frank and sincere nature, and has rapidly grown to one of the strongest and truest kind. Louise will tell you how long and carefully she has considered my proposal, and how well she has been able to do it through

the absolute trust and confidence which I have placed in her. And although she may be said to be impulsive regarding many things, I think in regard to this she has tried to be extremely conscientious and cautious in forming her decisions.

I know that the uncertainties that surround the life of a musician and the sacrifice he is called upon to make for his art will have little weight with you as compared to the unsettled character of my religious convictions. About this I can say but little. My life has been unusually free from religious influences and I see nothing beyond the relation of man to his fellowman and the life he lives on earth. But I hope that you will not regard me as a scoffer or as one who has not the highest reverence for religious conviction wherever it is truly felt.

I hope that you will find it in your heart to give your entire consent to our engagement, if for no other reason than because of the love and devotion which I have for your daughter, and which I believe she, in some measure, returns. I remain, respectfully yours, Sidney Homer.

In West Chester the letter was received in a crisis atmosphere and her mother, after carrying it to her room, remained for a long time in seclusion. "Your letter came to Mama this morning," she wrote him. "I do not know how she will write, tho' I am sure she will not withhold her consent and blessing, for she knows true love is sacred. . . . My poor darling boy! Others may tremble for me, but little do I fear that any unhappiness will result from our love for each other. . . ."

A few days later Sidney received her mother's reply, and at once was jubilant with relief. "I had such a beautiful letter from your mother," he wrote Louise. "She yields to your wish and tries to believe in your faith in me, and remembers me in her prayers." This somewhat ambiguous approval he interpreted as reason for "unbounded hope." "The word does not exist," he wrote, "that can express the way I feel. . . . That glorious chord in Isolde's death song, when she sees the spirit of Tristan, might come near it. . . ." Soon afterward, buoyed by the letter and feeling more confident, he made that trip to West Chester and in her view took the citadel by storm.

It seems, indeed, that she may have been too apprehensive all along about this confrontation, for in Boston they'd had such a different situation—lessons in his studio, evenings at the opera, walks together on the Common—and in that beneficent atmosphere had discovered a most complex involvement. But it was still a very new involvement, delicate, untested, barely realized, and she had been fearful of subjecting it too soon to such a diverse and lively household—the noisy children, the retired old folk, the Bibles everywhere, the jokes, the witticisms. However, it was a very human family, susceptible to warmth, especially to communication. And Sidney had, much more than perhaps she had realized, an unusual gift for communication. He could talk to Uncle Martin about politics, to young Fulton about high school—join in the jokes, solve the puzzles, present conundrums of his own. And while all this was going on Louise was content to remain blissfully on the perimeter, all but disregarded, while the various tensions unwound and the pieces were gradually knit together—Allie, so bright and witty, falling under his spell; Allie's husband, Will Husted, a quiet, careful man, a cashier at the bank, earnestly discussing finance; Daisy, the youngest of them all, as captivated by "the music teacher from Boston" as Louise had been, all those years ago in Philadelphia, by the tall, aristocratic figure of her Uncle Elisha Fulton.

During his visit her mother made it plain that though they could be engaged, there were many ironbound provisions and it was unlikely they could be married for several years. The most stringent of her stipulations was that he should be earning enough to support a wife, for his unconventional, seasonal and somewhat uncertain occupation was looked upon with great suspicion in West Chester. In addition they must have a home to live in, and Louise must have money saved for a trousseau. All this, of course, was considered perfectly reasonable. No careful mother of a daughter would expect less, and many couples waited patiently for years to attain these essential objectives. Therefore, in West Chester, their engagement was not taken too seriously,

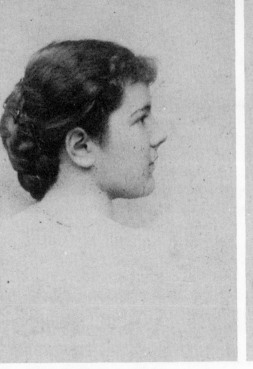

Louise in Boston in 1894.   Sidney Homer in 1894.

and when they returned together to Boston, at the end of his visit, it was still regarded at home as a rather vague and tentative thing.

Recently the Barrows boardinghouse had been sold to be made over into apartments, so in Boston Louise rented an inexpensive furnished room at 10 Brimmer Street. She had her choir position with the First Universalist Church and her lessons at the Conservatory, but she had lost all interest in all her activities, and simply went through the motions. For a while she continued with her harmony lessons, but those studies had become impossible to fulfill. The chords, the progressions, the difficult transpositions —her mind seemed unable to cope with the concentration and instead she would find herself playing at keeping house—sorting out his bachelor's laundry that had been delivered to the studio, turning the white silk ties that had yellowed, and the frayed collars of his shirts.

They felt as though they had invented love, and walked the empty streets penniless and distracted. But they were trying to be practical, and evolved together an announcement of his classes in the fall. This was a vital matter and she took down his dictation in shorthand, and wrote it all out afterward in a fine, flowing script. The announcement, when they had finished, was quite dignified in tone, with the heading "Season of 1894–95—Classes in the Analysis of Symphonies," a list of the composers to be studied and, to broaden the appeal, an assurance that the classes would be "adapted to amateurs as well as musical students, all the technicalities being eliminated as far as possible." The terms would consist of "ten lessons each, the charge being five dollars a term." Applications for membership were to be sent to "Mr. Sidney Homer, Hotel Pelham, Room 512."

This was a bad time for him, financially, since his season of classes had ended, but he had managed to borrow twenty dollars, giving in exchange a check dated some time in the future—a device often used among his friends, for that was the way they lived, in reasonable comfort, but on the edge of nothing. He had an income of five hundred dollars a year from the estate of his wealthy Uncle Sidney, and in a sense this had made possible his precarious existence. The small sums of money, arriving quarterly, had given him just enough freedom to break away from the accepted traditions, though his early education had been conventional enough—Boston Latin School and Andover. But when he was sixteen he had rebelled and protested passionately to his father that his school subjects were irrelevant, since it was surely unreasonable to spend years learning Greek when the greatest Greek literature could be read in translation. He had wanted to go abroad and study, and though his ideas had been vague and youthful, no more substantial than walking the streets he'd read about in books, his father had agreed.

With his income of five hundred dollars a year he had gone first to London, and there, coming from a house of silence (for both his parents were deaf-mutes), he had discovered music and gone on to Munich to study. But for years it had been an uncertain business, more in the nature of a deepening experience, an awakening passion, a series of miracles—the first orchestral concert, the first Beethoven symphony, in Leipzig a Wagner Festival with Anton Seidl conducting. A series of discoveries, but without any proper discipline, until, when he was almost twenty,

George Chadwick had helped him find his way, giving him first
a technique to work with, then sending him back to Munich to
learn harmony and counterpoint from the great master, Carl
Rheinberger. He'd planned a final year in Vienna, studying orchestration under the supervision of the director of the Academy,
Johannes Brahms. But when he was home on vacation (visiting
his sister in New Bedford, where his parents were also living),
his father had died suddenly of a heart attack—calling out in the
night, then falling in his arms.

Three times, while living in Germany, Sidney had dreamed
this experience, and so the shock was somewhat eased, the
dreams a gradual, perhaps beneficent, preparation for what was
to come. But the impact was profound, and he had been especially aware of the unusual loss to his mother, whose communication was so limited. So he'd sent his mother and sister abroad
in his place, to recover, with the diversion of travel, from the
shock of what had happened, and had decided that, for him,
the time had come to earn a living. But how does a music student
manage that? As usual he'd consulted with his great friend and
guide, George Chadwick, and it soon appeared that his only
prospect was to serve as a church organist. But he had instinctively, even passionately resisted that, for during his student years
he'd become a purist—acutely sensitive to chords and progressions, themes and modulations, hearing with his inner ear the
creations that moved him. He considered most church music
uncomfortably sanctimonious, and believed he would have more
artistic freedom as a teacher of harmony.

Though Mr. Chadwick had thought it unlikely he could earn
a living in such a precarious way, he had helped him get a start
—sending him his first pupils, encouraging, advising. And Louise
thought it an odd coincidence that the distinguished musician
who had seemed to her, when she auditioned for him, so severe
and unapproachable, had become, in fact, a trusted friend in
both their lives, helping her become established at the Conservatory, and sending Sidney, whenever possible, still another student
of harmony. Many of his pupils in music appreciation were
young ladies, often rather frivolous, wanting mainly to fill their
time. But he had, as well, several serious young men who were

hoping to become composers. As his reputation had become established, his earnings had improved. But it was still a precarious existence, and during the long summer months he could never be sure what the winter season would bring.

In the meantime there was nothing to do but wait, while devising a great many ingenious budgets, all proving how inexpensive it was to live. Otherwise time was standing still, the heat of summer so enervating that even the swans on the river seemed to droop, and when she sang in church the pews were half empty. In July Sidney became ill, with a vague kind of malady, a nameless fatigue, headaches, twinges of rheumatism and feelings of depression. He'd had such illnesses before and she cared for him tenderly, rubbing his forehead with witch hazel, making cooling drinks of fruit juices and sugar. She didn't understand the depressions, which seemed to have no connection with the circumstances of his life, and neither did he. But he'd had it all before—the apprehension, the sleeplessness, the vague, dispiriting malaise.

Before he had fully recovered she had to go to West Chester, and from there she wrote urging him not to have such "gloomy feelings," adding, however, that she "would not have him changed an atom for anything under the sun." Her letters were anxious yet confident, and soon he was able to reply that he was well again, "calm" and "serene," and in the future was going to do everything possible to prevent such "nervous prostration." When she was in West Chester she went through the little Saratoga trunk, tearing up calling cards and love letters, especially those from Mr. Calhoun, but saving other mementos from the past—packing away parts of her childhood into the satin-lined drawers, and turning the rest into wisps of paper, a confetti-shower of memories that seemed already to belong to someone else. "It has made me realize how different my life is and will be from the past," she wrote him. "It also makes me feel that I was much younger in those days, for life has so much deeper meaning for me now. Darling, I cannot go to sleep without telling you how dearly—*how dearly* I love you. Everything seems so insincere and unreal and meaningless, because nothing is real to me now but your love and I can think of nothing else."

Soon after that he came to West Chester and they returned to Boston together. But there was still to be overcome a dead weight of uncertainty and opposition. They had hoped to be married in November, but by that time nothing had changed—she still didn't have a trousseau, they still didn't have a home, her mother was still concerned about his "uncertain profession" and "part-time teaching," and even expressed, in her letters, a gentle hope that she would some day marry Mr. Calhoun—while in Arlington, Bess still favored Mr. Scott, who even now was unable to believe he had been rejected.

Louise hardly knew how to counter all these alien attitudes, but in November she persuaded Sidney to write her mother more fully about his financial affairs, and this he did, though tempering the distasteful task by observing, at the outset, that "there are other things of more importance than the support of the physical nature." Nevertheless, he managed to meet some of the objections, and in reply her mother wrote, "Your long letter in regard to the state of your finances has set my mind at rest, as I had feared somewhat, as Louise had only said, in regard to your affairs, that your lessons occupied mainly only two days of the week. She was so hurt at my last letter for which I am very sorry. But it was this that caused my anxiety, as heretofore I had depended on your judgement which I thought possibly you might set aside and give way to impulse."

Her mother's reference to "impulse" was intended, she knew, as a warning, and she had always been fearful herself of going into debt. But now she set aside those lifelong scruples and borrowed one hundred and fifty dollars from the First National Bank of West Chester for her trousseau, arranging the transaction with the help of Allie's husband, Will Husted, and giving in return a note which she would pay in installments from her church salary.

She had never before had so much money to spend on clothes, and consulted by mail with her friend Mrs. Paxton. Together they evolved "a practical basic plan," which would include a simple brown for travel, and black for evening. But when she went to the stores to buy the materials, and held up in front of the mirror a green wool or a lavender silk, the warm bright colors would at once become a foil, throwing into relief the deep gray of the eyes, the dark silky luster of the hair and, especially, the glowing, pearly texture of that marvelous complexion. So she had to write Mrs. Paxton that she had made some changes in their basic plan. "Instead of the brown for travel," she wrote, "I have a *green*, and instead of the black for evening I got a pink crepe de chine." She also described a "lavender china silk," which she would have made "very simply, V neck and a little heliotrope velvet," and a housegown which was to be "a *beautiful* shade of red India twill, trimmed with black lace," as well as "pretty pink and blue French flannel for short skirts. Will make these myself: tucks with feather stitching and lace."

It was while she was working on her trousseau that they finally found a home, none other than that same unheated top floor of the Barrows boardinghouse. Recently the building had been turned into apartments, and they found they could have the top floor, and a room in the flat underneath, all for only fifty dollars a month. The room underneath would be Sidney's teaching studio, and the chilly, ramshackle attic at once took on a new identity, becoming, in her letters as well as in her plans, "quaint," "cozy" and ideally suited to a "homelike" atmosphere.

The letters she wrote about her coming marriage were sometimes a puzzle to her friends, for they were all judiciously tailored. In Pittsburgh her godmother, Mrs. Dilworth, was surprised that she had been told "*nothing* of the fortunate young man, not even his occupation!" But a friend in Philadelphia was "delighted that the man you are going to marry is musical, for not to have sympathy in that line would be sad indeed." The oldest friend of all was retired now and living in Johnstown. "I have been thinking of you so much of late," Maggie Johns wrote. "My step is always lighter when I hear from my deare Louise."

For months she had been scaling down her wedding plans, abandoning first what she'd wanted most, a ceremony in the Spruce Street church in Philadelphia, and next a church wedding in Boston and a reception in Bess's house. The final plan was a simple service in Bess's living room, with just a few family members present. But it didn't matter anymore about the wedding, for they had picked the date, January 9, 1895, and planned to send, with the announcements, invitations to an "At Home" reception that they would give themselves, soon after they were married, in their own home on Boylston Street.

The ten days they would take for a honeymoon had to be scheduled so that Louise would miss only one Sunday in the choir, and Sidney not too many classes. They couldn't go far and he learned, through friends, of an exclusive hunting lodge in Georgetown, the Baldpate Inn. The lodge, though closed in winter, took occasional guests, and he wrote making inquiries, stressing in his letter the importance of a "restful" atmosphere, "good country food," "the use of a sleigh" and, above all, "quiet and seclusion."

Mr. William Bray, the proprietor of the Baldpate Inn, studied this letter judiciously, and concluded that he was to be host to an elderly gentleman with an invalid wife. He replied accordingly. "Would most respectfully refer you," he wrote, "to Professor Holt, of the Hotel Bellevue, Beacon Street. Please ask the Professor what he thinks of this place for someone feeling indisposed."

The Baldpate Inn was very old and had been furnished by its distinguished patrons with the finest of English antiques, old pewter, paintings and portraits. It had been built almost two hundred years before, had low beamed ceilings, many fireplaces and was situated on a small river, sheathed now in ice. There was no central heating, but Mr. Bray was confident that even for an elderly invalid the big corner bedroom could be made comfortable, with foot warmers for the canopied bed, the fire always lit and a chaise for reclining.

He met the train himself, taking a supply of carriage robes in the sleigh and standing for some time beside the snowy tracks. Finally there was the train, and only two people alighting; and when he saw them it was all he could do not to laugh out loud, and he was quite unable to suppress a huge smile of amazement and delight. The Baldpate Inn was isolated, the winter months uneventful, and for the staff it became a pleasure, anticipating the needs of such undemanding guests—a fine big breakfast in front of the fire in their bedroom, late in the morning, whenever they chose to ring; and the other meals, too, wherever they might choose to have them, in a windowed alcove overlooking the snowy hills, or perhaps before the fire in the oak-paneled library. It became a pleasurable experience providing an atmosphere of attentiveness and luxury, for in exchange they had, so unexpectedly, an atmosphere of romance, of joy and tenderness, that seemed to suit the fine old inn.

After their return, Louise had only a few weeks to prepare for the reception. But Tillie, the janitor's young wife, was able to help, and together they polished and dusted and arranged. She'd had an upholstered window seat made for the front room, where there was a coal fire. For the bedroom in back she had chosen a wallpaper that she thought the most exquisite she had ever seen—green and white, with a delicate vinelike pattern. And to furnish the Boylston Street apartment, Sidney's mother had given them some of her most cherished possessions, which had been in storage for years: the mahogany cabinet with glass doors, the Chippendale chairs, the delicate English china.

The cards, included with the wedding announcements, read:

At Home
Wednesdays
February the Twentieth and Twenty-Seventh
355 Boylston Street
Boston

These receptions would compensate for the plainness of the wedding, which had excluded all their friends and seemed already a dreamlike thing—the old white dress made over, the bits of tulle for a veil, and walking alone down the stairs in Bess's house, while Sidney's sister Georgie played a wedding march on the piano. She had been in such a daze that the wedding seemed already as hazy as sunshine on a misty day. And now they were to be properly "at home," with Tilly to help with the serving, and the ladies' wraps laid out in the room with the ivied wallpaper.

She wore the housegown of red India twill, trimmed with black lace, for the receptions. It had a small train, the first she had ever owned, and when everything was ready, and she was receiving her own guests in her own home, she felt as though she had stepped from one life into another.

Many of their guests were Sidney's friends—musicians, artists, pupils—and a good many were his relatives, who came in relays, Pierces and Nichols as well as Homers. It was a rather formidable family he had, and highly individualistic, but there was also a certain prevailing resemblance—the women often tall and plain and energetic, the men distinguished in appearance, and rather reserved.

It was a very Bostonian family, with some of the qualifying attributes—vacillation, procrastination, a tendency toward inertia—that can come, perhaps, from a long, attenuated line. But there was altruism, as well, brusque and forthright, often original, and years ago this kindliness had protected his mother, Anna Maria, when, as a young girl, she had been, as she was even now, small, fragile and too spirited for the silence of her world.

The marriage of George Homer and Anna Maria Swift had been arranged in the old-fashioned way, plotted over the teacups, with wisdom and foresight, by a bevy of resourceful Boston ladies. On one hand there was a bachelor of forty, a tall, bearded, blue-eyed man who worked in the Customs House and lived in Boston with his father and unmarried sister. When he was about nine, George Homer had lost his hearing, some said from diving too recklessly into the Charles River. Because lip-reading wasn't known at that time, he'd been educated in a school for the deaf, which had affected his ability to speak. But could his life be altogether satisfying when he must communicate with his hands? Then, by chance, there had recently come to Waltham, to live with her maiden aunt, a child who could not hear or speak—for though she was twenty-three she seemed a child, having been raised in that way, motherless and enchantingly dependent, growing up in New York and encouraged to be frivolous, with dancing school, balls and parties, and such a joyous love of rhythm, of color and variety, that the quietness of her world had been allayed.

Anna Maria had lost her hearing at the age of two, after an

George Homer, father of Sidney Homer. Anna Maria Swift Homer, his mother.

attack of scarlet fever. Her mother had died that same year, and she'd been cherished and pampered by her father and her older brothers. But then her father had died, her brothers had married and gone out West to live and she'd come to Waltham, to be cared for by a maiden aunt. Now the Boston ladies, chatting over their teacups, were concerned, for in the quiet New England town she had seemed to droop, the big dark eyes too solemn, the silence too unbroken. She had become listless, pale and lonely. And so it was arranged, and one day a fine carriage, with a coachman and four horses, clattered into the village of Waltham, and Anna Maria was persuaded to change into her prettiest silk gown. Then she descended the stairs in her aunt's house, to be introduced to two dignified ladies in black and a tall, bearded, blue-eyed man who could talk to her with his hands.

Marriage, and the loving guardianship of that marriage, had

restored her spirit, for she was a romantic and would take her two children all over Boston in search of color and adventure— to plays, to circuses, to exhibits of pictures and always to parades. Often they would stand for hours, waiting to see some great man pass, for though she couldn't hear the bands, she could feel the rhythms and see the colors and communicate to her children the buoyant wonder of that moment.

She had been protected in her isolation by her husband and his relatives, and whenever a child was born an old aunt would come to live with them and teach the baby to talk. The first child, a boy named for his father, had died at the age of three —a beautiful, speaking child, scratched in the eye by a playmate, the accident resulting in brain fever. A year later there was a girl, Georgianna, and four years after that another boy, named for his Uncle Sidney. And to the great astonishment of everyone, all the children could hear and speak perfectly.

Little Sidney had been three years old when his father bought a house at 27 Appleton Street, in Boston—an important milestone made possible through the help of his Uncle Sidney, a bachelor and importer who provided trust funds and small incomes for many of the needier members of the family. It was only a small house, but charmingly decorated, and his parents had delighted in caring for it. Almost every year something new would be added—pearl paper with a crimson border for the tiny hall, perhaps; a rosewood set for the parlor; or Chippendale side chairs with leather seats.

These were the furnishings that had been taken out of storage to decorate the apartment at 355 Boylston Street. And when their friends and relatives had climbed the four flights to the top they would discover a fire blazing in the open grate, and a most homelike atmosphere. And they all came to one or another of the receptions—Sidney's cousin Tom Homer, his second cousins Charles and Arthur and even his cousin Winslow Homer, who lived most of the year in Prouts Neck, Maine, and just happened to be in town. The presence of this artist cousin was a measure of the family loyalty, for he was something of a recluse, quite solitary in his ways and increasingly successful. Recently he had been awarded a gold medal at the Columbian

Sidney Homer when he was about twelve, a student in Boston.

Sidney Homer when he was studying in Munich and already wearing those white silk ties!

Exposition in Chicago for a seascape called "The Gale," and another by the Academy of Fine Arts in Philadelphia. Winslow Homer didn't seem at all as Louise had imagined an artist might, for in appearance he was rather formal, and wore, for the reception, a black cutaway and stiff derby hat. He was a smallish man and almost bald, though with a very large up-sweeping reddish moustache; in his manner he was reserved, not talkative, and for the most part remote and self-contained.

This advent of an artist in Sidney's family was not surprising, for though the family fortunes had been founded on importing and similar ventures, there were several who had strayed from the original tradition. Another of his cousins, Augusta Homer, was married to a sculptor, Augustus Saint-Gaudens, and his sister Georgie's husband, Frederick Diman, was a singer and conductor. Quite a few of his relatives were widely traveled and lived in handsome town houses on Beacon Street. So at the receptions the conversations ranged widely, and all this conspired to make Louise feel as though she had, indeed, stepped from one life into another.

Chapter IX

For over a year now Louise had been studying with Mr. Whitney. But though he was an experienced singing teacher, they weren't making much progress with her voice. Strangely, all the old problems were still there: the heaviness, the unruly resonance, the uneven placement. And it could be painful to struggle with an instrument that had so much potential, and was so beautiful at times, and yet so troublesome.

Mr. Whitney was puzzled himself by their lack of progress. But he was a teacher who believed he knew his limitations, and with her voice he was inclined to be cautious. He was afraid he might damage such a heavy, unwieldy instrument if he forced the high notes, and usually transposed her songs to a lower key, exclaiming, meanwhile, that if only she could study with his great master in Rome, Vannucini would know exactly what to do! He seemed to think his gifted Italian teacher would have some magic formula, some especially devised technique to send the high notes soaring and modulate the low ones. And that could be a tantalizing thing, to have a voice so flawed and difficult that only an old man living in Rome could provide the answer.

Mr. Whitney became very animated when he talked about

Signor Vannucini. How inspired he was! How intuitive! Thus creating a kind of mirage that made it even more discouraging to follow, day after day, the usual unprofitable routine. But this year there were other things to think about, for in the fall a baby would be born. And that first summer, when they had rented their apartment to a friend, and were given, by parents of a pupil of his, a tiny, one-room cottage at Kennebunkport, Maine, Louise could sit by the rocky shore, cooled by the breezes, buoyed by the changing moods of the sea, and sew on the Gertrude System Garments. These infant clothes were very modern in design, styled so they could be slipped on all at once, without pins or buttons, and a truly conscientious mother must sew every stitch herself.

The baby, a little girl, was born November 20th, in the room with the ivied wallpaper, and afterward they received from both their mothers many helpful letters of advice. His mother warned against "chilly sheets" and recommended "partridge" as a favored diet. And her mother believed "a month upstairs" would be "a great gain in the end." "Don't see much company," she wrote, "it makes for a cross child. Keep quiet, and don't read in bed. I love to commit you and your dear one to His tender care." It was an affectionate letter, though tempered, as usual, with a characteristic word of warning. "I hope you will feel," she wrote, "that this little one is to be trained for Heaven. It *may* be she is a *loan*, and He has the right to take her when He will." They named the little girl Louise, called her Baby and admired her extravagantly. With their first Christmas tree they had a most appropriate companion, a dark-eyed little daughter, sensibly attired in Gertrude System Garments.

Meanwhile Sidney's classes were growing in size. They were becoming more prosperous, and since he could arrange his schedule as he wished, his time was flexible, and when he was free he had only to climb a flight of stairs. It was an ideal situation, and with Tillie at home to mind the baby Louise could go about the city in a glow of contentment—across town, on Friday evenings, for choir rehearsal, or over to the Conservatory on Wednesday for her lesson with Mr. Whitney. Twice during the winter she took part in small recitals, one in Malden, and

Louise and her baby daughter in Boston.

one in New Bedford, and was paid twelve dollars each time. And she often sang at weddings.

The only shadow, if there was one, was that perennial trouble with her voice, which, by this time, she was quite accustomed to. But one evening, after an unusually frustrating lesson, with her heavy voice unable to respond, she sighed. It was just a small sigh, while they were both sitting close to the fire after supper, which they always did since it was their only source of heat, he with his pipe and stein of beer, talking over the events of the day. But he happened to hear, and asked, quickly, what was the matter. And she replied wistfully, "Oh, nothing, just the same old trouble with my voice!" and then went on to talk of other things.

But for him that muted sigh served as a catalyst, sparking an unforeseen idea, and he found himself wondering, on impulse, if they couldn't go abroad just as he had in his youth, so that Louise could study with the finest teachers, and learn how to sing. However, this idea was so unforeseen and so disturbing that he said nothing to her at the time, but wrestled with it secretly, in a rising fever of hope and anxiety.

Day after day he weighed the pros and cons of such a radical proposal—the dangers and the possible rewards. And when he tried to banish the whole rash project, it would return to haunt him the next day. The only money they would have would be his trust income of five hundred dollars a year. But it had occurred to him that they might borrow from wealthy friends and relatives, giving as a reason that they wanted to "further her musical education." If they could raise twenty-five hundred dollars in this way they would have enough, he believed, for two years in Paris, and while she was studying singing, he would have a studio and compose.

The greatest hazard in his plan was the effect on his own profession, for it had taken him five years to build up his classes —the private lessons in harmony and counterpoint, the group courses in symphony and opera and the advanced study with serious composers. Gradually he had managed to achieve a reputation in Boston, and was able now to earn a fairly liveable income. But if he had to close his studio, all his pupils would go to other teachers, and when they returned, after two years in Paris, he would have to start all over again. So it would be a risky venture, but to counter it there was that wistful sigh, and all the years she had been trying to learn how to sing.

However, he was still not ready to take the plunge. And so he hesitated, postponing from day to day the final step of sharing with her what he had now begun to call his "great plan." But one day she more or less forced his hand, by having a plan of her own, or at least an unexpected opportunity. It had come about at the Conservatory, when she was having her lesson, and she returned home that evening in a radiant mood, unpinning her hat, tossing it on the piano, then defying him to guess.

When she had something of moment to relate she liked to make an event of the telling—what he said, what she said, creating a drama. And now there was a characteristic air of mystery while she revealed that a distinguished gentleman had come to see her at the Conservatory, quite elderly he was, gray-haired and very solemn, chairman of the Music Committee for the New Old South Church, and—you'd *never* guess—he'd offered her a contract for twelve hundred dollars a year, just *twice* what she was getting now!

Although he made a pretense of sharing her joyful astonishment, he knew then that he would have to tell her about his plan. But the gradual unfolding, which he had plotted so carefully, turned into a shambles, for she thought that he was indulging in a comical bit of invention, and her laughter, echoing about the apartment, all but drowned him out. She had laughed just this way at the antics in *Charley's Aunt*, and tonight, with a fine new contract in the offing, she was in a mood for fantasy, and quite ready to go along with that fairy-tale world he was creating, in which they would all sail away to a beautiful adventure—just pack up Baby and sail away—just borrow money and give up the teaching and the choir and all the income, and sail off to Paris. . . . She thought his earnest manner comical, the outlandish scheme a fanciful bit of humor. And it was like a roller-coaster ride with a big bump at the end, when she finally discovered that he was serious.

He had been living so long with this dream of his that it had begun to seem quite feasible. But she was shocked, for she thought the whole venture flighty and irresponsible. She couldn't believe that he'd be willing to borrow money in such a heedless way, give up his profession and their home and go traipsing off to Europe, just so that she could study with someone he liked to call "the greatest singing teacher in the world."

Nevertheless, after that evening, they talked about it often. And when she protested that it would be unsafe for Baby, that she couldn't bear to leave her home, where they'd lived scarcely a year, that surely it would be unwise to forfeit his profession and his income, Sidney would respond by embroidering for her, night after night, his new vision of the future. And this he could do quite vividly, for during the past few weeks he had been living so intensely in a more expansive world that now their present life no longer satisfied him. Unaccountably, he had become oppressed by the sameness, the narrowness, and gradually he communicated that dissatisfaction to her. Especially this was so when he touched on that studio he hoped to have, and the composing, for she had always regretted that the teaching took so much of his creative energy. The work he did with his most serious pupils was so concentrated and strenuous that often at the end of the day he'd be exhausted. And time after time his own efforts to compose were put aside, so that he could help those to whom he was committed.

This troubled her, and now when she saw the signs of fatigue after a day of teaching, she would think of the studio he might have in Paris, the songs he would compose—the difference it might make in his life if he had that opportunity. She wanted him to have a chance, she didn't like to see his talents wasted, just as he was disturbed that she couldn't have the finest teachers. They both tended to live in each other's lives, and gradually this mutual dissatisfaction settled like a cloud over the day-by-day routine that only a short while before had seemed almost ideal, and they were no longer content.

His musician friends were shocked when they heard about the venture. It had taken him years to build up his classes, they said, and when he returned he'd have to start all over again. But it was the greatest friend of all, George Chadwick, who formulated the most obvious problem, pointing out reluctantly, one evening when they were all three walking together on Boylston Street, that there were no roles in opera for her voice—a statement of fact so undeniable that it fell flat as a stone into the quiet night.

Hastily Sidney replied that they "didn't aspire to Grand Opera," they just wanted to "give her a chance to see what she could do." But this, of course, was an evasion—for what else did they aspire to? Nevertheless, it was a fact that she didn't have the high notes for opera, or even for many of the songs and selections sung in concerts. She had an unusually limited voice, pitched too low, without the range or scope needed to repay the investment of borrowed money and lost income that Sidney proposed. But strangely, they circled about this central flaw without attempting to touch it, mesmerized now, in some mysterious way committed, and early in March they made their decision and started the appeal for funds.

He composed the letters artfully so that their requests would be made to sound both dignified and businesslike. He wanted their friends and relatives to realize that this was not an impulsive project, but a most carefully considered course of action, and many of them did. Her godmother, Mrs. Dilworth, wrote from Pittsburgh sympathizing with their aims, but unable to make a loan at this time. However, there were several who could, and within a few weeks they had the twenty-five hundred dollars of borrowed money that he had set as their goal.

Her relatives in West Chester were confounded when they heard about the plan, for it seemed to them that she was doing the same thing all over again—abandoning a safe and secure life for some foolish and flighty future arrangement that made no sense at all. However, when they took the baby to West Chester to show her off to the relatives before sailing for Europe, the talk was not of singing, but of the Gertrude System Garments, infant care and feeding and other maternal lore. This created an atmosphere so reassuringly domestic that even her mother's shocked dismay was somewhat eased.

Sidney's relatives had traveled abroad a good deal, so they could understand the project better. And it was his cousin, Augusta Homer Saint-Gaudens, who helped them with their plans. Gussie suggested Beatenberg, high in the Swiss Alps, for their summer vacation. And while they talked about it over tea, the ship they would sail on for Rotterdam—the S.S. *Maasdam*—the trip up the Rhine, the pretty, inexpensive inn where they would stay, it all seemed as evanescent as the sunbeams glittering on the teacups. But in only a few weeks there they were, breathing air spun fine as crystal, while the sheep moved about, cropping the grass, and a small brook, pearly and translucent, wandered through the hilly fields.

Louise was intoxicated with this sudden change in her life, the foreign atmosphere and especially the snow-covered mountains, majestic and so peaceful, that seemed to give the days an almost dreamlike quality. They had friends in the Beatenberg Inn —Monsieur Savard, a French composer, and his young wife, a companionable Swedish girl. Monsieur Savard was a prominent musician, winner of the Prix de Rome, and when Louise had sung for him, he started composing a song for her, using a poem of Verlaine's, "Le Crépuscule."

With the Savards there were picnics, and long walks through the countryside. But in the evening, when they were alone together, they would talk about the future. And then Sidney would outline for her the many theories he had evolved about music students living abroad. This was a favorite topic, for during his own apprenticeship he'd known many Americans who'd come to Europe to study. He'd seen the disappointments and the fail-

ures, and from all this he'd drawn a number of practical con-
clusions. One of his theories stressed the importance of proper
living conditions. Too many music students, he said, lived in
cheap furnished rooms or shabby hotels, and tried to exist on
black coffee and inferior restaurant food. This, he believed, was
especially disastrous for singers; how could they hope to succeed
if they undermined their health?

Another strong conviction was concerned with the matter of
a full schedule of lessons. Many voice students, he said, were
satisfied with just one singing lesson a week, but that could be
false economy, for it was well known that much of the work
a singer did on her own could be injurious to her voice. Therefore, since their resources were limited, Louise must have an
elaborate schedule of instruction, for there was no time to lose.

It didn't occur to either of them that his views might resemble
those of a gambler who believes in risking everything on the first
throw of the dice. All his theories had been most carefully considered, and while he explained them to her she would listen
intently, impressed by his wisdom and foresight. He had a way
of talking with great conviction, and she had a way of listening
and believing. His hands, big and square and clumsy, moved
when he talked. His strong dark hair, which he wore parted in
the middle, fell over the sensitive forehead. He was very tall,
broad-shouldered but otherwise knobbily thin—the features
rugged and rather plain, in the Boston way, the moustache neatly
trimmed, the eyes dark and expressive, and she thought him the
handsomest man she had ever known.

In Beatenberg the proprietor's fifteen-year-old daughter, Anna
Kindleman, helped care for Baby. And since her parents were
anxious that she learn both French and English, it was arranged
that she would come with them to France. So at the end of
August they left for Paris with the Savards and their little girl,
Anna and Baby, who was now nine months old, and described,
in letters home, as "a little round peach." They also took with
them many practical theories to help with that precarious and
evanescent matter of learning how to sing.

Chapter X

In Paris they looked for an unfurnished apartment, and found a big sunny one at 36 rue de Lubeck, across from the Trocadero Park. There was no central heating, and the place was brightly, starkly bare. But the rent was only thirteen dollars a month, and adventurously they undertook a transformation. They already had with them, from Boston, their rugs, books and silver, and they bought a few necessities—some secondhand beds and wicker chairs and a big tin tub for baths. Then, with a length of cheap cretonne, Louise made curtains for the windows, and covered the packing boxes to serve as small tables, washstands and bureaus.

All day long the rooms were full of sunshine, and once they were settled, their American friends, living haphazardly in hotels and furnished rooms, were astonished at how cheaply they had managed such a comfortable arrangement. Around the corner on the Avenue Kléber they rented an attic room for four dollars a month, and furnished it with a rented piano, a table and chair —this would be Sidney's studio.

Meanwhile Louise was auditioning every day, for anyone and everyone—singing teachers, musicians, friends of the Savards, friends of friends. Just as in Boston, there was interest and encouragement, only here, instead of recommending choir positions, they told her that she had "une vraie voix du théâtre"—

a true operatic voice. And this was said so often, with such sincerity, that she became every day more hopeful, and could hardly wait to begin.

But the selection of a singing teacher was the most crucial element in the entire spectrum of his "great plan." Nothing else was so vital, and with great caution he made inquiries, and settled finally on a most distinguished maestro, Monsieur Jacques Bouhy. Monsieur Bouhy's former pupils were on opera stages all over Europe and he agreed to give her lessons at the reduced rate of only four dollars an hour.

But she must have other training to supplement the singing, and in accordance with his theories, Sidney arranged for her quite an expansive program—two lessons a week in "action and deportment" with the famous Yersin sisters, two a week in French and diction and, so that she could take full advantage of his methods, three singing lessons every week with Monsieur Jacques Bouhy.

When she had her voice lessons, Sidney always went with her and listened closely. Throughout the hour he was quietly observant, and Monsieur Bouhy was a most impressive teacher— reserved, very formal and controlled. The Maestro's studio was in keeping with this restraint, a severe rectangle of mirrors and gilt chairs, the walls hung with photographs of grateful pupils. And the teaching was so stylized, and so exacting, that the lessons were sometimes a strain. But that was a small matter, for she was making progress, and within only a few months could write her friend, Marion Cock, that Monsieur Bouhy had said her voice was "beautifully placed," and she had only to learn to "*support* properly, with the breath, *without pushing*," which would make the soft singing "easy." She could also confide to her sympathetic friend that she had "learned the role of Orpheus by heart (in French)," and "almost finished Dalila," and that "Bouhy is already talking to managers about me."

Like so many of his pupils, she now revered Monsieur Bouhy, who had quietly taken command, not only of her voice, but also of her future. And so that winter in Paris took on a lovely cadence, and even before the leaves had begun to turn in the Trocadero Gardens, she was winging her way here and there in a veritable whirl of lessons and activities. In December the Paxtons came to Paris to live, so that Dr. Paxton could take charge of the "services d'ateliers" in the American Church on the rue de Berri. Quite often Louise would sing at these Studio Services, which were held on Sunday evenings for the colony of Americans —students, artists, musicians—living in the artistic quarters of Paris. Afterward there might be little suppers, or other informal gatherings, and this became the nucleus of many congenial friendships.

Among the new friends they met there were the Fidèle Koenigs. Monsieur Koenig was an engaging young Frenchman who served as "chef du chant" at the Paris Opera, and coached the singers in their roles; his wife, a charming young American, was a member of the Fay family in Boston. Monsieur Koenig would play the accompaniments when she sang at the Studio Services, and often, afterward, he would talk to her about her voice. He was an ebullient young man, tall, blond, disarmingly outspoken and inclined to stutter when he became excited, the French phrases falling over each other in comical fashion. But at the piano he became a different person altogether, relaxed, composed, un-usually intuitive. And after she had finished singing, he would tell her earnestly that he "envied her teacher the honor of spon-soring such a voice," calling it "velvet."

During the winter she sang Monsieur Savard's song, "Le Crépuscule," at a concert given by the Société Nationale de Musique—an affair sponsored by the musicians themselves, and considered, by certain purists in Paris, somewhat amateurish. Nevertheless the hall was filled, the applause was brilliant and the great success of the evening was a strange, vibrant piece that undertook to tell a story with an orchestra. Many people thought the novel idea outlandish, but the composer, Paul Dukas, con-ducted it himself, and at the end the audience applauded wildly and L'Apprenti Sorcier became a sensation.

Meanwhile Sidney was going with her to all her lessons and listening when she practiced at home, and one evening, when she was feeling especially content, and they were sitting, as usual, close to the fire, he started to talk, choosing the words very care-fully. Choosing the words so carefully that it was quite a while before she realized what he was saying, and felt the chill of the cold, empty, profitless winter. Though she mustn't be discouraged, he said. All voices responded differently to different methods, and next time they would make a better choice.

She was unprepared, she'd had no suspicion, and it was a shock to realize that a singer cannot truly hear herself. She is so close to the tones that she is easily misled, and watches, instead, her teacher's face, and listens for his approval. And meanwhile what was happening? Her voice was becoming smaller, he said. It was becoming "covered over," veiled in some way, and the brilliance was diminishing very fast. He had been going with her to all her lessons, listening intently, and recently with anxiety, for it seemed to him that Monsieur Bouhy's technique was damaging what she had had before. Though he had been recommended as the finest teacher in Paris, and had an impressive manner and a handsome studio and talked confidently about "managers," his method, which had been spoken of so highly, was muffling and constraining the natural qualities of her voice.

Once she had been able to assimilate the import of this disheartening revelation, she agreed that they would have to change teachers. But the break was a hard one to make, delicate and very painful. All Monsieur Bouhy's pupils had a regard for him approaching reverence, and they had been part of that magic circle, devoted to "The Master," as they called him, admiring, without reservation, a most distinguished friend. And now they must express dissatisfaction and turn to someone else.

It wasn't easy, for they weren't, now, quite so confident. But they made inquiries, and settled finally on an Italian singing teacher, Signor Juliani, who was highly recommended. And within a week or two they realized they had chosen well, for the difference was apparent almost at once—the high notes free and bright again, the veiled, "covered over" effect vanishing like magic. The difference in the method was apparent, too, for Juliana didn't have Monsieur Bouhy's reserve. He taught her to open her mouth wide, releasing, with unrestrained vitality, the resonance of the soaring tones. And he created, in his studio, an atmosphere quite the opposite of Monsieur Bouhy's hushed formality. Signor Juliani liked to make his pupils feel at ease, with jokes, blandishments, at times a bit of clowning. During the lessons he was relaxed, even jovial, and there was laughter in the studio. But he was a genius, as well, and his pupils spoke with delight of his engaging personality, and with extravagant admiration of his accomplishments—all the miracles he had performed and the lives he had transformed.

Louise responded instinctively to the relaxed, sunny atmosphere and had never been so happy in her work. They felt as though they had averted disaster—though perhaps just in time, for a good part of the money was gone. But meanwhile they'd found the right teacher at last, and during the lessons Sidney would listen carefully, at first with relief, and then, after a month or two, with anxiety again, for now something unfortunate seemed to be happening to her low tones. These had always been the treasure of her voice, its greatest asset—those deep low tones, so original in texture, weighted with timbre, dark as velvet and profoundly moving. But now, with this new technique, they were flattening out, becoming breathy, hollow, partially deadened, and that could be a catastrophe.

Again he had to tell her; she couldn't hear it herself. And afterward even the bright spring sunshine in the Trocadero Gardens took on a different look—all the flowers, the tall trees, the ladies with their pretty parasols, the small children, so lively with their hoops and satin hair ribbons, the charm of it a sad, disjointed thing because perhaps they didn't deserve it and shouldn't have come here and squandered their future.

This second setback wasn't as easy to deal with as the first one had been, for now much of that early confidence had faded. He told her anxiously that the next time they would be more careful and find a teacher who was a true scientist in the technique of the voice. But she had now the hurt, sensitive feeling of one who is inexplicably unable to conform, and finds herself mysteriously excluded from the inner circle of those who can meet the accepted standards of performance.

Now and then, at the Studio Services, Fidèle Koenig would hint guilelessly that he'd like to become her teacher. And this, too, had a hurting, belittling effect, for Monsieur Koenig wasn't even a voice teacher, he was just a coach. Although he'd had one

or two pupils, his profession was to drill the opera singers in
their roles. And even a lighthearted intimation that they might
settle, now, for some second-best, makeshift arrangement was
like an admission of defeat. When they left Juliani, Sidney would
say, whenever they tried unhappily to discuss this painful matter
—when they left Juliani it must be for someone at the very top.

But it was late in the spring, now, not a good time to make
a change, and they were hampered in their plans because their
money was almost gone. At the start they had been too prodigal,
and it was beginning to seem that his theory about not skimping
on lessons might have been a mistake—wise when it worked, but
a disaster when it didn't—for they had spent a thousand dollars
just on the lessons, and had almost nothing to show for it. When
Louise spoke or sang in French she was told that she had an
"accent délicieux," and she had become well versed in "stage
deportment." But what good was all that when she couldn't learn
how to sing?

However, Sidney still had his theories, and one of the most
unyielding was the importance of a summer vacation. Most of
the singing pupils they knew followed their teachers, in a sort
of retinue, to some mountain or seaside resort, and continued
with their studies. But he believed that everyone should have
some months each year of rest and relaxation. And it was true
that for Louise the winter had been strenuous, and the various
singing methods a great strain. Open the mouth wide, they said,
support with the breath—*without pushing*—stand this way, stand
that way, place the tone higher, place it lower, scales, arpeggios,
opera scores, language, diction, force, don't force, try the high
B flat, see how easy it is? Fine, Madame, fine. Now, we'll try
once more . . . The strain had been immense, she was wearier
than she knew, and when he said that she should have an interval
of rest, as almost always happened she believed him, and they
went by train to the Black Forest and stayed in a small inn in the
village of Schönwald.

However, this vacation was subdued and rather dreary. "Today it is raining again," she wrote her mother, "and it is horrid,
a summer hotel and rain, for everyone is around, and if we want
to be alone we must stay in our room. . . ." But the weather

cleared, after a time, and in Schönwald, when they took walks in the woods, the tall trees seemed to progress in clean, straight rows, majestic as trees on a stage set, and the forest had a beautiful stillness. "Yesterday we took a long walk to an outlook tower," she wrote her mother, "and climbed to the very top. We could actually see our dear snow mountains, the ones we loved so last summer. They are a hundred miles away but filled one quarter of the horizon like great fleecy clouds." And perhaps, in a way, this was symbolic, the high hopes of last summer belonging now to the past, the mountains, like the dreams, become as visionary as clouds.

However, Sidney was still trying to be quietly encouraging. The next time, he told her, they would find a teacher who was a true master of vocal technique. And sometimes he would try to analyze the complexity of the vocal instrument. There is the arch of the palate, he would say, the structure of the vocal chords, the diaphragm—the bellows that gives it power—the arrangement of the sinuses and antrums—the sounding board that gives it resonance—and of course the formation of throat and larynx: the whole interlocking mechanism so subtle and so delicate that only the most highly trained specialists could even begin to understand it.

But when she wondered unhappily if her voice might be out of adjustment in some way, he would reply that the singer's instrument is mysterious, and no one knows exactly how it works. A technique that is miraculous for one can be ruinous for another; and he might add that the word "miraculous" was used advisedly, for at times the proper technique could effect a miracle. So there they were, in the Black Forest, with the gray rain greeting them in the morning, oppressed now by the possibility of failure, but not ready, yet, to accept defeat.

However, when they had returned to Paris, they were still uncertain what to do. The next change would have to be the last, and they were half paralyzed by indecision, as well as by near poverty. Meanwhile she continued working with Signor Juliani, for within that familiar circle there were ties difficult to break. During the lessons and small recitals they had become great friends with the other singers, for Juliani's pupils were like one happy family, a small community of hopeful young artists, and all so devoted to their teacher that it would be an affront when they left, as well as an admission of failure.

There were social complexities, too, for the Julianis were among the group associated with the Studio Services on the rue de Berri. When a small musicale was arranged, there might be listed among the patronesses, "the Mesdames Paxton, Savard, Juliani, Koenig . . ." Quite often Louise would sing on these occasions, and now it had become a painful charade, for among these kind friends they must maintain a confident air and not admit that their money was almost gone, and they had no future here.

At home, too, they were trying to cling to a certain tempered equilibrium, and so it was disturbing when Madame Koenig came to see her, one morning in September, with a most unusual request. Louise was alone, that day, practicing her scales and exercises. Already there was an atmosphere of unhappiness in the apartment, overtones of failure. And now to that was added the strain of acute embarrassment, for such a request, so frankly stated, was a breach of etiquette. Teachers weren't supposed to court each other's pupils; no musician of stature would stoop to such a thing. Yet here was Madame Koenig begging her to study with her husband, pleading, with tears in her eyes, her voice trembling with urgency, "Madame Homer, if you only knew what he could do for you! If you only knew!"

Her own feelings were very fragile during this interview. While they talked she was herself close to tears, made acutely sensitive by all the months and even years of futile lessons. But she hardly knew what to say, for Fidèle Koenig wasn't a voice teacher, only a coach. They'd debated the matter often, and she understood the situation, but not how to refuse. So finally, to appease her friend, Louise promised reluctantly that she would speak to her husband when he came home from his studio for lunch.

But she knew already what he would say, and Sidney was most emphatic. They couldn't afford to experiment, he told her; the next teacher would have to be the last, and therefore they must find a man of the highest reputation, a true master in the technique of the voice. But how was she to explain that to Madame

Koenig when she came for her answer tomorrow? Their kind friends had placed them in a most delicate situation, and finally he thought of a way out—a compromise. They might agree, he said, to let Monsieur Koenig coach her in her operatic roles. For this they would pay him a dollar an hour, while at the same time she would continue her real voice lessons with Juliani at four dollars an hour. No harm would be done, and they'd be spared the embarrassment of an outright refusal.

Although this was hardly a flattering proposal, Fidèle Koenig consented at once. And the next day they went together to his studio, taking the opera scores. But Monsieur Koenig seemed to have forgotten that part of the stipulation, for after running his fingers lightly over the keys, he suggested that Louise start with a scale. And though she was surprised by the request, for she had imagined they would study the roles, she complied, singing the scale as smoothly as she could. And Monsieur Koenig nodded and smiled and said, "Fine, fine, now we will try again—no, do not open the mouth so wide—there, that is better, much better." And it was.

The next day there was another coaching session, and another the day after that. And Monsieur Koenig would say casually, "Today we'll forget about those chest tones, and get the voice up into the head. Now let us have a try. Let us carry it up, up, but gently, gently, there! you see?" And they saw. Every day they saw and every day they wondered, for she had never sung like this before.

After two weeks they dropped the lessons with Signor Juliani (the change wasn't, after all, too difficult to make), and Fidèle Koenig took over, and arranged for her a most unusual schedule of instruction. She would have a lesson every day, he said (still at only a dollar an hour), and never more than fifteen minutes of vocalizing by herself at home. Otherwise she must stay right away from the piano, and that was unheard of, a voice student who didn't practice endlessly at home. The contrast was startling: the piano so still, the sunny apartment quiet and the singer free to spend her time like any other wife and mother, sewing, chatting, playing with the baby. It was restful, and it was an adventure, for every day there was the lesson.

They were working now on the fundamentals of vocal technique, but oddly, these lessons weren't as demanding, or as taxing, as the other ones had been. Monsieur Bouhy had been so
rigid, so formal, that the singer was always under a strain, trying
anxiously to please, while Signor Juliani's atmosphere of energetic
good humor could be an effort to sustain. But Monsieur Koenig
was relaxed, composed, his touch on the piano an inspiration, his
manner so disarming, so unaffected, that the singer almost forgot
she was having a lesson, and the time flew by on wings.

It was apparent that he understood her voice, the assets as well
as the limitations. And she had begun to have great faith in his
judgment, until one day he undermined it all, and exhibited, quite
casually, a most appalling ignorance. And that was a great shock,
for the chemistry of faith between pupil and teacher is important.
She wanted to have confidence in Monsieur Koenig, but she was
badly hurt; indeed, if Anna Kindleman had calmly suggested that
they allow Baby to climb alone to the top of the Eiffel Tower,
she wouldn't have been more shocked, more stunned. Yet there
was Monsieur Koenig suggesting casually, "We will now do the
aria from *Le Prophète*, the big scene of Fidès in the fourth act."

She hadn't known he was so ignorant, she hadn't dreamed he
was so inexperiencd, and at first she was speechless with dismay,
the shock and the hurt mirrored in her face—mouth open, eyes
blazing and not far from tears, for with one stroke he had destroyed all her faith in his judgment as a teacher. But he didn't
seem to realize, and even began running through the accompaniment, murmuring hopefully: "We'll try a few bars, just one or
two?" But of course she had to refuse, flatly and with spirit, for
if she did as he suggested, she would seriously damage her voice.
And she thought Monsieur Koenig should have realized that.
She thought he should have known that this aria had been
written for a mezzo-soprano range, and even had long, sustained
passages of very high coloratura, impossible for a contralto. Indeed, this was a bravura piece with intermittent fireworks—great
sweeping passages, from quiet recitativo to soaring brilliance, and
huge breaks as well, from startlingly high tones to very deep ones.
The aria from *Le Prophète* required a voice with great flexibility
and enormous range. It was exactly the kind of thing she would

never be able to sing, and she told him so, flatly and with finality.

But he only smiled, shrugged slightly, as though it was a matter of small consequence, and coaxed, "Just a few bars, perhaps ten minutes, not much time wasted"—his manner so offhand, so bemused and casual, and so appealing, that finally to humor him she sang the opening passages, even worked them over once or twice. After that, at the end of each lesson, Monsieur Koenig would turn, for ten minutes, to the aria from *Le Prophète*, wasting time, of course, on this foolish, fruitless endeavor, until, at the end of a few weeks, she discovered, to her astonishment, that she could sing the whole of the big scene and aria from the fourth act of *Le Prophète*—sing it so easily, so effortlessly, that one might almost imagine that it had been written expressly for the purpose of revealing, to its best advantage, the unusual range, power and flexibility of her voice.

They both knew, then, that something not unlike a miracle was happening, but they spoke of it only rarely, not wanting to disturb such a tenuous equilibrium. The whole matter of the voice had become more mysterious than ever, but if she was finally learning how to sing, it had happened just in time, for their money was almost gone. They had miscalculated and been too prodigal, but fortunately the quarterly payment of a hundred and twenty-five dollars from his trust arrived in December to tide them over. There were no flowers in the Trocadero Gardens now, the sky was often gray, the air damp and chill; but there were lavender shadows when the gas lamps were lit, pearly mists in the early morning, and the city had never been so beautiful.

Chapter XI

In January the Saint-Gaudens came to Paris. Gussie had told them, when she was helping with their travel plans, that as soon as Augustus had resolved the matter of General Sherman's cloak they planned to come abroad. The Victory group was to stand at Fifth Avenue and Sixtieth Street, and for some time had been almost finished. But for years he'd been trying anxiously, and at times frantically, to devise a proper cloak. However, even after another year, there'd been no final resolution of the problem. So this winter, in desperation and at great expense, he'd had the whole enormous group—the angel, the General and his horse—packed up, crated and shipped to Paris, hoping that a change of scene would give him a new perspective.

The Saint-Gaudens had lived in Paris before, and Gussie was soon taking an active part in the group associated with the "services d'ateliers," attending the Sunday services on the rue de Berri, "Madame Saint-Gaudens" listed among the patronesses for the musicales. She was sociable by nature, positive, kindhearted and rather managing. But Gus was more volatile, an intense man, of medium height and middle age, his close-trimmed beard turning white, his hair still red. He was convivial at times, enjoying an evening at a café or a picnic in the country, but at other times he could be morose, withdrawn, obsessed with his work. The matter of the cloak, he told them, was more complex than it seemed, for he must find a way of conveying action, the General's cloak lifting, blown back by wind and movement, and whenever he attempted it, it resembled too closely the lift of the angel's wings. Again and again the ideal symmetry had eluded him, the cloak never quite in harmony with the concept he had in mind.

The winter was a busy one for all of them. When he could, Sidney went to his studio on the Avenue Kléber and composed songs—"Break, Break," with words by Tennyson, "Der Kosak," "Slumber Song"—then brought them home for Louise to sing. He also read the papers avidly that winter, for Paris was in the midst of a crisis revolving about an army officer, Captain Alfred Dreyfus, who many believed had been falsely convicted of treason. A trial was pending, the papers were filled with the case, and once, when they were walking together on the street, they saw the great champion of this cause, the French author Émile Zola, drive by in his carriage. It was evening, and the carriage was moving sedately, but at the corner a band of ruffianlike men, armed with clubs, darted out of the shadows and attacked—and then the driver whipped the horses furiously until they reared, plunged and finally escaped, galloping, like shadows, off into the dusk.

For Louise there were the lessons, and this winter the control she was learning with Monsieur Koenig was like a present—a surprise one—every day. It was as though her voice had been released from bondage, and at last was floating free. As though it had been imprisoned, and only partially available, and now finally was hers, without restraint. There was, for instance, that matter of the quiet legato singing—now, for the first time, she could convey the tenderness, the eloquent pianissimos, that had always been so difficult before. There were other techniques, too. Now she could leap two octaves, attack a single note, embrace a disembodied lyric phrase—all with seemingly careless precision. She could caress the trills, sustain the coloratura; and most astonishing of all, those distant high notes, so long out of reach, were falling, one by one, like stars into her orbit.

In December Fidèle Koenig arranged an audition for Mr. Maurice Grau of the Metropolitan Opera Company in New York. By chance they had seen a notice in the Paris *Herald* announcing that the Metropolitan would be closed this year, for the first time since its opening in 1883, and therefore Mr. Grau would be staying for a few weeks in Paris. Monsieur Koenig thought this providential. Such contacts were always useful, he said, and the manager of the Metropolitan might have some advice for a young American contralto. And so he made the arrangements, and when he learned that Mr. Grau didn't like to audition in a room or studio, he hired a small hall on the Boulevard Haussman, noting also, in that casual way of his, that she would, of course, sing what they now called her "showpiece"—the big scene and aria from *Le Prophète*.

And so she did, standing on the stage in an almost empty theater, with Monsieur Koenig to play the accompaniments, a ghostly expanse of empty seats and, far in the back of the hall, her husband and Maurice Grau, sitting side by side, listening. It was an odd situation, and perhaps she should have been nervous, but how could she be when the coloratura was floating out into the half-dark theater, rounded, lilting and so effortless? She had become like a performer in a circus who for years has been timid and earthbound, and suddenly discovers he can swing with ease, up near the top of the tent. It was exhilarating, the acrobatics and the subtleties—the low caressing tones, the crescendos, the flights of song. How could she be troubled when it was all suddenly so easy?

When they had finished Mr. Grau asked for more selections, which Monsieur Koenig just happened to have on hand. And so she continued singing, and afterward they all talked for a while on the sidewalk in front of the theater. Maurice Grau was an impresario with great dignity and reserve, distinguished in appearance, of medium height, partially bald, his beard neatly trimmed. He was impeccable in his demeanor, urbane, self-assured, and now he told them that she had a beautiful voice but of course she must have experience, for the Metropolitan never took debutantes. Keep in touch, he said, let me know how it goes.

Then he walked off into the Paris evening, leaving them to ponder that interesting word "experience." What exactly did it mean? When they were with the other singing pupils they heard a good deal of talk about "offers"—the "offer" some fortunate friend had had, the "offer" that might come some day, the "offer" that had sadly not been "offered." But in spite of all the talk, the whole business of opera still seemed evanescent and unreal, a kind of will-o'-the-wisp, more talk than substance. However, it didn't matter now, for they had entrusted not only her voice, but also the disposition of their lives, entirely to Monsieur Koenig. He had become the guardian of their affairs, and he understood, almost as well as they did, how precarious they were. He knew that they had, most unwisely, used up all the borrowed funds, and were trying to live now on payments of less than fifty dollars a month. He knew all about the widowed mothers at home, the little daughter to be cared for, the heavy burden of debt. And one day he said casually, at the end of the lesson, "Tomorrow we will go and sing for the Roberval Agency."

Tomorrow! It seemed to both of them too soon, but Monsieur Koenig only shrugged, in that offhand, so Gallic way of his, and told them it would be "nothing"—a "mere formality"—to let the agency know that she was studying in Paris. However, they understood that it would be an important formality, and decided that it would be better if Louise went alone—the presence of an anxious husband might be too disturbing.

Monsieur Koenig went with her, of course, to play the accompaniments, and she discovered at the agency that she would be singing for just one man, a Monsieur Perez. The room was rather small, and to be comfortable for the audition she removed the hat, the fur, and stood in the curve of the piano, the rich dark hair coiled low on the neck and fastened with tortoise-shell pins. And though it was a brilliant beauty she had, radiant, beguiling, it was also somehow touching, for there was an air of unselfconsciousness not often found in the audition room of the Roberval Agency.

Monsieur Perez sat at the far end of the room, and it seemed odd, at first, to be singing for just one man, in such a businesslike atmosphere. But when you have been living all your life with a voice too cumbersome and heavy, and suddenly discover another instrument altogether, an enchanting toy to play with, singing becomes sheer pleasure. As before, she was enjoying herself, and scarcely noticed that another gentleman had casually entered the room, a youngish man, though with white hair, who had gone directly to a window and was standing now, his back turned, looking down into the street. But she hardly knew he was there, for she had reached the recitativo, those marvelously controlled phrases, rounded in texture, silken in quality, that had been so impossible before. And then there were the fireworks, the great dark plunge and after it the flight, the top notes flooding the room, rising higher and still higher, the tone so lacquered over with the haunting gold of the contralto that the effect was ravishing.

But finally it was over, and when she had stopped, the gentleman with white hair turned from the window and said quietly, "Would it give you pleasure to sign for the summer season at Vichy?"

His tone was so casual that one wouldn't have imagined it would generate such an electrifying atmosphere—Monsieur Perez leaping from his seat, Monsieur Koenig blank with astonishment. However, Monsieur Koenig recovered quickly, and introduced her with ceremony to "Monsieur Bussac, Director of the Vichy Opera Company."

The Director bowed low over her hand, but still she scarcely understood, for though she could see on Monsieur Koenig's face a look of deep, controlled emotion, she had heard of Vichy only as a kind of water with bubbles, and didn't quite know what was happening. The audition room sparkled with astonishment, but there was so much rapid French, so much elaborate protocol, that she seemed more a witness than a participant. So now there was a kind of tableau, a moment of high drama: the young singer from America, dazed, bewildered, touchingly pretty, and hovering about her the three Frenchmen, all variously involved, and all engaged in conversation.

Monsieur Bussac, who had just happened to be strolling through the halls and had heard a voice that attracted him, was talking now of a contract—compensation, repertoire, the extent of the engagement. Monsieur Perez was agreeing fervently to everything; and Monsieur Koenig had assumed an air of great calm and dignity. Between them they were arranging her future, until finally she intervened to say that before she could sign an agreement she must speak to her husband. But that threw Monsieur Perez into a passion of agitation, and he began exclaiming, over and over, "But Madame, you do not understand! You do not understand!"—gesturing with excitement, keyed to a fine state of animation, until Monsieur Bussac cut him short with a wave of his hand, and said calmly that Madame was quite right. Before she could come to a decision she must confer with her husband, and meanwhile he would write the conditions on a piece of paper. In fact, he would draw up a contract and sign it himself, and she could give her answer to the agency in a day or two.

When that was done Louise tucked the contract in her muff, and Monsieur Koenig escorted her ceremoniously to the street. But once there he forgot his composure and reverted to that exuberant stutter. He even danced a little jig on the sidewalk, so jubilant he could scarcely contain himself. "But Madame 'Omair, Madame 'Omair, you do not know! You do not know what has happened to you!" he exclaimed. "The Vichy Opera never takes debutantes! They have the greatest artists in France, the finest conductors, a most distinguished audience, and I never for a moment imagined . . . !" Monsieur Koenig was so elated that the French phrases tumbled over each other in a staccato of stuttering confusion, and when finally they parted he was still in a transport of disbelief.

And she was still in a daze, for it had all been quite unexpected. They hadn't either of them foreseen anything like this, and it was while she was hurrying home through the Paris evening that she began to experience one of those moments of blissful awareness that can happen only now and then in a lifetime.

She knew Sidney would be waiting for her, and remembering all that talk about "offers," she plotted a fitting entrance for this moment in their lives. When she had reached the apartment, she stood in the center of the floor, flung wide her arms and exclaimed dramatically, "I have had an offer!" Then, rewarded with a look of blank astonishment, she made an event of the telling—what he said, what she said, even the decor of the Roberval Agency. She built her story in tantalizing sequence, creating mystery as well as suspense. And when she had arrived at a stirring climax, she withdrew from her muff—the contract.

No audience could have been more hypnotized by the drama, and no response could have been more eloquent, for the way had been long and treacherous, with failure lurking, unacknowledged, in the wings. And when they looked at the provisions that night, the French phrases seemed to dance in the firelight, giving substance to their dreams and casting in a very different light the way they might feel about all that money they had borrowed, the friends and relatives at home, the venture some people had thought foolish and flighty . . . here it was all summed up, and signed with a flourish by a Monsieur Bussac.

But the contract was a formidable document, and when Sidney studied it the next morning, clause by clause, he began to have some disquieting reservations. He realized, then, that there were many pitfalls, and was assailed by a characteristic reluctance to plunge too hastily into the unknown, for though he could be impulsive on occasion, he was also cautious, concerned, indecisive, apprehensive, and now he felt uneasily responsible.

The most obvious drawback to this undertaking was the great number of roles she would have to learn within the space of only a few months. In the contract they were all listed, and they made a formidable array: Leonora—*La Favorita*; The Queen—*Hamlet*; Dalila—*Samson et Dalila*; Ortrud—*Lohengrin*; Venus—*Tannhäuser*; Margaret—*Roi d'Ys*; Albine—*Thaïs*. In effect, there was the contralto repertoire, implacably set forth; to master it all so quickly would be an impossible ordeal, and also, he realized gloomily, unfair to her art.

Then there was the matter of the costumes. In the contract it was noted that the "compensation" would be four hundred and fifty francs (ninety dollars) a month, which was a modest salary, yet it was also stipulated that "the artist supply her own costumes." Since they had no funds at all, that provision alone cast a long shadow of doubt on the whole undertaking. There was also the matter of that strange place called Vichy. Would it be safe for their little girl? How about the milk? The water? The air? The living conditions?

But what was really troubling him was the sudden realization of her signature on a document drawn up by a Monsieur Bussac—an unknown manager who would then have her services at his command, and the next few months of her life at his disposal. For one who was very possessive, this was a disturbing prospect, and it was the relentless terms of the contract that were now bringing him face to face, for the first time, with the whole fact of his wife's becoming an opera singer. Oddly, he had never really thought the matter through before. When she had come to him in Boston, to study harmony, she had been a young church singer who suited her costumes, the pretty picture hats with the roses and trimmings of velvet, to the role, and her songs, the anthems and hymns, to the quiet church setting. That had been her life, and he had subtly altered it, introducing her to the color and drama of opera, and then, with his sudden inspiration, his "great plan," bringing her here to Paris to study.

But had that been altogether wise? Was it even fitting and proper for a young American girl from a religicus home to appear on the stage in a variety of costumes, some quite exotic, and sing all those impassioned operas? What did he know of the operatic world? The tenors and baritones she would have to sing with, the conditions backstage, the audiences in an unfamiliar place like Vichy—the whole demanding and still alien life of an opera singer?

He felt responsible, and now, with the contract waiting to be signed, he pondered, vacillated, weighed various alternatives and consulted anxiously with friends and relatives. Would this step be wise? he asked almost everyone they knew. And the replies were reassuring. Gussie Saint-Gaudens told them that Vichy was famous as a health resort and would be ideal for the baby; the costumer offered to take the payments for her costumes in installments from her salary; and Monsieur Koenig was certain she could learn the roles. All this quieted his apprehensions somewhat, and at the end of three days she signed the contract with Monsieur Bussac to sing the summer season with the Vichy Opera Company.

So now there was work to do, and as part of her preparation she started drama lessons with Paul Lhérie, a master of the art, who at one time had been known as "the greatest singing actor in Europe." Monsieur Lhérie had achieved his reputation by creating the role of Don José in *Carmen*. He had a mercurial personality, and a studio colorfully equipped with a variety of props—swords, crowns, robes and other operatic paraphernalia.

And for Louise, these acting lessons were almost as instinctive as breathing, for she'd always been susceptible to drama and had already many of the essential attributes—the graceful walk, so light and airy, the beautiful, natural carriage, and especially the quality hardest to define—the subtle gift that rivets attention, a presence, a magnetism, that can seldom be learned.

Because time was short, Monsieur Lhérie concentrated on the basic techniques, and showed her how to make a proper entrance, kneel gracefully, maintain the regal demeanor of a queen or, if need be, fall without injury in a faint on the floor. He taught her the classic gestures of welcome or dismissal, how to register expressions of anger, grief or joy. And he was such a consummate actor that while she was learning the roles he could assume, in an instant, all the other parts.

Julien, the costumer, was another mercurial personality, who wore, himself, an enameled face and a wig of lustrous black curls. When they consulted with him he tried ingeniously to moderate the cost by intermixing "tabliers" and other adornments in various imaginative ways. Nevertheless, the costumes—all the velvet and satin and chiffon gowns, the embroidery in silver and gold, the imitation jewels, the crowns and stomachers, the robes and trains—would cost altogether one thousand dollars. This was such a heavy burden that for a time they hesitated, looked at secondhand costumes and wondered what to do. Meanwhile Sidney wrote home for advice, and had, unexpectedly, a cable from a cousin offering to lend them the money.

It seemed to Louise now that almost everyone they knew was trying to help her in this tense and tenuous and arduous experience of becoming an opera singer. But not everyone approved, for in West Chester there was a different point of view, and a good deal of anxious concern. Her mother thought it was a sin to sing in opera, and Louise so regretted her mother's opposition that in her letters home she tried to argue away, with words, principles and beliefs that had endured a lifetime. "Why is it wrong, Mama," she wrote, "to put on historic costumes and sing, rather than sing in concert in a ball gown? They are all before the public!"

Hopefully she tried to involve her mother in all the new experiences, describing, in her letters, the auditions, the roles, the contracts. And when they were finally ordered from Julien, she described the costumes, the "purple brocade-velvet" for Hamlet's mother, the "blond wig" for Venus and the white satin gown for Leonora, "the skirt and waist embroidered with pearls, and mantle of pink satin embroidered with gold." She described the Dalila costume, which would have a "bodice of embroidered turquoise velvet," the satin slippers and gold sandals, the jewels and crowns and velvet cloaks, adding, finally, that she would have to have "a huge new trunk" to hold them all.

But though, almost overnight, it seemed, she had become an opera singer, only the summer was provided for, so in the spring she went again to the Roberval Agency for another audition. This time two dignified gentlemen from Angers were there, sponsors of a new opera company that was to open in the fall, and also the codirector of La Monnaie in Brussels, Monsieur Stumont. Afterward the gentlemen from Angers made an offer for the winter season, while Monsieur Stumont held out a tantalizing glimmer of hope—he would be pleased, he said, if she would sing for his associate, Monsieur Calabrese.

This presented a quandary, for La Monnaie was second only to the Paris Opera in prestige, a world-famous mecca for artists and musicians, whereas at Angers the singers would be young and inexperienced, and there would be no prestige at all. And so there was an interlude of hopeful suspense while they contemplated the dazzling prospect of the Brussels Opera House. But when Louise had sung for Monsieur Calabrese he told her, regretfully, that there was "no opening for a contralto at La Monnaie," which meant that she must slide way down the scale to a new little opera company buried in the very heart of France. But they didn't dare delay, for they needed the money to live on. "Perez told us I could get nothing as good if I waited," she wrote her mother, "so we thought 'a bird in the hand' and grabbed it. Angers is a beautiful city, they say, all surrounded with chateaux. We will buy a Baedeker and look it up." The contract with Angers was for six months at two hundred dollars a month, with a maximum of two operas a week—they would be able to live, she would be able to sing, and when they had bought a Baedeker they might know a bit more.

Though she had, now, a glittering array of opera costumes, her own wardrobe was very limited. But fortunately a wealthy American lady had left in her will a number of gowns to be distributed to needy students, for in the spring there was a flurry of occasions —a concert at the Salle Charras with two other Americans, another concert at the Baroness de Hagerman's home for the American ambassador and still another at a Mrs. Grey's. From the gift to the students Louise was able to select a ball gown of black lace over rose silk that was ideal for these social affairs. And before she left for Vichy Mrs. Paxton made her a present of her first "Paris creation"—an afternoon costume of pale gray broadcloth piped with white satin (the vest lined with satin embroidered with tiny flowers)—made to order for twenty-five dollars by one of the finest French couturiers.

Before they left she sent her mother a postcard, dated May 10, 1898. "We are so busy with final errands and lessons," she wrote. "Today Helen and Jim Paxton come to lunch, at four I sing at a musicale ($20.00), and this evening we dine with our cousins, Mr. and Mrs. Saint-Gaudens. Tomorrow will be devoted entirely to trunks. I am so anxious to get to the country! My debut will be the first week in June. . . ."

The Saint-Gaudens had a big, makeshift, rather shabby apartment, which they were able to rent quite cheaply. And at this farewell dinner, they had, as always, when they spent an evening with their cousins, an uncommunicative but vigorous companion—General Sherman astride his horse, at the far end of the big studio room. The General was still without a cloak, for that tormenting problem hadn't yet been resolved. But there was that evening a certain mood, as of many things pending. Gussie planned to return to America to fetch their young son, Homer, from boarding school, and Augustus planned to enter his Equestrian Group in the Paris Salon as soon as it was finished. Then there were the songs that had been composed in Paris—would they ever be published? And an opera debut, early in June. Gussie was quite hard of hearing, so they talked of all these matters in voices slightly raised, while General Sherman, at the far end of the room, waited for his cloak, so that he, too, could go prancing off—perhaps to victory.

Chapter XII

They had come early to Vichy, so that they could be settled and rested before her debut, and within a day they had found a comfortable place to stay. "Just found a house, half a house," she wrote her mother on a postcard. "Address all mail: 16 Rue Callow, Vichy, France. How fine to be in the country!" The half-house was a small villa called Les Violettes, and a French maid was included in the rental. But this was actually a strange and alien place for such an eventful episode in their lives. The very fact that they had never heard of Vichy might indicate how far removed it was from their plainer, simpler orbit, for it was actually a very famous resort, one of the most fashionable in Europe. But it was a town with a schizophrenic nature, much of the time quiet, almost somber, closed, careful, cautious, but blossoming for a few months into a frenetic brilliance, with the hotels suddenly open and the visitors arriving. Like a flock of starlings, they would migrate from some other habitat and settle about the place, bringing with them their stylish carriages, their huge trunks filled with the latest word in fashion, and their retinues— a veritable invasion of personal maids, valets, coachmen and footmen. When that happened, with the effect of a prairie fire, the casinos would open and ply their vivid trade on the broad Esplanade bordering the Allier River, while on the outskirts of the town there would be horse racing, bullfighting and other colorful diversions.

Vichy had three main assets to attract this profitable migration. First there was the Vichy Springs, owned by Monsieur Fair —a natural endowment of sparkling water that was especially prized as a cure for rheumatism, digestive troubles and a host of other ailments. Then there was the unique social status of the town. The Prince of Wales, Albert Edward of England, was one of those who had "discovered" Vichy, and it had since become a favored resort for the aristocracy of Europe. During the summer season the chief criterion was a show of great wealth, as well as a feverish pandering to pleasure, and inevitably those of lesser rank came to see and be seen.

The final drawing card, greatly prized by the citizens of the town, was the Vichy Opera, which was perhaps the most distinguished of all the provincial opera companies in France, a reputation so jealously guarded that the taxpayers even contributed a subsidy to maintain such a valuable asset. Everything about the opera company was closely watched, and when, in April, 1898, Monsieur Bussac, the manager, published in the papers his plans for the coming season, there was consternation, for to the astonishment of everyone, he had included among his leading artists a debutante. This was a flagrant breach of the traditions they treasured. Not for a generation had there been a debutante in the company, for the Vichy Opera could attract the most celebrated singers in France. Yet there it was, in the list of principal singers, the name of an unknown American contralto who had never even appeared in opera. And there was instant opposition, for such a radical departure was interpreted by the citizens of Vichy as an insult to the company, and, worst of all, a threat to their prestige.

Monsieur Bussac had, perhaps, underestimated the effect of this departure from tradition. But the citizens were outraged, fearing, especially, the effect on the *abonnés*, the subscribers, when they came for the season. These valued patrons would be certain to resent the slight to their opera company. And so it was the pocketbook that was threatened, as well as the opera, and after the matter had been debated with great heat in all the cafés about town, a delegation was appointed to protest to Monsieur Bussac. But the manager refused to reconsider. He had signed in good faith, he said, and he wouldn't go back on his word.

Following this futile protest, the town had split up into two factions, those who upheld the manager's right to his own discretion, and the majority who opposed him. Day after day the arguments swirled up and down the Esplanade, and the controversy became so heated, and the resentments so bitter, that it was decided, finally, to stage a demonstration, and boo and hiss the unknown singer as soon as she appeared on the stage, for only in that way could they show the stubborn manager exactly what they thought of him.

Although Louise and Sidney were entirely innocent of this controversy, they may have sensed an alien atmosphere, and perhaps for this reason they dreamed up other things to worry about. Sidney was concerned because a group of Spanish bull-fighters had rented a villa just across from theirs. Spain was now an enemy country, at war with the United States. Recently Admiral Dewey had won a great victory in the Philippines, and he was afraid the gloomy matadors, who sat constantly on the steps of the villa, staring across the street, and would be performing throughout the season in an arena on the outskirts of town, might resent this defeat of their country, and retaliate by kidnapping the baby. Their little girl was two and a half now, and much of the day she played in the garden, under the fierce gaze of the Spanish matadors. She was a pretty child, graceful and appealing, the dark curls brushed by Anna into glossy ringlets, and she seemed to him such a ready target for the wounded patriotism of their neighbors that he arranged elaborate procedures, with Anna and Marie, the maid, always in attendance when he wasn't there himself to guard her—though the gloomy matadors never did disturb the baby.

And Louise was troubled because she had discovered that she would have to make her debut on a Sunday. She had never imagined that opera would be given on the Sabbath, and she knew how shocked and saddened her mother would be. Moreover, here such a requirement was especially distressing because the opera hall was housed in the most elaborate of the casinos, not far from the gaming tables and glittering social rooms.

When they'd first come to Vichy the town had been very quiet. "The place is nearly empty," she'd written her mother, "people just beginning to arrive." But once they had arrived it had seemed an alien migration, the fashionable ladies sitting hour after hour in the square in front of the luxurious hotels, attended by their maids, embroidering with hoops and eyeing each other's elegance —the lace gloves, the ostrich-plume hats, the elaborate bustles— and the men attending the horse races and bullfights, crowding about the gaming tables or pacing the broad Esplanade overlooking the Allier River.

And so there was a strident, glittering social atmosphere when Louise went to the opera house, on June 23, 1898, to make her debut as Leonora in *La Favorita*—regretful, because it was the Sabbath, but never dreaming that here in Vichy so many were aligned against her, the townspeople incensed by her presence in the company, and the *abonnés*, just as everyone had feared, outraged by this slight to the renowned Vichy Opera. They had been kept carefully in the dark about the situation, but it had been simmering for so long that it had become explosive, and when Sidney took his seat in the hall he realized at once that something was wrong.

He had left her in her dressing room, with a dresser, a coiffeur and others to help her, and already there was that invisible barrier—a kind of wayward concentration—creating a certain distance between the one who would perform, and the one who would be watching. She was thinking about the songs, the arias, the crescendos, the gestures, and he was thinking about her.

He had been afraid his nervousness and anxiety might add to her trepidation, and so he had left her and taken the seat Monsieur Bussac had given him in the center of the hall. And almost at once he had noticed the agitation, which he interpreted as some sort of political crisis. He knew the French were very political as well as excitable, but he was disturbed, for all over the hall men in black evening suits and high silk hats were congregating in groups, gesticulating angrily, or jumping from their seats and calling back and forth. The talk was in such rapid French that he couldn't understand the import, but he was disturbed by the air of conspiracy—the excited bursts of conversation, the abrupt decisive gestures and the hard look on the faces, many of them closed, angry, cynical.

He tried to tell himself that he was foolish to worry. The role of Ferdinand was being sung by Scaremberg, one of the finest tenors in the Paris Opera, and the rehearsals had all gone well. The other artists, most of them so experienced that they scarcely needed rehearsals, had been good-natured and very kind about forgoing their usual diversions to work with a beginner. For many in the company the Vichy season was regarded as a vacation, a chance to picnic with their families, and fish from the banks of the neighboring rivers. But they had cheerfully consented to the added hours of rehearsing and patiently helped her with her roles.

This experienced cooperation had made her work much easier, and he knew it was unreasonable to feel so anxious. But when the curtain rose he was unaccountably overwhelmed by a feeling of dread. She wouldn't appear in this scene, where, in the courtyard of the monastery, Ferdinand relates the story of his newfound love to Balthazar. But she would be waiting in her dressing room, and now that it was too late he wondered whether it had been wise to let her make her debut in a strange French city. They were very isolated here in Vichy, with the Spanish matadors across the street and the hotels and casinos thronged with fashionable members of society, and she'd been unhappy about singing on the Sabbath. But she was happy with her gown—the white satin embroidered with pearls, the pale spangled chiffon of the sleeves, a vision of a gown, like nothing she'd ever worn before. She was happy, too, with her role, but he wished now that they weren't so far from family and friends, for the atmosphere in the hall was hectic and very strange. He had imagined that once the opera had started the agitation would subside, but instead, during the brief intermission it became more noticeable, the angry muttering and even abrupt signals back and forth. He knew she would be waiting in the wings, and had, now, almost a feeling of panic, for that ominous air of conspiracy still hung

about the hall, veiled and threatening, even after the curtain had
risen to reveal the Island of Leon, where Inez and her maidens
were gathering flowers and singing sweetly together, then wel-
coming Ferdinand, removing his blindfold and retiring gracefully,
leaving him to look about, wondering and waiting . . .

So then they were all wondering and waiting, in an atmosphere
hushed and painful for him, and for others in the audience frenetic, resentful, harsh, poised, until suddenly from the wings,
she appeared, arms outstretched, singing triumphantly, "Mon
idole! Mon idole!" singing, singing, the voice so shimmering
bright, so young and free that it struck like a shaft of light, stunning the fevered pulses. On and on she sang, the tones soaring
throughout the agitated hall, tones so original in quality, so
frescoed with silver and gold, that the listener hesitated to
breathe, not wanting to lessen the rapture. And in this way, unwittingly, the fevered will to protest was scattered into fragments
of rapt attentiveness, and no one moved or spoke. The outraged
patrons had had an honest cause, good reason to rebuke their
director. But they were, most of them, connoisseurs of opera,
more than anything they valued a beautiful voice, and now they
were so hypnotized by the grace and brilliance of the singing, so
stirred by the depth and power and radiance, that when she had
sung her duet with Ferdinand, and vanished again into the wings,
the whole fevered situation exploded into pandemonium—hoarse
cries of "Brava! Brava!" and thunderous applause. All over the
house the men in black leapt to their feet, calling out fervently,
"Encore! Encore!" and the ovation was so sweeping and so pro-
longed that after a time she had to return again from the wings,
radiant in the white satin and pearls, arms outstretched, triumphant because she had found her love, "Mon idole! Mon idole!"
and sing the duet with Ferdinand all over again.

Not until nearly the end of the season did the other singers tell
them about the heated controversy that had almost made a
shambles of her debut. And they realized then that the resentful
mood might well have had a pendulum effect, emotions keyed to
fever pitch reacting as fervently in the opposite direction, the
debut made more dramatic than it otherwise might have been.
From this she profited, for all over France the newspapers carried

As Leonore at her debut in Vichy, June 23, 1898.

With her small daughter in Vichy.

stories about "the sensational debut in Vichy of Madame Louise Homer, the American contralto." The critics wrote that she had "great dramatic fire," "a marvelous voice" and "extraordinary beauty." Toward the end of the season a special performance of *La Favorita* had to be arranged so that the leading patron of the opera company, Monsieur Fair, owner of the Vichy Springs, could come from Paris to hear her.

But though all this was rewarding, Vichy never became a congenial place to live. The peacock atmosphere in the square in front of the luxurious hotels seemed to Louise a waste of the summer, and she discovered a small park, bordering the river, where they could take their little girl and where there was even an old man tending a herd of goats—a pretty place, and so disregarded that they had it almost entirely to themselves. Throughout the summer she pasted all her clippings and programs in a ten-cent copybook, and at the end of the season made a list: ·4 *Favorita*, 3 *Hamlet*, 2 *Dalila*, 1 *Roi d'Ys*, 1 *Lohengrin*, 2 *Thaïs* —13 performances.

Then, almost overnight, it seemed, the visitors and their elaborate retinues vanished from the scene. Like the noisy starlings migrating with the seasons, the whole glittering facade, the sleek carriages and the elegance, went spiraling off again, to swoop down on Baden-Baden or some other fashionable resort. Once again Vichy was "nearly empty," and after a two-week vacation at Escoule le Bas, on the coast of Brittany, they went to Angers, where Louise had signed for the winter season.

But now they regretted this commitment to sing with a new, untested opera company in a remote area of France. They wished she had waited until after her debut and taken a chance on finding something better, for they were afraid that after the brilliance and éclat of Vichy, the whole venture in Angers would prove to be a mistake and a disappointment. However, there was no alternative, for she had signed a contract, so they came early in September, to be settled before the season opened. But Angers was an inhospitable city, and they couldn't even find a house to live in for the winter.

They had been assigned two noisy rooms over a store in the center of town, which would be impossible for her singing, his composing, the baby's sleep and play. But in Angers there was no scattering of small villas like the ones in Vichy; in fact there was nothing at all, although they trudged back and forth, day after day, through streets where the walls were high and the houses turned blank faces of stone or brick or stucco.

Black Angers, it was called, in the very heart of Royalist France, a cold place, regulated, hemmed in by tradition. In Angers people lived and died in their homes, and they didn't rent them out. In time the houses became filled with heirlooms, ancestral treasures to be guarded with great caution and not entrusted to strangers. It was a very remote city, austere, self-contained, and as they walked disconsolate through the streets, they wondered if they would ever feel at home here. But one day they came across an empty house, boarded up and deserted. Anxiously they inquired and found that it could be rented for ten dollars a month, and one of the stores in town would rent them furniture for another ten dollars a month. There was no central heating, and during the winter weather they would have to run shivering through the icy halls, but they had a house again, with a garden and a gate.

The leading patron of the new opera company was the Comte de Romain, an aristocrat whose ancestral chateau was a great pile of stone, with an avenue of trees, on the outskirts of town. The count had engaged as his director Monsieur Breton, a quite elderly opera manager who had come out of retirement for this undertaking. Monsieur Breton was so gentle and unassuming that it was difficult to believe that he could create an opera company, and just as they had feared, most of the singers were young and inexperienced. The audiences were also without experience, and a town so regulated by tradition isn't easily seduced by something new. So the people of Angers came warily to the opera house and sat through the performances, stolid, glum, waiting to be shown.

But they had some beautiful voices in the company—a tenor whose ringing tones could soar to the rafters, a fine young baritone with a flair for drama. And to compensate for the inexperience there was, it became increasingly clear, the sure touch and impeccable taste of their wonderful director. Monsieur Breton was very gentle, almost a fatherly, or grandfatherly, figure to his artists, but he schooled them with such sensitive insight, such true musicianship, that with each production there was notable improvement, until the company had taken on a glow, a brilliance, that even this seemingly cold and inhospitable town found irresistible.

The people of Angers had come warily to the opera, at first, waiting to be shown, and indeed they were, for as the repertoire unfolded—*La Favorita, Hamlet, Le Roi d'Ys*—and the performances became more assured and more compelling, the audiences, almost in spite of themselves, responded. And with the production of Saint-Saëns' musical drama, in which Louise sang Dalila, the people of Angers were won over. For almost ten years *Samson et Dalila* had been a favorite in France, and in Angers it became feverishly popular. Extra performances had to be scheduled, and always the theater was filled, for no one seemed able to get enough of it—the seduction, the deception, the fearful climax at the end. They identified with the singers, and responded ardently when Dalila conveyed the shifting moods of the delicate aria, "Amour! viens aider." This was an ideal role for her voice, and the long lingering notes, so lustrous, so weighted with languor and tenderness, seemed reaching out to seduce them. So in the town there was now a deepening affection for the young American contralto who had become, so unexpectedly, a part of

their lives. They thought her costumes marvelous, the long garlands of roses braided into the long dark hair, the beautiful clear
profile, and when she went shopping for a new bonnet for the
baby, or needles and thread, or something for the house, she
would be recognized and several ladies would hurry to wait on
her. There would be a ripple of astonishment throughout the
shop, a flutter of whispered comments, of pleasure and affection,
and she would think, with surprise, can this really be me?

The experience was very different here in Angers. In Vichy
there had been a splintered effect, the audiences, the opera company, the home all spinning about in separate orbits. But here in
Angers the town embraced the opera company, and the opera
company was an extension of the home. And since they were all
caught up together, there was a certain mood, a certain buoyant
spirit not easy to define. In her letters home she tried to describe how simple and valid and almost humdrum life backstage in an opera company could be, hoping this would reassure
her mother. She explained about the "salon for the chorus," and
the "salon for the artists," and pointed out, especially, what a
"family" occupation an opera company in France really was:

> For instance, there are fifty in the chorus, and they are
> almost all married, and both husband and wife sing. They
> are each paid $40. a month, and by both singing they can
> live very well. There are often whole families—the father
> in the orchestra and the mother and daughters in the
> chorus. They all bring their sewing and knitting to the re-
> hearsals, and when they are not singing they are sitting in
> the salon for the chorus, working. The artists, too, are the
> quietest set of people you ever met. The wives always come
> when their husbands sing to help them dress, and if you
> could peep in the salon for the artists during a performance
> you would see a jolly happy family. We were perfectly
> astonished at it all, as we had imagined artists and singers
> were different from anyone else. If they are different at all
> I can see only one way, and that is that they seem perhaps
> lighter-hearted and happier. We all chipped in and gave
> M. Breton, the director, a Christmas present. Everyone
> loves him, he is so kind and thoughtful.

After Christmas Monsieur Breton added *Aida* to the repertoire, and Louise began the study of Amneris. This would be the
first role she would interpret without Monsieur Koenig's guidance, and working alone in the Angers house she evolved a quite
original Pharaoh's daughter. Amneris is a challenging role for a
contralto, and one of the most rewarding in the whole literature
of opera, for the character is complex and the motivations intricate. It is Amneris who dominates the big scenes—in the palace,
the courtyard, the temple—and much of the drama and conflict
stems from the moods, whims, passions and jealousies of the
Egyptian princess. But within this context there can be variations, and she made the underlying mood more human, the
frantic jealousy not an evil but a tormenting thing, Amneris not
the imperious, vindictive character so often associated with the
part, but one who was younger and more vulnerable, a distraught, impulsive princess, too despairingly in love and too
tragically destructive.

In Angers they couldn't have the grand processions and spectacles usually associated with *Aida*. But they could have the
illusions created by their wonderful director, and the people
loved it. The notices were filled with praise, the whole season
had become a brilliant success. But there was one troublesome
aspect, for it was a success buried deep in the provinces, and
didn't hold much hope for the future.

They were inexperienced in these matters, and hadn't understood that at first. But now they were discovering singers with
beautiful voices who had sung for years in the provinces because
they had no place else to go. Conversely, the great stars in
America—Nellie Melba, Lillian Nordica, Emma Eames—after
their studies in Paris, had been wafted straight to the top: to
Covent Garden, La Monnaie or the Paris Opera House.

It seemed that once you had become identified with the provincial opera houses you were likely to be stranded there. If
you stayed too many years, the small opera houses could become a kind of trap. So when Monsieur Breton offered her
a contract for the coming season, they hesitated, for they didn't
want to be exiled too long in France, and success in Angers
would mean nothing in America. What she must have now was
the prestige of a major opera house, and with the cooperation of

Monsieur Koenig she went to Paris in January and auditioned at the Roberval Agency for Monsieur Gailhard of the Paris Opera. There was then an interval of suspense, but within a week or two Monsieur Gailhard wrote that he had recently engaged a contralto and had "no further openings" at the Paris Opera House. Also, on impulse, during the winter, Sidney wrote Maurice Grau, describing Louise's debut in Vichy and her success in Angers, and then watched anxiously for a letter from the Metropolitan Opera in New York. But there was no reply.

Meanwhile they needed the security of a contract and were so content in Angers that they believed that was where they should stay. But still they hesitated, for they knew that if they remained too long in this remote city, there would be a feeling of fading hopes and aspirations. They would become like the Comte de Romain, who had shown them, one day, the rooms in his great chateau, reserved for visits from the king. Not for years had there been a king in France, but every day this beautiful suite of rooms was dusted, polished, the linen changed, fresh flowers arranged—so that all would be in readiness when Royalty was restored and the king returned to his throne. Meanwhile the Comte de Romain was waiting, patient, serene, confident . . . just as they were waiting . . . until, unexpectedly, another letter came from the Roberval Agency to say that an audition had been arranged with Monsieur Calabrese of La Monnaie; and once again they were hopeful, for the Brussels Opera House had great prestige. Also the prospect was promising, since she had already sung for Monsieur Calabrese. So it was arranged that she would go to Paris (alone, to save the price of a ticket) after their performance of *Dalila* in Tours.

Monsieur Breton had been taking their popular production of *Samson et Dalila* to a number of neighboring cities, and the performance in Tours was the final event in a gala anniversary celebration. It was a brilliant though somewhat ponderous occasion, the auditorium hung with flags and emblems, the senators and deputies wearing their finest array of rosettes, medals and the crisscross of satin ribbons. Following the performance there would be a State Dinner, with all the prominent dignitaries attending, and during the performance the distinguished deputies became, like Samson, so susceptible to the charms of Dalila, that a delegation was appointed to wait on the American contralto in her dressing room and request her presence as guest of honor.

Monsieur Breton and the Comte de Romain were both deeply honored by this invitation, and so Louise became the only woman present at the State Dinner, which went on and on and on while one after another the bemused and eloquent guests rose to their feet and made a toast in her honor. Ceremoniously they saluted her in rotation around the table; gallantly, at the end of each speech, they all rose to drain their glasses with a flourish; and graciously she acknowledged the tributes, smiling, smiling, while above the flower-decked banquet table the audition for Monsieur Calabrese hovered like a wraith, mingling with the fumes of the wine and the curling wreaths of tobacco smoke.

It was almost dawn when she was able to retire, and daybreak when she rose to take the train for Paris. During the trip she vocalized, did the breathing exercises, the scales, the arpeggios. And Monsieur Koenig was there to meet her at the station and escort her to the Roberval Agency.

Monsieur Calabrese was a round little man, rosy, plump and quite elderly. He sat with his hands folded across his stomach, among an array of gold watch chains, fobs and decorations, and listened quietly while she sang. And all the eloquent tributes in Tours may have gone to her head, for she felt supremely confident, and when she had finished turned with assurance to Monsieur Calabrese, who said quietly, "Fine, very fine, Madame. I think you should sing another season at Angers. Then come to me again, and we shall see."

Another season at Angers. The casual, kindly words were unexpected and she was dismayed, for why had Monsieur Calabrese asked her to come so far if he was going to tell her that? But perhaps he was afraid of hurting his good friend and fellow manager, Monsieur Breton? The thought came to her in a flash, and she said, with spirit, "Monsieur Calabrese, I don't know where I'll sing next year, but it won't be in Angers!"

The reply, made on impulse, had its effect, for at once, as if by magic, the atmosphere changed. Unexpectedly Monsieur Calabrese started to laugh. His plump little stomach shook when he laughed and the gold chains and decorations jangled. "Where's the contract?" he shouted. "Monsieur Perez, what are we waiting for?"

But the bright mood of that return to Angers with the longed-for contract in her pocket was soon overshadowed by news of a tragedy at home. Word came to them in a cable, and then in letters. Sidney's sister Georgie's husband, Fred Diman, had stepped from a train in the Arlington station into the path of a moving train, and had been instantly killed.

The shock and sorrow of this disaster were heightened by the separation. Sidney could imagine, only too vividly, the situation at home—his widowed mother, in her world of silence, so dependent on his newly widowed sister, who had also in her care two little boys, now fatherless. The thought of so much unhappiness was intolerable, and he started at once formulating a plan. He knew that his sister and his mother both loved travel. Their natures responded instinctively to new sights and places, and he imagined that living abroad might mitigate their sorrow. So he wrote urgently: Sell the Arlington house and come here to us. And before long it was arranged that his mother, his sister and the two boys would join them in Europe in another month or two.

But the timing of this new responsibility was precarious, for their own summer plans were uncertain and they were again entirely out of funds. They'd had to turn to Julien for still more costumes for *Hérodiade, Princesse d'Auberge* and other operas. The outlook wasn't too promising that day when a letter came, delivered in the usual way but so unexpected that it might have dropped straight out of the clouds into the garden at Angers.

The postmark was London, and the glossy cream paper was adorned with a royal crest in gold. But the tone was prosaic and businesslike, for it seemed that Mr. Higgins, director of the Royal Opera Company, was writing to say that Mr. Maurice Grau of the Metropolitan Opera was going to manage their summer season and had asked him to inquire if she would be free for an engagement at Covent Garden this summer. If that was possible, would she perhaps audition in Paris for his codirector, Lady de Grey, some time within the next two weeks? When they had recovered from the first astonishment, they understood that this was Mr. Grau's reply to the letter Sidney had composed so carefully, early in the winter.

Fidèle Koenig arranged the audition for Lady de Grey, as he had all the others, with impeccable finesse, engaging this time a salon at the Paris Opera and inviting a number of distinguished guests. Thus, for a leading member of London society, the audition was turned into a social affair, an elegant little party, with waiters hovering discreetly about with trays of wine and little cakes, and a decor of gilt, satin and brocade.

In the midst of all this the audition was more in the nature of a lyric entertainment. And when, wearing a corsage of pink roses to complement the fashionable pale gray of her "Paris creation," Louise sang the dramatic scene from the fourth act of *Aida*, the haunting contralto, the sheen, the radiance, were not so much on trial as an artless offering to anyone who happened to be present, including, of course, the guest of honor, codirector of Covent Garden.

Lady de Grey was striking in appearance, almost six feet tall, brusque, charming and formidable. In London her salons were famous, for there the leaders of society mingled with the most celebrated in the world of the arts. In her home Albert, Prince of Wales, might dine with Nellie Melba or Lillian Nordica, and it was said that the impromptu music at Lady de Grey's sometimes outshone the brilliance of an evening at the opera.

This rare combination—an understanding of the arts, a flair for business and a position in society—made her invaluable at Covent Garden, where she had a liaison role. And now, when the American contralto had finished her selections, Lady de Grey got down to business. She had with her a pencil and paper, and informally, while the party continued around them, she discussed the terms of a contract. She could offer, she said, a hundred dollars a week, for a season of eleven weeks—would that do? And when those terms were promptly agreed to (by one who hadn't, in fact, two cents to rub together), she outlined the repertoire, which would include *Die Walküre, Aida, Lohengrin* and a number of other roles.

She promised to send the formal contract in a week or two, and just as she was leaving turned to ask, "You will, of course, sing *Aida* in Italian, and *Lohengrin* and *Die Walküre* in German?" And just as casually Louise replied, "Why, of course!" for though she'd never sung in either of those languages, even a slight hesitation might have marred, just a little, this dazzling occasion.

In Angers, when it became known that she wouldn't be returning for another season the people protested bitterly to Monsieur Breton, holding him responsible for the loss of their contralto. And indeed, there was a feeling of loss on both sides, for in Angers she had found something that had affected her profoundly —a realness, a quality of constancy, that seemed to be crystallized in that remote French city.

At the close of the season, to please Monsieur Breton, she gave a farewell concert. But it wasn't easy to sing in an opera house so weighted with emotion. Throughout the evening flowers were brought up the aisles, until it seemed that all the flowers in the province must be banked about her on the stage. And during the recital there was the kind of sadness that derives from nearly perfect happiness, the nostalgia associated with something that can never be repeated—a voyage, a vacation, a season of opera.

She had, then, two weeks in Paris to prepare for the Covent Garden season, and it became a marathon of concentration, studying the roles with Fidèle Koenig, and the languages with an Italian teacher in the morning and a German teacher in the afternoon. But there was still time for friends, and before they left for London they had another farewell evening with the Saint-Gaudens. As before, they dined informally in the big studio apartment, but this time there was no equestrian statue riding away at the end of the room, for Augustus had finally resolved the matter of General Sherman's cloak.

During the winter he'd hit on the plan of having Gussie make a variety of cloaks in cloth. He'd then tried them on the General until he'd found one that satisfied him. Oddly, the final cloak had been the simplest of the lot, the most unremarkable, the least notable. But Saint-Gaudens had, at last, the symmetry he'd been trying for years to achieve, and the judges had been so favorably impressed that General Sherman and his victorious angel now had the place of honor at the Paris Salon.

Chapter XIII

In London they put up at a boardinghouse and tried to find a proper place to live. But this time it would have to be a neat trick, indeed, for though they had almost no money, they must find a place big enough for Sidney's family, too. It seemed an unlikely quest and they had almost despaired, when one day they were told that a Mr. Rutledge had reduced the rental of his town house on Regent's Park by half. This made the town house even cheaper than the boardinghouse, everything considered. And the result was a kind of Arabian Nights effect, for though they still had no money, not even enough for a horsecab, they were suddenly living in the most fashionable area of London, in a setting of quite astonishing grandeur, with a library paneled in red Morocco leather, a gold-lacquered grand piano in the drawing room and hunting prints with riders in elegant red coats prancing up and down the beautiful winding stairs.

But the gilded piano couldn't compare with another treasure in this house, for between two bedrooms, Louise wrote her mother, there was a fine dressing room with "a white enamel tub"—the first they had had in three years—"so you can imagine our joy!" Then there was Regent's Park, which she described as "the most beautiful of all London parks—*huge*, and both wild and cultivated, and right at our *front door*. We are going to rent wheels," she wrote. "Living here will be a *real vacation!*"

This vision of flying about the park on wheels was meant to compensate for the fact that they would have to spend the summer in the city. She so much preferred the country that she felt constrained, even unnatural, when she had to remain inside on a balmy, sun-filled day. Nevertheless, there she was, and when she went to the opera house to begin the preparations, she discovered that rehearsing at Covent Garden was rather like trying to hold a wedding, or perhaps a formal reception, in the grand concourse of a busy railroad station, with the guests for-ever jostled from their places, rival conductors vying for the stage and the many travelers hurrying here and there, throwing the meticulous ceremony into disarray—one singer, a tenor per-haps, yielding his place to another, casual "stand-ins" for the most important roles, and bystanders, those loiterers in the big railroad stations, wandering about, cheerful and noisy, enjoying the proceedings.

At Covent Garden the bystanders were known as "monitors," and they seemed to be remarkably idle young men in morning coats, many with monocles, who would drop in at the opera house between card games at the club as a means of passing the time. Perhaps in imitation of the Prince of Wales, they liked to fancy themselves connoisseurs of opera, but they rarely listened to the singing at the rehearsals and would stand about in groups, talking loudly, gay and convivial.

But quite apart from the onlookers, there was monumental confusion at Covent Garden, with singers and musicians from all over the world arriving to take part in the summer season, and half a dozen languages spoken in torrents of voluble, rapid-fire instruction and dissension by conductors and directors of various nationalities. In the midst of all this Maurice Grau's of-fice was somewhat in the nature of the information desk in the big railroad station, an oasis of assumed calm, with the heroic clerk re-routing the distracted travelers here and there, quietly and with a show of authority. But even Mr. Grau couldn't create order out of such a chaotic situation, and meanwhile many of the most celebrated singers in the operatic world—Jean de Reszke, Nellie Melba, Lillian Nordica, Pol Plançon—were arriv-ing day after day, bringing with them a striking interplay of varied personalities, vivid temperaments and conflicting desires.

As a result, even the repertoire had fallen into disarray, and Louise was told that several of the operas she had been engaged to sing wouldn't be given at all. Mr. Grau then asked her to learn quickly, since they would be performed almost at once, two new roles—Lola in *Cavalleria Rusticana*, and Maddalena in *Rigoletto*; and after hearing her at a musicale at Lady de Grey's, the fine conductor Luigi Mancinelli asked her, as a favor, to learn the prologue of his new opera, *Ero e Leandro*.

On May 9, 1899, she sang the small role of Lola, and afterward *Punch* found "Homer-Sweet-Homer a fascinating Lola," while others commended her "beautiful presence," her "powerful voice" and her "consummate ease." But the performance of *Aida*, on May 13th, was the one she thought of as her "real" debut at Covent Garden, and then there was an ovation, as she wrote her mother, "in the *middle* of the act," and in the reviews they said that she had "true dramatic fire," and a voice that was "fresh and brilliant, and a gait and gesture both exquisite."

She sang *Aida* with three different sopranos—Mme. Litvinne, Mme. Gadski and Miss MacIntyre. Late in the season a new baritone came from Italy to sing the role of Amonasro. His name was Antonio Scotti, and he had such a stirring baritone voice, and such a warm, engaging personality, that he soon became a great favorite.

Rigoletto was intended as a vehicle for Nellie Melba, and when they rehearsed together the famous soprano was touchingly kind to the young contralto. "The moment I sang a note," Louise wrote her mother, "she went up to the conductor, Mancinelli, and Sidney heard her ask all sorts of questions about me. Then she asked to be introduced." There followed a quiet conversation, while Melba questioned her about her studies, her repertoire, her engagements. The Australian singer was considered by many to be unapproachable, as cold and glittering as her famous jewels. But on this occasion she seemed genuinely concerned, saying finally, "We will talk later, there is much I can tell you."

However, before the performance Melba became ill, and *Rigoletto* had to be canceled. *Aida* was hastily substituted, which

meant that Louise sang that night to a half-empty and disconsolate opera house, for the public had become impatient with the
many illnesses in the company. "Another disappointment—the
word is a hackneyed one this season," wrote the reporter for
the *Telegram*, while the *Graphic* suggested that "the authorities
adopt stringent measures to exorcise the demon of ill health that
appears to have gained a foothold in the theatre. First it was the
turn of M. Jean de Reszke, and now Madame Melba has succumbed to the prevailing sore throat."

Artists came from many countries to sing at Covent Garden,
and then they were affected by the uncertain climate and couldn't
appear. Yet in no other company were the great singers so essential to success, for here performances revolved about two interlocking orbits—royalty and the stars. Audiences in London
demanded a Jean de Reszke or a Nellie Melba, caring more for
the great names than for the operas or even the performances.
And they came to see the aristocracy. Queen Victoria was in retirement on the Isle of Wight and never appeared in London. But
the Prince of Wales was a devotee of opera, and when he occupied the royal box with Princess Alexandra, attendance at the
opera soared, as did the brilliant display of tiaras, jewels and
lavish gowns. All this created at Covent Garden an artificial
atmosphere that seemed to pervade much of the art.

The uncertain repertoire made her own responsibilities heavier,
for she didn't dare "succumb to the prevailing sore throat," and
as the summer progressed she began to feel more and more like
a restless prisoner in her handsome English drawing room. Day
after day, through the elegant French windows she would see
all the fortunate families lolling about in the park, picnicking,
playing games, free as birds. But she had to worry about catching
cold, and so that vision of whirling through the park on wheels,
and having "*a real vacation!*" had faded into weeks of increasing
frustration while she remained inside, with her gilded piano, in
the guise of a prima donna.

However, she did escape occasionally, and one afternoon took
her little girl to the zoo, where they rode on the camel and then
on the elephant, clinging precariously to an array of velvet
pillows. The ride on the elephant was the most perilous, for he

stopped en route to nibble the leaves of a tree, "and then I nearly died from fright and she from joy," she wrote her mother. "I was sure he would decide to sit down and eat in peace!" At that moment, when the elephant raised his trunk to nibble the leaves and they clung together, their laughter floating in terrified spirals up into the tree, Louise didn't look like a prima donna, nor did she feel like one. But she didn't imagine, either, that she might be telescoping into that single exuberant occasion more eloquent enjoyment than that experienced during a summertime of outings by half the people she'd been envying in the park.

In July Sidney's family arrived to stay with them and begin the absorbing task of discovering "Dickens' London." Day after day they went sight-seeing, in a pleasant whirl of activity, and in many of her letters home Louise urged her mother to come, with Daisy, for a similar visit, and see some of "the outside world." "Daisy could study history and music and languages," she wrote. "I love West Chester, but I don't think it's good for a girl to live all the time in one small town."

However, none of these suggestions were taken seriously, for in West Chester there was a certain routine that didn't allow for unpredictable adventures. But her friend Marion Cock seemed to understand better this life she was living abroad, and in her letters to Miss Cock Louise often included descriptions of his music. "Sidney just called me up to his room to hear a new song," she wrote. "It is *beautiful*! To a Hood poem called *Autumn*. Also the other day he wrote one, so lovely, to another of Hood's poems—*It was the Time of Roses, we plucked them as we passed.*"

He composed the songs with her voice in mind—the range, the texture, the color. And when she sang them for him they would experiment together with the tempi, the phrasing and the inter-pretation. However, his composing had always been a very private occupation, and he dreaded exposing his creative work to what he thought of as the "commercialism" of a publisher. But he had promised her that he would, once they were in London, so on almost the last day of the opera season they went together, with a selection of his songs, to Great Marlborough Street, a small publishers' lane, and spoke with the London agent of the B.

Schott Söhne Company, a German firm. There they were told
that Herr Dr. Strecker, manager of the firm, was summering on
the Belgian coast, not far from Heyst-sur-Mer, where they planned
to spend two weeks in August, and would be pleased to come
and see them and hear the songs.

B. Schott Söhne was a very large firm, with branches all over
Europe. The company published music magazines, were the
publishers of Beethoven and Wagner and had done a monumental
job of transcribing the famous first edition of the *Nibelungen
Ring*. All this made Sidney increasingly apprehensive. But Louise
was so confident that there could be no evasion, and when the
Covent Garden season had ended in the middle of August, and
they had all gone to Heyst to stay in a small cottage on the shore,
Herr Dr. Strecker came to hear the songs.

He was a most distinguished music publisher, and while Louise
sang he sat quietly listening, impassive, intent. They stopped for
lunch, then she sang again, many of the songs more than once,
while the composer played the accompaniments, and for Sidney
it was an interlude of intense anxiety. He was thirty-four now,
and had been composing since his student days in Germany. But
he had guarded the output timidly, half persuaded that he preferred to keep his music a solitary occupation. Nevertheless, here
they were, turning the little parlor in Heyst-sur-Mer into a concert stage.

When it was finally over Herr Dr. Strecker made an offer. He
would buy all the songs outright, he said, and publish them with
both German and English texts. And for the anxious composer,
who had been for so long apologetic about his work, and haunted,
too, by a certain feeling of unreality, this was a moment of profound relief. He had never imagined he would receive such a
sweeping proposal, and nothing could have been more reassuring.
But after some days of elation and uncertainty he decided to
refuse, for this was the old-fashioned way—buying a composer's
work outright, without royalties, the copyright belonging to the
publisher. He preferred the newer method, with the composer
receiving royalties and retaining the copyright. So finally he declined, though with gratitude, for Herr Dr. Strecker had done
him a valuable service.

In Brussels they rented a small house at 9 rue de la Presse, and an apartment around the corner for Sidney's family. But this year the domestic arrangements were more difficult, for their devoted friend and helper, Anna Kindleman, must return to Switzerland. During her stay with them she had learned both French and English, and now she would go back to Beatenberg and help her family run their inn.

Louise made her debut at La Monnaie in *Aida*, with the great baritone Marcel Journet as Ramfis, and the celebrated tenor Imbart de la Tour as Radames. Then came *La Favorita*, and then *Lohengrin*. The role of Ortrud was the most difficult in her repertoire, one she had always approached with anxiety. It seemed, indeed, that Wagner had made his music for Ortrud as treacherous as his queen, with a mezzo-soprano range soaring almost out of reach, and a tone that must be lacquered over with hate, gilded with venom and geared to a hissing vengeance that was a great strain to convey. But here in Brussels the dreaded role of Ortrud was, she wrote her mother, "suddenly *so* much easier."

She hardly knew why this was so, but at La Monnaie all the roles seemed to take on a new depth and a new focus, perhaps because the company was run with such grace and precision that it might almost be considered a university of opera. This was an experience she hadn't had before, for her training had been fortuitous and somewhat uneven. In Vichy she'd been the only debutante among singers so accomplished that they didn't need rehearsals; in Angers the entire company had been new, while in London there had been great stars and great confusion. But here in Brussels even the most famous artists were creating opera in a spirit of rare cooperation, under the guidance of gifted leaders in the field.

The rehearsals at La Monnaie started every morning at nine, and all four leaders attended—Monsieur Flon, the conductor; Monsieur Amanz, the stage manager; Monsieur Calabrese and Monsieur Stumont, the codirectors. Throughout the morning they would sit together on a platform above the orchestra pit, analyzing at length every position and inflection, every phrase, every gesture and every bar of music. At La Monnaie there was no stress on the individual bravura performance the way there had been at Covent Garden, or even Vichy. Instead they were all involved together in seeking out the drama, the hidden motives and the brilliant effects. Even the most distinguished artists complied with the system, and afterward in the salon for the artists, the "Green Room," they would discuss the various methods and techniques. And from these long, penetrating sessions, Louise found that she was learning a more coherent and more perceptive approach to her art.

Although they had great stars at La Monnaie, they didn't have the "star system." Instead the Brussels Opera Company was noted for the most finished performances, and it was this that made it so popular with composers. Those sensitive and beleaguered artists liked the prospect of the many careful rehearsals, the impeccable artistry and devotion when their works were introduced to the public. And this year the big event of the season would be the world premiere of Massenet's *Cendrillon*.

Jules Massenet was one of the most celebrated of French composers. He had already achieved fame with *Manon* and *Thaïs*, and to be entrusted with the original production of a work by such a distinguished composer was considered an honor for the company. Louise would have the role of Madame de la Haltière —Cinderella's vain, foolish mother—Charles Gilibert would sing Pandolphe and the costumes would be spectacular. "They will cost $200.," she wrote her mother, "and I must have an auburn wig ($49!). But they say it is an honor to create a role at La Monnaie." And of course it was, but when she went to the opera house to rehearse she soon found herself in a quandary, for she'd had no experience with a comic part. There were no guidelines, since the opera had never been presented, and she'd had no training in the subtle timing or witty inflections that can make an audience laugh.

Massenet himself came to many of the rehearsals, and when he was there it was an added strain. There was something inhibiting about working under the anxious eye of the composer, and this was especially true since she was struggling with every phrase, trying to understand the subtleties and skirt the perilous line between comedy and farce. Her big scene was "getting ready for the ball," and for this she had a superb costume of green satin with lavish embellishments—an overskirt of rose satin, a bodice of silver lamé, puffed sleeves, silver lace, gold embroidery and a great many green satin bows encrusted with pearls. Throughout the comic scene, in a spirit of agitation and vast excitement she would add to this vivid ensemble various adornments—lace gloves, bracelets, earrings, brooches, necklaces and finally a triumphant headdress with two tall plumes—one red and one white. She was meant to be a foolish woman, vain, flighty, talkative, showy, and Pandolphe her bumbling, pompous husband. But she scarcely knew how to convey, in French, the double entendre, the arch or humorous connotation. All this was strange and treacherous territory, until Charles Gilibert became aware of her dilemma and cheerfully took over.

Gilibert was one of the greatest of French baritones. He was a big man, with a squarish yet mobile face, a born actor, with a splendid voice, who had been ten years at La Monnaie. He could manage the part of Pandolphe with the greatest ease, and had an ebullient nature. But for this occasion he became very deliberate, very patient and consoling, coaching her with infinite finesse until she could mimic his methods—the gesture, the turn of the head, the extravagant response. When she understood that he was "creating" her role for her, she complied at once and became an ardent pupil, practicing over and over the various subtleties, until they had devised together fascinating scenes, filled with dash, verve and comic invention.

The opera opened with considerable fanfare on November 6, 1899. Monsieur Cain, the librettist, came from Paris for the premiere, and approved the work they had done, for they had, together, a buoyancy that lit up the stage, so that as soon as they appeared there would be a spark, the beginning of hilarity. And that was a new experience, the ripple of laughter out there in the dark, the audience responding with a roar of delight. The opera was hailed by the critics as a brilliant achievement, and the whole affair was a spectacular success. "I wish you could have heard all they said," she wrote her mother afterward. "M. Massenet, and M. Cain, too, when they came to my dressing room. Well! Now they will give this opera about three times a week for a month or two. Friday was the first, and tonight is the second."

However, the immense popularity of *Cendrillon* crowded out

other roles she had hoped to sing more often. Now, instead of appearing as the beautiful Leonora, or the seductive Dalila, she had to don, night after night, the absurd costume and comic mannerisms of Madame de la Haltière. But it seemed that every season had its surprises as well as its disappointments (at Covent Garden she hadn't sung half the roles she'd been promised). And then, in the middle of this one, not long after Christmas, Monsieur Stumont, their codirector, suddenly died. He had been elderly and very kind, his death was a great shock, and soon afterward Monsieur Calabrese announced his retirement.

After so many years of continuity, this unforeseen change affected all the artists in the company. The two directors had been paternal in their attitude, creating for their singers a safe, comfortable operatic world. But now that world was suddenly in question. And once more they were discovering how precarious a singer's life could be, with the future always subject to matters of chance—casts, repertoire, contracts, managers and many factors that could never be foreseen.

After a time it became known that several in the company had signed contracts with Maurice Grau of the Metropolitan Opera House. Charles Gilibert, Imbart de la Tour, Marcel Journet, even their brilliant conductor, Phillippe Flon—all these noted artists would make their debuts next season in New York. But others were not so fortunate, and now, when they gathered in the Green Room, there would be an air of sober constraint. Unwittingly the artists had become rivals, each wondering who might be engaged for another season. Cut suddenly adrift, their old camaraderie had split apart into little eddies of anxiety, and throughout the company there was a disconsolate wariness, a malaise that stemmed from the loss and the uncertainty.

The most sensitive element was the one of prestige, and the artists at La Monnaie understood that very well. Sign with some lesser company and the singer might find himself on an operatic toboggan, sliding away into oblivion. Yet there were only a few opera companies in Europe with prestige enough to serve as a springboard to the top.

Meanwhile Louise was corresponding with Mr. Higgins, hoping to sing another summer in London although many people believed that Covent Garden would be closed this summer because of the Boer War. The situation in South Africa was approaching a crisis, with Baden-Powell under siege in Mafeking, and it was said that the social season in London would be curtailed. However, Mr. Higgins seemed confident that the opera would continue and in his letters was proceeding in the usual way. "I advise you to study Azucena (*Il Trovatore*)," he wrote, "which we will do with Slezak, a new Bohemian tenor, now at Breslau." He also noted that her roles would be somewhat limited, since they wouldn't be giving *Favorita,* and had "no tenor for *Le Prophète.* . . . If I had more roles for you," he wrote, "I could pay more."

That was where matters stood, the future still obscure, until one day a letter came from Mr. Higgins that was not unlike the one that had dropped so casually out of the clouds into the garden at Angers. This time, however, the magic was smudged and blotted, a hastily scribbled postscript under the manager's signature at the bottom of the page: "Mr. Grau has asked me to inquire of you what terms you would accept for next winter at the Metropolitan."

The writing was almost illegible, but unerringly they deciphered it from beneath the blots and smudges, for this was what they had wanted all along. They were homesick, and they wanted to go home. But without an opera contract that would hardly be possible, for they couldn't return to Boston now and reassemble his classes—that life seemed remote and long ago. Almost unwittingly they had become dependent for their livelihood on her singing, and the debts still loomed large. But now there was this postscript from Mr. Higgins, and in a buoyant mood Sidney set about devising ideal terms for a contract, while Louise wrote her mother, "I think it is pretty sure that next September will see us in America."

Maurice Grau's reply was for the most part favorable, though he pared down the terms and added some provisions of his own. "The extreme limit that I could pay," he wrote, "would be $800. a month, to sing an average of ten times a month." He also stipulated that it would be impossible to give her "the privilege of singing in concerts," since he must have "absolute control of the entire time and services of all artists that are engaged with me." He stated firmly that he would require the option of renewing her contract "for a second season at $900. a month, and for a third at $1000."

The additional clauses disturbed Sidney a good deal—the "absolute control," and especially the three-year option, for the Metropolitan went on long tours, both fall and spring, and this was an obligation he hadn't foreseen. However, there were many compensations, especially the promise of that name, "The Metropolitan," and after some hesitation he composed a letter for Louise to send, agreeing to all the terms that had been stipulated.

In his reply, Mr. Grau was most understanding. "You must remember," he wrote, "that having an option on you for more than one season will be to your advantage as well as mine, as I will then have every reason in the world to do all in my power so that you will have the greatest possible success." He also agreed to pay "travel expenses for two" on the long tours, as well as their boat fare to New York. In a postscript he added, "Your position in my company will be that of one of the *leading* contraltos for the French and Italian operas. As for the German operas, I have Madame Schumann-Heink, on whom I have a contract for another three years."

A few weeks later the manager of the Metropolitan sent a formal contract listing all the roles she must be prepared to sing: Amneris in *Aida*; Martha in *Mefistofele*; Maddalena in *Rigoletto*; Lola in *Cavalleria Rusticana*; Urbain in *Les Huguenots*; Siébel in *Faust*.

Sidney studied this important document with great care, and he was surprised to find that Mr. Grau had included those last two roles, for they were both small parts, not usually sung by a contralto—Siébel, a gentle youth in love with Marguerite; Urbain, a page to the Queen, who greets the courtiers with that sparkling aria, "Nobil' Signori, salute!" In France, both roles were sung by a second soprano, and while he pondered them he had gradually that prickling sensation that precedes intimations of disaster.

Not all at once, but insidiously, the implications took hold, for it was plain that if Louise sang these roles she would have to appear on the stage of the Metropolitan in boys' clothing. And this was a situation he found impossible to imagine, for

in all her operas she'd worn only the most feminine attire—
velvet robes, trains and satin gowns.

The boys' costumes he envisioned as the close-fitting tights
worn in circuses and carnivals, revealing the pretty curves and
contours for all to see. Such a display would, he felt, be wholly
out of character, and he composed a letter for her to send asking to be relieved of the boys' roles. But Maurice Grau flatly
refused.

So then they were faced with an unforeseen and most disturbing dilemma, for though he didn't want to deprive her of
her contract, he felt he must protect her dignity. And on a
deeper level he just plain didn't want her on the stage in such
costumes. He felt angry and sick that as a husband and protector he had been faced with such an alternative. But he
couldn't so lightly dismiss her future, and wrote long, anxious
letters to friends and family in America asking their opinion
of this painful impasse.

He wrote George Chadwick in Boston, and others of his
friends there. And she wrote her mother, explaining the situation, though at the same time trying to make it seem not quite
so serious. "As many times as I have seen Scalchi in those same
roles," she wrote, "I never even noticed she was in boys' clothing, and I imagine the rest of the public is like me."

But her mother sided strongly with Sidney's views in the
matter, and even thought the boys' costumes "unchristian." And
when her mother forwarded a letter Bess had sent to West
Chester that was critical of opera and filled with barbs and
sarcasm, Louise was deeply hurt. In reply she wrote hurriedly:

I have just this minute received Bess' letter and must write
you a letter to send her. Bess says, "Many people have expressed surprise that she has avoided it for so long," but
you see I haven't avoided it at all. Those roles were written
by the composers not for a *contralto,* but for a second soprano, and it is only Grau in the whole world that has them
sung by a contralto. Bess says very positively that she would
never have gone on the stage herself, but how can she be
certain how she would act under circumstances she has
never experienced? I know very well Bess, with her husband

in business in Boston, could not very well leave her family and go on the stage, but my circumstances were so different I hardly think it is logical to compare the two. . . .

On and on this letter went, the tone defensive and deeply wounded, for it didn't occur to her to employ in rebuttal the barbs and sarcasm she was trying to refute.

Sidney, also, was unhappy with this partisan stand in West Chester, and wrote her mother, "One thing I do not agree with you in, and that is that Christianity is involved in this matter of costumes."

He then resorted to logic in her defense. "Christianity lies in the *reason why* we do a thing," he wrote, "more than in the act itself. A person may wear a costume in order to impersonate a noble character or increase an impression of art intended to do good." But though he was troubled by the criticism in West Chester, the matter of the boys' costumes had cast a blight over the whole Metropolitan contract. There were many drawbacks to those ironclad provisions, and one of the most serious was the long hectic tours that he was afraid would break down her health. In almost every letter Mr. Grau had complained about the sickness in his company, sounding like a man on the verge of exhaustion. "Pardon my delay," he'd written, "but I've been so upset by a lot of illness in my company. . . ." And a few weeks later, "I have been terribly upset by the great amount of illness that has existed in my company this season." Emma Calvé, Milka Ternina, Andreas Dippel—in city after city, Montreal, Toronto, St. Louis, the leading singers had become ill and couldn't appear.

Vividly he could imagine the disrupted homelife, the trains, the hotels, the inevitable sickness, and wrote a long letter to her mother explaining why the engagement with the Metropolitan was "objectionable." "In the first place," he wrote, "Mr. Grau wants absolute control of Louise for *three years*. In the next place comes the roles in boys' costumes. Besides this Mr. Grau travels all over the country for more than half the season, and his singers are sick and tired most of the time. To be tied down for *three years* to such a roving hard life seems to me altogether too much for her to undertake."

Meanwhile there were long, anxious discussions in the little house on the rue de la Presse. And though Louise felt quite differently, and wasn't troubled by the matter of the costumes or the traveling, she didn't try to override him. She didn't insist and take control, as she easily might have done. She wasn't reconciled, but nevertheless she was prepared to let the future slip away. (A decade later the writer Willa Cather would try to define this quality in her nature. In an article for *McClure's Magazine* entitled "Three American Singers, Louise Homer, Olive Fremstad and Geraldine Farrar," she would compare the inner needs and life-style of the three singers, attributing to the two sopranos fame achieved on the crest of a compelling ambition, whereas for the contralto she would discern a lesser ardor. "Her freedom from vanity frees her from self-torture," she would write. "She has set herself no goals it would break her heart to lose." But in her assessment, Willa Cather may have overlooked the poignancy of relationships too valued to be sacrificed on the operatic shoals.)

And so the matter stood—a torment of indecision—until one day, in desperation, Sidney suggested that they consult with Monsieur Calabrese. The manager of La Monnaie might be able to advise them, and in any case he urgently needed someone close at hand to talk to. In a mood of great distraction they took a horsecab to the Brussels Opera House, feeling now somber, constrained, with the future hanging in the balance, for in his view it was "damned if you do, damned if you don't," and he was outraged that Mr. Grau had placed him in such an untenable situation.

But Monsieur Calabrese calmed their agitation at the very start. Quietly he listened to the whole disjointed story, and then, to their astonishment, he began to laugh. Just as at the Roberval Agency, when Monsieur Calabrese laughed all the gold fobs and medals bounced about on his round little stomach, only this time he shouted, not for the contract, but for the head costumer, exclaiming meanwhile, "You will see, my dear children, it is not at all as you think!"

The head costumer was a birdlike little woman given to brilliant flights of imagination, a genius at her craft. And when Monsieur Calabrese had explained about "the beautiful con-

tract with the Metropolitan in New York," she echoed his
words, "But my children, it is not as you think!" adding, with
an air of vigorous disdain, "Those little soubrettes, with their
closefitting tights, they are all wrong!"

Then she described the costumes she would make herself,
embroidering the flights of fancy with a lovely array of detail.
For Siébel, she said, there would be a long satin tunic with
ruffles of velvet, and loose satin trousers to buckle below the
knees. For Urbain, a coat of white velvet trimmed with gold
braid, and white kid boots that buckled at the knee. The coat
would come to the top of the boots, and there would be a wide
collar of stiffened cream lace to frame the beautiful face, and
for the dark hair a cap of pearls.

White velvet, loose satin tunics, creamy lace—the pretty
phrases were wonderfully reassuring. And now that he could
picture her modestly wrapped about, with knee-high boots, lace
collars, gold embroidery, pearl caps, velvet ruffles and all the
other feminine adornments the costumer had described, his apprehensions faded right away. Oddly, once the matter of the
boys' costumes had been righted, the other matters took on a
different guise. The disadvantages became less apparent, the
tours might even be an adventure, and they cabled Maurice
Grau that very day, accepting his terms provided they could
have her costumes made in Brussels. And from New York
Mr. Grau wired in reply, "I was very pleased when I received
your cable. Let us therefore consider the matter settled, and we
shall sign the contracts in London. I shall do everything in my
power to meet you in all your desires."

In Brussels it was rumored that she wore her own hair when
she sang in opera, and a reporter for *La Réforme* came to in-
vestigate this unusual custom. In her story she described the
American singer for her readers:

She is dark, as a contralto should be and it is true that Mme.
Homer acts with her own hair instead of a wig. What beautiful hair she has! She is quite slim, which contradicts the
popular belief that contraltos must be stout. Her face has an
animated but tender expression, and she has large fearless
dark eyes. Her profile has a beautiful surety of line, and her

luxuriant dark hair falls without restraint from her forehead. She has an expressive and serious look, which is
softened by a brilliant smile.

They had been subletting the Paris apartment on the rue de
Lubeck, believing it would be a profitable asset when the Paris
Exposition opened in 1900. Now, finally, it *was* the year 1900
("everyone is asking, is this the end of the nineteenth century
or the start of the twentieth?" Louise wrote her mother on New
Year's Day), and the apartment was conveniently there for
Sidney's family, who much preferred living in France. Meanwhile, for them, there was London, and they stayed this summer in a boardinghouse just five blocks from Covent Garden.
As before, when Louise began preparations at the Royal Opera
House there was great confusion, and in the midst of it, this
season, an undertaking that she approached with misgiving, almost with dread, for she would be singing the role of Ortrud
under the great Austrian conductor Felix Mottl.
So far she had sung *Lohengrin* only in French, with French
conductors. She had had no experience with the German traditions, very little with the German language, and Herr Mottl was
a foremost interpreter of the Wagnerian operas. He had conducted the *Nibelungen Ring* at Bayreuth, and for years had been
director of the Karlsruhe Opera. He was himself a composer,
with a brilliant reputation, and at the start of the *Lohengrin*
rehearsals she was apprehensive, for the role was the most difficult in her repertoire.
But when Felix Mottl discovered how anxious she was to
learn, he gave her many private rehearsals. Together they explored the subtleties of this towering and devious role (which
is, like Amneris and Dalila, a catalyst of the tragedy, but so
much more evil). He showed her in the study sessions how to
broaden the tone into hatred, how to build, very gradually, to
a crescendo, how to wrest from the scenes the utmost in drama.
During this absorbing interval of creation she was supremely
content, for though her education had been limited, she had
derived, from her father perhaps, the concentration, the passion
for learning and the receptive mind of the scholar. She had
never wanted "just to know how to sing"; she had always wanted

A photograph taken in Brussels in April, 1900, while the contract with the Metropolitan was a matter of debate.

to delve deeper. And when she could have the guidance of an inspired teacher, there was at once a response, an intelligence, a commitment that could be a valuable asset for a singer in opera.

Herr Mottl became so interested in her voice that he asked her to sing several of his songs at a private musicale, a brilliant social affair with Sir Henry Irving, Ellen Terry and other notables among the guests. And when she sang Ortrud at Covent Garden he had added immeasurably to her interpretation of the role.

It had been predicted that the social season, and the opera season, too, would be curtailed by the conflict in South Africa. But actually the reverse had happened, and more people were staying in London this summer, caught up in the drama of the Boer War and following, with mounting suspense, the situation at Mafeking. There, for almost a year, a small band of valiant Englishmen, with their heroic leader, Baden-Powell, had been under siege. Meanwhile Colonel Mahon was struggling to reach the embattled scene and rescue his beleaguered countrymen. This was the scenario—a battalion of brave men refusing surrender, holding out against desperate odds, a heroic attempt at rescue and the whole of London, indeed the whole of England, caught up in the drama.

Mafeking was adding a brilliant dash of patriotism to the social season. And when Louise sang a "command performance" at Buckingham Palace, the hero of the hour among the aristocratic guests was Sir George White, who had distinguished himself at the siege of Ladysmith.

The "command" was in the form of a letter from Sir Walter Parrott, music director to Queen Victoria: "I am commanded to ask if you will sing at the State Concert at Buckingham Palace on July 25th, 1900. . . ." The other soloists, all from the opera, were Suzanne Adams, Pol Plançon and Fernando de Lucia. They also had the orchestra and chorus of the Royal College of Music.

But the occasion was so weighted in protocol that the music was almost lost in the formalities. No applause was allowed at a State Concert, no backs could be turned on the royal family. When the Prince and Princess of Wales made their delayed entrance, they were preceded by twenty chamberlains in medieval costumes, walking backwards, bent almost double at the waist. The seats for the guests were arranged in tiers along each side of the glittering hall, and this was a dazzling assemblage, earls and duchesses, diplomats and admirals, and Indian princes in robes of woven gold, with strands and ropes of rubies and

emeralds and diamonds falling almost to their feet. For the
singers, seated on an improvised platform, it was a strange,
exposed situation, and while Louise was waiting to sing her solo,
Dalila's aria, "Mon coeur s'ouvre à ta voix," she was reminded
of another solo she had sung, just thirteen years ago, a stirring,
tragic song, "The Diver," and a similar situation, sitting on the
platform with Miss Spicer, watching the audience take their
places in Horticultural Hall, and thinking, with surprise: Can
this really be me?

The singers were rewarded for their work with forty guineas
apiece, a few kind words of appreciation from the royal couple,
who spoke individually to the soloists before they left the hall,
and a midnight dinner in a private dining room in Buckingham
Palace, where they were served a marvelous variety of rare
delicacies on gold plates, by an impressive array of footmen
and waiters in resplendent uniforms.

More than ever, this season, attendance rose and fell at
Covent Garden with the presence of royalty. And on May 17,
1900, when Louise sang her second performance of *Lohengrin,*
with Felix Mottl conducting, the opera house was almost filled
with a brilliant audience come to see the princess in the royal
box, and only incidentally the queen pouring out her flights of
gilded hate on the stage.

Nevertheless she had a tremendous ovation that night, following her big scene in the second act. Again and again she was
called back to bow, in the midst of wave after wave of applause,
and from the galleries cries of "Brava!" and excited expressions
of approval. Throughout the theater the mood was electrifying,
and that could be marvelously rewarding for a singer who had
worked so faithfully, with Herr Mottl, to achieve this new and
more compelling Ortrud.

But strangely, the enthusiasm didn't last. In the next scene
it was apparent that interest had begun to flag. And during the
final act, when she had to stand motionless for long intervals
beside the River Scheldt, Louise discovered, with surprise, that
the Prince of Wales and his Princess had left the royal box.
She didn't often become aware, from behind the footlights, of
what was going on in the darkened auditorium. But now it was

As Ortrud in *Lohengrin* at Covent Garden in 1900.

inescapable, for many in the audience were leaving right in the middle of the opera. They were standing in the aisles, their backs to the stage, and the rustle of conversation throughout the theater seemed very far removed from Ortrud's bitter triumph and the swan boat gliding sedately on the river.

When the opera had finally petered out to only the faintest smattering of applause, Sidney was waiting in the wings to tell her what had happened. At the start of the third act, he said, the Prince had received a stirring message—Mafeking had been relieved. The news had spread throughout the theater and many in the audience had lost interest in the opera—caring more for the victory celebration in the streets.

When Louise had dressed hurriedly, and they were prepared to leave, they discovered that this demonstration had already reached mammoth proportions. Because Colonel Mahon had so bravely rescued his gallant countrymen, the whole of London was converging now on the central part of the city, moved to express their relief and joy in a display of fervent patriotism.

The size and ardor of the crowd were almost frightening, and when finally they plunged in they were caught up and all but trapped in a demonstration of gigantic proportions. They had to go only a few blocks to reach their boardinghouse and be with their little girl. But even one block was a monumental task in this dense and frantic atmosphere. All about them the elated crowds swirled in eddies of excitement, and the disorder was intense, with horses reined in, pawing the air, snake dances, war dances, the streets a seething mass of lights, noise and furious elation—flaring gas lamps, bonfires, screams, shouts, horns, flags, banners, carriages trapped and overturned, lampposts shinnied, speeches hurled jubilantly into the night.

The mood was one of mounting hysteria, and the great throngs of people were so frantic with joy that the distance they had to traverse might have been five miles, progress was so perilous and slow. Again and again the surging crowds threatened to sweep them off their feet, until in the end it took most of the night to go the five blocks to the boardinghouse where their little girl was sleeping. And it seemed now as though they had been living abroad for a very long time.

Chapter XIV

The eventful years in Europe ended, as they had begun, with a visit to West Chester. And, as usual, time seemed to have stood still in that quiet Quaker town, though in fact there had been changes, and the household on South High Street was much smaller. Auntie Fulton had died, Ella had married, young Fulton had gone west to Chicago. Now, in Sarah Beatty's home, there was only Daisy, who was nineteen, and Aunt Kate, almost eighty. But there still seemed to be a crowd around most of the time, with Allie and Ella coming every day with their husbands and children, and everyone sitting about on the porch, enjoying the tall shade trees and the presence of friends and relatives. Louise had worried about her mother when she was away. "Do you get very tired, Mama darling?" she had written from Brussels. "Now you are sixty-three, but with so few at home I thought perhaps you would have an easier time." She had been gone more than four years, and it was reassuring to find her mother so much the same.

The Opera Train was to leave New York November 2nd,[7] and travel first to Los Angeles for three performances, then on to San Francisco, where Louise would make her debut in *Aida* on November 14th. So it seemed they had an adventure in the offing, but meanwhile much of the attention centered about their little girl, who was seeing her grandmother for only the second time. She had been an infant when they left, and now she was almost five years old, a graceful, dark-eyed child who seemed to her American cousins quite foreign, for she spoke French, in a lovely patter of "accent délicieux," and wore, of course, the French dresses, bonnets and shoes.

Bess had agreed to board their little girl and her nurse while they were on tour. So from West Chester they went to North Newton, Massachusetts, where Bess now lived, to get the child settled and visit a few days with friends and relatives in Boston. And it was in North Newton, just two days before they were to leave for New York to board the Opera Train, that Sidney woke in the morning, desperately ill.

The onset was very sudden. In the evening he was visiting with friends, enjoying a reunion after many years away, and the next morning, at dawn, he was stricken with a raging fever and paralysis. In the North Newton hospital his illness was diagnosed as an acute attack of rheumatic fever, and while the doctors struggled to keep him alive, Louise wired Maurice Grau that she wouldn't be able to come to New York to join the Opera Train.

Then she sat by his bed, willing him to live, caught up too suddenly in a nightmare world of imminent disaster. From New York Mr. Grau sent her a ticket to San Francisco, with a request that she come directly there to make her debut in *Aida*. But that she could never do when Sidney was so ill, and meanwhile the struggle continued, with day and night nurses, other doctors called in for consultation, his cousin, Tom Homer, coming out from Boston to be with her in this crisis. He wasn't, himself, aware of all this, for much of the time he hovered between delirium and unconsciousness. During one interval he had what he would afterward recall as a "strange vision"—a spirit in the dark sky, a beautiful face, "the eyes full of sorrow and sympathy," an angel, taking him by the hand. When he woke from this "vision" he felt suddenly happy and calm. But that brief oasis of healing "calm" flared into passionate alarm when he discovered that she was still in the hospital.

At once he began to protest. Why was she still here? Why

wasn't she on the Opera Train? Now there was barely time and she must leave at once and go direct to San Francisco for her debut. Eloquently he pleaded with the doctors, insisting with the poignant lucidity of the very ill—weak, feverish, the voice barely a whisper, the agitation burning away every last remnant of strength. They owed it to Maurice Grau, he protested, the manager who had been so distracted by all the illness in his company the year before. Mr. Grau had paid their passage to America; he had been a good friend, encouraging, considerate, and they owed him this in return.

Above all, he couldn't endure the thought of the lost debut, and in his efforts to have his way he became so agitated, so disturbed, that the doctors were alarmed. He must have rest, they told Louise. He was somewhat better; the most acute crisis was past. But if he continued in this state of agitation the fever would surely rise and he would have a critical relapse. So there it was, neat and inexorable—finely honed, sharpened enough to pierce the heart. And finally, so that he might have some rest, with great reluctance and strong misgivings, she boarded the night train in Boston.

As the doctors had foreseen, as soon as she had left, he fell into a deep, healing sleep. With his mind at rest there was immediate improvement, and knowing how anxious she would be, he composed a reassuring telegram to be sent to a station along the way. But to those in charge it seemed a burdensome plan, trying to intercept a speeding train on its way across the country, and the telegram was never sent.

She was alone on this trip, and as soon as the train had left the Boston station she was overwhelmed with the knowledge that while she was away, he would die. This presentiment became more acute with each passing mile, until the dread and remorse were so vivid and relentless that she could hardly eat or sleep. There was no one to share the grief. And every hour became a day, every day a week, while she traveled farther and farther away from him, across the plains and the prairies, half paralyzed with the sick misery of apprehension, distraught with an anguish not unlike that of the minstrel Orpheus when he finds that by weakly yielding to the passionate pleas of his beloved, he has caused her death—*che faro, che faro*, across the plains and over the mountains, fearing he was dead.

In San Francisco she rode in a horsecab, an ominous casing of fear and dread, up the hill to the Occidental Hotel. And there she found telegrams saying he was getting well, and finally she could weep.

But not for long, since there was now only one day for preparation and rehearsals. The next night, November 14, 1900, she made her American debut in *Aida*. Her old friend Mancinelli was the conductor, and afterward the reviews paid glowing tribute to the new American singer. "The pretty young contralto was a stranger who came comparatively unheralded," wrote the critic for the *Evening Post*, "but ere her first scene was finished the audience was hers to command. She has the advantage of youth and beauty, a voice of rich quality and remarkable range, and a dramatic force that is irresistible." "Her voice is unlike any contralto we have heard in years," wrote the reviewer for the *Bulletin*. "It will be a wonder if Louise Homer does not become a very great prima donna contralto." "Remember the name," warned the *Examiner*. "It is going to spell something big in the years ahead."

She clipped all the reviews and sent them to him, like a bouquet, to decorate the bedside table. And he shared them willingly with the doctors, the nurses and any other captive audience. But he was concerned that she had had to endure such fearful suspense on that trip alone across the continent and wrote her:

> I have been wild with indignation that you should have suffered unnecessarily through the carelessness of others. While you were on the train I was anxious about you, so I wrote a telegram for them to send. They promised to send it to the train and I waited every day for an answer, with what feelings you can imagine. And at the end of the week they informed me that the telegram had never been sent! Don't say anything, but wasn't it cruel? . . . Your success has given me happiness I cannot describe. You are all the

world to me. You are in my thoughts from morning to
night. . . .

The next night, on November 15th, she sang Siebel in *Faust*,
with Nellie Melba as Marguerite, and wore for the first time the
new costume of satin and velvet ruffles. But after that there
would be no more performances for ten days, and when the opera
patrons of San Francisco learned the circumstances of the young
American contralto, they gave her, in effect, the keys to the city.
The Spreckels, the Oelrichs, the Popes—they were strangers at
first, but soon they became friends. And during her stay she
was all but overwhelmed with kindness and attention, her room
at the hotel always filled with flowers, a carriage at her disposal,
luncheons, dinners and other diversions arranged when she was
free. It was a very genuine hospitality, impulsive, unaffected,
and before long she felt reassuringly at home in the big, ornate
houses on the hill, with the portes cochères, the fountains, the
elaborate statuary and that breathtaking view of the bay.

There was a spirited, unpolished air among leaders of society
in San Francisco that seemed almost to belie the show of wealth.
And this had always been a city in love with opera. As early as
the eighteen forties, when the first charter was granted, there
had been opera companies coming to perform. Colonel Maple-
son, Theodore Thomas, Henry Abbey—all the distinguished im-
presarios had been accorded a fervent welcome in San Francisco.
And though the Mission Street Opera House wasn't large, the
acoustics were perfect and the decor a luxurious, jewel-like setting to provide a glittering frame for the extravagant, even
fabulous gowns and jewels that San Francisco audiences liked
to parade on opera nights for all to see.

She sang Schwertleite in *Die Walküre*, Maddalena in *Rigoletto*
and another Siébel. Then, on December 3rd, she boarded the
Opera Train for the first time. That colorful caravan had
blazoned on the side of each car, in letters a foot high, the name
METROPOLITAN OPERA HOUSE. But without Sidney she was
lonely on this tour, for many in the company were foreigners,
and they settled down at once to their accustomed diversions—

the men playing cards, the women crocheting and knitting, the gossip flying about in a dozen different languages.

However, there were some old friends, and a few who were American—Suzanne Adams, with whom she had shared the State Concert at Buckingham Palace, Lillian Nordica, who was now at the pinnacle of her fame. Louise had sung with Nordica both seasons at Covent Garden, and their training had been somewhat similar. They had both studied in Boston, at the New England Conservatory, with George Chadwick as mutual friend and advisor; and they had both gone to Paris to learn opera.

But there were divergences, for Nordica, who had come originally from Maine, had had an ambitious, strong-willed mother as catalyst of her career, a passionate partisan at home, arranging her musical education from earliest childhood. Since then her beautiful soprano voice had carried her far, and after achieving stardom she had become noted for her extravagant costumes, her unusual marriages and a certain superb arrogance. The five-thousand-dollar tiara given her by the Metropolitan was famous, and so were her hats, which had become noted for a spectacular array of furs, feathers and flowers. As an opera star Lillian Nordica had created an image for herself and was greatly admired for her extravagance, but there was another side to her nature, and she could be, with those who knew her well, responsive, warm and genuinely kind.

Many of the cities they visited had never seen opera before, and Grau's celebrated artists had to make do with some dismal situations. In Denver the theater was so small that the chorus and ballet could scarcely be accommodated on stage, while in Kansas City, Convention Hall was so huge and barnlike that it all but dwarfed the more intimate operas like *Bohème* and *Lucia*. In Lincoln, Nebraska, the auditorium was still being built when they arrived, and the dreariest conditions of all they encountered in Minneapolis, where Exposition Hall was declared by the critics unfit for opera and such a disgrace that the civic leaders vowed, right then and there, to tear it down and build another (which they did in exactly one year).

Louise appeared as Urbain in *Les Huguenots* in Minneapolis, and sang the delicate solo, "Nobil' Signori, salute!" an aria so

graceful, with such lovely vocal acrobatics, that at the very outset there would be a ripple of contentment, a sigh of pure enjoyment, and at the end a spontaneous outburst of applause. In the
audience on this occasion there were many old friends—and
others who remembered her father's ministry. But it was a
strange, even eerie experience, for this was the same Exposition
Hall in which she had sung when she was fourteen, one among
a thousand children, packed into the chorus, until a bolt of
lightning had turned the whole place into a holocaust of terror.

After Minneapolis the somewhat weary caravan turned toward New York, where they would arrive on December 17th.
Louise was to make her Metropolitan debut in *Aida* on December 22nd, which meant that she would have only a few days to
find an apartment for her family if they were to be settled in
their own home on Christmas Day.

This was the somewhat precarious plan that she had been
evolving during the tour. The last months had been disturbing
—all the visiting about, the illness, the separations, the loneli-
ness. And she believed that she could erase all that, and turn it
around and set it straight with that most desirable of all fulfill-
ments—the simplicity, the privacy and the blissful communication of Christmas Day in their own home.

She had already bought the presents in the Chinese stores in
San Francisco, and Sidney had promised to meet her in New
York. For several weeks he had been out of the hospital, con-
valescing and gaining strength, and the doctors had told him
he was well enough to travel. But he was reluctant to make the
trip alone, and at the last minute sent a telegram to Minneapolis
asking her to come instead to North Newton. So then her ardent
plan became more difficult. But she was still mesmerized by that
prospect of a family Christmas tree, and undertook a kind of
marathon, winging her way here and there with the mythical
ease of Santa's reindeer—first up to North Newton, to see him
and reassure him, then back again, alone, to New York, to rehearse at the Metropolitan and find a place to live.

In the midst of all this she took a carriage to Thirty-ninth
Street and donned the regal robes of Amneris for her debut. The
cast was undistinguished that night (two of the newcomers

wouldn't sing with the company a second season), but throughout the performance the contralto was radiant with relief, for on that very day she had found a home for her family (some furnished rooms on Fifty-seventh Street), and bought a Christmas tree and tinsel. When the curtain had fallen there was just time to catch the night train to Boston, and the next morning the trolley to North Newton. After that there remained only the instructions from the doctor to list carefully, the trunks and the warm coats, the hired carriage, the trip to New York with their little daughter and at last the stocking hung in an unfamiliar place, and a tree in their own home on Christmas Day.

Two weeks later, on January 7th, there was another *Aida* which seemed a more authentic debut, for the cast was brilliant and Sidney was in the audience to hear her sing. This time she could look up into the rosy glittering tiers and believe finally that she was appearing at the Metropolitan in New York. The cast that night included Jean de Reszke as Radames, Edouard de Reszke as Ramfis, Johanna Gadski, Marcel Journet, Antonio Scotti, some of the finest of Grau's singers, and throughout the evening the performance unfolded with an almost hypnotic artistry.

Much of the applause that night was for the beloved tenor, who for years had been an idol of the opera public. Jean de Reszke hadn't sung at the Metropolitan the year before, and there had been persistent rumors that he had lost his voice. With a great tenor there are often these apprehensions, a sense of personal concern amounting almost to hysteria, and when he had made his first appearance of the season, as Lohengrin, on New Year's Eve, an enormous audience had come, many with great anxiety, to find that there was no truth at all in the bleak predictions. Nevertheless, it was believed his career was drawing to a close, and this was, in fact, the last *Aida* he would sing in New York, the last Radames at the Metropolitan, the final portrayal in that role of a certain poetic quality which he alone could convey.

The great Polish tenor, Jean de Reszke, wasn't, like his brother Edouard, a commanding personality, big, powerful, exuberant. Instead he was of slighter build and quieter temperament, dark and romantic in appearance—a marvelous Romeo and an ideal Hamlet. Originally he had been a baritone, and had retrained his voice to a higher range—a rare achievement that had given his singing an air of exquisite discipline, the tones melodious and tempered, the texture so modulated, so finely grained, that the effect was almost hypnotic. Jean de Reszke's lyric high notes didn't blast the galleries and stir the pulses—instead they stilled the heart, communicating with unique artistry, a restrained but fervent passion. In time there would be another tenor at the opera house, another Radames to bring the audience to their feet with the fire and splendor of a magnificent vocal talent. But the echoes of that quieter genius would remain, for all time, among the glories of the past.

Throughout the season the Metropolitan commuted to Philadelphia for a series of performances in the Academy of Music, which was, unlike its plain and forthright name, a very pretty, rococo, cream and gold and velvet-red jewel of an opera house, almost Mozartian in flavor. And when Louise found that she was to sing *Aida* in Philadelphia on January 15th, she felt as though she couldn't bear it if her mother didn't come to hear her.

She had never been reconciled to her mother's disapproval, and now she launched a campaign of persuasion—arranged for tickets, enlisted her sisters as allies, wrote long, pleading letters home. This urgency precipitated a crisis in West Chester, and Sarah Beatty spent long hours in prayer and meditation, seeking guidance. From earliest memory she had been taught that opera was a sin, but finally, unable to deal such a hurt, she consented to come.

This was a generous gesture, perhaps too generous, for when Louise knew her mother would be there she was assailed by a confusion of second thoughts, and wondered if it had been wise to insist. Now that it was too late, she could imagine how Grand Opera might seem to one who had had no experience with the theater, how colorful, perhaps crude, and so violent—a too exotic tapestry of marching warriors, chanting priests and the handmaidens of Amneris adorning her with garlands of flowers.

Throughout the performance, aware that her mother was in the audience, she was half sick with anxiety, and when finally

Taken in 1901, during the first season at the Metropolitan.

she had sung the last mournful song above Radames' tomb, she hurried to her dressing room to meet her mother there. They were both in black at that moment for Sarah Beatty had worn only black since she was widowed, and Louise was in the somber black of grieving repentance. Now, in the midst of the black veils, and the tears, and the ardent reunion, her mother exclaimed, "My child, you have converted me to opera!" And nothing could have been more reassuring or more eloquent, for this was the language of religion, of inward change and true conviction.

Louise was singing in several operas with Nellie Melba—*Rigoletto, Les Huguenots, Faust*. Like Jean de Reszke, the Australian soprano planned to remain abroad next season. It seemed she wouldn't be returning to the Metropolitan, and in March, Melba asked them to visit her in her apartment in the Ansonia Hotel, for, as she had said at Covent Garden, "there were things to talk about."

Nellie Melba had been eight years at the Metropolitan, and her dazzling flights of song were considered, by the opera public, a unique treasure. She had come from a plain home and a remote town some distance from Melbourne, and had had very little musical education. But she had been born with a voice so perfectly placed that from the very first she could sing like a bird. Therefore, in her experience there had been no arduous training, no anxious search for a reliable teacher, no miracles of technique; her voice was simply there—high, bright, supple and silvery, scaling the heights and manipulating the trills with an ease that was truly ravishing.

It was a limited voice, better suited to the lighter roles. When she tried Brunhilde in *Siegfried* it was a disaster, and the critics complained that her acting was wooden. But all this was forgiven because of those high, high skylarking trills, a passionless ecstasy of song so pure, so cold, so birdlike, so rare and so hypnotic that almost as soon as she started to sing she became the darling of the opera public, courted by the aristocracy, feted and adored.

They went to see Nellie Melba in her home in the Ansonia Hotel, a suite of rooms richly decorated with velvet drapes, jade boxes, marvelous enameled Easter eggs and pretty porcelain figurines. All these luxuries, the silk sheets and satin pillows, the brocaded table covers and delicate gilded ornaments, Melba carried about with her, back and forth across the Atlantic, when she traveled. Throughout her career on the stage she had been petted by society, the favorite of kings, rewarded with jewels and valuable gifts. But she had also been lonely, beset by nerves and illnesses that interfered with her singing. She was now just forty years old and still beautiful, the hair a rich red-brown, the eyes dark and on this visit very kind, for she had sensed, when she was first introduced to the American singer, a certain naïveté, an impulsive, trusting nature that was in her view incompatible with the complicated and often treacherous world of opera. She had wanted to counter this with a warning, some wisdom from her own experience, and talked to them earnestly about managers, contracts and the many protective devices that a singer must have at her disposal to guard against the pressures and perils of public life.

She spoke of rivalries, intrigues, the exploitation of the vocal artist, and they listened without really comprehending. It wasn't that they doubted her advice; it was just that the things she said seemed to them remote, even unreal. They were reminded of the managers they had known—Maurice Grau, Monsieur Breton, Monsieur Calabrese—and easily dismissed the urgent warnings, remembering best the tribute at the end, when, just as they were leaving, Nellie Melba said quietly, "My dear, you have the most beautiful voice in the world."

If the most gifted artist of them all could speak in this way, there was reason to be elated, and returning to the apartment on Fifty-seventh Street they talked about the future, and also about Sidney's songs. He was fully recovered from the convalescence following his illness, and throughout the winter had been rearranging his work, and postponing, week after week, the moment when he would take his compositions to an American publisher. But now the exhilaration following that visit with Madame Melba had its effect, and he decided right then that the next day they would consult with G. Schirmer & Sons.

This was often the only way he could act—on the spur of the moment, after months of indecision. Let's go, he would say, and they did, taking a carriage to Union Square and the songs in a valise, so that almost before they realized what was happening, they were being shown to a room on an upper floor for a conference with Mr. Gustave Schirmer, son of the president and founder of the firm. Mr. Schirmer was rather a young man, with dark brown eyes and a quiet, attentive air. The fact that he and Sidney were exactly the same age—thirty-six—created a certain feeling of rapport while they spent a leisurely morning discussing his work and singing his songs, which Louise did with a touching air of pride and confidence. When they were through, Mr. Schirmer said that his company would publish the songs, and selected a group of eight Tennyson lyrics as a beginning. Royalties and contracts were discussed, terms quite simply arranged; and a little later he walked out again into Union Square—a man with a profession.

For both of them this was one of those occasions that happen only now and then. At breakfast this morning he had been a musician working alone, without recognition, perhaps even wasting his time. And now, only a few hours later, he was a composer, taking his wife to the Brevoort Hotel—luxuriating over a pipe and a stein of beer while she sparkled across from him and the implications gradually sank in.

In April Mr. Grau took his company on a short tour of some eastern cities and Chicago. And that could be an adventure—singing opera with friends and family in the audience. In Boston it was like coming home again, and here it was said that "she made a beautiful Amneris, and after the immortal 'love duet' there were calls of 'Alone! Alone!' and Madame Nordica gently pushed her forward. Again, in Act IV, her intensely dramatic agony of remorse, and denunciation of the priests was superb and excited a dozen recalls."

They were almost a week in Chicago, where all her brothers were living now, and where they gave a performance of *Les Huguenots* that the critic for the *Journal* called "extraordinary." "Never in the history of opera in this city," he wrote, "has there been such an audience and such a performance. Hundreds of persons were turned away from the doors." The cast that night included Nellie Melba, Lillian Nordica, Edouard and Jean de Reszke, Scotti and Plançon, and it was said that as Urbain, "Louise Homer burst upon the sight of her audience, a vision of loveliness in white, gold and delicate hues, and stunned them with the grace and beauty of her singing." "The opera was too long for the singer to respond to encores," noted the *Chicago Journal*, "save in the exquisite aria by Urbain. But Madame

The costume created in Brussels for the page, Urbain, in *Les Huguenots*.

Homer went so directly to the hearts of her audience that she was fairly compelled to give it a second time."

However, in Pittsburgh her friends there found it impossible to believe that "one of the Beatty girls" was really an opera singer. They had watched her grow up, and knew their minister's family so well that they couldn't quite credit this new status, and so she was welcomed there with a certain affectionate condescension as well as genuine warmth. Judge and Mrs. James Hay Reed gave a reception in her honor, in their Amberson Avenue home, and in the society columns it was reported that she "received in a beautiful gown of pink chiffon and lace."

She appeared as Urbain in Pittsburgh, and the next day the reviewers commented on an atmosphere of genuine surprise. Exclaimed the *Press*:

> Who ever would have thought that a Pittsburgh girl would receive such an ovation! Respectable mediocrity was all that most people expected, but after the first few notes were sung a perceptible breeze bespoke the interest, and as the work progressed, finally breaking into the beautiful "Nobil'

Signori!" aria, a stillness that betokened a storm of applause to come, fell over the opera house. Then, just as the last notes were sung, the storm broke. It is doubtful if anybody ever made such an impression on Pittsburgh.

"The people sat up in surprise," admitted the *Times*, "when her round full voice was heard, thrilling in its salute to the company." "Favor gave way to surprise," reported the *Post*:

> when, with a voice of pure velvet, she tripped airily through the mazes of Meyerbeer's music, intoning perfectly, trilling superbly, putting a ravishing touch of color here and there, concluding with an outburst of song that brought wild and glad acclaim. Few singers have received such an ovation in Pittsburgh, and in the end the entire aria had to be repeated.

After the opera tour there was a Festival Tour, which meant huge auditoriums or outdoor arenas, very large orchestras, enormous amateur choruses, often numbering in the thousands, and an audience that was unsophisticated, for the most part, but keyed to an ardent participation. The music festivals had now really taken hold, and were being presented all over the country, from Bangor, Maine, to Ann Arbor, Michigan, in St. Louis, Worcester, Cincinnati and many other towns and cities.

The mainstay of these festivals was the amateur, for in 1901 there weren't any adequate inventions to reproduce vocal or instrumental music. If you wanted to hear music you had to make it, and almost every town had its amateur choral and orchestral groups. Often groups in neighboring towns would band together and rehearse throughout the year. And it was the enterprising manager who turned all this into a festival—engaged professional soloists, provided a conductor and sometimes an orchestra, hired the halls and made the whole thing work.

The manager of Louise's Festival Tour was George Stewart, a leading director in the field. The conductor was Emil Mollenauer, and the other soloist was a fine young baritone, Emilio de Gogorza. Together they toured the festivals, which was rather like taking part in a series of immense houseparties, with, perhaps, a touch of the revival meeting and a leavening of carnival atmosphere as well. But what was most notable at these events was the earnestness, the genuine rapport. There was an airy eminence for the soloist at a music festival, and perhaps because they felt that Louise had somewhat mysteriously graduated from her own choral group, but was, in fact, one of them, a heightened sense of participation. Wrote a reporter in Saginaw, Michigan, "Such an ovation has never before been heard within the walls of the Masonic Temple. The members of the chorus were most persistent. They were waving a thousand handkerchiefs, and when she bowed and kissed her hand to them, the men in the chorus stood up and cheered." Wrote a reviewer in Ann Arbor:

> She was met with a storm of applause, and coming forward to bow was handed two huge bouquets of red and white flowers. She has a winning manner that cannot but affect an audience the minute she steps on the stage. Last night her soft brown hair was arranged low on her neck, and she was beautifully gowned in creamy satin and pale blue brocade. The conquest was half made before a note was uttered, and after the encore she won the hearts of everyone in the chorus by waving to them with her white-gloved hand.

In the summer they went to Cornish, New Hampshire, to be near their cousins the Saint-Gaudens. And it seemed that the intervening years had been eventful for both couples. In France, General Sherman, with his perfect cloak and victorious angel, had been awarded the Grand Prize at the Paris Salon. Saint-Gaudens had been made an Officer of the Legion of Honor, and all these accolades and tributes had established Augustus Saint-Gaudens as the foremost of American sculptors.

This summer Augustus had brought the victory group back with him to Cornish, and was designing a pedestal for its final resting place at Fifth Avenue and Sixtieth Street in New York. He also planned to have it gilded, a project his friends strenuously opposed. They were afraid the effect would be cheap and showy and that the handsome bronze statue would be ruined. But Saint-Gaudens was stubborn almost to the point of obsession, an artist truly consumed by his craft. Once, some years before, when the casting of the Robert Louis Stevenson bas-relief had been delivered to his studio, he had discovered a slight error in the fold of the blanket and became so distraught that he'd seized a mallet and would have smashed the Stevenson medallion if his friends hadn't intervened and forcibly restrained him.

Now it was the gilding of the Victory. In spite of all the protests he couldn't be dissuaded, and when it was done it seemed to everyone exactly right. For much of the summer it stood in a field behind the sculptor's studio, against a wooded background of dark green pines, a strange and marvelous sight in the quiet New Hampshire countryside. In the evening the slanting rays of the sun would set the gold ablaze, and then the General would seem to be taking flight, the whole equestrian group as shimmering and unsubstantial as a dream.

The Saint-Gaudens had been coming to Cornish for years, to live in a greatly loved home, Aspet—an old brick farmhouse which they had gradually embellished with pergolas, porches and grape arbors. They had had artist friends to visit who would sometimes return to rent or build homes of their own, until a small community of artists and writers had evolved in Cornish. The recreations, often at the Saint-Gaudens' home, were simple and spontaneous—tennis, croquet, charades and sometimes music around the old upright piano in the living room.

Mr. Grau had asked Louise to learn Venus in *Tannhäuser* for next season. But the ceilings were too low for vocalizing in the small farmhouse they had rented, so she put her piano in an open corncrib in a field above the studios. There she rehearsed the *Tannhäuser*, and was astonished, one day, to hear a fine basso profundo voice floating up the hill. The resounding lyric phrases were almost as powerful as those of Pol Plançon, and one would hardly have imagined that Augustus, with his slight build, would have a voice of such quality. But he did, indeed, have deep tones of almost operatic timbre and resonance, and he liked to sing when he worked. Meanwhile she was rehearsing the Venus. "Geliebter, komme!" she would sing in the radiant contralto. And sometimes the two voices would rendezvous in the sunlit field for an impromptu duet.

Saint-Gaudens usually worked on a number of commissions at once, and had a bigger studio near his own for his assistants. One of his projects this summer was a statue of Phillips Brooks, which was to stand beside Trinity Church in Boston, and he wanted to have, as part of the memorial, a shadowy figure of Christ, in the role of guardian and friend, behind that of the great preacher. Many of his symbolic works were derived from composites, and now he perceived, as a model for some aspects of the Christ, the brow and the contours of the head of his cousin Sidney Homer. To this end several photographs were taken—stark, unretouched ones, which the sculptor placed around his studio at different angles. And when the work was completed, there, in the serene and brooding figure of Christ, was that sensitive, suffering forehead, and the distinctive, quite subtle modeling of the head.

There were many new friends that summer in Cornish. Most were artists or writers, and one was a tall, dark young novelist, Winston Churchill, whose Civil War novels were all best sellers, and who was much better known than his distant cousin in England, a correspondent for a London newspaper. Another youthful artist, Maxfield Parrish, told them he was unhappy with his work and discouraged about his health. Whenever Sidney encountered someone who was disheartened, he would be beguiled by a certain formula, a kind of cut-loose philosophy. So now he urged, persuasively, "Go away, find a new climate and a change of scene! Go to Arizona! It will be an inspiration!" And the artist did, and it was, and within a decade scenes of wide blue skies, airy spaces and graceful ladies in swings were decorating half the parlors in the country.

The goldenrod was tall in the fields, a nostalgic foil for the gleaming gold of the Sherman, when they took their little girl to stay with her grandmother in West Chester and joined the fall tour of the Metropolitan.

Chapter XV

The 1901–2 fall and spring tours of the Metropolitan would go down in operatic history as the most extensive ever undertaken, either before or since. This was a true marathon, as the extraordinary record makes clear: 145 performances of 30 operas in 27 cities in 15 states and Canada. Never again would the opera company tour in the fall, or undertake such an ambitious program, and Henry Krehbiel, the distinguished music critic of the *New York Tribune*, writing in 1908, says of this period in opera: "Grau's dictatorship was brief; but while it lasted it was probably the most brilliant operatic government the world had ever known from a financial point of view, and its artistic highlights were luminous in the extreme."

The tour started in Albany, then progressed to Toronto, where Louise sang Ortrud in *Lohengrin* for the first time in America. The critic for the *Toronto Star*, describing her portrayal of Ortrud as she had evolved it with Herr Felix Mottl in London, wrote:

> The rich, vibrant texture that is noticeable throughout her great range has a fascination for the ear, a sort of haunting power. When Ortrud pleaded, the round voice had a caressing note. When she hated the tones broadened with a fearful, encompassing reach. When she exulted the notes rang out like bells. It cannot be told how Louise Homer

accomplished such a climax. Voice built on gesture, and gesture on voice, the structure growing ever, until the audience, able to resist no longer, burst into applause before the scene could draw to a close.

She sang Ortrud again a few nights later in Syracuse, and in both these performances of *Lohengrin* Marcella Sembrich sang the role of Elsa. But this was an unusual occurrence, for the Polish soprano rarely sang Wagnerian roles, and was best known as a Lucia, an Elvira or a Violetta. Marcella Sembrich had first sung with the Metropolitan the year it opened, in 1883, and had a coloratura voice of unusual beauty. Among vocalists she was unique, for she was an accomplished pianist, as well as a virtuoso with the violin, and this rare musicianship extended to her singing, which was incomparable in its technical perfection. Sembrich was a small woman with great charm, proud, self-contained, somewhat aloof, yet with a generous, sympathetic nature, and this long tour together was the beginning of a friendship that would span the years.

The Opera Train continued on its way—Louisville, Nashville, Memphis, Atlanta, New Orleans—*Carmen, Lohengrin, Manon, Roméo et Juliette*. Just unloading the scenery was a feat in itself, and it was a great relief when they finally settled down in San Francisco for a stay of almost a month. Here Grau asked Louise to learn the role of Brangäne in *Tristan und Isolde*, and for this she plunged into a period of concentrated study, working first with the repetiteur, Hans Morgenstern, and then with the conductor, Walter Damrosch. This was the first work she had done with Damrosch, who was a true master of German opera, and just as with Herr Mottl, the experience was creative and absorbing.

Walter Damrosch was still rather a young man, not yet forty, but already he'd had a varied and quite dramatic career. He had been just twenty-three when his father, Leopold Damrosch, was both manager and music director of the Metropolitan. During the season, when his father had become fatally ill with pneumonia, he had taken over and conducted, without previous experience, performances of *Tannhäuser* and *Die Walküre*, believing his father would "die happier" if these duties were fulfilled. Since then Walter Damrosch had survived numerous intrigues and power plays at the Metropolitan, and had even had an opera company of his own. But perhaps he didn't have the ego or the concentrated drive of the true manager or impresario, for his nature was a rare blend of vitality, integrity and imagination, with a fine leavening of humor. Inherently he had a gift for living, and this, too, was the start of an enduring friendship.

During the long study sessions in San Francisco, they evolved together an interpretation often remarked as unlike any other, a Brangäne misguided, perhaps, but swayed by tenderness and devotion, and very human. This is a complex role that weaves its way throughout the opera, a counterpoint as well as a catalyst of the tragedy. And in the portrayal there must be unusual subtlety, for each facet—the nuance of the voice, the gesture, the pose, the tempo—is a piece in a mosaic that is not Brangäne's, but belongs, essentially, to Isolde. "Habet acht, habet acht!" The voice from the tower was haunting in its foreboding, the warning cry almost unearthly. But the character was real and valid, a yearning and anguished accompaniment to the immortal love story.

They took to the road again on December 5th, leaving the comfort of the hotel for the confinement of the Opera Train. But when the engineer had to stop for coal and water in some small hamlet on the way, the singers would abandon their Pullman Palace cars for the snow-strewn desert of Wyoming. They made the most of these occasions. Released from the monotony of the Opera Train, they would respond to the recess like children let out of school, Walter Damrosch wearing a conductor's badge proclaiming him supervisor of Car B, Schumann-Heink clowning a bit with the big baritone Pol Plançon, Suzanne Adams, for a lark, climbing up into the engineer's cab.

There were many imponderables on these tours—changes in repertoire, mislaid costume trunks and, especially, inhospitable theaters. In Kansas City the critics complained that Constitution Hall was unfit for opera. The huge, drafty auditorium had been built in a matter of months to house the Democratic Convention, and could add very little to the drama and illusions of Verdi.

Maurice Grau's singers relax and clown a bit during the tour in
1901. Marcella Sembrich has her arm about Louise's shoulder;
Sidney is beside them.

And in Indianapolis the theater was so icy cold that the matinee
had to be canceled, and throughout the evening performance of
Lohengrin the audience huddled shivering in their winter coats.

They were two days in St. Louis, where Louise sang both
Tannhäuser and *Aida*. There a critic reported that "As Venus
she wore a gown of white satin, with pearl embroidery, touches
of silver, and radiant pink chiffon. Louise Homer is a great
beauty," he noted, "and one of the few singers able to suggest
why the German minstrel would linger so long in Horselberg."
The Tannhäuser who shared the rosy grotto with her at this
performance was Andreas Dippel, a good-looking, wavy-haired
German tenor, who was an unusually versatile singer, experienced in many facets of opera and very popular with the other
artists.

Maurice Grau opened his New York season with *Tristan* on
December 23rd, but he gave his contralto a few free days for
Christmas with her family before she must return to appear, on
January 4th, in *Faust*. Though Grau was a manager who kept

Maurice Grau, manager of the Metropolitan Opera, who toured the country from coast to coast, and included among his strenuous ventures two summer seasons at Covent Garden in London. (Courtesy *Opera News*)

his own counsel, Louise had the comfortable assurance that he was doing all he could to further her career. Gradually he was adding new roles to her repertoire—a few smaller ones, like Emilia in *Otello*, and especially the bigger German ones, Ortrud, Venus and Brangäne, which she sang with the marvelous soprano Milka Ternina.

She was also singing the great religious music—Bach's *Passion Music* at the Metropolitan's Sunday night concert, with Walter Damrosch conducting, and a week later Handel's *Messiah* at Carnegie Hall, with the New York Symphony Orchestra and

As Brangäne in *Tristan und Isolde*.

Frank Damrosch conducting, She had an affinity for the spiritual music—the Bach, the Mozart, the Brahms, the Handel—and to sing it with the great conductors and finest orchestras could be a moving experience for the singer as well as her listeners. In the lyric passages there would be a haunting intimation of latent power tenderly restrained, the tones falling almost to a whisper, then rising, perhaps in a minor key, to an interval of conviction so radiant and so weighted with the faith of the singer that many in the audience would be uniquely touched—saddened, elated, moved at times to tears.

One of the most beloved figures in the world of music at this time was the Polish pianist Ignaz Paderewski. Ever since his American debut ten years before, Paderewski had been the idol of the American public, adored as much for his romantic appeal as for his brilliance at the piano. Susceptible ladies "swooned" at Paderewski concerts, others framed his photographs, and they came in droves to hear the Polish pianist with the pale, stern, uplifted profile, and the wonderful mane of red-gold hair.

Paderewski had written an opera, *Manru*, which had been

produced abroad and would have its American premiere at the Metropolitan on February 14, 1902. Louise was to have a leading role in this opera, that of Hedwig, the abandoned wife. But though Paderewski came to many of the rehearsals, he was so diffident about his work that these sessions, with the composer looking shyly on, weren't at all like the ones for *Cendrillon* under the exacting, authoritative presence of Massenet.

The libretto for the opera evolved about the trials of a gypsy, Manru, who is seduced by the wildness of his nature and his love of roaming into forsaking his wife and child and following into a tragic fate a maid of his own race. In this not too original story Marcella Sembrich was Ulana, the alluring gypsy maid, and the title role was sung by a singer imported for the occasion, von Bandrowski. Henry Krehbiel found the music of *Manru* "brilliant," much of it derived from the "melancholy and passion" of Hungarian and Magyar folk songs, but the libretto he considered "silly" and unworthy. The audience was "the most numerous and brilliant of the season," and it was Marcella Sembrich who finally coaxed the diffident composer out of his parterre box to acknowledge the "fervent" applause. *Manru* was performed four times in New York, and five times in other cities during the spring tour. But it never caught on and was then dropped from the repertoire.

Maurice Grau provided his subscribers with some notable casts that season, but none to equal the all-star evening he arranged for the Gala Performance on February 25, 1902, in honor of His Royal Highness, Prince Henry of Prussia. For this unique occasion Grau paraded all his principal singers in their most favored roles: Gadski, Schumann-Heink and Edouard de Reszke in Act 1 from *Lohengrin*; Calvé and Scotti in Act 2 from *Carmen*; Homer, Eames and de Marchi in Act 3 from *Aida*; Milka Ternina and the great baritone van Rooy in Act 2 from *Tannhäuser*; a scene from *Le Cid*; and a scene from *Traviata*, starring Marcella Sembrich. Seldom had so many celebrated singers sung so many celebrated roles. Yet strangely, no one listened.

The singers might have been singing into a vacuum for all the attention they received, but it was a marvelously arrayed vacuum, for the whole of the Metropolitan's auditorium had been decorated in honor of Prince Henry and transformed into a twinkling bower, with carloads of lush green smilax imported from the South and massed along the front of all the boxes and balconies, up and down the proscenium arch, hung from the chandeliers. The entire opera house was smothered in it, and to add to the fragrance and illusion the dark green smilax was studded with miniature bouquets of dainty marguerites, white azaleas, and tiny green and white lights.

The royal box created for His Royal Highness might have come straight out of the Arabian Nights. For this the partitions of the five center boxes in the Golden Horseshoe had been removed, the interior draped with crimson velvet, the front massed with American Beauty roses and a canopy constructed of white satin, crimson velvet and gold fringe. An elaborate standard was affixed to the apex of the proscenium arch, with American flags and shields on the right, and German on the left. The program for the Gala Performance was a work of art in itself, printed in royal blue on a length of heavy white satin, bordered in gold braid and creamy fringe. At the top was a portrait of Prince Henry (with his medals, trim beard and waxed moustache), surrounded by cupids, muses and the flags and state seals of the two countries. And at the bottom another muse, attired in Grecian robes, reclined on a marble bench and strummed her lyre in the midst of the national anthems, "Die Wacht am Rhein" and "My Country, 'Tis of Thee."

New York society had been in a ferment all winter over this visit to New York of Prince Henry, brother of Kaiser Wilhelm of Germany. It wasn't often that royalty came to America and competition for the royal favor had been intense. Mrs. Vanderbilt was the fortunate hostess who would entertain the Prince at dinner, and when her plans were made known, Mrs. Astor, piqued by this coup on the part of her greatest rival, sailed for Europe. J. P. Morgan won the Prince for a lavish luncheon; Mrs. Ogden Mills would entertain him at an elaborate breakfast. But many could not be included, and so that everyone could at least bask in the royal aura, the Gala Performance was arranged at the Metropolitan to serve as the grand climax of his visit.

Grau's program was much too long but this hardly mattered,

for most of the attention was riveted on the other side of the opera house, where Prince Henry was holding court. "At no public affair in my time," reported Krehbiel of the *Tribune*, "has New York had such a display of gowns and jewels." The program he called "a generous rather than a dainty dish to set before a king's brother," adding that "it was very late when the curtain of smilax and light fell on the last act, and the Prince had left the house long before."

In the summer Sidney and Louise took a cottage at Lake Placid and settled down to await the birth of a baby, who would be born in October. They had never intended their little girl to be an only child. They wanted more children, and had reasoned that the fall would be an ideal time for such an event, since she would miss only a few weeks of the opera season. Sidney had his piano in the pump house, that summer, and wrote several songs that would be widely sung in concerts: "Prospice," "A Woman's Last Word" and settings to Holmes' "Last Leaf" and Stevenson's "Sing Me a Song of the Lad That Is Gone."

All this time his family had been living in the Paris apartment. His sister, Georgie, had married a young Frenchman she'd met at a seaside resort, and they'd seemed quite settled there. But now Georgie wrote that she, too, was expecting a baby in October, her husband couldn't find employment and things weren't going well. When Sidney learned of this he cabled at once: "Come here to us," and in August they all arrived—his mother, his sister, her two boys and her new husband.

In the fall they all went together to West Chester, and in that hospitable town of many available homes they rented two houses across the street from each other. But almost at once they were plunged into a period of crisis by an epidemic of typhoid fever. Georgie's oldest son had it first, then Georgie herself, following the birth of a baby boy, and finally their own little Louise, who was now almost seven years old.

The little girl was delirious with fever; there were several days of intense anxiety. And in the midst of all this the baby son was born, on October 20, 1902, and named Sidney Jr., for his father. So then, with the crisis past, and all the invalids finally recovering, it became a time of regrouping shattered forces, and also a time of thankfulness. The doctor advised a long convalescence, for the birth had been attended by complications, and Louise was quite willing to comply. Her mother and sisters could come for long visits, and the quiet cadence of West Chester was ideal at such a time.

But then there was a telegram from Maurice Grau that was in the nature of a bolt out of the blue, to shatter with chagrin the serenity, to edge with discontent the contentment: Would she sing *Carmen* at the Metropolitan the first week of the season, on November 29th?

Nothing could have been more unexpected, and yet there was a certain logic to the request, for she had learned *Carmen* two years before in Brussels. Mr. Grau had requested it for a performance at Covent Garden. And since she would have appeared with several of the artists then at La Monnaie, Monsieur Calabrese had arranged a dress rehearsal for them, and she'd sung the haunting tunes and danced the provocative dances with Marcel Journet, Charles Gilibert, a brilliant cast. Many of those same artists were now at the Metropolitan, and they'd have the same conductor, Phillippe Flon. So this would be an ideal opportunity to sing that most fascinating of roles, except that the doctor said definitely no.

It had been a great disappointment that *Carmen* was never given in London, and here in America the role belonged exclusively to Emma Calvé. The French soprano had become famous for her portrayal of the part, but this season she wasn't appearing at the Metropolitan. So here was a chance that might not come again, and for Louise the disappointment was more acute because so many of her roles were dark and heavy. It was the contralto range of her voice that cast her as a jealous princess, or a vengeful queen. How often did she have a chance to wear bright poppies in her hair, and, as a wanton gypsy, dance with a tambourine? But, in fact, the role of Carmen arouses tingling aspirations in almost all opera singers, perhaps because it is the very essence of opera. Here is a part that has everything —gaiety, seduction, vibrant color, melodies that sing themselves and caress the voice, drama that unfolds from vivid passion to a crescendo of violence, and as a start the acacia flower between the teeth, the flaunting, the wildness, the mocking and the tempting. Yet the doctor said definitely no.

But while she was trying to be reconciled, and the decision was still pending, right there in the midst of that tranquil domestic scene she was betrayed unwittingly by an odd illusion, the pink bed jacket, with its lace and ribbons, taking on the guise of a Spanish shawl bright with color and long fringe, while the baby bottle, held tenderly above the contented little face, might have been a tambourine. And perhaps that was the ultimate treachery, the associations, buried deep and all but forgotten, the little girl, just five years old, twirling faster and faster in the parlor at Shadyside, her pinafore swirling about her knees, her hazel eyes brilliant with excitement, singing and dancing with her tambourine for Maggie Johns. All this affected the situation in various subtle ways, and on a wave of determination she wired Mr. Grau accepting the part. A few days later, when the baby boy was less than a month old, she went to New York with a friend, to stay in a hotel and prepare for the opera season.

That meant, of course, that she had rejoined the company, and would have other roles as well. And so there were many rehearsals, and on the opening night of the new season, November 24, 1902, she sang Emilia in Verdi's *Otello*, with a brilliant cast, Emma Eames as Desdemona, Albert Alvarez as Otello, Antonio Scotti as Iago. But the strain was too much, and after this opening performance she had a severe relapse and was very ill—too ill to sing *Aida* on the 27th, or *Carmen* on the 29th. Camille Seygard had to sing it in her place.

Within two weeks, after an interval of convalescence, she was able to appear as Maddalena in *Rigoletto*, with Marcella Sembrich as Gilda. But the chance to sing Carmen didn't come again. Just as she had feared, Emma Calvé returned to take back her cherished role, and that bright, brief opportunity was lost forever.

However, she did sing a number of new parts this year— Waltraute in *Götterdämmerung*, Ulrica in *Un Ballo in Maschera*. And in the spring there was a towering new role to learn, one to stir the imagination and challenge the dramatic powers—a vivid characterization that, like the other big ones in her reper-

As Azucena in *Il Trovatore*.

toire, Amneris, Ortrud, Dalila, was central to the theme and catalyst of the tragedy. Oddly, this too was a gypsy role, but otherwise almost the antithesis of the one she had lost, for Azucena was a gypsy dressed in somber rags, a tormented mother, a commanding and fateful figure in Verdi's darkest opera, *Il Trovatore*. In this stirring drama she portrayed a wild, embittered soul, whose frantic life is doomed by vengeance, and by the other side of that livid coin—suffering.

She appeared in *Il Trovatore* for the first time on March 11, 1903, with Nordica, Campanari and Journet, and when she had sung the dramatic "Stride La Vampa" aria ("Fierce flames are soaring") it was said that "the gallery and the entire house erupted in wild applause." "The Azucena of Louise Homer was a surprise and a triumph," wrote the critic for the *Evening News*.

An overworked and almost worn out word is intense, and yet there is none other that can convey the concentrated, wild, fiery, passionate, ungovernable nature of the old gypsy woman as she bore in upon her audience. . . . She conveyed thrillingly and commandingly the horror, the woe and the despair of the past, the affection and devotion of the present, and the hunger for vengeance and retribution in the future. It was a grand dramatic achievement of voice, facial illumination and action indicative of indomitable revolt and defiance . . . and should be ranked among the greatest Azucenas of the world.

She sang *Il Trovatore* on the spring tour, in Boston and several other cities. But now this was a touring company with an uneasy, transient air, for Maurice Grau had resigned from the Metropolitan. The reason given was ill health. The long tours, the two summer seasons at Covent Garden and the strenuous dual seasons in New York and Philadelphia had taken a heavy toll, and Mr. Grau announced that he would retire to his summer home, a beautiful chateau at Croissy-Chatou, on the Seine near Paris.

Grau's singers had had confidence in his artistic judgment, his rare ability, his loyalty as a manager, and now, just as at La Monnaie, they found themselves suddenly cut adrift. This was especially true since there was, at this time, no permanent organization to which the singers belonged, no "Metropolitan Opera Company" but just an "opera house" leased by the Board of Directors to various managers. Now The Maurice Grau Opera Company had been dissolved, and in the spring, to the surprise of almost everyone, the directors announced that they had leased the Metropolitan to a manager who was almost the direct opposite of Grau—Heinrich Conried, manager of a small German theater on Irving Place, who had recently been giving theatrical performances in universities around the country but who was an impresario with no opera experience and no musical background.

Nevertheless, Heinrich Conried had a forceful personality, and it was this energy and business skill that had recommended him to the directors. He was a man who had great confidence in his own ability, and he convinced them that he could make even the rarefied world of opera a paying proposition. So during the winter leases were signed and arrangements made for "Conried's Opera Company at the Metropolitan in New York." And in the spring Mr. Conried came to the opera house to negotiate with Mr. Grau for the scenery and other properties, and with the singers for the coming season.

Louise and Sidney went together for this interview, which was carried on in an atmosphere so feverish with activity that coherent communication was all but impossible. Throughout the conference messengers dashed in and out, the telephone rang incessantly, assistants came for advice, and in the midst of all this Heinrich Conried launched into a fervent description of his unhappy financial situation. He was a big man, an imposing figure behind the familiar desk—flamboyant in appearance, with brilliant dark eyes, unruly dark hair, a rather fleshy nose and chin. And he spoke with great emotion of the overwhelming demands that made it impossible for him to give her an increase in salary.

This was a disappointment, for they had hoped for better terms and believed that with the added years of experience she was entitled to a more favorable contract. But Mr. Conried was so overwrought that they couldn't help sympathizing with his predicament. It was evident that he was anxious to have her in his company, and finally, because they were reluctant to add to those heavy financial burdens, they agreed to a three-year contract. There would be no increase in salary the first year, but substantial raises the next two, and once the contract had been signed, Mr. Conried expressed the most fervent gratitude. He became, then, quite effusive, and only afterward did they realize that there had been no mention of her voice, or even of roles or repertoire. In the confusion of all those harried interruptions, all they had really talked about was money.

Chapter XVI

The new contract with the Metropolitan gave the future a continuity it had lacked before. Now finally it would be practical to have a permanent home in New York instead of the makeshift places they'd been renting month by month. And that meant they could send to Boston for the furniture and personal possessions that had been in storage all these years. Especially it was reassuring to know that they could continue to combine the home life and the opera life without too many complications.

For the summer months they went to Onteora Park in the Catskills, where they were soon part of a congenial community. But then there was an alarming development, for the baby boy became mysteriously ill. By nature he was placid and cooperative. But suddenly, almost overnight, it seemed, he wouldn't eat or sleep, cried constantly and even screamed with pain when they as much as touched him or tried to change his diaper. None of the local doctors could tell them what was wrong—all the remedies, the paregoric, the medicines, were ineffective. So finally, in desperation, they sent to New York for their own baby doctor, Henry Chapin. Responding to their frantic pleas, Dr. Chapin took the train to Onteora Park; there he examined the wailing child, recommended treatment and took the next train back to the city. Nevertheless, to the distracted parents it seemed like a miracle, for within a week the baby was his old placid self again, though the only treatment their doctor had advised was three ounces of orange juice twice a day.

Much of the life at Onteora Park centered about the tennis courts, where everyone gathered to watch the matches, and especially the tournaments. But this summer the handsome college athletes, in their blazers and white flannels, were faced with a dilemma, for again and again they were being beaten at their game by a youngster still in short pants. The members of the Onteora Club took their tennis seriously, and displayed their silver cups with modest pride. But young Billy Tilden was everywhere at once, like a flashing windmill on the tennis courts, and it all but spoiled the summer for the confident college champions to be losing all the tournaments to a little boy who was only ten years old.

In Onteora there were new companions, and two especially who became lifelong friends, Mr. and Mrs. John Alexander. They met first at a children's party, and that could be a pleasurable experience, sitting about near the lake discovering mutual interests, while the little girls played hide the thimble, making, with their exuberance, their colored hair ribbons and dainty frocks, a lively ring of pastel colors. John Alexander was an artist noted especially for his portraits. But he had a distinguished reputation in other fields, and had done work in the theater as well—most recently the color and lighting effects for the actress Maude Adams. He had created murals for the Carnegie Institute in Pittsburgh, was a prominent member of the National Academy of Design and one day he would design for Louise a most notable opera costume.

Emilio de Gogorza, the fine young baritone she had often sung with at the festivals, came to see them one weekend when the summer was almost over. And it seemed he had a most unusual mission, for he had come to ask her if she would sign a contract with the Victor Talking Machine Company to sing into a horn.

Signor de Gogorza stayed two days, swam and watched the tennis and talked almost constantly about his unusual project. But it all seemed to them very strange and quite unreal, for they'd never heard of an opera singer making mechanical music.

And to Sidney, especially, the whole idea sounded somewhat disreputable. A serious singer was supposed to have a certain standing in the world of the arts, and he found it hard to believe that an artist who valued her reputation would sing into a horn.

However, Signor de Gogorza didn't seem too surprised by this reaction, and during his stay at Onteora Park he tried to persuade them that his company's talking machines would be quite unlike the cheap and tawdry form of entertainment provided some years before by Thomas Edison's "cylinders." Those big, garish contraptions had been put on display in drugstores, hotel lobbies, country fairs and other public places, and for a while they had been quite a fad. You put a nickel in a slot, some earphones over your head and heard a Philip Sousa march, or some popular little ditty like "The Mocking Bird," all in a squeaky tone that was almost impossible to decipher. Recently a new version had appeared, using discs instead of cylinders, but the sounds were still garbled and tinny, the display had a carnival atmosphere and it was all very far removed from the world of the serious artist.

Sidney pointed all this out, as tactfully as he could, and Signor de Gogorza was most understanding. But he earnestly defended his own talking machine. Some day, he said, they hoped to be able to record stringed instruments—violins, cellos, whole orchestras. In the meantime, with their newly invented "diaphragm," which so improved the "acoustic machine," they believed they could do justice to the greatest of operatic voices. And so he had been delegated to make Louise an offer. If she would sing for them, he said, they would pay her her concert fee and a commission on every "record" sold (for that's what they were planning to call the discs they would make).

Though it was hard to imagine that "commissions" on those things he called "records" would ever amount to much, Louise thought it might be an adventure to sing into a horn, and was quite willing to agree. But Sidney was afraid that such a strange venture would endanger her status in the musical world. It wouldn't be wise, he pointed out, for her name to be coupled with music-hall singers. An artist's dignity must be protected; her reputation, her most valuable asset, must be guarded at all times. So in the end they declined the offer. But Signor de Gogorza refused to be discouraged, and asked cheerfully if he could come again and see them in New York. Then he took his departure, promising another visit soon, and the next week her vacation came to an end and she left Onteora Park on a festival tour that was, in its way, a marathon.

Her concert manager, Mr. Wolfsohn, had planned an ingenious schedule so that she could appear in two New England festivals at the same time. But the arrangements were precarious, and hardest of all on the local managers, who must wonder constantly if a train would be late. Wrote a reporter in Worcester, Massachusetts, "Like 'Sister Anne,' there were many who were casting anxious glances down the road. But the singer finally arrived, not at all fatigued from travel, to take part in the morning rehearsal. . . . This morning at 1:30 she left for Portland, Maine, where she will sing tonight." Wrote a Portland reporter, "She was not at all tired from her travels, and caused a sensation at the morning rehearsal of the Music Festival. She was in perfect voice and sang with thrilling effect the aria from *Les Huguenots*."

There were festivals in Vermont and New Hampshire, too, and many in the audiences would have come long distances, in their carriages and wagons, from farms and communities far back in the hills. Not more than once a year did most of them experience something like the aria from *Les Huguenots*, sung with full orchestral accompaniment and a voice that soared straight up into the clouds. And for the artists at the festivals there were the hectic schedules, the slow, jolting trains, the big hatboxes, the trunks with gowns, the morning rehearsals, the roses pinned in the hair, and finally, from the platform, that sea of waiting, often ardent faces—and for them, too, it was a unique experience.

After the festivals there was the matter of finding a home in New York, and this was a milestone after so many years of living here and there. They'd had the apartment on Boylston Street in Boston, and the apartment in Paris, furnished mainly with packing boxes. And there had been a good many rented places with a variety of decor—some, like the house on Regent's Park in

London, too splendid, and others too drab. But it was years since they'd had a place of their own. Now they sublet a small house on West Ninety-second Street in New York, and sent to Boston for all the furniture that had been in storage for so long. And they were in the midst of all this moving and settling when Signor de Gogorza again came to call, this time bringing with him Mr. Calvin Child, Director of Artists for the new Victor Company.

So then they sat down among the packing boxes to discuss the new venture, and Mr. Child described most persuasively the special status his company had evolved to differentiate between ordinary "popular" music and offerings of an operatic or classical nature. For the opera singers, he told them, the Victor Company was going to have what he called "Red Seal" records. These records would be quite unlike the ordinary ones, they would sell for a considerably higher price, and to distinguish them from the cheaper records they would have red seals, instead of blue.

Then Mr. Child said something else that put into an altogether different light this strange undertaking, for he told them that Victor was planning to sell their "talking machines" at a very low price so that individuals could afford to buy them and play them in the home. Their new Red Seal records, he said, would be heard not in hotel lobbies or country fairs but in the privacy and seclusion of the family living room. And in this setting, among the packing boxes and the familiar furniture, still in disarray, and the children's voices in the hall and on the stairs, that word "home" had a powerful effect. It seemed to Sidney, then, a most dignified, even idealistic thing these gentlemen were doing, and before their visitors left that day, Louise became one of the first to sign a contract with the Victor Talking Machine Company.

For some years the Victor Company had been engaged in a patent suit with Edison that had only recently been settled in their favor. And they were still competing with the Columbia Company in Bridgeport which, during the summer, had tried to record the voices of several Metropolitan singers, including Marcella Sembrich and Antonio Scotti. But the results had been so garbled and of such poor quality that the singers had been upset, and Columbia had decided to abandon the whole undertaking and revert to the lighter, popular music.

Nevertheless, Victor was a company in a hurry. The directors had faith in the future of their project, and they had set out to corner the market in opera singers, and in effect blanket the field. So on September 12, 1903, Louise went with Signor de Gogorza to make her first recordings. The studio was Practice Room No. 826 in Carnegie Hall, used with an adjoining room where the machinery was installed. This arrangement wasn't too practical, for when anyone happened to be practicing in the vicinity all the operations had to be suspended. But many problems hadn't yet been worked out, for the venture was still new and experimental.

She found that to make the recordings she would have to sing into a horn on one wall which was fastened to a tube that went through the plaster to a machine in the next room. She would have a piano accompaniment, since the "diaphragm" couldn't yet cope with other instruments, and at first they had to test the volume, resonance and power of her voice in relation to the delicate vibrations of the acoustic machine. It was this that had defeated the Columbia Company. But the Victor technicians worked out an ingenious system, and it was decided finally that she would stand close to the horn only for the pianissimo passages of a song; then she would move back a step or two for the stronger notes; and for the soaring high tones she must turn around and sing to the opposite wall, otherwise they sounded in the machine like the shattering of a ton of glass.

During that first session in the Carnegie Hall studio she made five recordings, which were among the first Red Seal records released by the Victor Company: "He Shall Feed His Flock," from Handel's *Messiah*, sung with a serene and most moving conviction; "Annie Laurie," a nostalgic air that always seemed to delight her audiences when she used it as an encore in her concerts; "Nobil' Signori," the air that so enchanted them when she "burst upon their sight" in the costume of white velvet and gold in *Les Huguenots*; "Le Parlate d'Amor" from *Faust*; and "O

As Maddalena in *Rigoletto*, which she sang at Caruso's debut
performance, the opening night of the season, November 23,
1903.

Toi Qui M'Abandonne," the aria from *Le Prophète* that had been
Monsieur Koenig's talisman, all those years ago in Paris.

She had worked hard and cooperated patiently with the
hopeful young technicians. Nevertheless, it seemed a rather odd
mechanical adventure, sandwiched in between more serious
commitments—the festivals, a concert tour and finally the
opera. This year she was to sing Maddalena in Verdi's *Rigoletto*
at the opening of the new season, on November 23, 1903.

Marcella Sembrich would sing Gilda, Antonio Scotti had already become noted as a most dramatic Rigoletto, and the part of the Duke of Mantua would be sung by a new Italian tenor who was making his American debut—Enrico Caruso.

For the opera public the evening was notable because the Metropolitan had a new regime, a new manager, Heinrich Conried, and especially because the opera house itself had an entirely new decor. Not for some years had there been any changes, but now the whole interior had been altered and refurbished in a most remarkable way.

The work had been done over the summer by two talented designers from the Ecole des Beaux-Arts, associates of the distinguished architect Stanford White. John Carrere and Thomas Hastings, with almost unlimited funds at their disposal, had been able to effect a transformation of the elegant but rather sedate appearance of the auditorium, and their alterations had included almost every aspect of the interior decoration. Most notably, they had added ornate gilded plaster reliefs to the faces of all the boxes and balconies, and installed throughout the hall upholstered seats, hangings and drapes of deep crimson velvet. This overlay of lustrous gold and deep warm crimson gave the hall a rich, baroque, Edwardian grandeur that was, in its way, very subtle, for while it created an ideal background for the diamond tiaras and jeweled gowns, it seemed also to envelop the entire audience in an almost homelike sensation of satisfying warmth. Although there was richness and glitter, there was, as well, a most harmonious atmosphere, and all this had been achieved through many innovations. Now there was a Golden Horseshoe in fact as well as fancy, new gilded medallions had been arranged above the softened contours of the proscenium arch, while high above the rising tiers of gold and red a sunburst of dazzling light had been installed, a massive chandelier, marvelously arrayed in a crisscross pattern that was also made of gold.

The critical appraisal of the new tenor, though favorable, was somewhat restrained. In the *Sun*, W. J. Henderson noted that "Mr. Caruso's clear and appealing high tones set the bravos wild with delight," adding, however, that "connoisseurs of opera saw

Enrico Caruso as the Duke of Mantua in *Rigoletto,* in which he made his Metropolitan debut, November 23, 1903. (Courtesy *Opera News*)

more promise for the season in his mezza voce." But it seems the "bravos" may have been right all along, the fervent response from the galleries a forerunner of what was to come, for that night when they sang Verdi's marvelous quartet, "Bella Figlia dell'Amore," with its intricate pattern of emotions—Gilda's heartbroken sobs, Maddalena's beguiling coquetry, the Duke's romantic response, Rigoletto's towering rage—there was a new quality to the blending of the voices, a new and more stirring contrast, a smooth, vibrant, glowing tone that soared eloquently to the topmost galleries with an almost celestial ardor.

Conried had asked Louise to learn two new Wagnerian roles this season, Fricka in *Die Walküre* and Erda in *Siegfried*. These were parts that had been sung by Madame Schumann-Heink, but the German contralto wasn't with the Metropolitan this year. So two nights later, on November 25, 1903, she sang Fricka for the first time, in a performance of *Walküre* that was Olive Fremstad's debut at the Metropolitan. The brilliant American soprano had been trained by Lilli Lehmann, had sung at Bayreuth and would become famous for her Wagnerian roles.

With these two notable debuts the season was under way, and Conried was greatly helped at the start of his regime by the accident of his new tenor. Actually Maurice Grau had arranged Caruso's contract the year before, and it had lain on Conried's desk for months while he debated whether to sign it. But when it became apparent that Enrico Caruso was fast becoming a star of the first magnitude, he called all the reporters together to discuss with them his great "find."

He had also engaged a new American contralto, Edyth Walker, who had been singing at Covent Garden and would make her Metropolitan debut November 30th in *Aida*. About this there had been rumors circulating for weeks, hints and innuendos that Louise found very hard to credit, though they were repeated again and again, by friends, other musicians, her dresser, her coiffeur and various people at the opera house, in the form of direful warnings and predictions. And what they were saying was that Edyth Walker had been given by the new manager "absolute control" of the contralto roles.

There was ample opportunity for more than one leading contralto, but the hints and innuendos implied something else altogether. What they were trying to tell her was that Conried had downgraded her status as an artist, and if that were true it would mean that she had been tricked into accepting an inferior position in his company.

Now, with misgiving, they were reminded of that hectic conference in the spring, when there'd been no mention of her voice, or even of roles and repertoire, and all they'd talked about was money. And they recalled, too late, Nellie Melba's warnings, all that talk about rivalries, intrigues and the exploitation of the vocal artist. Down at the opera house there was a cynical explanation. Louise Homer was known as "Grau's artist," they said, and the success of her career would add nothing to Conried's prestige. But Edyth Walker would become known as "Conried's artist." Her presence in the company would enhance his status as an impresario, and to that end he had offered her, as an inducement to sign with him, "absolute control" of the leading contralto roles.

Meanwhile, assuming good will on the manager's part, Louise had signed a three-year contract and done nothing to protect her interests, though it seemed likely that Conried had been planning, even then, to diminish her status in his company—put another American contralto in her place as Amneris and Ortrud and Brangäne, and simply use her as a convenience, to sing the smaller parts.

It had all been quite legal, but also a form of trickery. And she believed so passionately in honest dealings that she didn't feel she could continue under such a cloud of exploitation and callous disregard. She felt the way she had at the Penn Charter School when Mr. Jones had blandly asked for her resignation. She had signed in good faith then, too, intending to keep her part of the bargain, and it was a chilling thing to find that she had been so casually made use of.

So far, in her experience, there'd been no dissension, and no backstage intrigues. Always, in the five years she'd been singing in opera, she'd had a manager she could trust. Now, because he seemed so ruthless and unconcerned, she wanted to have it out with Conried, and if she had been tricked, break her contract.

But when they talked about it in the house on West Ninety-second Street, night after night, in an atmosphere of considerable distress, Sidney tried to calm her fears, and counseled patience. If she would only regard this as a temporary setback, he said, and not let it affect her singing, it might all work out in time.

Nevertheless it was a serious setback, and in the end the house itself played a part in her decision. They had only recently moved all their furniture from Boston. Sidney had his studio on an upper floor and was composing; their little girl was going to a school nearby, and the baby boy spent much of his day in a carriage in the park. Now the welfare of her family must be weighed against the hurt, the pride, the anger, for she wasn't like those singers who lived in suites in the Ansonia Hotel and could take off at a moment's notice. Because of the commitments at home she didn't have the leverage many singers enjoyed, the freedom of action to pit one manager against another, sign with Covent Garden to assure a more favorable contract with the Metropolitan, invest in a brilliant success abroad to up the salary at home. She had to work within a narrower margin in dealing with the complex matters of contracts and prestige, for always there was, on the other side of the ledger, the home, the children and, especially, his tranquility and peace of mind.

So finally she decided to do nothing at all about Heinrich Conried's evident deception. And though it was disheartening, when she returned from an unprofitable day of work the little house on West Ninety-second Street would be a refuge, the activity and creativity there a solace for the disappointments at the opera house, for she wasn't like those singers who must carry their burning hearts to a suite in the Ansonia Hotel and think of all they had sacrificed for a career.

Even before her debut in *Aida* Edyth Walker was announced for future performances as Amneris, Brangäne and Ortrud, and at the opera house it was assumed that the two American contraltos were cool toward one another. There, a certain hostility was taken for granted when two singers were competing for the same roles, a jealousy attributed most often to the sopranos, and dramatized by the critics, who liked to write at length about

the rivalries at the opera house. Now there was a situation made
to order for this bitterest of battles: two American contraltos,
one an Amneris already acclaimed by the public, the other an
interloper from abroad, a classic confrontation, with the old
Amneris naturally resenting the new one.

But Louise was unhappy with this atmosphere of ill will and
backstage intrigue. Edyth Walker was a handsome, dark-eyed
young woman, and very charming. At Covent Garden they had
been friends, and it seemed a pity that they must now be pitted
against each other all season long. This fortuitous, latent antagonism was very hard to live with, day after day at the opera
house, and when they talked about it together, Sidney felt as
she did. They both wanted to overcome the coolness and the
resentment, those vague but treacherous feelings everyone assumed must exist. But what they finally found to do was a great
shock to Miss Walker, who had come only recently from Vienna
and was staying at a hotel near the opera house. And it seemed
to her a most alarming intrusion, for suddenly, on the very
afternoon following her debut as Amneris in *Aida*, there they
were, standing on her doorstep, as casual as a neighbor couple
dropping in to pay a call—just standing there, unexpected, unasked and certainly most unwelcome, in the anteroom of her
hotel suite.

Their presence at this time seemed to her a most disturbing
development, and she was uneasy, fearing some unhappy confrontation. Her debut the night before had gone well, and the
reviews had been, for the most part, favorable. "Miss Walker is
comely," Henry Krehbiel had written, "and the possessor of a
voice of lovely quality though not of great volume. There is a
decided charm in her singing, the most artistic grace of which
is the perfect evenness of tone. . . ." The reviews were favorable, and Edyth Walker knew all about the situation at the
opera house. Many people had told her that in Grau's opera
company Louise Homer had been considered *the* Amneris, a
brilliant, fervently acclaimed interpreter of the role. She suspected, also, that there had been some trickery on Conried's
part, so it was alarming to find them suddenly right here in
her home, though they were smiling, the singer marvelously

pretty in a black sealskin coat, a trimming of flowers on her hat, her husband tall, angular, dark-eyed. They were even pretending an air of friendliness, but she was suspicious of their intentions, expecting unpleasantness, perhaps even a confrontation, and surprised when they began at once to talk about her debut. Warmly they praised the beauty of her voice, and spoke in glowing terms of her performance. Then they seated themselves, in relaxed and casual fashion, in her living room, and asked about her experiences in Vienna, all with such genuine and unaffected interest that she found herself replying in kind, and before long they were all talking together with animation about various musical matters.

And that was when she understood that they *were* just a neighbor couple dropping in to pay a call. And she was so astonished by the discovery, so moved, so curiously elated, that she never forgot this moment in her life, and spoke of it often to friends, and many years later to her singing pupils, for it seemed to her an extraordinary thing that her greatest rival should have become, so simply and naturally, a friend.

Heinrich Conried had a talent for the bravura gesture and early in the season announced, with considerable fanfare, the first American production of *Parsifal*. This launched a highly publicized copyright suit with Cosima Wagner, for the composer had forbidden any performances outside of Bayreuth for a minimum of fifty years. Inevitably the ensuing battle filled columns of news. But Conried went ahead with the undertaking, and *Parsifal* was unveiled on Christmas Eve, 1903, and given again on New Year's Eve. It was hailed as an "artistic triumph," and the critics wrote that with this production alone the manager had justified his first season at the Metropolitan.

Louise sang "The Voice" in the first performances of *Parsifal*, a very small opera role, but one of the most exposed—a single disembodied phrase floating through a shaft of light. Meanwhile, just as she had feared, she was singing many of the smaller roles this season: Lola in *Cavalleria Rusticana*, Maddalena in *Rigoletto*. Only by chance did she sing the bigger ones—Amneris, late in December, with Caruso as Radames, and not until January Brangäne, with Milka Ternina as an exquisite Isolde.

As Waltraute in *Götterdämmerung*, which she sang first under Grau in 1903.

She was also singing the two new Wagnerian roles, Fricka and Erda. And though they both had beautiful music, they were contrived so as to be for the singer a great strain and an ordeal. She especially dreaded Fricka's entrance in *Die Walküre*, for then she must ride onto the stage in a little goat cart, clinging to the reins and maintaining the regal poise of a goddess. The long switch in her hand, painted in stripes of silver and gold, was to crack in rippling waves above the heads of the poor little mountain goats as evidence of her willful, indomitable nature. Meanwhile she would feel the eyes rising above her, tier after tier of staring eyes, and be afraid that when the time came she wouldn't be able to alight with the proper poise and dignity, for the cart was very flimsy and her gown was much too long.

Wagner had devised the silly entrance, but he had also provided marvelous strains of music to rise from the orchestra pit like a hypnotic shield and make the foolish appear dramatic, the impossible possible, the quaking goddess imperious. Down among the rocks in his armor and winged helmet, Van Rooy, as Wotan, would be waiting for her, a troubled god, wary and affectionate. And after alighting from her rickety cart she must advance with a measured, majestic gait, and in the guise of a strong-willed, domineering woman proceed to shatter the visionary delights of all the gods in the *Nibelungen Ring*. "Wo in Bergen du dich birgst . . ." She must implant with conviction the seeds of doom, in a voice weighted with authority, a velvet spiral of nagging and bad temper, before she could finally clatter off again in the same perilous goat cart, back to the familiar refuge of the wings.

Erda in *Siegfried* was another ordeal, and a very lonely one. For this she must go with her dresser down into the cellar of the opera house, a place that made her shudder, vast and gloomy and full of lurking perils—huge spider webs that dangled from the beams, coiled ropes, planks and hooks, to snag or trip the unwary. There, in her shroudlike gown, she must climb into a small cage like a dumbwaiter, and wait, clammy with anxiety, while the "veil of frost" was put over her head, and above them the music echoed like distant thunder. Two stagehands would be standing by, with ropes and pulleys, to haul her to the surface of the earth, and an assistant conductor, with score and baton, to give the cue.

It was this sense of isolation that made Erda such a painful role to sing, for when she finally did appear on earth she would find herself in a cloud of blue steam, curling mists wrapping her around and the veil of frost over her head, so that she could hardly see the Wanderer, Van Rooy, with whom she must sing, or even hear the music, which seemed to come from a great distance. Meanwhile she must strain to catch her cue, caught up in swirling mists of anxiety, vague sensations of alarm. But finally: "Stark Ruft das Lied" ("Great power hath song")—the reluctant goddess, from within her mysterious cloud, would respond to the magic summons. And at that moment in the opera the haunting cadence of the beautiful voice, the glowing texture, muted at first but rising finally to an impassioned plea, "Löse des Zaubers Zwang!" ("Loose thy constraining spell!") would become for the listeners in the audience an enchantment, woven with a penetrating sadness into the spell of Wagner's music.

The critics had praised Conried's initiative in bringing *Parsifal* to New York, but it soon became apparent that he knew very little about music, and throughout the year they printed stories about his artistic limitations. There was, for instance, the time he had protested, in an interview with Henry Krehbiel, that he could no longer listen with patience while the chorus in *Lohengrin* sang in two languages at once. (It seemed he had failed to distinguish between "in sogno," a dream, and "un cygno," a swan.) Another time, at a rehearsal of *Die Walküre*, he interrupted the proceedings with an outburst of rage at the man in charge of the lighting effects—all because he had been following, in the promptbook, the wrong act of the opera.

This lack of musical background was a great burden to Heinrich Conried, and perhaps the reason why he operated much of the time in an atmosphere of crisis. Because he was a forceful man, he usually managed to compensate for his limitations. But the effort required a high degree of intensity, and he was in a crisis mood one morning, early in March, when he burst into a rehearsal room to ask Louise if she would sing Fricka in *Das Rheingold* that evening. Olive Fremstad, who was supposed to

An imposing portrait of Heinrich Conried, who became manager of the Metropolitan in 1903. (Courtesy *Opera News*)

sing the part, had suddenly been taken ill, he had no one else and begged her to do him this favor.

But as it happened, she had never sung Fricka in *Das Rheingold*—in *Die Walküre*, yes, but not in *Das Rheingold*; that wasn't one of her roles. So she had to explain regretfully that she'd never learned the part or sung it in her life.

Conried then became thoroughly alarmed, and created a scene of mammoth proportions. The conductor, Alfred Hertz, was with them that day in the rehearsal room, as well as one or two others, and the manager was so distraught that it might have been comical if it hadn't been so disturbing, the scene he managed to create, striding up and down the room, the picture of tragic despair, almost in tears, insisting the role must be in her contract, it had to be, and in any case she must learn it, otherwise he would be ruined, for all the seats were sold, and if she didn't comply he would have to close the opera house and turn away the subscribers . . . On and on the tirade went, though it seemed an extraordinary thing he was asking, to learn an entire role in one afternoon. But she had never known how to stand up against onslaughts of emotion, and now the discordant jangle of nerves created such a numbing confusion that finally, to end the scene, she weakly agreed. At once the atmosphere lightened, Conried became effusive in his gratitude, and a grueling ordeal got under way.

She worked with Alfred Hertz throughout the long afternoon, in an opera house that could be at such times a dreary place, filled with ghostly rustles. The tension made the learning more difficult, but at the end of several hours of concentrated study she believed she had mastered the part. After a light supper in her dressing room she had her costume fitted—a luminous gown, sprinkled with sequins, that was believed appropriate for a goddess who would "waken in a flowery meadow" to see for the first time the spires and turrets of Valhalla. It was while the garment was being pinned into place that Alfred Hertz came in, sat down at the piano and suggested that they run through the score "one last time."

He was by this time in evening dress for his role as conductor, an imposing but reassuring figure—almost bald, with a full beard, rimless spectacles and a gentle air of authority. Quietly he struck a chord and played the opening passage, but when she started to sing she couldn't remember a single note. Out in the auditorium the ushers in their smart liveries were already leading the way down the network of carpeted aisles. But in the dressing room there was a stricken silence while the stunned goddess stood helplessly waiting, all the sequins and satin pinned into place but her mind suddenly a blank, for the role had simply vanished. Hertz, not wanting to stampede her into a panic, was very calm. Again and again he played the opening passage, until, very slowly, it began to come back.

They had had no rehearsal of the action or the *mise-en-scène*, but Anton Van Rooy, an impressive Wotan in his silken beard and coat of shining mail, coached her as they went along. And when the mists had cleared and the landscape brightened to reveal the god and his consort awakening from a long sleep, and in the distance the spires and turrets of Valhalla, her voice rang out with authority: "Erwache dich, Wotan, Gemahl . . ." Fricka was a goddess who never faltered in her determination, keeper of the hearth and home, upholder of morals, and now she must give no sign that she had never before crossed the bridge to Valhalla, or heard the Rhinemaidens mourn the loss of their gold.

The company went to Chicago in March for a two-week engagement, and there Louise stayed with her brother Will, while Sidney remained in New York with the children. But he knew she was somewhat disheartened, and there were many letters back and forth. "I have just been playing with Baby," he wrote her, "and he laughs so at anything silly I do that I'm in danger of growing foolish. Every morning he wants to talk to his 'Mama' through the register. . . . I'm glad you and Fremstad sang *Die Walküre* opening night. You were very cheerful about wading through drifts at one in the morning! . . . If you are near the store that handles Schirmer's music, will you stop in and see how many of my songs they have on hand?"

Schirmer had now published two more collections of Sidney's songs. The most recent was a group of Robert Louis Stevenson lyrics, and Emilio de Gogorza and Marcella Sembrich were both using one of these, "Sing Me a Song of the Lad That Is Gone," on their concert tours. He was also beginning to receive critical notice. "Homer's efforts were encored," wrote a Boston critic, with, perhaps, a trace of condescension, adding that the songs had a "strong melodic line" but were, at times, "too declamatory." While a critic for the *Boston Courier* wrote that "Homer's setting of Browning's *Prospice* is one of the great ones—conceived on a scale so austere as to seem statuesque. A long search might not find anything to compare with its classic atmosphere."

Herbert Witherspoon, a concert artist with a fine bass voice, was singing many of his songs in concerts. "This afternoon," he wrote her, "Witherspoon came to the house and sang some of my songs for me. He had an accompanist with him,

"Every morning he wants to talk to his 'Mama' through the register . . ." A photograph taken in 1904, before she went to Chicago.

and he sang the *Prospice*. Well, the way he sang it took my breath away. It was tremendous! The whole man went into the song, voice, heart and soul. If he sings it this way in public it will be a sensation. . . ."

From Chicago she wrote him that her brother Will had one of the new "talking machines" and was playing her records. And that, indeed, was the saving grace of this dreary winter— the unexpected popularity of the talking machines. The Victor technicians had already left Carnegie Hall, to escape the inconvenience of the neighboring practice rooms, and now had their recording studio at 234 Fifth Avenue. In February, Enrico Caruso had gone to the new location to make his first Victor records. And in March, Louise went there for another session and made several more recordings, including the aria from *Samson et Dalila*, "Mon coeur s'ouvre à ta voix."

The first royalty check had far exceeded their expectations, and because it seemed in the nature of a windfall they were surprised and grateful. In the summer, when they went to Cape Cod, they were able to buy Sidney a studio—a small portable house that could be set up among the dunes, then folded away in the winter. With the added income they could pay back the last of the debts and feel, now, a little more secure.

When she returned to the Metropolitan for the 1904–5 season there were two new roles to learn—Laura in *La Gioconda*, and Magdalene in *Die Meistersinger*. They started with the *Gioconda*, a complex opera, with a great variety of melodramatic devices including stabbing, poisoning, suicide and arson. It is, in fact, a most operatic opera, a vivid pageantry of violence and action. But it is Ponchielli's masterpiece, and very popular, for it is filled with a sumptuous array of Venetian costumes and scenery, and a great wealth of fascinating music— duets, arias, choral and crowd effects, ballet, the lovely "dance of the hours" and a rich, sustained symphonic texture.

They had a distinguished cast for their first performance— Lillian Nordica as Gioconda, Caruso as Enzo, Pol Plançon a most evil Alvise, Giraldoni a fierce Barnaba. Edyth Walker was La Cieca, the blind mother, and Louise sang the role of Laura, "the superb lady of Venice, and rival of Gioconda," who at the end must go into a trance and lie still and lifeless in

As Laura in *La Gioconda*.

her coffin for most of two scenes, rising finally from the dead to flee the ruined palace with Enzo, the Genovese nobleman.

This doom-laden plot had to be rehearsed many times, which was perhaps most arduous for their tenor, Enrico Caruso, who had already become so popular that the demands on his time were heavy. But as a rule he was good-natured and compliant, though he had a volatile personality—one moment in high spirits, relieving the boredom with coin tricks to amaze the stagehands, and perhaps, soon after, in a state of gloom. Caruso had an ingenuous nature—open to experience, to emotion, and without too many protective devices. He was often nervous before a performance, and subject to a certain fatalism, as though the naïveté of his spirit had never quite caught up with his situation. But already his dynamic presence had worked a transformation at the Metropolitan. Previously there had been a certain social air, with often many gallery seats unsold and, in the early scenes, the rustle of taffeta as the boxes filled slowly with members of society. But now a whole new class of music-lovers were flocking to the opera house to hear Enrico Caruso—arriving early, crowding the galleries and hurling their bravos with fervent abandon. And this more emotional response had affected both the repertoire and the underlying spirit at the opera house.

On December 3rd, they gave their first *Meistersinger*, and after the *Gioconda* no contrast could have been more notable, for Magdalene is a lighthearted role in an opera that has no melodrama and very little action, though there is, to recommend it, sheer inspiration. Wagner has woven into *Die Meistersinger* a most subtle design, a pageantry of affirmation, a quintessence of thought, mood and gentle irony. Underlying the humorous episodes there is a profound philosophy, and with his music he has welded the whole into a masterpiece.

As Magdalene Louise wore a quaint medieval costume—velvet bonnet, modest church attire. She played the part with a warm and sparkling touch, being properly forgetful in the church, properly helpful in the town square and singing with the others, in Hans Sachs's workshop, a wonderful quintet of contrasting moods and emotions. Magdalene is a lighthearted role, demure and artfully contrived, a bright mosaic in a tapestry of marvels.

In February, Conried staged a performance of *Die Fledermaus*, which the critics called "a curious affair." In this production all his leading singers were required to take part in a second-act ball, sitting about at tables, pretending animation, and occasionally singing. Louise sang the quartet from *Rigoletto* with Caruso, Nordica and Giraldoni at the *Die Fledermaus Extravaganza*, as it was called, but the critics thought the whole affair shoddy and pretentious. "The truth seems to be," wrote Henderson of the *Sun*, "that people were asked to be astonished at the lavishness of expenditure, and to gape at the appearance of Caruso, Nordica and the rest, in a cafe chantant spectacle at a masquerade ball." Conried charged double the usual price of tickets for his extravaganza, and Henry Krehbiel maintained that "all Mr. Conried's artistic energies in his second season were expended on the production of *Die Fledermaus*, which he gave for his own benefit."

As Magdalene in *Die Meistersinger* she wore a quaint medieval
costume.

Chapter XVII

The opening performance of the 1905–6 season would go down in operatic annals as an event of sorts, for over the summer the old red curtain had been replaced with a new one of heavy gold damask—the first gold curtain the Metropolitan had ever had. Louise was to sing on this opening night, November 20th, in *La Gioconda*. Meanwhile, early in the fall, they had moved to a house on Eighty-ninth Street, with a backyard overlooking a livery stable, which proved endlessly fascinating for the little boy, who could watch the horses being fed and watered from his nursery window. This rural atmosphere impressed the reporter from the *Mail and Express*. And when she came, the morning of the opening at the Metropolitan, for an interview, she wrote:

> Calmest of the principals in tonight's cast was Louise Homer, who in private life is wife of the composer and mother of two children. Today she was quietly going about her household duties, singing a few scales now and then, but keeping the balance between the work of a famous contralto and the routine of a happy home life, in a comfortable house west of Central Park. Tonight she will drive down to the Metropolitan and be transformed into the faithless Laura who is helped to a successful elopement

with Enzo Caruso by her erstwhile rival, Nordica Gioconda.

Though she was, perhaps, not as calm as the reporter imagined, there was this contrast in her life—one moment the high melodrama on the stage, and soon afterward the sunny, lively little house, the crescendo and discipline of music, and the responsibilities at home—a complex of emotions and situations made possible by an elusive quality she had, a kind of radiance, that she carried about with her throughout the day so naturally that it seemed, in fact, to be a part of her.

Early in the season Engelbert Humperdinck came to New York for the first Metropolitan production of *Hänsel und Gretel*. Louise was to sing the role of the Witch, and this beguiling little opera proved to be one of Conried's most successful contributions to the repertoire.

Hänsel und Gretel is an entrancing drama, for though the mood is one of childlike enchantment and simplicity, the score is filled with ingenious and fascinating melodies, and the orchestration is almost Wagnerian in texture. Humperdinck had been a disciple of Wagner's, absorbing the Master's grand design. And for his homespun little opera he had composed music that was ideally contrived—subtle, powerful, tenderly persuasive. The emotions in *Hänsel und Gretel* are valid—fear, distress, consolation, enchantment—and the structure, with its interplay of mood and emotion, whimsy and climax, is all but perfect.

Louise created the role of the Witch under the guidance of the composer, and between them they made it a bewitching part, one that brought squeals of ecstatic horror from the children in the audience, and built to a memorable and fiery climax. Since the opera relies for much of its charm on a certain naïve realism, she devised for herself a fearsome costume, a hooked beak of a nose, a pointed chin, a wretched mat of straggling hair. And when she sang the "Hocus, pocus, Hexenschuss!" not only the children on the stage, but those in the audience as well, were all but hypnotized.

They gave their first performance on November 25, 1905, and the critics approved this blend of the comic and the macabre. "Give me the Witch for my money!" exclaimed the *Telegraph*, "with her broom, her wild ride, her hideous leer, and her appetite for small boys." While in the *Times* it was noted that "Louise Homer was a blood-curdling Witch of fearful and wonderful appearance."

Hänsel und Gretel became so popular that it had to be given ten times that first year. Meanwhile, Conried had returned *Il Trovatore* to the repertoire. Once again Louise was singing Azucena, with Lillian Nordica as Leonora; and she was also appearing throughout the season as Amneris and Ortrud and Brangäne, and Magdalene and Fricka and Erda and Laura. Though there was still, under Conried's direction, a certain air of caprice, she had more than regained her old status in the company and now was singing regularly all the big contralto roles.

In the spring she learned the role of Nancy for Friedrich von Flotow's *Martha*, a light opera that had been a favorite for years all over the world. In their production Caruso appeared as Lionel, Pol Plançon as a jovial Plunkett and Sembrich as a delectable Harriet. Together they all went to the Fair, exhibited a fine confusion in the farmhouse and sang their sparkling spinning-wheel quartet. Marcella Sembrich interpreted most wonderfully the beautiful Irish folk song "The Last Rose of Summer," and their performance of *Martha* became immensely popular.

As soon as the New York season had ended, Conried sent his company off on a spring tour that was far more extensive than any he had attempted before, with engagements in Washington, Pittsburgh, Chicago, St. Louis, Kansas City, and finally a trip to California, with two weeks in San Francisco. They traveled under the expert guidance of the assistant manager, Ernest Goerlitz, and gave performances of *Lohengrin*, *Martha*, *Hänsel und Gretel* and many other operas. But coming at the end of an exacting New York season, this long tour seemed to many of the singers an imposition. Throughout the company there was a general feeling of letdown and malaise, and for Louise the long spring tour was especially trying because she was expecting another baby in October. Little Sidney Jr. would soon be four years old, and they believed three children would be an ideal number. So now she was looking forward to a restful summer ahead, and trying to conserve her strength.

But meanwhile she had to sing *Martha* in St. Louis, and another *Martha* in Kansas City. And it was a relief when they finally reached San Francisco and could settle down in comfort in the Palace Hotel. As was their habit, they had soon turned their big hotel room into a home away from home, with music strewn about, and pictures of the children on the dresser. Their room was furnished in French Provincial style, with a huge wardrobe, heavily carved, a most impressive piece of furniture, reaching all the way to the ceiling. They also had a wood-burning fireplace, and because Louise was tired from the trip they took many of their meals there. She would have two days of rest before she had to sing Ortrud in *Lohengrin* on April 18th. And it was most enjoyable to dine in front of the crackling fire, with liveried waiters hovering discreetly about, unfolding with a flourish the spotless linen cloths and raising silver covers from the steaming dishes.

And, in fact, there wasn't a hotel in the country more noted for an ambiance of luxury and attentiveness, for a homelike atmosphere and supreme comfort, marvelously combined with elegance and grandeur. The Palace in San Francisco was one of the most famous hostelries in the world and over the years had played host to a notable array of celebrities. Sarah Bernhardt had stayed there, with an entourage that included a baby tiger, and Lily Langtry had danced divinely in the ballroom. Henry Irving had visited there, and Ellen Terry, and Oscar Wilde and Mrs. Patrick Campbell. Rudyard Kipling had been a guest, as had Ulysses S. Grant, General Sherman and President Theodore Roosevelt.

The Palace Hotel had become noted as an apotheosis of the extravagance, the exuberance, the eclectic imagination that characterized the city of San Francisco. But it was also supremely comfortable, even, in its way, homelike, and the management had become adept at entertaining celebrities and catering to their whims. Some years before, it had been Ellen Terry who didn't like the design of her marble wash basin (the hotel had nine hundred, all individually designed). Now it was Enrico Caruso, unhappy with the interior decoration of his Suite No. 622. Every room in the Palace had a different decor, ranging from Edwardian elegance to Byzantine splendor, with many variations between. Caruso thought the redwood paneling and heavy drapes in his suite too gloomy, even funereal, and was much happier with No. 580, which had walls of California laurel overlaid with maroon satin, an English marble fireplace, French chandeliers, Persian bedspreads and Turkish carpets.

The hotel itself was a huge, rambling structure, covering almost three acres of ground. It had been made, when it was built, thoroughly earthquakeproof, with brick walls two feet thick, massive pillar foundations more than twelve feet deep and reinforcing bands of steel throughout the walls. The Palace had more than eight hundred wood-burning fireplaces in the individual rooms, and to guard against fires it also had its own firefighting system. Huge tanks of water had been installed on the roof and in the basement, and five miles of piping had been built into the walls. Each room had an individual fire alarm, and an army of watchmen patrolled the halls, signaling with electric buttons the various points on their rounds. Due to these precautions a number of small fires had already been easily extinguished, and in San Francisco it was said that if the Palace Hotel ever burned, the city would go too.

The Metropolitan opened its West Coast engagement on April 16th with *The Queen of Sheba*. Edyth Walker and Andreas Dippel sang the leading roles, but the opera was new to San Francisco, and not well received, one headline noting, "Opera crowd cold." However, the performance the next night was a brilliant success. This was *Carmen*, with Caruso and Olive Fremstad, and the Mission Street Opera House was filled that night with a distinguished audience and a dazzling array of pearl and diamond chokers, and glittering tiaras. Elaborate parties had preceded the opera, for this was the great tenor's first appearance in San Francisco, and there was no presentiment of disaster while they applauded wildly Enrico Caruso's soaring eloquence as Don José.

More parties followed the opera, and the streets were lined with fine carriages and liveried coachmen taking their fashionable occupants here and there. All over the city there were festivities, including a champagne party at the Palace, where the artists, Hertz, Scotti, Caruso and others, were in high spirits. But even those who were celebrating had ended their revelries and were in their rooms at 5:15 the next morning, when the San Andreas Fault suddenly split apart, ripping and tearing the earth and the buildings and emitting a shrill, unearthly wail, like a thousand off-tune violins, a harrowing crescendo of shrieking cymbals and whining cellos, a weird orchestral din that flooded the region like the crack of doom, then ceased abruptly, leaving in its wake a damaged city, and a smoldering, breathless silence.

The Palace Hotel still stood, after the earthquake, though it had shuddered under the impact, the plaster cracked and shredding from the walls, doors jammed, floor heaving, the massive furniture tossed and careening here and there. But it still stood, and in Suite No. 580 Enrico Caruso, stunned by the fearful violence, moaned in terror to his friend Alfred Hertz that he had surely lost his voice, until finally Hertz commanded him to sing, and the impassioned strains of that soaring aria of Don José's, rising now to a crescendo of emotion, electrified those, standing shocked and stunned, in the corridors and on the street, who heard it. Meanwhile all over the city people were fleeing to streets made dangerous with falling cornices and snaking, sputtering electric wires. Afterward Hertz would recall that "the streets presented an amazing series of grotesque sights. Most people had fled from their rooms without stopping to dress, many of them a little less than naked. But excitement was running so high that nobody noticed or cared."

In that vast hostelry, with its thick walls and miles of corridors, they had known nothing about the festivities following *Carmen.* So that Louise would be rested for *Lohengrin* the next night they had dined in their room and gone early to bed, for Ortrud was a demanding role and this was especially so when there was a baby on the way, for then it was an added strain to stand almost motionless throughout that long first act, in heavy train and crown, maintaining all the while the regal pose of a queen.

This was a part that required physical endurance, and she was trying, on the spring tour, to conserve her strength. But she would never sing that performance of *Lohengrin* at the Mission Street Opera House in San Francisco. And when they were awakened by the earthquake, and enveloped in that harrowing crescendo of wailing, shrieking sound, they were also transfixed by an extraordinary sight, for it seemed that the huge wardrobe in their room was doing a little dance. Back and forth it swayed; here and there it jiggled. And when it finally fell, plunging full length across the room, it fell in an unearthly silence, the noise of smashed and splintered wood drowned out by the horrendous wailing of the San Andreas Fault.

The noise stopped suddenly, with an abrupt and shocking silence, and Sidney's first thought then was to get Louise out of the hotel, which he feared might collapse at any moment. But all her clothes were trapped in the smashed wardrobe, which had fallen across the bureau, demolishing everything. He had two suits and a bathrobe on the chair beside his bed, and dressed hurriedly, snatching up what he could. But she had only her dressing gown, and so was one of those who had, as Hertz noted, "fled from their rooms without stopping to dress." Nevertheless, they were among the first to leave the hotel and discover a stricken city and a strange, almost breathless silence. But gradually more people emerged from the shaken buildings, to join those already in the street. James Hopper, a reporter for the *Call*, would describe the "dishevelled" people those first hours after the San Francisco earthquake. "In the garish morning light," he wrote, "I saw many men and women with gray faces. All of them had a singular hurt expression—not one of physical pain, but rather one of injured sensibilities, as if some trusted friend had suddenly wronged them, or as if someone had been rude to them."

The streets were dangerous, but they made their way, finally, to St. Francis Square. And there she felt so strange and distressed, standing about in a public place in her nightclothes, that she went behind a bush and put on his extra suit. Then she sat on a bench, and an old Italian gentleman looked at her, and smiled, and gave her a piece of candy.

Most of the buildings were still standing, and much of the damage was, at this time, invisible. But it was there, for under the ground the water mains had been cracked, and the telephone and electric wires severed. San Francisco was entirely cut off from the outside world, but gradually it was becoming known that a great catastrophe had taken place, and military forces were being mobilized, though not always wisely. The city was stranded, and so were the people in it, each individual or group isolated in a small eddy of anxiety and loss. Meanwhile fires were already starting among the wooden buildings on the bay, and since there was very little water to fight them with, they were spreading rapidly, up Market Street and other avenues, and a good many were trying to flee the flames by escaping into the hills.

Looking for some kind of refuge, they became part of this exodus, and after several hours in St. Francis Square were able to persuade a hackdriver to take them up Pacific Avenue to the home of the George Popes. Here they were warmly welcomed, and Louise was given some borrowed clothes to wear. But while she was trying to change hurriedly, in a first-floor room, still fearful of another quake, the Chinese houseman knocked discreetly on the door, and called out, apologetically, "Pardon me, Mister and Missus, but I regret to inform you that the house is on fire."

Coming just when she was trying to regain her equilibrium, this was an added shock and, alarmed and shaken, they ran outside. But their hosts, somewhat embarrassed, quickly reassured them, for it had been only a small kitchen fire, easily extinguished, which seemed to their friends an amusing coincidence in the midst of a disaster like an earthquake. But it was, in fact, neither amusing nor a coincidence, for in time these small kitchen fires would burn down the city. Most were caused by cracked chimneys or dislocated flues, and since they flared up when the breakfasts were started they would be known as the "ham 'n egg fires." Because of the severe shortage of water many of the conflagrations couldn't be contained, and these were spreading gradually, from one house to another, and then from one block to another, finally engulfing whole areas.

They breakfasted with the Popes on the lawn in front of the house, for no one wanted to remain indoors; and they could see, from their refuge on the hill, the many fires flowering in the heart of the city. Here and there the flames were visible, flaring poppy-red among the gray and yellow buildings, and a spreading pall of smoke hung like a cloud over the city they all loved.

But among the refugees streaming up the hill, dragging their possessions in small carts, baby buggies, anything on wheels, there was now a shift in mood from the early shock and apathy, even a kind of exhilaration, defiant, resilient. "Don't be downhearted!" read the signs on the carts and buggies, "Cheer up, it might be worse!" Already the earthquake had spawned a variety of jokes, to be passed up and down the lines of refugees. And during the long day they stood by the road, giving cups of coffee to those who were most exhausted, especially the mothers with small children. But even this had to be carefully rationed, for the Popes, too, were almost out of water.

That night, while their hosts put their four small children to bed on mattresses near the front door, Louise tried to rest in the big touring car that stood on the lawn in front of the house. But though she was enormously fatigued, it was a nightmare rest, for the sky was lit with a brilliant glare from the burning city, and at intervals there would be huge explosions, shaking the ground and showering sparks and pinwheels into the sky. These were from the dynamite that was now being used to contain the fires and turn San Francisco into a perilous battleground. Because of the desperate shortage of water the firefighters were trying more violent methods, and large blocks were being blasted away to halt the spreading flames. But much of the work was so wantonly performed, with so little expertise, that more often than not the haphazard destruction spread the fires, or started whole new conflagrations.

General Frederick Funston, commander of the Presidio, was one of those most dedicated to the use of dynamite, here, there and everywhere. Within an hour of the devastating earthquake General Funston, acting on his own initiative and without authority, had put San Francisco under martial law. He had ordered companies of soldiers to patrol the streets, called in reserves from outlying districts and issued a great many ironclad and often conflicting mandates. The soldiers were ordered to shoot on sight anyone caught looting, and more than one innocent citizen was killed while trying to rescue a few of his own possessions, or help a friend. Under such severe pressure some of the soldiers became trigger-happy, and this was now a dangerous city to walk through. Meanwhile the mayor and his "committee of fifty" were retreating before the flames, setting up headquarters here and there. But with all the lines of communication disrupted, even the most valiant efforts to distribute food, care for the injured and temper the chaos were pitifully ineffective.

By morning many of the refugees who had streamed up the hills, trying to flee the flames, were now streaming back down again, hoping to escape by ferry to Oakland. Clearly this home was going to burn, and soon after dawn the Popes packed their four small children, their servants and the few possessions they could carry into the big touring car, and drove away to their place in the country. They'd had no alternative, for there was no water left, inevitably their house would be destroyed and they had to protect their children.

So now, once again, they were stranded in a paralyzed and burning city, and scarcely able to imagine that only a short while ago they had been pampered guests in a luxurious hotel, preparing for a performance of *Lohengrin*. It seemed almost forever that she'd been wearing borrowed, ill-fitting clothes, and trying to make do with shoes that hurt her feet, and find some rest where there was none. And, in fact, she might have been strong enough to withstand the shock of the earthquake without any subsequent illness if she had been able to have some rest and repose not too long afterward.

But as it was, they had to think about escape, and went finally to some other friends, the Blisses. Here they received a most touching and reassuring welcome in a home where there seemed to be an almost buoyant atmosphere, as though the very nature of the catastrophe had uncovered a reservoir of grace and kindliness. In this home they were treated like honored guests, served a delicious breakfast, offered, in effect, the keys to the city. And for a time, with these rare friends, there was an illusion of safety, a temporary respite, like the brief lyric interludes in a violent opera, when the music lulls the listener and makes him more vulnerable.

But it was only an illusion, for in the heart of the city the great landmarks were going one by one—City Hall, the St. Francis Hotel, the Fairmont. For a while a desperate effort was made to save the Palace, using the huge tanks of water on the roof and in the cellar. But finally that, too, was engulfed in flames, and one spectator would note, with awe, a patriotic bit of byplay as the American flag flying over the Palace Hotel tried valiantly to avoid the flames. Again and again a shower of sparks from a nearby building would rain down upon the emblem, giving the appearance of a fiery fringe. But repeatedly the threatened flag would shake off the sparks, as if unwilling to succumb. However, the hotel was doomed, and later Oscar Lewis would describe the final hours, when there remained just "one last sinister guest" in the abandoned hotel, who, during the morning hours, "began stalking through the corridors, the lobby, the banquet halls, mounting stairs, entering the hundreds of rooms. Trailing his scarlet robe, he advanced inexorably, permeating every corner of the structure, silently at first, then more boisterously, until presently the grand court vibrated with an immense humming roar."

By this time the "sinister guest" had, most likely, entered their room as well, to play casually with the opera scores, the music, the pictures of the children, and consume the huge wardrobe as it lay prostrate on the floor. But though it now seemed a long time ago that they had been transfixed by that eerie, silent plunge, they still hadn't escaped the confused aftermath of the earthquake. Every moment the fires were coming closer; before night this home, too, would burn, and after some anxious consultation it was decided that they should try to walk to the harbor, and then cross the bay on a ferry. The Blisses had relatives in Oakland who would take them in. And to guard against the dangers of this expedition their host, who was well known in the city, gave them a calling card on which he wrote: "To whom it may concern—Please take care of Louise and Sidney Homer, and help them any way you can." They were also given all the provisions they could carry—blankets, sandwiches, cakes, champagne (there was no water).

Thus equipped they started out, walking through a city that was oddly disheveled—subdued, threatened and threatening. The soldiers patrolling the streets had been ordered to shoot on sight anyone doing anything amiss. But the groups of people camping out in the squares and small parks in makeshift tents, or trying to cook on makeshift stoves, seemed to making of this strange disaster a sort of impromptu picnic. There was still a resilient mood, a certain defiant air. But they were themselves very close to defeat, for though they stopped often to rest, it was plain she could never walk so far. They had miscalculated, not realizing she was too ill for such an arduous undertaking. And finally, in desperation, Sidney stopped a driver with a small truck going in their direction and begged him to take them to the harbor. But the man had been forbidden by his employer to take any refugees in his truck, and told them that if he disobeyed, he would lose his job. So now there was a long moment of delicately balanced pressures, while she stood there, numb with fatigue, the beautiful face dazed with exhaustion, Sidney continued to plead frantically for help, and the man looked at them, hesitated and finally said, "Get in."

The city of San Francisco was now ironbound, with mandatory orders of evey kind and description—pasted on walls, bruited about, enforced by the patrolling soldiers. But this had done nothing to allay the confusion, and on their way to the harbor they passed a great many hurrying people trying now to escape across the bay. Though there was some disarray, most of the men wore dark suits and derby hats, the women voluminous skirts, straw boaters or bonnets with plumes. And in this accepted mode of dress they ran headlong over the cobblestones, or rode in jolting carts, trying to flee the burning city.

The ferry-house still stood, for it had been protected through-

Fires were already starting among the wooden houses on the bay, and there was very little water to fight them with . . . (Culver Pictures)

Some of the soldiers had become trigger-happy, and this was now a dangerous city to walk through. (Culver Pictures)

out the day by fireboats that were playing a constant stream of water on the sturdy structure to preserve it. But the heat from the fires was so intense that the air was stifling. James Hopper, the reporter for the *Call*, has described this scene at the ferry-house. "People spoke very little," he wrote, "or if they did, it was in low tones. The silence was acute. Everybody seemed to be overwhelmed by the terrible magnificence of the spectacle that was being enacted all around. . . . Women in opera cloaks dragged trunks. Bands of Chinese, dazed and helpless, drifted along with the mass of refugees. It was incredible what foolish things people clung to."

Meanwhile, a monumental evacuation was in progress. In addition to the regular ferries, a director of the Southern Pacific Railway had mobilized a fleet of launches to transport the refugees to Oakland. All along the waterfront everything available was being pressed into service—skiffs, rowboats, coal and cargo lighters, launches and boats of all kinds. And though there was some profiteering in this mad shuttle back and forth, much of it was voluntary. The Southern Pacific ran all its rescue operations free of charge, and transported hundreds and thousands of refugees from the disaster area in boats and trains, at a cost to the company of more than half a million dollars.

Crammed into one of those shuttling ferries, they finally reached Oakland. There, with relatives of the Blisses, they were again accorded a most touching welcome, with many new friends hovering anxiously about. But though the Opera Train was to leave that night, and it seemed they were finally safe, all the kindness and concern couldn't help very much, for now she was seriously ill. However, their overwhelming desire was to go home, so he went at once to the station to inquire about trains. And there he discovered that their manager, Ernest Goerlitz, had performed an astonishing feat of organization and logistics—rounding up his scattered company, arranging transportation and bringing some semblance of order out of chaos.

When the earthquake first struck, Goerlitz had tried to ignore it. He had even gone straight to the opera house to prepare for a matinee performance of *Figaro*, with Marcella Sembrich. But while the stagehands were sweeping up the plaster, an entire wall had caved in on the stage. So then he'd abandoned that project and turned to the rescue of his company. With Prussian efficiency, he'd had messengers running here and there, trying to locate the singers and musicians. And he'd already arranged for a special section of the Overland Limited to leave for Chicago that night, with first-class accommodations for his principal singers, and many of the accustomed luxuries.

Nothing had been overlooked, and when the big train pulled out of the Oakland station, all the members of the company were accounted for. A few would come later, but all were safe. And on the Opera Train, they were able to unwind after the long ordeal, and while relating their adventures regain, gradually, their equilibrium.

Marcella Sembrich was already planning a benefit performance to help the musicians replace their instruments; and Edyth Walker had undertaken to help the women of the chorus during the first frantic hours following the earthquake. Alfred Hertz had spent the night in a borrowed bed in Golden Gate Park, and had been wakened by a terrifying roar, to find that he was right beside the lion's cage; Pol Plançon was bemoaning the loss of a dozen hand-tailored silk shirts he'd never even had a chance to wear; and Caruso was exclaiming fervently that he would never again set foot in San Francisco (and he never did). Sharing the adventures put them in perspective, and on the Opera Train the talk was voluble and unrestrained, for here there was safety, comfort and companionship.

But for Louise there was no such relief from tension, for now she was dangerously ill. And the stress and poignancy of their situation, on a speeding Opera Train, with a miscarriage imminent and all the other members of the company in a relieved, even holiday mood, was underscored by the extreme reticence in vogue at this time. Such matters were never openly discussed, and in fact were shrouded in a kind of Victorian mystery. But finally Sidney confided, with great discretion, in the manager's wife, Mrs. Goerlitz. A telegram was then sent ahead to Des Moines, Iowa, and while the Opera Train waited on a siding, a Dr. McFaul came to examine her. But this only confirmed their apprehensions, for the doctor told them it would be impossible for

In Chicago, while she waited behind drawn curtains, "the reporters came in droves to interview the singers, who posed gallantly for pictures, and . . . later it was remarked how superbly poised they were, in their furs and feathered hats. . . ." Caruso and Marcella Sembrich are at far right in the picture. Others in the group include Edyth Walker, Bella Alten, Robert Blass and Ernest Goerlitz. (Courtesy *Opera News*)

her to travel as far as New York. So it was arranged that the doctor would wire ahead to her brother Will Beatty and have an ambulance meet the train in Chicago.

Meanwhile newspapers all over the world were carrying stories about the dramatic plight of the Metropolitan artists. And when the train reached Chicago the reporters came in droves to interview the singers, who posed gallantly for pictures, and related their adventures. Later it was remarked how superbly poised they were, in their furs and feathered hats, and how good-natured and cheerful, in spite of the ordeal. While all this was going on, Louise waited behind drawn curtains. But when finally there was some semblance of privacy, a stretcher was brought to her stateroom, and she was rushed by ambulance to the Wesley Hospital. There she lost her baby, for several days it wasn't certain if she would live, and merged with the illness were nightmare memories of the earthquake, as well as great sorrow and regret.

When the reporters came to interview him at the hospital, Sidney was properly evasive. And because he was so reluctant to reveal the true cause of her illness, all the accounts were variously contrived. One, after listing the well-known singers on the Overland Limited, noted that:

> Every member of the troupe was in good condition, with the exception of Madame Louise Homer, who suffered a shock as the result of her experience in San Francisco. As the train sped through Iowa Dr. W. D. McFaul of Des Moines was asked to board the train. He advised the singer's immediate removal to a hospital upon her arrival here.

Another reported that:

> Louise Homer is recovering from injuries suffered in the San Francisco earthquake. As soon as she was found, near the St. Francis Hotel, slightly harmed, she was hurried to Chicago for treatment. Every effort to aid the wounded singer has been made in order that she may be able to sing at the Cincinnati Festival next week.

While still another wrote that:

> succumbing to the nervous strain of the last few days, Louise Homer reached Chicago yesterday only to be taken to the Wesley Hospital on the verge of a nervous breakdown. So sharp was the reaction after the singer left San Francisco that it became necessary to place her where she might have constant care. An ambulance met the Oakland Limited and conveyed her directly to the hospital, where an operation was performed by Dr. Reed.

Inevitably these garbled accounts were repeated, year after year, in the operatic annals of the Metropolitan. And it is still being written today that the American contralto Louise Homer was the only one in the company unable to withstand the shock of the San Francisco earthquake.

Chapter XVIII

Conried sustained heavy losses as the result of the earthquake—in scenery, equipment and costumes, as well as expected revenue—and it was generally agreed that he acquitted himself under pressure with unusual skill and generosity. When news of the disaster was first flashed to New York, he had taken his place at the switchboard to reassure distraught relatives and friends. He had been most considerate of the welfare of his artists. And later in the summer he sent Ernest Goerlitz back to San Francisco to make refunds, in full, on every ticket sold—at a cost to his company of over a hundred thousand dollars.

But at the start of the 1906–07 season Conried was hard-pressed, and when the reporters questioned him about replacing the lost scenery, he snapped back at them, "I'm not Oscar Hammerstein, and cannot have these things done without time!" —a sarcastic reference to the rival impresario who, almost overnight, was building another opera house just five blocks away.

Never before in its history had the Metropolitan had competition, and it seemed a daring venture. But Hammerstein was a formidable opponent. He was calling his new theater the Manhattan Opera House and building quite an elaborate structure, in a pseudo-Georgian style, faced with marble and brownstone trim. In spite of all the embellishments the new opera house was rising with astonishing rapidity on Thirty-fourth

Street. And almost every week Hammerstein would call the reporters together and announce some new plan to intrigue the public.

Oscar Hammerstein had many of the very qualities Heinrich Conried lacked—subtlety, wit and style, and to top it all, genius. For the reporters he was superb copy—urbane, provocative, a man of vision and ideas, daring and resourceful. However, Conried had some notable advantages on his side of the ledger —the prestige of the Metropolitan, the boxholders, the subscribers, above all, most of the stars. And so, with considerable fanfare, they had squared off for what Henry Krehbiel liked to call "this merry operatic war."

To open his new season Conried had a most important new star, whose contract, like Caruso's, had been arranged by Grau some years before—the American soprano Geraldine Farrar. Farrar made her Metropolitan debut on November 26th, in *Roméo et Juliette*, to considerable acclaim, and would appear next in the title role of Puccini's *Madame Butterfly*, which was to have its American premiere February 11, 1907. Puccini was coming to New York to oversee this production of his opera. And for the premiere performance Louise would sing the contralto role of Suzuki. Caruso was to be Pinkerton, Scotti would play Sharpless, Albert Reiss, Goro—a cast called by Aldrich of the *Times* "the strongest forces the company can command."

Geraldine Farrar didn't come to New York unheralded, for she already had a reputation as a star at the Royal Opera House in Berlin. And the fact that she was known to be a favorite of the Crown Prince added a certain touch of glamour to her renown. But she was also very American, and a serious artist, who had worked long and hard, with a devoted mother at her side, to attain a position in the opera world. As a singer she had unusual insight, and could evaluate her strengths and compensate for her limitations. Later she would write of herself that she wasn't "a true dramatic soprano" but a singer "who could manipulate so as to convey the accents of drama." She felt that "the power of suggestion" could compensate for "vocal resources never over-strong," [8] and perhaps for this reason created her roles with remarkable subtlety and finesse. In the middle register her voice was darkly colored and unusually beautiful, and this "power of suggestion," combined with rare talent, grace and charm, soon made her a star.

To prepare for *Madame Butterfly* Farrar spent many months studying the figures on Japanese vases and prints and working with a Japanese actress, Madame Fu-Ji-Ko, so that she could perfect and make instinctive certain poses and gestures—the meekly bowed head, the modest composure, the small, shuffling steps, the serenity and grace characteristic of young Japanese women. And in the scenes that she and Louise shared they worked together in this way, creating a duet of the actions as well as the words—gestures that would be subdued yet eloquent, every slightest movement part of a picturesque whole. Americans, at this time, had only a vague, idealized image of the faraway country of Japan, and it was this exquisite remoteness they were trying to convey, the delicate pictorial quality within the poignant unfolding of the drama.

The staging for *Madame Butterfly* was done by that most revered of theater directors, David Belasco, and Puccini directed the rehearsals himself. So there were many high-powered personalities involved, and no work Louise had ever done under the guidance of the composer was a greater strain. Wrote one music critic, in his column, "So much has Puccini accomplished by pushing and prodding at rehearsals, and insisting so strenuously on his demands, that once, at least, he had Geraldine Farrar and Louise Homer in tears."

Although *Madame Butterfly* had received great acclaim in Paris, it had failed miserably when it was first produced in Milan. Perhaps for this reason the composer was in a high state of nervousness and exertion during the rehearsals. But afterward he was rewarded, for the performance at the Metropolitan, on February 11, 1907, was a brilliant success. In his review, Richard Aldrich of the *Times* noted "the fine Italian hand of Mr. Puccini himself, who had molded it according to his own ideas . . ." and found most provocative "the delicacy, the shifting pictorial beauty, the completely penetrating atmosphere that gives perhaps greater delight in this opera of Puccini's than in any of his others."

The "Duet of the Flowers" from Act II of *Madame Butterfly*.
Geraldine Farrar, as Cio-Cio-San, is in the tree, with Louise
Homer, as Suzuki, kneeling beside her. The composer, Giacomo
Puccini, supervised the production and received an ovation when
he was presented on the stage.

Meanwhile Louise was going once or twice every season to the Victor studios to make a new selection of records, and gradually the whole process was being improved. Most notably, the technicians had finally found a way of recording orchestral instruments—violins, cellos, even wind instruments. And the year before, in 1906, she had gone to the studios and remade many of her old records with orchestral accompaniment.

Now, in the spring of 1907, they were going to try another experiment—four operatic voices on one record. Nothing so demanding had ever been attempted before, and for the new venture the Victor Company selected the famous quartet from *Rigoletto*, "Bello figlia dell'amore," with, as singers, Enrico Caruso, Louise Homer, Antonio Scotti and Bessie Abott, a young soprano who had been two years with the Metropolitan and had what Krehbiel called "a winning voice of lovely timbre and impeccable quality."

Recently the recording studio had been moved to the company's main factory and office building in Camden, New Jersey. They traveled there on a special train, almost filling the car with a retinue of relatives and accompanists and secretaries and managers. Scotti and Caruso were great comrades, and had between them an array of jokes and repartee to relieve the tedium—Scotti the steadier of the two, a calming influence, Caruso more emotional, often in a crisis state of mind. But in fact they were all in a crisis state when they finally faced the horn.

The acoustic machine had now been placed in full view (the surface noise having finally been moderated). But the music still had to be focused, and this required great ingenuity. The singers were positioned first, directly in front of the horn. Then the violinists were crowded close in behind, with small devices on their bows to direct the sound. Those with flutes and wind instruments arranged their chairs on the tops of tables along each side, and the conductor then wedged himself in front, with the technician at his elbow.

The situation was not unlike a carefully crowded elevator, and in the midst of it they had to do a kind of tribal dance to modulate their voices—back, forth, turn around—back, forth,

Posing with the latest model of the Victor Talking Machine.

turn around—that might indeed have been comical if it hadn't been so subtle and so serious. Their biggest problem was the tender diaphragm that could so easily be blasted by too much power or resonance. So they sang in an atmosphere of suffocating tension, keyed to a monumental control. But they were rewarded, for the quartet from *Rigoletto* became one of the wonders of that year. Victor charged six dollars for their record (an unprecedented sum for only four minutes of music), and hailed it as the forerunner of many more to come.

They made their trip to Camden in the midst of quite a controversial opera season, for to everyone's great surprise the new Manhattan Opera House was giving the Metropolitan some notable competition. The press and the public were beginning to enjoy "the battle of the opera houses," and at a performance of *Aida*, when Louise sang Amneris, with Caruso and Emma Eames in the cast, a reporter noted with interest that the Metropolitan was only half full. Then he hurried to the Manhattan, where *Aida* was also being given, to relay his information to the performers there. At the Manhattan, where they had a splendid audience, the news was greeted with rousing cheers, and during an intermission the singers and their conductor, Campanini, joined hands and did a little dance of triumph on the stage.

The Manhattan had a tenor, Alessandro Bonci, who was almost as famous as Caruso, so there was a "battle of the tenors" to intrigue the public. But Hammerstein's ace in the hole was his conductor and music director, Cleofonte Campanini, who had taken a hastily assembled company of singers and musicians and created, almost overnight, a distinguished opera company. Campanini's choral effects in *Aida* were stunning, and his working habits were prodigious. He inspired in his artists a fervent loyalty, and with his rare talents contributed to a season that was now casting its long shadow all the way to Thirty-ninth Street.

Henry Krehbiel was inclined to feel that much of the success of the first season at the Manhattan Opera House was due to "fascination with the audacity of the undertaking." The public had great sympathy for the "undaunted manner" in which "this difficult and dangerous enterprise" was carried out, and audiences were in a mood to overlook inadequacies. When Nellie Melba joined the company in the spring and sang *La Traviata* and *La Bohème*, some of the most distinguished subscribers deserted their boxes at the Metropolitan and journeyed to the Manhattan to hear her. Then in March, Emma Calvé came to sing *Carmen* and encroach once more on the regular patronage at the Metropolitan.

And so the battle was joined, with each manager free to raid the other's resources; and this they did, right and left, for there was nothing to stop them. No ground rules had ever been laid down to guide competing opera companies. Throughout the spring there were lawsuits, predictions, proclamations and, perhaps most troublesome of all for Conried, rumors. Hammerstein announced that he had signed Madame Schumann-Heink and Lillian Nordica; Conried countered by signing up the Manhattan's popular tenor, Alessandro Bonci. Hammerstein then tried to break that contract with a lawsuit and an injunction;

but two could play the legal game, and Conried used the same method to prevent any future performances of *La Bohème*, claiming he owned exclusive American rights to all Puccini's works. In his dealings with the temperamental singers Hammerstein had a flair for the dramatic gesture: in Paris, when he was trying to sign up Nellie Melba, he went to her hotel with a suitcase full of money and strewed the green bills like leaves over her carpet—a gesture she found so irresistible that she signed a contract the next day.

Inevitably Louise was caught up in this musical maneuvering, and it was rumored in the papers that she'd signed with Hammerstein. But she couldn't take proper advantage of the "merry opera war," for another baby was expected in December. Her singing next year would have to be curtailed, and finally, after some temporizing, she signed a contract to sing the last half of the season at the Metropolitan.

For the vacation months they went again to Craigville on Cape Cod. And this was an idyllic summer, a benign contrast to the one the year before, when she'd been recuperating from the illness and loss following the earthquake. As usual her family came in relays to visit—her mother, her sisters and their children. Sidney's family came, too, and at times there would be as many as a dozen of them at table, or sitting about on the porch in the West Chester way, the conversation witty, relaxed, a comfortable stream of nothings floating blissfully out to sea.

In the mornings Sidney would go to his studio on the dunes, and sometimes bring back a song for her to try. He was working this year on poems by Christina Rossetti, which he found "fascinating, exquisite and spiritual." And when she sang them for him—"Ferry Me Across the Water," "When Windflowers Blossom on the Sea"—the songs would have a lyric quality, innocent and fanciful, that seemed to symbolize the mood of that summer.

But in September Louise became seriously ill, and they had to hurry to New York. There the doctor found the complications, the kidney trouble and edema, so severe that he felt the pregnancy could not be continued. Such an acute toxic condition was hazardous to them both; now her life was in danger, and that of the child as well. So after waiting as long as he dared, the doctor induced labor, and on October 15th a baby girl was born, two months premature; ten minutes later, still another baby girl was born. ("What have we here!" exclaimed the doctor, astonished.)

The twin babies were born in a brownstone house on East Eighty-ninth Street. But when Dr. Chapin was summoned hastily to examine them, he predicted, with quiet resignation, that the littlest one was too small and too weak to survive. However, he was optimistic about the older twin. "This one," he said, "will live."

So there it was, except that the frantic father couldn't accept the verdict, and in a state of great excitement bullied and galvanized the two doctors—Dr. Brodhead, the obstetrician, and Dr. Chapin, the pediatrician—until a feverish battle got under way. A bottle or a wet nurse? All day they argued, with Dr. Brodhead favoring the wet nurse, and finally one was found. Meanwhile the furnace was stoked to heat the room to 98 degrees, the babies bathed in oil and wrapped in cotton wool, and the entire house plunged into a crisis (she's *got* to live!) atmosphere, so unreasonable, so overwrought, so adamant, so strenuous, that in the midst of it even that tiniest one clung tenaciously (and exuberantly) to life. And at the end of a week, to the surprise of almost everyone, it became apparent that they would both survive.

At first Louise was too ill to fully understand what had happened. But when she realized that she had twin daughters, she secretly equated the two experiences. In her view the birth of twins was a benign and most fitting consolation for the loss and bereavement following the earthquake.

When it was certain both babies would live, they were given names. The older was called Katharine Hun, for an ancestor of his who had settled in Albany; the younger was named Anne Marie, for his mother, Anna Maria Homer, who had died the year before. And for the parents there is something beneficent about twins—a certain miracle feeling they have when they look at them and think: Can this be true?

The press seized on the event with enthusiasm, soon dubbing

the babies "the famous Homer twins." Many of the opera stars came to call on them (Schumann-Heink jokingly told reporters she was going to "adopt" them), and for a while they were a kind of seven-day wonder. But many in the opera world didn't share this view, for it was feared that the birth of twins might have damaged, or in some way altered, the contralto voice. Among musicians they were regarded as a serious hazard, and many thought the maternal risk a great pity. At this time the public was constantly beset with rumors that some singer had "lost his voice." In a sense a voice belonged to the public, and the fact that a certain familiar contralto might never again be heard in its full estate, in the songs and arias assigned to Amneris and Ortrud and Azucena, was a matter of real concern.

It was decided that Louise would return to the Metropolitan on December 18, 1907, as Ortrud in *Lohengrin*. But the doctor was cautious, and most of the preparation had to be done at home, which turned the brownstone house on Eighty-ninth Street into a lively tangle of the domestic and the operatic. Alfred Hertz, the conductor, came to rehearse, and Emma Eames, who was to sing Elsa, and Otto Goritz, to run through his scenes as Count Frederick of Telramund. Meanwhile the governess went back and forth, taking the little boy to the park and the oldest girl to school. The accompanist came every day, and the costumer many times, for the old Ortrud costumes, lost in the earthquake, were to be replaced with new ones, the most elaborate a rich red velvet and heavy white silk, embroidered with mother-of-pearl medallions. The doctor came to check on the infants, and then Louise would consult with him and record in her notebooks the number of ounces gained and any change in the regime, and return, radiant and relieved, to continue the rehearsing. Those who came—costumers, conductors, accompanists, nurses, singers, friends—may not have found the elegance usually associated with an opera star. But in spite of the confusion they found warmth, friendliness, vitality, even a certain underlying serenity, and at the heart of it that quality she had, a realness and a radiance that was in its essence a distillation of many things.

When she finally took her place behind the footlights, a regal

". . . many thought the maternal risk a great pity." Katharine is on the right, Anne on the left.

queen beside the River Scheldt, there was a certain unease in the opera house, for all those rumors about the "lost" contralto voice were now to be put to the test. And so the mood at the start of the *Lohengrin* was apprehensive, and during the entire first act there was no confirmation either way, for she hardly sang at all. To the audience her appearance was reassuring, the beauty still luminous, as touching as before. She looks the same, they said, but can she still sing? There was speculation during the intermission, and some anxiety. But finally the curtain rose on the scene with Frederick on the steps of the cathedral, and then with Elsa on her balcony, and at last there was the spine-chilling outburst: "Entweihte Götter!"—the golden notes soaring at will, shivering upward like flames, vibrant with emotion, the great pealing tones that many had feared would be lost forever. At that the whole opera house burst into a storm of applause, a crescendo of relief, hoarse cries of "Brava!" an ovation that went on and on and on. And perhaps it was absurd, but singing is very mysterious, and who can ever know?

After the *Lohengrin* she started rehearsals for a performance of *Tristan und Isolde* which would be the Metropolitan debut of the great Viennese conductor Gustav Mahler. And this was an absorbing experience, for the new conductor made of Wagner's music something to lift the heart, a vision, an orchestral beauty sublime in its connotations.

Mahler was a very intense musician, somewhat melancholy in appearance, with rimless pince-nez, wavy dark hair and a sensitive, vulnerable face. The critics found his interpretation of Wagner's masterpiece "inspiring," and they gave their production of *Tristan* five times at the Metropolitan that season.

They also took it to Philadelphia for a performance on January 28th, and that could be a trial, those shuttle trips in the middle of winter, when the children might so easily be catching cold or coming down with something. But usually she would make a tour of inspection before she left, after the practicing but before the train, hurrying through the halls on the wings of the music, to make sure that all was well at home. And this time she found the little boy in the kitchen, dressed for his outing in the park.

He was sitting on a chair, waiting for his nurse, which for a five-year-old seemed rather subdued. And she thought he looked uncomfortable in the leggings, the heavy coat, the cap with ear-laps, so hot and flushed that with foreboding she felt his cheeks, then removed the cap and ran her fingers through his hair. "Why this child has a fever!" she exclaimed angrily. And the nurse, that indispensable enemy, replied with self-righteous smugness, "You know you always say they must have their afternoon of play in the park."

The kitchen was below street level, facing a courtyard, and had only an inconclusive view of the cold gray January sky. But the nurse was dressed as usual for her outing, in the big plumed hat, the veil, the fur, the long skirts sweeping the ground, the dark gloves. And now she had a strategic advantage, for in an hour a special car would leave the Pennsylvania Station, with Olive Fremstad, their Isolde, Heinrich Knote, their Tristan, Van Rooy, who would sing Kurvenal, and of course the conductor, Gustav Mahler. If there was to be a performance of *Tristan* tonight Brangäne would have to be on hand, as well. So now Louise could linger only briefly in the kitchen, to remove tenderly the child's heavy coat and say urgently to the nurse, "He must be put to bed at once, and be sure to call the doctor."

Often, during the winter, the children had these colds and fevers, and there were others at home to care for them. Nevertheless, it was distracting, a familiar distress when she had to leave at such times, and there was a residue of nagging worry all during the engagement in Philadelphia, and afterward a moment of light and airy relief when very late that night she could make another inspection and find the little boy lustily asleep, and not really sick at all. And all this made a kind of frame about their performance of *Tristan*, which had been illuminated this year by the great Viennese conductor Gustav Mahler.

Conried had also added the Russian baritone Feodor Chaliapin to his rolls. Chaliapin was a wonderful basso, said to be "of marvelous stature," and he made his debut on November 20th in *Mefistofele*. But in spite of these additions to his rolls, Heinrich Conried was losing ground to the Manhattan Opera House.

Increasingly the "opera war" was cutting into the Metropolitan's patronage and profits, and in part this was because Oscar Hammerstein was offering the public, this season, such a sparkling and original repertoire. *Thaïs, Louise, Les Contes d'Hoffmann, Pelléas et Mélisande*—these were some of the striking new productions at the Manhattan Opera House, and often they overshadowed the more familiar presentations at the Metropolitan.

To counter the imagination and vitality of Hammerstein's repertoire, Conried had the stars, especially a galaxy of sopranos, and the critics sometimes complained that he allowed these brilliant singers to all but "run the show." This frenetic custom of Conried's may have derived, in part, from inexperience and a certain deep-seated sense of insecurity, for he allowed himself to become involved, as no other manager had, in the intrigues and rivalries at the opera house. He didn't have the necessary aloofness or authority, and when he was planning the schedule of roles and repertoire for the coming weeks he would often have on hand, as willing accomplices, several of the leading sopranos in his company. Nordica, Eames, Fremstad, Sembrich, Farrar—they were all authentic stars, each with a devoted following. And while the schedule was being arranged they would sit about the manager's desk stating preferences and opinions in an atmosphere that could become quite animated. Usually each singer would have a partisan along, to help with the negotiations—a mother, a husband, perhaps a manager, and sometimes a pet dog as well (Nordica favored poodles; Eames, dachshunds). These were vibrant personalities, all with a certain elegance, and in the manager's office there would be a fine array of feathered hats, furs and jewels to add a pretty flair to the proceedings, while Conried, striving to placate or please each one, arranged his schedule of roles and repertoire for the weeks ahead.

Meanwhile Oscar Hammerstein, with seemingly boundless vitality, was regaling New York with a wonderful array of novelties. And Conried, beset by his rival's brilliant tactics, was losing prestige and a great deal of money. The Metropolitan was now heavily in debt, and the directors were so unhappy with the situation that they were beginning to question the whole system of "renting out" the opera house. Recently Otto Kahn, a banker and great devotee of opera, had been making trips abroad to study the methods and management of opera there. And gradually there was beginning to evolve a new philosophy to guide the destinies of the Metropolitan. Originally, in 1883, the opera house had been built as a showcase for the elite. In those days, leaders of society had been most concerned with the unique status of their boxes in the Golden Horseshoe, while the performances had been left up to the experience and judgment of whatever manager happened to be in charge at the time. But now there was to be a more fundamental aim, with the Metropolitan becoming an entity in its own right, a cultural asset to the community and a more serious house of opera.

In February the directors issued what they called an "historic bulletin," announcing the formation of a *Metropolitan Opera Company*. The new company would be under the control of a Board of Directors, and in the bulletin it was noted that "the traditional system of having the manager share in the profits will be abolished. The manager will have a fixed salary and neither he nor any employee will have any financial interest in the affairs of the company." Conried's contract was bought back at a sum said to be seventy thousand dollars. And on February 11, 1908, Heinrich Conried announced that, because of the sciatica that had been troubling him all year, he would retire at the end of the season.[9]

In an aura of some secrecy, Otto Kahn and others had been negotiating with Signor Giulio Gatti-Casazza, the manager of La Scala in Milan. Meanwhile rumors that the Metropolitan might have a manager from abroad were stirring up a good deal of alarm. Opera-goers feared the intrusion of a foreigner, and many of the singers were opposed to what they called "the Italian method," procedures which they defined as a generally disordered atmosphere with haphazard scheduling, last-minute rehearsals and other unhappy practices to make the singers' work more difficult.

The directors were aware of this cloud of apprehension and moved with caution, devising finally an ingenious compromise arrangement. In the spring it was announced that the Metropolitan would have, next year, a "joint-management" with Signor Gatti-Casazza of La Scala as "general manager" and the popular tenor Andreas Dippel as "administrative manager." It was tactfully pointed out that "At Mr. Gatti's side there will be Herr Dippel, long known and liked by the New York public as a sterling artist of remarkable musical ability." During the negotiations the manager from La Scala had included, as a condition, that he must be allowed to bring his own conductor to New York. So in the same bulletin it was announced that for the coming season "Gustav Mahler and Arturo Toscanini have been engaged as joint musical directors."

In all this a genuine effort had been made to balance the unknown with the familiar, and make the transition more acceptable to the public and the artists. But backstage at the opera house alarm was not forestalled. Especially among the sopranos, who had been so comfortably in command during Conried's regime, there were gloomy predictions. In Italian opera houses, they said, there was no efficiency and no system; performers were ordered about at will, health was undermined and, most ominous of all, the slipshod "Italian method" was "ruinous" to the voice. Therefore, with all this to look forward to, they began at once pinning their hopes for the future on their old friend and compatriot Andreas Dippel.

In May, Signor Gatti-Casazza came to New York to look over his new opera house and plan the coming season. Herr Dippel had been making halfhearted attempts at arranging some contracts, but everything was up in the air, and there was apprehension regarding the new manager. No one knew what to expect, or even how to employ his curious double name. Did you say Signor Gatti? Or Signor Casazza? Or both at once? And what was going to happen now? At the opera house the atmosphere was one of confusion, with many decisions pending, when the manager from La Scala came to New York and with an air of quiet authority took command.

As usual Louise and Sidney went together for this interview, and found a manager not at all like the one they had had before. In appearance Gatti-Casazza was of medium height, with close-clipped beard and dark, rather melancholy eyes. He had been only a few days in New York, and was in an unfamiliar office in a vaguely hostile and quite formidable opera house, but he had the air of a man who knew his business, exactly what he wanted and where he stood.

He said very little during the interview, his attitude one of courteous reserve, but he seemed to know all about her voice, her roles and her position with the company. She had already been negotiating with Herr Dippel, who had been reluctant to agree to certain concessions. But Signor Gatti-Casazza, with a wave of his hand, a gesture of most courteous acquiescence, put an end to all the quibbling and granted her every wish, then signed the contract with a certain quiet flourish.

Chapter XIX

Five years before, in 1903, when Louise had sung the opening night of the season at the Metropolitan, with a new manager and a new regime, the occasion had been made more historic because of the new decor—the lustrous gold and crimson revealed for the first time. Now, in 1908, there was a similar situation, for this year, again, she would sing the opening night of the season with a new manager, a new regime and many alterations in the opera house. Perhaps they weren't as visible as the gilt and sparkle had been, but they were just as fundamental, for under Gatti's direction improvements had been made in the structure and efficiency of the stage, the orchestra pit and the general design.

The work had been going on all summer, and in the main it had been devised to enhance what the new manager viewed as "the total effect" of opera. Gatti wanted a more dramatic frame for the music and the golden voices, more color, illusion, vividness, grandeur. And this was, in essence, a new concept at the Metropolitan. Maurice Grau, with his belief in the "star system," had been inclined to slight the chorus and orchestra, while Conried had at times contemplated expansion without ever being able to achieve it. But Giulio Gatti-Casazza, working with his companion creator, Arturo Toscanini, included in his overall design many interacting factors—lighting, scenery, costumes,

Giulio Gatti-Casazza, who came to the Metropolitan in 1908 and, "with an air of quiet authority, took command." (Courtesy *Opera News*)

chorus, orchestra, soloists—the whole sweeping panorama of grand opera.

Many of the changes were structural, with new machinery behind, under and above the stage, to allow for more varied theatrical effects, and machinery installed under the orchestra pit, so the entire orchestra could be raised and lowered. New elevators were built to the galleries, and the orchestra pit had been made much larger so the orchestra could be expanded. In addition to all this, new costumes had been created for the choruses, and a great deal of most evocative new scenery had been designed. But though he favored the "total experience" of music drama, Gatti was practical and realistic in the changes he made. He understood the mechanics of opera and initiated at the Metropolitan a double orchestra to lighten the burden of rehearsals for the musicians, and two entirely separate choruses —one for German opera, and another for French and Italian.

Meanwhile rumors had been circulating about the sweeping changes at the opera house, and this particular "opening night at the Metropolitan," on November 16, 1908, had taken on the aura of an historic event. The opera was to be Verdi's *Aida*, with Arturo Toscanini conducting, Caruso as Radames, Scotti as Amonasro, Homer as Amneris and a new soprano, Emmy Destinn, in the title role.

Before the start of rehearsals, Louise had a brief session alone with Toscanini and ran through her role for him, with piano accompaniment, in one of the smaller salons. This was a deceptively serene occasion, for he seemed quite satisfied, and asked only for different tempi here and there, and one or two small changes. The new conductor from La Scala was a rather small man, quick-moving, intense, with a sweeping moustache and dramatic dark eyes; he listened intently while she sang, and afterward spoke quietly of the beauty of her voice. But this benign first impression was misleading, for once they had started rehearsals his demands were many and imperious. On the podium, though he was of slight build and stature Toscanini seemed to tower above his artists, who could be made to feel, at times, impaled on a pin in the midst of the surging musical arena, transfixed by that piercing gaze.

Arturo Toscanini was passionately committed to what he called the "composer's intentions." Unlike many conductors, he would allow no slightest liberty with the score—no interpolated grace notes or long, sustained high tones, to thrill the galleries and indulge the singer. Once, when he was a very young man, he'd traveled hundreds of miles to ask Giuseppe Verdi about a single "ritardo" that had become an intolerable obsession. So in a sense he was a beleaguered intermediary between the composer and his music, for once a concept had been burned into his brain he must transfer it to an unwieldy canvas, a diversified company of singers and musicians, all with human failings. And since he had no use for compromise, this was a discipline that required a devastating concentration, a tension, a sometimes violent, slashing, relentless rehearsal session that was often, for the singers, a nightmare.

But Toscanini was also an intermediary between the artist and his art. With his compelling insight he could discover new gifts in his singers and musicians, unsuspected powers, hidden resources. Under his guidance they might awake from the night-

As Amneris in *Aida* at Toscanini's debut performance.

mare astonished, invigorated, inspired, with an altogether new vision of this role they were going to sing. And it was that way with the Amneris. Louise had sung the part first at Angers, and under many conductors since. But now she was learning all over again this many-textured role. Torn apart, for a while, by the new conductor, it was all coming back together again, into a more persuasive whole.

Every seat in the great hall was taken for their opening performance on November 16th. In his review the next day Richard Aldrich of the *Times* noted, especially, the "gorgeous scenic effects" and the "highly colored and vivid" orchestral performance. "The spirit that pervaded it was clearly instilled by the new conductor," he wrote. "He is a strenuous force, a domineering power, a man of potent authority, a musician of infinite resource." There was eloquent praise for the new soprano, Emmy Destinn, a singer with a hauntingly beautiful voice, as well as rare musical intelligence. And of her Amneris the critics wrote that "Louise Homer was more than brilliant," "looked the daughter of a thousand kings," "gave the greatest singing performance of her career" and "made the role of Amneris a glory."

The new manager, Gatti-Casazza, was reserved, aloof, an im
presario who kept his own counsel. But Louise felt more at home
with his regime than she had under Conried's somewhat flamboy
ant rule. The routine might include a certain formality and re
straint, but it was also more predictable. Conried had been
capricious manager, laboring under a pressing weight of enter
prises and rivalries. . . . But Gatti was calm, consistent and
perhaps most important, innately musical, an artist in his thinking

However, not everyone felt as she did, and some in the com
pany were already in revolt. Backstage, trouble was brewing, an
chief among the rebels were the sopranos, who had been s
favored by Conried, so free to choose what and when they woul
sing. Gatti had a certain sphinxlike quality, a way of going calml
about his business. Never did he allow a singer in his office whe
he was planning the roles and repertoire, and if there was a con
troversy he would listen courteously, then, as a rule, continue a
before.

He was somewhat impassive, but firmly in control. And thi
disturbed the singers who had been counting on the co-manage
Andreas Dippel, to protect their interests. Dippel was himself
singer, an old and valued friend, and even more pliable tha
Conried. But early in the season, they began to hear rumors, an
what they heard was that the Board of Directors had already of
fered the manager from La Scala a three-year contract—one tha
would give him full authority and reduce Andreas Dippel to
lesser status.

This was a prospect they couldn't accept, and just ten day
after the brilliant opening performance of *Aida*, several of th
singers wrote a formal letter addressed "To The Board of Di
rectors of the Metropolitan Opera Company"—a document c
concern and protest which was signed by five of the leading star
in the company: Geraldine Farrar, Marcella Sembrich, Emm
Eames, Enrico Caruso and Antonio Scotti.

In the letter they wrote that they had "heard of a movemen
to grant Messrs. Gatti and Toscanini a contract of three years
duration" and wanted to be assured "that Mr. Dippel would b
granted the same privileges under contract." "Our confidence i
the managerial and artistic capabilities of Mr. Dippel," the

wrote, "gives us sufficient reason to associate ourselves firmly with his ideas."

This letter caused a sensation in musical circles, for though it was sent privately, the directors released both the letter and their reply to the press—a maneuver that incensed the singers, for they hadn't meant to advertise the dissension openly. But by airing the protest the directors underscored their views in the matter. In their reply they stated firmly that it was impossible "to administer an organization like the Metropolitan under two heads," and therefore Mr. Dippel's functions "must be subordinate to those of the general manager, Mr. Gatti-Casazza, who is the supreme executive head of the organization."

It was generally believed that the two men involved, Caruso and Scotti, had become somewhat reluctant signers by means of feminine persuasion. Scotti was more than a little in love with Geraldine Farrar, and it wasn't in the nature of such gallant gentlemen to refuse support for the beautiful sopranos. Meanwhile the entire upheaval was neutralized since Gatti himself took absolutely no notice of it. Throughout the controversy he remained courteous to the singers, issued no statements to the press and went methodically on his way. This tended to minimize the dissension, and before long some of the letter writers had second thoughts. On December 11th Farrar, Scotti and Caruso issued a statement to the press explaining that their letter had not been suggested by Andreas Dippel and they had intended no "animosity" towards Mssrs. Gatti and Toscanini. And a little later, when Marcella Sembrich announced her retirement from the Metropolitan, she expressed in an interview a certain regret at her part in the proceedings, making clear that her retirement, planned long before, was in no way connected with the controversy.

On February 6, 1909, an unprecedented Farewell Performance was given to mark Marcella Sembrich's departure from the stage. The beloved coloratura had made her debut with the Metropolitan the year it opened, and her most ardent adherents in New York turned out to "pack the house to suffocation" and pay tribute. Scenes from several of Sembrich's operas were given, and at the end, while Gustav Mahler conducted the march from

Figaro, Madame Sembrich entered on the arm of Signor Gatti-Casazza, followed by the leading members of the company, and there was a ceremony, gifts and speeches, ending with "a final shower of rose petals that covered all the guests on the stage."

A few days later Sembrich was again honored, at a banquet at the Astor Hotel. And this time her colleagues devised a bit of a caper that "caused delighted comment for days afterwards, and quite confounded the newspaper reporters." Louise had a part in the entrancing little ruse, which began with a hasty rehearsal before the dinner. Sembrich had become noted for the great number of roles in her repertoire, and those conspiring so artfully included Walter Damrosch, Frank Damrosch, Geraldine Farrar, Caruso, Scotti, Homer, Dippel and de Gogorza. But they were secretive about their project until, in the middle of the dinner, with Marcella Sembrich at the head table, her countryman Paderewski at her right and almost all the great of the musical world in the big banquet hall, a chord was struck in an anteroom. Then, casually, to the tune of *The Merry Widow Waltz*, they began to sing the titles of the operas in the form of a round, beginning with "*Rigoletto, Puritani, Huguenots*," all the familiar voices responding as if by chance from different parts of the room. "As the song went on amazement grew," wrote Henry Krehbiel. "The last motif was sung in harmony by Farrar, Homer, Dippel and de Gogorza, and at the end there was an uproarious demand for more." So then they began again, this time with "*Il Barbiere, La Lucia, La Bohème* . . ." and to the astonished diners it seemed an impromptu and most exhilarating recital, a mysterious bit of high jinks that was the talk of the town for days.

Marcella Sembrich had been planning for some time to retire, but for Emma Eames the end of her career was directly related to the new management at the opera house. "To continue at the Metropolitan under the Italian regime," Eames would write later, "would have been impossible for one with my artistic ideals." [10] The beautiful soprano had made her Metropolitan debut as Juliette in 1891, and ever since had had a most devoted following. But she was a very sensitive artist, and now could not be reconciled to what she considered "the lack of a logical system" at the opera house. So only a week after the Sembrich farewell, on February 15, 1909, this very great artist, only forty-two years old, retired from the stage forever after a performance of *Tosca*, the scene at the end most affecting, when she stood amid offerings of flowers, her ardent adorers in tears, and told them, with emotion and quiet dignity, "In the eighteen years that I have sung here, I have endeavored to give you my best. My love I leave with you. Good-bye!"

There are always regrets when a beloved singer leaves the stage, and this year at the Metropolitan there was the sense of an ending as well as a beginning. Farewells were said to several beautiful voices (Nordica, too, would soon retire, somewhat at odds with the management). But meanwhile there was Toscanini, weaving his spell, and for Louise his coming had been an unsuspected boon, for he seemed to have a special affinity for the quality of her voice, and wanted her, whenever possible, in everything he did. This included the *Götterdämmerung*, in which she sang the part of Waltraute. That the new conductor should choose to do this opera surprised the critics, since there were already two conductors for German opera at the Metropolitan, Mahler and Hertz. But at La Scala the *Götterdämmerung* had been a cornerstone of Toscanini's repertoire. He also wanted her in his performance of Verdi's *Requiem Mass*, which was given first on February 21, 1909. The soloists were Destinn, Homer, Martin and Witherspoon, and their interpretation was so transcendant that they had to give their *Requiem* four times within a few weeks.

It may have been the *Requiem* that turned Toscanini's thoughts, that winter, to still another role for her—something in her voice when she sang the great religious music, in her pose, her face, her demeanor, a certain intuitive response that was profoundly moving. In any case, he evaluated the roles she was singing that season with the four different conductors—*Il Trovatore* and *Rigoletto* with Spetrino, *Tristan und Isolde* with Mahler, *Die Meistersinger*, *Die Walküre* and *Siegfried* with Hertz and, with Toscanini himself, *Aida* and *Götterdämmerung*. A great variety of dramatic roles, but not one that was fully in accord

with the singer's true nature. Then he consulted with Gatti and
they devised a plan, a vehicle to convey ideally the quality of her
art and provide for the artist the ultimate in fulfillment.

They told her of their decision one evening late in March
when she'd come to the opera house for a performance of *Siegfried*. A message was sent to her dressing room: Would she see
Signor Gatti in his office? And there the two friends, with somewhat the air of conspirators, outlined their plans. The sets, they
told her, would be created in Paris by the distinguished designer
Jacques Pacquereau, and painted by the French artist Paul
Chauvanne. No expense would be spared, everything possible
would be done to create an inspiring revival, next season, of
Gluck's *Orfeo e Euridice*.

They were rewarded for this bit of managerial plotting with a
look of ineffable astonishment. And afterward, down in that vast,
gloomy cellar under the opera house, she'd felt as though she
were walking on air. All about were the coiled ropes and huge
spider webs she'd always dreaded, but when she'd climbed into
Erda's rickety dumbwaiter, and was waiting, through those
treacherous moments, to make her perilous ascent to earth, she'd
found herself actually in the clouds. How had they known that
Orfeo was the one role she had always wanted to sing?

Chapter XX

"Mon coeur s'ouvre à ta voix"—Dalila was wooing Samson and the round voluptuous tones traveled through the rooms of the Cape Cod house and out to the nursery where the twins were having their lunch. Miss Ames was feeding them from china hot plates, and today she was vaguely irritated. She didn't quite know the source of her irritation, which made it worse, but it had something to do with status.

As the voice rose higher the notes seemed to take flight. They peeled off by themselves and flooded the room with a brilliance that was dark gold in texture and marvelously seductive. This aria had become a showpiece for the singer, almost her signature. No audience at a Homer concert was entirely satisfied until, at least as encore, she had sung "Mon Coeur." And now, as the dramatic climax drew near and the yearning tones soared higher and higher, one of the twins pushed away the spoon and regurgitated a mouthful of peas. The slimy green stuff ran down her chin onto her bib and Miss Ames stood up. Her irritation had deepened and she had to take some action, though it wasn't the singing, really. It was something else—an attitude. In this household she felt dispossessed. Even when the mother was away there was an atmosphere of waiting, of incompleteness. And when she was home her presence was everywhere.

Miss Ames didn't know that she was the victim of an ambiv-

alence that had never been resolved. But she felt shorn of the
proper degree of power. As a rule the nurse in a household had
her own small area of authority, a minor dictatorship, apart from
the kitchen and the downstairs, a comfortable niche where she
could hold sway. And she'd thought, when she came to work for
an opera singer, that this arrangement would be assured.

But it hadn't worked out that way, and increasingly she felt
deprived—even more so because she had no obvious complaint.
Her employer was reasonable most of the time, but she never
let go the reins. She was always too much there, so that no matter how busy and harassed you were, you felt superfluous. It was
a subtle distinction that Miss Ames didn't altogether understand,
but now she stood up, put the twins back in their cribs and
walked through the halls to the parlor. She knew the singer was
getting ready for a concert tour and had a program to prepare,
and in a vague way this increased her determination as she
rapped sharply on the door and heard a rather surprised "Come
in."

The surprise in the voice made her hesitate, but only for a
moment. Then she opened the door and saw that the children's
mother was standing beside the piano, with one hand on the
keys, her face a little flushed, her hair in some disarray. She was
wearing a plain cotton skirt that fitted nicely over the hips and
flared about the ankles, and a shirtwaist of pink china silk that
complimented the silky texture of the most beautiful complexion
Miss Ames had ever seen.

A concert audience might have been captivated at that moment, for the dark gray eyes were still brilliant from the emotion
of the song, and tucked into the lively brown hair was a tea rose
that had been plucked from the breakfast table that morning.
"I'm sorry to disturb you," the nurse said flatly, "but Anne threw
up her lunch." Then she stood stolidly in the doorway watching
the radiance fade away.

To plummet so swiftly is like riding a roller coaster higher
and still higher, then dropping suddenly, long before you're
ready. You can become a little dizzy from the downward plunge,
and now she had to adjust her mood to this new dilemma, and
leave her music and hurry through the halls to the nursery. Any

illness in the family distracted her, and there'd been a time like this long ago, when she'd been seven years old and had run out into the hall to tell her father that she was learning to play the piano. "Papa, Allie is teaching me to play the piano!" She'd been almost bursting with excitement, but he hadn't answered. Fleetingly his hand had touched the top of her head, but he'd said nothing, just climbed the stairs, holding to the rail, his head bent so that his beard seemed to lie heavy on his chest. And something in his face had silenced and frightened her.

Now, when she discovered the twins bouncing around in their cribs, looking reassuringly healthy, the relief was so dazzling that she forgot there'd been any interruption, and played with them and jiggled them on her knee, and the mingled shouts of laughter floated out onto the dunes and attracted others in the family. The little boy came in, with a pail of sand, and the older girl, with her tennis racquet, and soon they were all playing with the babies, right in the middle of their interrupted lunch. This was a development Miss Ames hadn't foreseen, though she realized, too late, that she should have, for everything was higglety-pigglety in this household. There was no discipline, no orderly procedure, no proper situation for a nurse. And yet a nurse was indispensable, and so you had an ambivalence against which the singer had no adequate defense. Now, in the twins' nursery, Dalila's impassioned appeal had vanished utterly, wafted far out over the gray expanse of ocean. But a shadow still remained from the sudden turmoil, a wisp of memory, for what had frightened her even more than the waxen color of her father's face was something no one else seemed to see—a going-away look, almost a peaceful look.

She was absorbed this summer in the study of *Orfeo e Euridice*, which made her, perhaps, more vulnerable. This was for her a time of intense creativity. Day and night she was living the part, and often she would walk for miles along the shore, caught up in those luminous scenes. But sometimes she would be distracted, and as she walked the long stretches of sand she would instead discover Maggie Johns, and hear the lilt of that long-ago voice telling her who she was: 'What a pretty baby!" "What a happy little girl!" and experience a certain adventurous feeling they used to have, when they would make a game of fitting her mother's new Sunday gown to the dress form, all the hooks and eyes, the velvet ribbons, the deep blues and greens, and then step back to admire their creation, and all the while, in the sewing room, a certain easy mood, a lightness. Or she might be distracted by intervals of remembered anxiety, a stern sadness in the home, the muted Sabbath, all suffering a punishment for sin, which surely couldn't be; or find herself bemused by his too eloquent defense of agnosticism, the plainly rational views of one who didn't know, though the songs he would compose for her seemed to say otherwise, which wasn't easy to reconcile; and sometimes she would recall her father's voice, and hear again those great descending arpeggios, the marvelous tones dropping down, down, down, so dark, so powerful and melodious.

In Craigville, when it rained, water dripped from the eaves and gutters, a gray mist hung over the horizon and time seemed to stretch endlessly for those who were vacationing. The older children said, "What will we do?" the visiting relatives sat about on the porch and before she could shut herself away in the parlor the singer must make plans. A tea party for the oldest daughter, who was thirteen, an awkward, restless age; a ride in a hired carriage for her mother. She must consult with the cook and order meals for a varied household. Only then could she go to the parlor, shut the door and open the score of *Orfeo e Euridice*.

"Chiamo il mio ben cosi." She rehearsed with the rain washing against the windows, singing the phrase thoughtfully, not in full voice, but with a brooding eloquence. In the melancholy tones and the accents of the music there seemed to be a quiet radiance. For such a sorrowful lament it was a surprising association and she wondered if it could be a clue. Had Orpheus, even in bereavement, had a radiant fidelity?

Already she had discovered that one of the miracles of this opera lay in the stark range of emotions. Although it was a short music drama, with a small cast and a rather slight libretto, the composer, Christoph Gluck, had found a way of encompassing the heights and depths of human experience. Side by side he had arrayed the ugly and the sublime—the terrors of the underworld, the "pure light" of ineffable bliss. With the genius of poetry and economy, he had pitted the most deadly and fearsome horrors against the radiant power of love, and then transfixed his listeners with music so inspired that they were caught up irresistibly in the eternal conflict.

But though she was absorbed in the role, she couldn't confine herself to the *Orfeo*, for she had other commitments this summer. In the fall there would, of course, be a concert tour. And perhaps the most pressing of the obligations was a recital they were going to give together at the Lyceum Theatre in New York —a performance devoted entirely to his songs. The concert would be a matinee for the benefit of the MacDowell Club, many critics would be there, many friends and musicians, and Sidney had become so apprehensive about the venture that he often wished he could banish the entire project and send it sailing, like the driftwood on the beach, far out to sea.

It was his nature to shrink from such ordeals, and her role to sustain him. Together they worked, day after day, exploring the dynamics of each song, and for him this collaboration was indispensable. But it wasn't easy work, for a composer can have moments of acute self-doubt. And when they had had enough she would change to her taffeta bathing suit, and out on the sands they would find a pretty scene, the ladies with their parasols, the little girls with their stiff, pastel hair ribbons, the fleecy clouds, the dark blue sea. Then, once again, she would find herself engaged in a poignant debate in the crystal quiet of the Greek hills.

She carried the score with her when she went on tour, and studied it every day when they'd returned to New York. But meanwhile there was his concert on November 2nd. And he had become so uneasy about playing the accompaniments that finally he arranged an ingenious backup plan, with Richard Hageman, an assistant conductor at the Metropolitan, at his elbow, to turn the pages and take over the accompaniments if need be. For her part, she must compensate for his intense shyness by providing the warmth, the poise, the spontaneity that is the essence of a solo concert. And when finally she could persuade him to come forward and take a bow, she would be touchingly content.

The reviews the next day were reassuring. In the *Press*, Max

Smith wrote that "Homer is at his best, it seems to us, in words that ask for the simplest treatment—the tender love of a mother, the confiding, ingenuous devotion of a child for its parents, . . ." while Richard Aldrich wrote in the *Times* that "he has gained some of his strongest effects in the employment of a free declamatory style, united to an accompaniment whose characteristic expressiveness and pregnant harmonies, often dissonant and unconventional, are skillfully employed to heighten the emotional coloring. Such verses as Browning's *Prospice* and *A Woman's Last Word* he treats in a vividly effective manner, and he has done little that is more seizing than his setting of Tennyson's *Thy Voice Is Heard*." This last song had a breathless quality that she conveyed with startling effect, for he had devised it so that the singer must plunge at once into tempestuous emotion, keyed to the rolling drums and the confusion of battle, with, as a counterpoint to the fiery drama, an underlying tenderness, a mood of quiet reflection, the two themes mounting irresistibly to a most moving resolution.

Only a few days after the recital she would have what seemed a marathon of opera openings. The first was to be in Boston, on November 8, 1909, where she would sing *La Gioconda* with Lillian Nordica; then, the next night, November 9th, she would sing *Aida* in Philadelphia, with Gadski and Caruso, and on November 15th open the New York season at the Metropolitan with another *Gioconda*, this time with Emmy Destinn and Caruso—and all this must take place in the midst of a marathon of private rehearsals with Arturo Toscanini, for now, day after day, and step by step, they were creating, with the greatest finesse and the most delicate precision, the *Orfeo e Euridice*.

She hadn't known about the Philadelphia opening when she agreed to sing in Boston, but she would have wanted to in any case, for this was the dedication of a new opera company, and a beautiful new theater. After all these years of visiting companies coming to perform at the old Mechanics Hall, Boston was finally to have an opera company of its own, and a Boston Opera House. The new theater had been dedicated the year before, on November 30, 1908, when, in an impressive ceremony, "Mr. Eben Jordan, president of the Boston Opera Company, in the presence of numerous dignitaries, including Governor Guild, laid a Deer Island granite cornerstone and smoothed it over with a silver trowel." It was also noted that "in the cornerstone were phonograph records by Caruso, Homer, Farrar, Alice Neilson and others, and documents from many Boston musical societies." Henry Russell was director of the new opera company, and he had wanted two American singers who had begun their musical studies in Boston—Lillian Nordica and Louise Homer—to sing at his opening performance.

For a city that was usually somewhat reserved, this was a festive occasion. Almost all the elite were there from the Beacon Hill area, not with the tiaras and jewels of a San Francisco audience, but with the rustle of dark silks and quiet assurance. The mood was brilliantly responsive, and at the end of the opera, when the chandeliers flashed on to reveal the pristine elegance of the new opera house, there was such an endless parade of flowers that one reviewer reported afterward that "the flunkeys would not suffice, and the supernumeraries brought bouquets and baskets and armloads, until the stage was banked with them."

For a brief time, in the midst of this fragrant bower, the soprano and the contralto joined hands—Gioconda conveniently recovered from her tragic suicide, Laura returned from her mad flight with Enzo. It should have been a time to linger and bask in the warmth of old friends and a new opera house, but, like Cinderella, she must escape into the night at the appointed hour and board the train for Philadelphia, no matter how bright the lights, how endearing the festivities. And so the crowds, gathered outside to watch the celebrities come and go, saw an automobile at the stage door, with its motor running, a chauffeur alert at the wheel, police on horseback holding back the crowds, until finally the stage door opened and they caught just a glimpse, a tantalizing swirl of dark sealskin fur and lavender velvet, a diaphanous veil, a radiant smile—all too soon gone, yet worthwhile, too, in its way, like discovering, for an instant, a jewel in the dark snowy night.

She had the score of *Orfeo* with her on the train, and when she woke in the morning, to go directly to a hotel and prepare for *Aida* that night, it seemed a long time ago that she had arrived in just this way, in the cold gray of the South Street Station in Philadelphia, come from Arlington with such trepidation, after the broken engagement with John Calhoun, to pick up her life again at the Arch Street boardinghouse.

Toscanini conducted their opening performance of *La Gioconda* at the Metropolitan on November 15th. And he also undertook a new presentation of *Tristan und Isolde* in which she sang Brangäne. Once again she had to restudy a role she had been singing for many years, and afterward the critics found Toscanini's presentation "filled with emotional fervor," and "waves of turbulent orchestration that surged in inspired grandeur."

They gave a second performance of *Tristan* on December 8th, with Lillian Nordica as Isolde, and this would prove to be the great soprano's last appearance at the Metropolitan. But though some were leaving, there were many new singers at the opera house, and one, this season, was the Czech tenor Leo Slezak, with whom Louise sang *Il Trovatore*. Slezak made his Metropolitan debut as Otello, and was said to be so "gigantic" that "the audience fairly gasped when he made his entrance." He was also called a "splendid actor," "with a voice of fine power, used with discretion."

They would give their revival of Gluck's *Orfeo e Euridice* late in December, and almost every day she went to the opera house for private sessions with the Maestro. They worked in one of the smaller rehearsal rooms, and usually she would arrive early, with the score and the interpolations he planned to use—"Divinités du Styx" from Gluck's *Alceste*, a trio from the composer's *Paride e Elena*, a chorus from *Echo e Narcissa*. Many versions of the *Orfeo* had drifted down through the years, and these decisions were an important part of the conductor's role.

When she arrived for the study session she might walk up and down the room for a while, breathing deeply. Then, after removing the pins from her hat, and placing it, with her muff, on one of the chairs, she would strike a chord on the piano and sing an arpeggio, a routine exercise to limber up the vocal instrument, letting the voice start quietly, but with a depth, a patina of tone so original that it could have belonged to no other singer, and scaling upward, higher and still higher, releasing, at the top of the flight, a shower of sparks, then drifting slowly downward, sinking softly, but with a firm underpinning and a haunting tone. During this exercise she would remain standing, for she almost always stood when she sang—relaxed, absorbed, the harmonious planes of the face conveying a touching composure. She might then sing a second arpeggio, a half tone higher, another lilting spiral, another drifting shower of sparks. And perhaps at that moment Toscanini would enter, walking quickly, go directly to the piano, open the score, and at once there would settle over the rehearsal room an atmosphere of extraordinary dedication.

They were studying, with the greatest intensity, every phrase, every bar of music, every gesture, every change of mood—probing, testing, evaluating, with the tremulous precision of jewelers faceting a diamond. Writing with a blue pencil in a firm clear script, Toscanini would note in the score some of his directions: "Agitato"—"con passione"—"vibrato"; and frequently she would add reminders to herself: "con dolcezza"—"caressingly"—"keep intensity"—"great repose."

In part the fascination of this opera stemmed from the fact that it was the oldest in the repertoire. Before Gluck composed his *Orfeo*, music drama had been a stylized offering of spoken lines and trills, intended as a vehicle for the singers, with the libretto, the plot, of little consequence. But with the genius of inspiration, Christoph Gluck, writing in 1760, had created a work in which the drama unfolded through the music, and for the first time in opera the human situation was irresistibly involved. This was an unheard-of innovation, and to attain it he had transformed the rococo concoction of ballet, song and flowery episode that passed for opera in his day, and created a unified form in which the score was faithful to the text, the whole an integrated work of art. And he had done this with such luminous integrity that *Orfeo e Euridice* had become the forerunner of the whole tradition of opera.

The composer had used great subtlety to attain his ends, though for the most part it was the subtlety of inspired simplicity. In the opening scene, for instance, he had created, from those stricken cries of bereavement—"Euridice—Euridice—Euridice"—a revelation of the underlying intent of his opera. Imposed against the tranquil resignation of the chorus, with the shepherds and shep-

herdesses engaged in their plaintive laments, those anguished
cries had been made into a stark and most poignant confrontation, the third cry a dissonance, against a background of chords
of diminished intervals, a searing discord of unreconciled grief.

At home Louise worked with an accompanist. But meanwhile
she was singing many big roles this season, performances of
Ortrud, Brangäne, Amneris, Azucena, in Brooklyn and Philadelphia as well as New York. Every hour of time had to be carefully
rationed. And there was one day when she was rehearsing that
most beautiful aria of grief, the "Che Faro," just as the oldest
daughter returned from school and wanted to hang about, the
way a young one of fourteen sometimes does, looking a bit lonely
and forlorn. This was a familiar dilemma, but never an easy one.
Finally, not wanting to send her out of the room, she thought
of a way of combining the two, the mothering and the rehearsing,
and suggested, on impulse, "Why don't you pretend you are Euridice? Lie down on the floor as though you were dead, and I'll
sing my lament to you!" But though the young daughter, happy
to be a part of the drama, assumed at once a properly theatrical
pose, the plan was a dismal failure, for after only a few bars of
the mournful "Che Faro" the singer, overcome by emotion, burst
into tears and exclaimed to her accompanist, "I can't go on. She
looks too dead!" And indeed she did, there on the living room
floor, in her Peter Thompson uniform, her head cradled touchingly in one arm. The effect was too pitiful, and the child too un-
naturally still, for a singer who was trying to convey, in accents
of profound grief, the treacherous eloquence of Gluck's music.

They began their ensemble rehearsals in December, and then
Toscanini, with the orchestra at his command, could enforce his
most imperious demands. They hadn't always agreed about the
interpretations, and most especially she felt that she should give
full rein to the soaring note of lyric anguish in the "Che Faro."
But Toscanini wanted the phrase made shorter, in keeping with
what he considered "the composer's intentions." And at the first
ensemble rehearsal, when she tried to have her way, and let her
voice expand and float endlessly in that impassioned climax, the
conductor abruptly crashed the orchestra into silence, making,
with his expressive hands, an imperious gesture of command, and

leaving her all alone up there, to commune with the gilded sunburst. As he had intended, it was a too-conspicuous solitude, and
in later years Toscanini would gleefully recount this operatic
episode as proof that he had maintained, at all times, an iron
control over artists.

Meanwhile there was the costume, which she had always imagined as a flowing Grecian robe. But the color, the texture, the
design, all this would require imagination. And because the costume would be an integral part of the illusion, it was being created for her by the distinguished artist John Alexander.

Ever since that summer at Onteora Park, John Alexander had
been a valued friend, and now he would play a valuable part in
this role she was going to sing. But the costume he created was
not at all as she had imagined it, for instead of the flowing robes
he had designed a simple tunic, ivory-white in color, falling to
just below the knee. The lines of the tunic were natural and free,
the trimming a plain geometric border of gold, and interwoven
in gold, the suggestion of a girdle. To this he had added a short
cloak of dark gold velvet, with simple classic lines, a wreath of
deep blue leaves, sandals with gold thongs wrapped to the knee.
The design was imaginative, and also, in its way, dramatic, for
in this attire the Greek minstrel would have the subtle and powerful appeal of a most touching and unaffected simplicity.[11]

In December the scenery arrived from France, and Gatti, who
made all the arrangements, was more than satisfied. Nothing
quite like it had been seen on the New York stage before—the
atmosphere translucent, the flow of light and color dreamlike and
strangely moving. The scenery had been designed by Jacques
Pacquereau and painted by the famous artist Paul Chauvanne,
and Gatti called it "exquisite and full of poetry."

In the cast Johanna Gadski was singing the role of Euridice,
Bella Alten the part of Amor, and Alma Gluck, a lyric soprano
new to the Metropolitan, was to be the Happy Shade. Gluck had
a lovely voice, haunting, seductive, tender, a voice ideally suited
to the lyric bliss of the Elysian Fields, and by chance she brought
her six-year-old daughter, Marcia, with her to the dress rehearsal.
This impressionable child was so affected by the stark range of
emotion in *Orfeo e Euridice* that she would remember it always

As Orpheus in 1909, the one role she had always wanted to sing.

as a turning point in her life. Writing years later, as Marcia
Davenport, she would describe Toscanini "driving the demons
with his flailing right arm"; the dance of The Furies, "the rage,
hate, violence a seething boil of motion," and afterward the won-
drous beauty of the Elysian Fields "bathed in a silvery light" and
her mother "seated at a harp . . . a vision of comforting loveliness." She would come to believe that this dress rehearsal had
"colored" her "life" and her "mind"—Gluck's music, Toscanini's
"fanatical" involvement and the magic on the stage creating for
her a fateful experience.[12]

They gave their first performance on December 23, 1909.
Because the occasion was eventful, their old friends Jim and
Helen Paxton came to hear her and sit with Sidney in his box,
and her dressing room was full of flowers and telegrams and messages. But already there had begun a certain detachment, and
when she finally stood on the stage, in the tunic, the sandals, the
wreath of leaves, head bowed, in an attitude of profound despair,
she had become Orpheus.

This mystical experience had never happened to her before,
and it was so absorbing that there was almost no awareness of
the curtain rising, the great darkened auditorium and the audience already spellbound, caught up in the magic of the poetic
setting, the eloquence of the music, and moved by something in-
candescent in the poignant isolation, the pose and stillness of the
minstrel Orpheus.

Even the isolation of grief had become a somber reality—the
cypress grove bathed in a twilight calm, the torch beside Euridice's tomb reversed, symbolizing death, all about the shepherds
and shepherdesses moving quietly and, finally, a song of such
enduring fidelity that even the gods were moved, and miracu-
lously, within a luminous cloud, Amor, the god of love, appeared holding a golden lyre. In his song Orpheus had pleaded
with the powers of darkness that he would go himself to the
Underworld and there defy the "fiendish ghosts of the night" to
withstand the music of his lyre, and his desperate pleas had been
heard. Stirred to compassion by the beauty of the song, the gods
had sent Amor to tell him that he was to be the first to brave
the terrors of the Underworld.

But the terms of the reprieve were harsh, for if he should succeed, and, with the power of song, move to pity the Rulers of the Dead, toward Euridice he must feign a cold indifference. He must not look at her or give any sign of affection—just one tender glance and his love would be lost forever. This was the gods' decree.

With the coming of Amor the twilight gloom of the cypress grove had been transformed. Now there was everywhere a pearly light, and at the end, holding his golden lyre before him like a cross, Orpheus strode forth on his quest. Higher and higher he climbed the rocky hill, and this was an inspired moment at the Metropolitan. Toscanini was carried away, the orchestra crashed with eloquence, and as the curtain closed there was a sweeping torrent of applause. Afterward many in the audience were weeping; others were too moved to speak. Throughout the opera house there was an atmosphere of awed astonishment, as though something unforeseen had happened.

According to legend, trees would uproot themselves and rocks become loosened from their ledges so that they might follow the incomparable music of Orpheus, son of Apollo. And during the second act of *Orfeo* the audience is made as susceptible as the trees and rocks, for here the composer has devised a tingling tapestry of terror—the gloom of night, the pitiless glare of the leaping flames, and in the murky atmosphere the hideous monsters and the great black dog, Cerberus, blocking the passage to the Elysian Fields. "Che vuoi?" they snarl. "Che mediti?" ("What do you wish? What is your purpose?") And for the hushed audience there is a moment of poignant confrontation when Orpheus pleads with the monsters and they cry back at him, "No! No! No! No!" the music building to a fiery passion of rebellious hate, then modulating into a mood of feverish wonder when the Furies wilt before the eloquence of his plea and Orpheus descends into the writhing mass of the doomed. Fiercely they leap about him, with frightful menacing gestures, but resolutely he continues on his way, the orchestral incantation a crescendo of horror that breaks finally into triumph and tenderness as Orpheus, still holding high his golden lyre, passes through the flaming gates into the mysterious world beyond.

This transition from the murky nightmare of the Underworld

to the serene beauty of the Elysian Fields is one of the most astonishing achievements in opera. For his Blessed Spirits, Gluck has created music of divine simplicity, and a flute solo of ravishing sweetness. Marvelously he has conveyed the sunlit fields, the luminous sky, the tranquil felicity. Everywhere there is a radiant gladness, and when Orpheus enters he exclaims, in astonishment, "Che puro ciel!" ("What a pure light!") It is this unfolding of abject terror into ecstasy that is the ultimate expression of Gluck's genius. Orpheus, transported, sings of the radiant sky, the whispering streams, the rustling breezes, the singing winds. And the audience shares in the transport, the awe and the wonder, for everywhere there is a silvery light, an atmosphere of peace, repose and blissful tranquility.

Nothing that comes after quite equals the powerful illusion that pervades this scene in the Elysian Fields. If the opera is flawed, it is in the third act, when Orpheus, leading Euridice up the stony paths to earth, must turn away from his beloved while she pleads desperately for his affection. Perhaps this situation is too unlikely, too artificial, to be made wholly convincing. And when Euridice sinks back into death because Orpheus, distracted, has turned to look at her, even the beautiful "Che Faro" is too resigned an expression of grief to convey the shock and despair of such a moment. The ending of the classic opera —the intervention of the god Amor, and the lovers reunited on earth through the caprice of the gods—is perhaps somewhat arbitrary. But throughout the final scene, in the gardens of the Temple of Love, Gluck's magic weaves a light and airy spell, a luminous and most moving affirmation. And of the performance it was said, in the reviews the next day, that "last night's astonished audience left the doors of the Metropolitan, enthralled. . . ."

The day after her first appearance in *Orfeo e Euridice* was also the day before Christmas, which meant that the reviews had to be shared with a great flurry of belated preparations. This added a certain buoyancy to the trimming of the tree, for all the critics paid glowing tribute. In the *Tribune* Henry Krehbiel found the opera "powerfully appealing to the imagination." "Toscanini's treatment of the music was reverential," he wrote, "more than reverential, it was loving, and his spirit had its coun-

"The day after her first appearance in *Orfeo e Euridice* was also the day before Christmas . . ." The two-year-old twins in 1909, Anne at left, Katharine at right.

terpart in that of Madame Homer. Hers was a lovely impersonation—lovely to the eye, in figure, pose, movement and gesture—and equally lovely in song and voice." In the *Times* Richard Aldrich called their revival "certainly one of the most perfect productions ever put forward in New York," and noted, of her role, that "her portrayal of Orpheus is a strong and moving presentation, first of despairing grief and then of ecstasy. Nothing that Louise Homer has done is likely to rank higher in importance." Others wrote that "the tender beauty of exalted singing was the prelude to Homer's finest achievement in the passionate *Che Faro*," and called the opera "a moment of triumph for the brilliant artist."

Chapter XXI

The kaleidoscope of opera in this 1909–10 season had a variety, a vitality, a shifting panorama more diverse and more tumultuous than ever before, and would become known, in later years, as an era of unprecedented expansion in the operatic world. The Metropolitan now had seven full-time conductors, a double complement of orchestras and choruses and more principal singers than ever before. And the pace was being set by Oscar Hammerstein, who, all by himself, was initiating an astonishing operatic explosion, and leading the directors of the Metropolitan down a garden path of tempting aspirations.

Having established his Manhattan Opera House in New York, Hammerstein had undertaken the building of a new opera house in Philadelphia—a handsome granite and marble structure at Broad and Poplar streets. He'd then compounded his audacity by having his gala opening the very night of the Metropolitan's opening at the Academy of Music, thus confronting Philadelphia's social leaders with a tantalizing dilemma and quite a few had managed, by juggling the acts, to attend both opening performances.

Hammerstein had then proceeded to include Baltimore in his grand design, and it was to counter this that the Metropolitan acquired the Lyric Theatre for a competing Baltimore season. In Boston it was the same; there, to forestall their rival's ambitious projects, arrangements were made with Eben Jordan for a liaison with the Boston Opera House.

Andreas Dippel's efforts to employ his displaced talents in cities outside of New York were in part responsible for the expansion. This year he was concentrating much of his activity in Chicago, which was another hotly contested area. Here Oscar Hammerstein had fired an opening salvo with an extravagant presentation of Mary Garden in *Salome*. But Dippel had managed to counter this and, soon after, the directors had announced "the recent formation of the Metropolitan-Chicago Opera Company," which was described as "the entering wedge in the Great West." They were even contemplating opera seasons abroad, and to this end had elected to the Board of Directors of the Metropolitan both Henry Higgins of the Royal Opera in London, and Count San Martino, president of the Royal Conservatory in Rome. Promotion and expansion had now become the order of the day, and momentous plans were in the making to further what Henry Krehbiel called "a truly Alexandrine ambition to conquer the spacious operatic world."

Though Louise traveled, occasionally, to Philadelphia, Boston and Brooklyn, most of her performances were in New York. And there, on February 16, 1910, she sang the role of Dame Quickly in Toscanini's revival of Verdi's *Falstaff*. Emmy Destinn appeared as Mistress Ford, Antonio Scotti was a marvelous Falstaff, and their brilliant tapestry of comic art was indelibly stamped with the Toscanini signature.

Afterward the critics wrote that she "wore a comical wig of corkscrew curls" and "gave the audience a rollicking good time," her pretty curtsies a lively counterpart to the beguiling harmonies. As a work of art *Falstaff* might be compared with Shakespeare's *The Tempest*, or perhaps Wagner's *Die Meistersinger*, for in all three there is a departure from the usual pattern of creation, a distillation of genius without the mantle of tragedy, a stirring affirmation of life almost at the end of life. Verdi was eighty years old when he wrote *Falstaff*, yet he composed a score filled with airy invention, a true masterpiece of comedy.

A month later, on March 18, 1910, Louise sang the leading role in the first work by an American composer, and the first work sung in English at the Metropolitan—*The Pipe of Desire* by William Converse. But her role in this pioneer opera was a thankless one, for the libretto was maudlin and unconvincing, an overwrought fantasy in which a shepherd, Iolan, impatient to see his bride-to-be, impulsively snatches a musical instrument from the King of the Fairyfolk. As his loved one, Naoia, she must rise from a sickbed, irresistibly attracted by the magic "pipe of desire," and struggle over rocks and streams to his side. There she is "stricken with a fever, her mind is turned awry, and she dies in his arms." This opera was called by Krehbiel "a jumble of operatic shreds and pieces," with music that had "moments of beauty," but was "too derivative."

In April the policy of expansion was extended to the spring tour, which was split into two parts to provide a wider coverage. For the first time in its history the Metropolitan would have two separate touring companies, with a double complement of principal singers, orchestras and choruses giving simultaneous performances in widely scattered cities. This unique arrangement was called a "split-tour," and Louise was assigned to "split-tour No. 1," which would be based primarily in Chicago, while "split-tour No. 2" would encompass Pittsburgh, Detroit, Cleveland and many other cities.

She would have to be away from home a month, and they decided to turn the occasion into a lark and call it a "second honeymoon." Her mother came to stay with the children, and in Chicago they sublet a furnished apartment with a balcony overlooking the water. In this beneficent atmosphere, one morning, while she was at the opera house rehearsing, Sidney wrote a song called "The Banjo Song." But he wrote it too easily, and the tune was too catchy and much too "popular" to be included in the work of a serious composer. The poem, which was deceptively simple, was from a collection called *Bandanna Ballads*, the work of a Southern poet, Howard Weedon. And when he consulted his musician friends—Hans Morgenstern of the Metropolitan, Kurt Schindler and others—they all warned him that such a lighthearted piece would damage his reputation. Nevertheless, a year or so later "The Banjo Song" was published and became immensely popular. Perhaps because it did have such a simple, in-

genuous air, the quality of a ballad, a folk song, it was sung
widely in concerts, sold thousands of copies and is still being sung
today by soloists and choruses all over the world.

The directors of the Metropolitan had arranged a week of
opera in Atlanta early in May—the first that Southern city had
ever had. It was said of this new undertaking that Atlanta could
offer "more friendly warmth" than most Northern cities, and more
"get-up-and-go" than most Southern ones. This was a city suddenly in love with opera, and for the Metropolitan artists it provided, with its "mantle of dogwood and azaleas," its memorable
parties and vivid hospitality, an enchanting interlude. In Atlanta,
Louise sang Ortrud and Amneris, and had a part in what would
become an annual event.

But the adventures weren't over yet, for now Signor Gatti-
Casazza planned to take his company across the Atlantic Ocean
for a season of opera in Paris. And so that she could have a part
in this pioneer undertaking, he offered to pay the fare both ways,
not only for the singer, but for the entire family—her husband,
all her children and two nurses.

The Paris venture had been planned by Gatti and Toscanini as
a means of extending to French audiences the talents and methods
of an American opera company. But the mechanics of such an
undertaking were formidable. All the principal singers had to be
transported, as well as stage managers, lighting technicians and
others. And an immense amount of scenery and equipment had
to be packed into the hold of the ship for a notable repertoire of
operas—*Aida, Cavalleria Rusticana, Pagliacci, Otello, Falstaff.*
The moving vans were kept busy, and one reporter noted "a
gigantic baby carriage, leaving the Metropolitan on top of a
wagon load of trunks, and proceeding down the gang plank with
the scenery and costumes." Although the twins' double carriage
wasn't really "gigantic," it was made of wicker, and was, in fact,
quite spacious.

The prospect of sharing an ocean voyage with so many opera
stars attracted a number of celebrities, and their departure, on
May 10th, was described by a reporter for the *Press*, who wrote:

> There sailed on the Kaiser Wilhelm 11 yesterday the
> greatest tenor in the world, the greatest dramatic soprano,

the greatest contralto and the greatest baritone. In addition
there was the greatest dancer, one duke, full grown, one infant duke, two duchesses and the daughter of the richest
man in the world. The officers of the North German Lloyd
Line say they have never seen such a crowd in Hoboken,
and as the great liner was slipping out into the river, the
end of the pier was a solid mass of human beings waving
handkerchiefs and canes. In that crowd, and totally unnoticed, was John D. Rockefeller, who had come down in
a hired coupé to bid his daughter goodbye. But the crowd
on the pier was not looking for Mr. Rockefeller—it was
looking for Caruso and Scotti and Homer and Gadski and
Fremstad and Farrar and Destinn and Amato and a dozen
other grand opera stars known to be sailing on what playful
Caruso calls "The High Cs Express." Out of the passenger
list might be picked the greatest all-star grand opera cast
in American history.

However, in Paris the directors of the Metropolitan were
confronted with some grueling obstacles, an array of frustrations that included a dilapidated theater, a second-rate orchestra and an antagonistic press. The hall they had engaged, the
Châtelet Theatre, was discovered to be an old barn of a place,
incredibly dirty, an utter shambles. To make matters worse, a
melodrama called *The Man with Two Heads* was still in progress,
and when the hall was finally available the Metropolitan's technical director, Edward Seidl, had just two days in which to form
a bucket brigade of Parisian workers, lay ground cloths brought
from New York, brighten the interior, install the heavy scenery
mountings and make the theater presentable for opera.

Meanwhile Toscanini had barely a week in which to train the
orchestra. But he worked so tirelessly, with such insight and
precision, that at the end of the first rehearsal session the musicians themselves gave him a standing ovation, and by the time
the Paris season opened it was said that he had performed a
"miracle" with his makeshift orchestra.

Most of the antagonism in the press was initiated by certain
elements in Paris who resented what they called "this Italian
invasion." The French newspaper *Gil Blas* took the lead, and

there was a growing chorus of attacks, insinuations and malicious rumors. It was believed that much of this had evolved from the unhappy experience of the French contralto, Madame Marie Delna, who had sung during the winter at the Metropolitan and fought so bitterly with Toscanini that she hadn't been asked back. It was this slight to a favorite opera singer that incensed her supporters and inspired the slanderous editorials. In the vicious attacks the Metropolitan was never mentioned. Always it was "the Italians," and in one spiteful editorial *Gil Blas* accused Gatti and Toscanini of coming to Paris "angling for a Legion of Honor decoration."

But in spite of all the drawbacks, the start of the Metropolitan's Paris season was such a glamorous occasion that the demand for tickets for the opening-night performance of *Aida*, on May 21, 1910, far exceeded the number of seats available. Finally, to accommodate all the notables, a gala "dress rehearsal" was given two nights before, and attended by a galaxy of celebrities. Many had come from America expressly for this festive opening—the Vanderbilts, the Potter Palmers, the Stotesburys. There were members of the French aristocracy—princesses, dukes and duchesses—the diplomatic corps, headed by Monsieur Briand, and some of the most noted in the artistic world, including the Jean de Reszkes and Gabriele d'Annunzio. Exclaimed the newspaper *Figaro*, the next morning, "What a hall! What a public! What cascades of precious stones! What charms, enfin!"— while Cartier estimated the worth of the jewels at more than three million dollars.

But though the dress rehearsal had been a brilliant occasion, at the official opening, two nights later, some in the audience weren't so well disposed toward the "Italian invasion" from America. They came waiting to be shown, only too ready to voice their displeasure, and this undercurrent of resentment was aggravated because quite a few were kept waiting out on the sidewalk during the entire first act. It had been ruled that no one could be admitted while the opera was in progress, and so they had to mill about, in a rising fever of frustration. And when the doors were finally opened, at the start of the second act, these latecomers stormed the galleries, flailing and shoving and turning the place into an uproar.

How much of the furor resulted from impatience, how much from a latent antagonism, would never be known. But for some time the second act was delayed, to allow the disturbance to subside. However, moment by moment, the violence increased, until finally, to distract the rioters, it was decided to continue the performance. Toscanini then walked out into the embattled hall, white-faced and grim, and took his place on the podium in the midst of a "tumult of boos and hisses, screamed epithets and curses." Defiantly he raised his baton and started to conduct. But the music was drowned out by the wild demonstration, for those who wanted to hear clapped furiously for silence, only adding to the din, until finally the entire house was seething with disorder.

Although Louise would have the opening scene in this act, the one in the luxurious royal apartments, where Amneris, in regal attire and exalted mood, is adorned by her handmaidens for the triumphant return of Radames from the field of battle, her dressing room was so far in the back of the theater that she was innocently unaware of the disturbance in the hall. For some time she had been ready, in her costume of rose and gold and long garlands of roses. But she hadn't known about the attacks in the newspaper *Gil Blas*, or the undercurrent of animosity in Paris, for they'd had other preoccupations. In the main these had been concerned with adapting the children and their nurses to life in a foreign country and a strange hotel. Was the milk safe for the twins? Was the governess too timid about taking the children to walk in the Bois de Boulogne? Their hotel on the Champs-Elysées wasn't entirely suitable for two-year-olds, and many breakables had had to be put out of reach.

And so she had been preoccupied, her life, as ever, an airy seesaw between the domestic and the operatic. Now, though she was surprised by the long wait, she wasn't too concerned, though it was a relief when finally the callboy came to fetch her. Behind him Mr. Speck, the stage manager, was calling out "Hurry! Hurry!" but when she asked the reason he only answered "Listen!" And then she heard it—the noise of hundreds of stamping feet, a sound like a kind of echoing roar from within the darkened auditorium.

He told her that the audience was tired of waiting, and hurriedly she took her place in the royal apartments, half reclining on her satin couch, with the chorus, her slaves and handmaidens, grouped gracefully about. Then the curtain rose, and for the first time she saw the tumult, the galleries in an uproar, the whole opera house a struggling mass of humanity, armies of shadowy, writhing shapes surging back and forth, and an unearthly noise of stamping, hissing, whistling, shouting. At that first, fearful moment, she told a reporter afterward, her "heart almost stopped beating." But if that was the case it wasn't apparent to the members of the chorus, who were so terrified they wanted to run away at once and leave the stage, which would have made a shambles of the performance. Forcefully she commanded them, "Sing! Sing! Sing as loud as you can!" and sang herself, their parts as well as her own, ignoring the pianissimos, pouring out a forte tone.

But their voices were drowned out by the fearful din, and so was the surging orchestral music. Toscanini seemed now like a puppet conductor, ashen pale and tense, flailing, flailing, his arm rising and falling, the musicians playing, playing, without making a sound. Nothing seemed able to stem the mounting violence, and finally she left her couch, walked down to the footlights, flung out her arms and sang for that seething mass of humanity at the very top of her voice. But this, too, was useless, for there was no audible song, and to the audience she seemed a puppet Amneris, standing there behind the footlights, arms outstretched, singing, singing, her mouth opening wide, then closing again, all without making a sound.

In the auditorium, Sidney had a seat not far from the stage. And when he saw her so close to the footlights, he snatched up his coat and was tensed and ready, prepared to leap to the stage if there was any sign of distress. But there was no such sign. She was Amneris still, a regal princess, and when, for a moment, there was a brief lull in the tumult, a slight hiatus, the way there sometimes is in an angry, clamoring mob, while each one struggles to catch his breath, into that sudden vacuum her voice soared. Like velvet streamers the lyric tones floated throughout the disordered hall, serene and unafraid. And instantly, as if by magic, a spell fell over the opera house. The effect was almost eerie, for it was as though the fevered audience had been suddenly transfixed, as though the contralto voice, so rounded and controlled, without a sign of tremor or distress, the timbre of it, the ravishing texture, soaring here and there with a careless and soothing cadence, had hypnotized her listeners.

The intense stillness continued until she had finished her aria. And then the opera house exploded again, but this time into a standing ovation, cheers and bravos and applause that went on and on and on. In its account of the Paris riot *The New York Times* called this applause "an ovation amounting to an apotheosis," noting that the audience "was cheering the American singer for her coolness and daring, as well as her marvelous art." In all the New York papers there were headlines: "Homer quells disturbance"—"Contralto stills angry Parisiens"—"Gallery in an uproar; savage cries and furious cat-calls; her courage and art wrest ovation." It was also reported that the rest of the performance continued "without incident," and the Metropolitan's presentation of *Aida* was hailed as a brilliant achievement.

The Paris season continued, with *Pagliacci*, *Otello*, *Falstaff*, and in spite of its difficult beginning, the entire engagement became a dazzling success. All the performances were sold out, new ones had to be added and, to the surprise of the Metropolitan's directors, they took in $10,000 a night. The baritone Pasquale Amato fascinated the French, who flocked to the opera house to hear him. And in Paris they gave their first performance of Puccini's *Manon Lescaut*, with Toscanini conducting. For the title role of this opera Gatti engaged a new soprano, at the moment in Paris, a brilliant and fascinating Spanish singer, Lucrezia Bori. Eventually, when she was free of her other commitments, Bori would become a great star with the Metropolitan in New York.

At the end of their season the Metropolitan artists gave a "Gala Benefit Performance" at the Paris Opera House for the survivors of the ill-fated submarine *Pluviôse*. Their program included scenes from several operas, and when Louise sang Brangäne in the second act of *Tristan* at this Gala Benefit, with Olive Fremstad as Isolde, it was the first time in forty years, since the start of the Franco-Prussian War, that a work had been sung in German at the Paris Opera House.

In Paris there was a reunion with the Koenigs, and then they

could relive the adventures, and convey some of the gratitude
for all that had happened since. But they took off for Switzerland as soon as the opera season was over, anxious to shake the
children free of the too-sedate Champs-Elysées hotel. And in
Grindelwald there was a concierge with a secret weapon, for if
the twins made too much noise when they were supposed to be
asleep, he'd tell them calmly that if they didn't stop he'd throw
them in the fountain. And the babies had seen the water in the
hotel fountain and knew that it gushed right out of the mouths of
two very large stone lions.

They lingered almost too long in Europe, for in the fall
Louise would have an extensive concert tour, throughout much
of the South. Then, just before they were to sail for home, on the
S.S. *Cecelie*, there was one of those family crises, when Katharine,
one of the twins, suddenly ran a high fever. For a time everything hung in the balance while they debated whether to sail.
Contracts had been signed, the financial situation was acute,
and on the final day the baby's fever dropped just in time.

When one twin is ill the other is inclined to even up the odds
by being as troublesome as she can. On the boat coming home
Anne followed this useful rule, and when her nurse told her that
if she ran away to her mother she'd get a spanking for sure, she
ran away anyhow, and her mother gave her, instead, a warm
hug, a radiant smile and a small doll (part of a present-a-day
packet they had on the boat)—thus bestowing on the nurse a
familiar irritation, and on the defiant two-year-old a mantle of
triumph, a kind of secret armor, to carry about with her forever
after. But they'd cut the time too short, and when they reached
New York an assistant manager of the Metropolitan was on the
pier with the scores of two new roles to learn—the Witch in
Humperdinck's *Königskinder*, and La Haine in Gluck's *Armide*,
which would open the opera season. She then had just four
days in which to settle the children at home, rehearse with a
new accompanist, Evadna Lapham, pack up the bags with the
concert gowns, the matching satin shoes, the scores of the new
operas and board a train for the long Southern concert tour.

Chapter XXII

In 1910 the solo concert tour was just coming into its own. For years there had been concerts in the big cities, and recitals (many of them amateur) in the smaller towns. Then the "talking machine" had come along, and the managers had been apprehensive. They had believed that if people could listen to music in their own homes, they would no longer pay to go to concerts, but actually the very opposite of what they'd feared had come about. Now people all over America were listening to opera singers on their talking machines. Famous names were becoming familiar names, famous voices familiar voices. And from this nucleus of new music lovers, anxious to see their favorite singers on the stage, a new audience had emerged.

The talking machine had revolutionized musical life in America, and the concert managers were reaping the rewards. In small towns and cities, as well as the big urban centers, they were making elaborate plans—hiring halls, arranging contracts, selling subscriptions, printing posters. Often they were over-zealous, and tried to fill auditoriums much too large for the surrounding population. Most of these solo tours were pioneer efforts, with inexperienced managers, makeshift halls and unsophisticated audiences. And it was the artist who must take these unpredictable ingredients and somehow make them work.

Louise had never before toured for so long without Sidney,

A photograph taken in 1910.

and after the summer in Europe the transition was too abrupt. From Asheville she wrote him, "Darling, I'm so crazy to see you and be with you, I can't see how I can last another week. I'm not usually homesick, only I love you so, and we did have such dear times together this summer." In reply he wrote, "I sort of realize that I was just about going to sleep for the rest of my life in the fall of '93, when a spark of life jumped in and set things afire. I don't care about being without that spark of life a *minute*."

But, in fact, he was without it. And so that they could communicate by telegram thoughts and feelings as well as facts, they devised a secret code to confound the hotel clerks. And no doubt they succeeded, for her wire from Spartanburg began: "Porker than ever porkissimo codessamo," while the one from Asheville ended: "Grin Porkie dump coderest." During the long train rides she scribbled little notes. "How thankful I am every minute," she wrote during the trip to Bristol, "that you aren't *here*. The noises and jolting and heat, I don't mind them one bit, but I can just see how your dear face would become more tired every hour." Another time she wrote, "I have been committing the new roles, so I can come home all ready for my season, and have nothing to do but look at my sweetheart. You have a *beautiful* face, darling. I don't wonder Augustus wanted it for his Christ! I wish I had a real picture of you, here with me now, but I have one in my heart."

Every performance, she found, was different. The concert in Memphis, she wrote him, was "just ordinary," but the one in Nashville was "memorable." "When I walked out onto that bare dirty stage last night," she wrote, "and saw this awful big ugly hall that holds 7000 and only about 2500 there, it looked discouraging, and when I first began to sing I felt a big echo. But I soon felt the intense earnestness and joy and intelligence of my hearers. . . . Everything was perfect from beginning to end, I can't tell you just how or why. Their faces were so animated and joyous, the applause so spontaneous, I was *perfectly* happy and content."

When she returned home there was just time for a joint recital in Worcester with the brilliant pianist Josef Hoffmann, and a concert at Carnegie Hall with Walter Damrosch and the New York Symphony Orchestra. Then she began rehearsals for Gluck's *Armide*, which would open the 1910–11 season on November 14th.

Toscanini was their conductor, and once again at the start of the new season the management of the Metropolitan had undergone a change. Over the summer there had been a reorganization, this time in the direction of retrenchment, stabilization and control. Signor Gatti-Casazza may have had the new status in mind all along, and during the feverish expansion the year before had simply bided his time while Andreas Dippel moved grandly from city to city, proliferating opera far and wide. Meanwhile the double complement of orchestras and choruses and the great number of principal singers had been so costly that at the end of the hectic season the directors of the Metropolitan had found themselves heavily in debt. The grandiose plans had proliferated more problems than rewards, and so they had decided to abandon their dreams of an opera empire, and scale everything down to size.

In "the merry opera war" Oscar Hammerstein had also been

losing money, though not as much, and at the end of his season he had told his Manhattan audience, with his usual debonair wit, that "while my losses have been enormous, I am proud of knowing that those of my adversaries have been much larger." Throughout the season competition from the Manhattan had cut drastically into the Metropolitan's receipts, so in a sense Hammerstein had won the first round of the conflict. But his finances were now precariously out of balance. And at the start of the 1910 season the directors of the Metropolitan offered Oscar Hammerstein $1,250,000 just to retire from the scene of battle.

This was a flattering offer for the brilliant impresario who had invaded New York entirely on his own and created such sparkling competition. In effect the offer was a ransom, to exclude his formidable talents, and when he decided to accept, an agreement was drawn up that would end, for all time, the "opera war." The terms of this celebrated agreement were largely negative, for in return Hammerstein simply promised to retire and give no more performances of grand opera in the vicinity of New York, Philadelphia, Boston or Chicago for a period of ten years. Edward Stotesbury arranged to buy his Philadelphia Opera House, and at the Manhattan he would be limited to light opera or operettas. So after opening the season at the Manhattan with what Krehbiel called "an exceedingly bright little piece," *Hans, the Flute Player*, Oscar Hammerstein sailed for England, to build an opera house in London and compete, this time, with Covent Garden.

Meanwhile, under increasing pressure, Dippel had resigned his position and gone to Chicago to manage an independent Chicago Opera Company. The brilliant conductor Gustav Mahler was devoting his entire time this season to the New York Philharmonic Society, which he had completely reorganized and transformed. And at the Metropolitan everything was reduced to more modest proportions, with the company giving outside performances in only a few cities, like Atlanta, where their expenses were fully guaranteed.

After the opening performance of Gluck's *Armide*, Henderson of the *Sun* called the production "a new laurel in the crown worn jointly by Messrs. Gatti-Casazza and Toscanini," thus defining, implicitly, the new regime. Full authority was now vested in the manager from La Scala. And though the hectic pace had been slowed, and some visionary projects abandoned, this hadn't dimmed the luster of the New York season. Gatti had a brilliant conductor and a wonderful roster of singers. Under his innately artistic and quietly controlled management, the Metropolitan was embarking now on what would become known as an especially shining chapter in the Golden Age of Opera.[13]

Like Maurice Grau, Gatti had a showman's instinct in the matter of casting. In December, that year, Geraldine Farrar made an enchanting Goose Girl in *Königskinder*. And in February, after a performance of *La Gioconda*, it was said that "one of the largest audiences of the year revelled in the delicious blending of the voices of Enrico Caruso, Emmy Destinn, Louise Homer and Pasquale Amato. . . . The opera might almost have been written with these soloists in mind, so admirably is the work suited to those great singers now in New York."

In the role of La Haine in Gluck's *Armide*, Louise had, as so often in opera, to portray evil, and mine from her voice those dark and threatening tones. Wrote a reviewer, "Though she could more easily be compatible with the character of Love than of Hate, Louise Homer called into play all her rich dramatic possibilities, and never forgot the classic nobility and poise that has made her *Orfeo* a thing to be remembered as long as one remembers the history of Grand Opera in this country." And that, indeed, was a leavening factor, for now she had a compensating opera. They gave their *Orfeo e Euridice* seven times that season, including performances in Brooklyn and Philadelphia, and each time she could experience again that poignant debate in the Greek hills.[14]

In June they went together to the Norfolk Music Festival, an event that had become a valued part of their lives. The Norfolk Festivals were sponsored by Mr. and Mrs. Carl Stoeckel and held on the grounds of their estate, White House. Artists of the highest caliber were engaged as soloists—Ossip Gabrilovitch, Alma Gluck, Albert Spaulding, Efrem Zimbalist, and in previous years Eames, Nordica, Sembrich. Each season an original work was commissioned for the Festival from some noted composer—Chadwick, Parker or perhaps Sibelius.

The concerts were held in the "Music Shed," and the artists

at the Festivals were treated like honored guests, provided with a luxurious private home, catering by Delmonico's, a key to the wine cellar, carriages and automobiles for drives through the countryside. In this beneficent atmosphere they had a kind of annual house party, with charades, costume parties and companionship, in the midst of an inspiring interlude of music. No tickets were ever sold to this so eloquently contrived event. They were all given away, and were so highly prized that audiences came from great distances to attend the Norfolk Music Festival.

After the Festival there would be an extended vacation, for another baby was expected in December. They had believed their family was complete, and four children an ideal number. But now they revised their estimate upward, and on December 12, 1911, a baby girl was born, and named Hester Makepeace for an ancestor of Sidney's who had come over with the Puritans.

Meanwhile there had been speculation about the contralto's "temporary retirement," one reporter noting that "her absence from the stage has deprived opera goers of musical rewards that have become almost indispensable. It is not unusual," he wrote, "for travellers from distant cities in the West to visit New York solely with a view to hearing Enrico Caruso and the beloved American contralto."

There had also been the usual apprehension about this "domestic interlude," and when Gatti told her she might return in any opera she wished, predictably she chose *Orfeo e Euridice*, and made her first appearance on January 25, 1912. Wrote a critic for the *Press*:

> Before an audience distinguished by the presence of the Duchess of Connaught (Queen Victoria's daughter-in-law) and Princess Patricia, Louise Homer made a triumphant return to the lyric stage last night. Would the singer be as beautiful as when she last appeared? Would her voice have all its former glory? These were questions in the minds of many. But whatever doubts may have been felt were dispelled quickly and effectively when her voice soared out into the vast ranges of the auditorium. . . . In that beautiful voice, so much an instrument of the heart, though guided by fine intelligence and artistic taste, there were poignant

accents, subtle shadings of feeling that it had never revealed before. During her temporary withdrawal from the stage she has grown to be a greater singer, a greater artist.

Meanwhile she was rehearsing for the title role in the Metropolitan's new "Prize American Opera," *Mona*. This was a patriotic project that had been initiated by Gatti when he first came to New York. Perhaps the manager had reasoned that he would be suspected of favoring Italian opera, and had countered by suggesting to the directors, in 1908, that the Metropolitan offer a prize of ten thousand dollars for a "full-length Grand Opera" by an American composer. The contest had sparked a good deal of interest, and a distinguished panel of jurors had been appointed, among them Alfred Hertz, Walter Damrosch, Charles Loeffler and George Chadwick.

Over a period of three years more than thirty scores had been submitted anonymously, and the prize had been awarded, in the spring of 1911, to Horatio W. Parker, Professor of Music at Yale University, and his librettist, Brian Hooker, also a Yale professor, for a full-length opera called *Mona*. The premiere performance had had to be delayed, as one music columnist delicately pointed out, because "the star of the prize opera was engaged with a half season devoted to domestic affairs." But now it was to be given on March 14, 1912, with a cast that included Rita Fornia, Albert Reiss and Herbert Witherspoon.

Mona wasn't an easy role to sing, for the inexperienced authors had made their opera top-heavy with exposition and long declamatory passages, and their heroine a kind of primitive Joan of Arc, a princess of the Druids, in early Britain, leading a revolt against the Romans—in effect a lady warrior in graceful, flowing robes, carrying a sword and sacrificing love on the altar of patriotism.

But though there were artistic problems, this advent of a first full-length American opera had attracted lively speculation. One music columnist noted that "Broadway has already named the Metropolitan's prize novelty '*Mona Louisa*.'" While another, describing a Sunday morning dress rehearsal as "an all-star occasion," wrote:

Caruso sat in the audience room with Composer Parker,

Librettist Brian Hooker and the invited members of the
Kneisel Quartet; Leo Slezak stood talking with Frank Damrosch, who used to rehearse those new German operas with
his father twenty years ago. The star of the opera took advantage of the quiet Sunday morning to let some of her
famous grand opera family see her in the heroine's role.
Nine year old Sidney Jr. was there, and the Homer twins,
Katharine and Anne, sat in the front row, their eyes shining
in the dark. "The best part of the show," said Master Sidney,
when interviewed later, "is the fight. Only there isn't enough
of it."

The premiere performance of the prize-winning opera was a
dazzling occasion, described afterward as "brilliant," with "forty
curtain calls," "tumultuous applause," "roars of approval" and
"an overwhelming display of laurel wreaths and floral offerings."
In the reviews her portrayal of Mona was called "heroic in spirit,
with aspects of tenderness, exaltation and savage fury . . ."
and her contribution "a masterpiece of dramatic art." But this
may have been said as much in sympathy as approval, for in spite
of the opening night ovations, the prize opera received lukewarm
notices from the critics, several complaining of "interminable
dialogue" and "static interludes." However, Henry Krehbiel
hailed the work as "a significant experiment in the field of native
opera," and felt that the authors should have been given a
chance to revise their prize drama "once the weaknesses were
disclosed. . . . The merits of the poem and score were so
great," he wrote, "that an attempt ought to have been made to
save it." However, there was no such attempt, and after four
performances *Mona* was retired from the repertoire.

In the spring Louise went to Atlanta for *Il Trovatore* and *Aida*,
and to hear a thrush sing. "When she heard the first few notes,"
commented a surprised reporter, "she asked the chauffeur to
stop the car so she could hear that bird-song to the end." However, this wasn't really too surprising, for it was her way to
listen to the music of many things in life, especially the small
quiet music. But meanwhile she was often involved in elaborate,
quite grandiose occasions, and in July went to Philadelphia to

The New York Times dubbed this "the first reading of the prize opera, *Mona*." Alfred Hertz, the conductor, is seated; standing, Horatio W. Parker, Gatti-Casazza and Brian Hooker.

help inaugurate the huge new Constitution Hall—an affair decked out with flags and bunting, celebrities, great fanfare and enormous crowds.

Constitution Hall, designed to house the national conventions, was a mammoth building. And for the dedication the city fathers had wanted two singers who were considered "native Philadelphians"—the fine baritone, Henri Scott, and Louise Homer, the contralto. They planned a three-day *Sängerfest*, with a chorus of six thousand men, and a double orchestra, under the direction of Eugen Klee. All the leading dignitaries would be present as guests of honor—the mayor, the governor and, on the final day, President and Mrs. William Howard Taft.

But though the entire city was exhilarated by the event, the entertainment was rather solemn, with many long classical selections. Louise was the only woman on the program, and it was said that when she sang, as an encore, "a tender, nostalgic *Old Black Joe*," she "electrified the great throng." Another critic, commenting on the aria from *Le Prophète*, called her voice "altogether indescribable," and then attempted a description. "From its lowest depths to its ringing heights," he wrote, "it has that wonderful quality of 'ivory and white velvet.' . . . More like a violoncello than any other instrument you can imagine, it has a power almost organlike. But her voice must be heard, and even then it is incredible."

The huge crowd responded with a roar of approval when President Taft sent word that he would like to have her visit in his box. While she was being escorted up the aisles "the great hall dissolved into ripples of applause," and there were "cheers every step of the way, and another mighty outburst when she was seen seated between President and Mrs. Taft, all three chatting together until it was time for her to sing again." The crowd was so enormous on this historic occasion that outside the hall "the mob packed the asphalt from curb to curb." And when it was time for President Taft to leave, it was reported that "his turbulent journey to his motor car had to be made by means of the 'old rules football variety,' with the Secret Service forming a 'flying wedge' to get him through."

But the tumult in Philadelphia had to be played out against a certain undercurrent of sadness, for in May her mother had had a stroke, and was now partially paralyzed. All at once that warm bright stream of conversation had been stilled, the effort to communicate made halting and garbled. Then, in June, Sidney had gone to a health resort at Kerhonkson, in the Adirondacks, for an interval of rest and quiet that was meant to cure the attacks of dizziness, the nervousness and insomnia that had recently been troubling him.

At this time it was the fashion to take "rest cures," and there were many fine health resorts scattered throughout the country. In the main they offered their guests a careful regime of diet, rest and recreation. There was a doctor to supervise (his was a

Dr. Foord), and for recreation invigorating walks in the piny woods, tennis and canoeing, and in the evening bridge and other quiet games. He was underweight, too easily fatigued, and the spells of vertigo that had started a year or so before, though they may in fact have been caused by some trouble with the inner ear, were at the time considered a mysterious symptom, and seemed to accentuate a tendency he had to be apprehensive about undue excitement, big crowds, a variety of circumstances. Seeking relief from these enervating anxieties, he had gone to the Adirondacks for an interval of rest.

He was in Kerhonkson when she was singing at the *Sängerfest*, but a little later he came home for the remainder of the summer. However, he believed he had benefited from the relaxation, as well as the ordered, reassuring routine, and in the fall returned to Kerhonkson, still trying to allay those mysterious demons of tension and anxiety. In the Adirondacks he could more easily avoid the exertion and undue excitement that he dreaded. And so the health resort had become a refuge, a reasonable retreat from pressures that could loom too large for one who was too easily engulfed.

Chapter XXIII

The gas logs were burning brightly, and didn't move, but while rehearsing the *Orfeo* she was gazing at them so intently that it seemed they must have. "Del mio barbaro dolor"—"My overwhelming sorrow"—she turned to the burning logs when she sang this phrase, for at home the fireplace represented the Underworld. It was an ungainly mantel, the green Italian marble and heavy English oak a poor substitute for the fiery pit on the stage, and it was in the front room of a brownstone house on East Seventy-eighth Street.

The house had a high front stoop and basement steps as well, leading into the kitchen, the servants' dining room, a labyrinth of dark useful rooms. Outside her door a narrow flight of carpeted stairs led to other rooms above, restless with the coming and going of many people. *Con passione*, Toscanini had written into the score. "Del mio barbaro dolor"—"My overwhelming sorrow." She turned to the gas logs and heard the children on the stairs, the running feet, the shrill childish voices, and was overwhelmed with intimations of mortality.

She had become vulnerable this year in part from the strain of trying to fulfill too many divergent roles. At the opera house they were calling rehearsals right and left—for *Götterdämmerung*, *Die Meistersinger*, *La Gioconda*—and Gatti had asked her to learn the role of Marina for Toscanini's American pre-

miere of Moussorgsky's *Boris Godunov*. Meanwhile she was
visiting Sidney in Kerhonkson as often as she could, and sending a steady stream of letters, as well as packages to provide for
his various requests—the special silk underwear he preferred,
his favorite brand of tobacco and cigarettes, warm clothing for
the winter months in the Adirondacks. And day after day she
was sharing, vicariously, her mother's pitiful battle with paralysis.

In the fall she had taken a house in West Chester, so she could
be near her mother for a while. "I stay with Mama as much as
possible," she had written him at Kerhonkson. "We sit in her
room and talk together. We find she is lonely when we leave,
and she seems to understand all we say. She looks so *lovely*
in the lavender robe I bought her. The twins' birthday is Tuesday, and I have bought them dollies and bracelets and an automobile."

In West Chester she had settled her family, for a brief stay,
in one of those familiar brick homes. "I have been ordering
things that are necessary," she had written him after that move,
"like a small gas stove, irons that aren't rusted, washboard, and
electric button in dining room fixed. We are training Hester to
eat with us. We are so few that we have to *keep together* all we
can."

In November she'd had to move them all back to New York
for the opera season, and at once had been engulfed in performances and rehearsals and the children coming down with
stomach upsets, one after the other. "Hester has it now," she
wrote him. "It is my fault, I started giving her whole milk too
soon. She woke last night and cried pathetically for hours, but
by two o'clock she was asleep in my arms. Then this afternoon
at five Morgenstern came to put me through some stunts on
Gotter and *Meister*. But I'm *tired* of all these rehearsals. *Meister*
tomorrow at 8 P.M., *Gotter* Friday evening, *Gioconda* Saturday,
Gotter with orchestra Sunday A.M. and I forget what Sunday
evening. If the latter can be changed I'll go to West Chester Sunday afternoon to see Mama, and come back Monday. . . ."

She was troubled because she had so little time free for the
children, and was almost persuaded that they should try to evolve
some other way of life, and give up the opera altogether. "Yester-

A visit to Kerhonkson in the middle of a tour, bringing along the flowers from the night before.

day," she wrote him, "I went to church all alone and heard a most beautiful sermon. Then I came home and played a game of tit-tat-toe with the twinnies. They were *so* amused! Then I drew a pig with my eyes shut and they were *convulsed*! It made me feel sad that I play with them so seldom. *Next year* we'll give to each other and our darlings!"

But it wasn't next year yet, and now and then, when it was raining and they couldn't play in the park, she would take the twins with their nurse to the opera house for one of the shorter rehearsals. They were five years old now, and would be reasonably quiet, sitting on one side of the half-dark stage. Meanwhile she would run through passages from some opera, with one or two of the other singers, all of them in street clothes, the atmosphere informal. If Toscanini was the conductor there would be a scattering of spectators in the darkened hall, musicians and students of music who came faithfully to all his rehearsals, so that they might experience his way with a score—the insight, the fervor, the infinite precision. But if Toscanini was the conductor the sessions sometimes became too long, while the Maestro rapped again and again on the podium, bringing the orchestra to a strident halt, his imperious voice demanding some subtle change in phrasing, or tempo, or modulation, or rhythm. And at one of these rehearsals the strain became so great that she began to weep, just a little, a few tears, wiped hastily away. In fact, this was not an unusual occurrence at rehearsals, when anxious, weary singers were struggling to comply. But when the five-year-old twins saw their mother in tears they turned into a catapult of wailing, sobbing protest, avenging furies in smocked dresses and pastel hair ribbons—hurling themselves across the stage, throwing their arms around her skirts and screaming at Toscanini, "Don't you make our mother cry!"

Toscanini responded to this impassioned plea with a smile and a benign wave of the baton. And for the spectators in the darkened hall, it made a beguiling bit of drama—the wailing little girls defending a tearful mother, and the conductor so indulgent and amused.

But for the singer it was a discouraging reminder of the many pressures that had been building up this year. Especially she was troubled because Gatti wanted her to sing the role of Marina, the alluring Polish aristocrat, in the American premiere of *Boris Godunov*, and there was also talk of returning Toscanini's *Falstaff* to the repertoire. All this would mean another series of rehearsals while she was trying to make those trips to Kerhonkson and West Chester, and care for the children at home. "I talked with Gatti yesterday," she wrote him, "and begged him to release me from the *Boris*. Among other things I told him that I had been at the opera house almost every day all season, and had no 'vie chez moi' at all, and I couldn't stand it, and I dreaded the *Boris* rehearsals, and also the *Falstaff*. He said there would not be many *Boris* rehearsals, and *if* they gave *Falstaff* it would not be until April. That 'if' is what I am hanging on to!"

As it happened, they didn't give the *Falstaff* that year. But the American premiere of *Boris Godunov* was presented on March 19, 1913, and hailed by the critics as "a remarkable disclosure of novelty in subject, method and style." She had only two scenes in this masterpiece of Slavic art, so teeming with life and somber

"She made her love scene . . . shine glitteringly in a garden of shadows." As Marina in *Boris Godunov*.

Slavic grandeur, and of her role it was said that "she made her love scene with the false Dimitri shine glitteringly in a garden of shadows."

In a sense her own life had now become "a garden of shadows," for she was trying to provide for her family a serene and ordered life, while her own was caught up in the hectic complexities of opera. And she had become discouraged because this feat was so difficult to achieve. "I have been thinking of all you wrote," she wrote him at Kerhonkson, "and when you are here I want to have 'dolce far niente,' time to be *together*. I will be glad when the winter is over!"

Perhaps it was a special dispensation that her voice, this year, had attained a certain pinnacle, more or less on its own. In several letters she noted this herself. "The singing has never been so easy . . ." she wrote him. "My voice is so clear and facile this year . . ." And the critics, echoing this view, were writing eloquent reports of the "marvelous sheen," the "scintillating brilliance," the "flawless beauty," while the noted critic and composer Reginald de Koven called her Orfeo this season "for me the most beautiful performance ever given in New York."

But Louise was disheartened, and late in the season wrote a hurried little note, in her dressing room, before the final scene in *Aida*. The next day it was said of this performance that "her voice was dazzling in its brilliance and beauty," the part of Amneris "invested with great tragic significance." But meanwhile the singer was scribbling, "Have you loved me as happily today as I have you? My make-up is off, and my street shoes are on. But the stage will be dark, and no one will know!"

So there it was—Amneris, shrouded from head to foot in deep black veils, her contralto voice blending from above with the voices of Enrico Caruso and Emmy Destinn, imprisoned below— but all the while poised for flight, ready to run away, as soon as she was free, from the opera house, and perhaps from opera.

Throughout the winter Sidney had been coming and going— home for Christmas, then back to Kerhonkson for several months, home again for Easter. When he was home he was most content when he could have a serene atmosphere and her constant companionship. But meanwhile she was singing in Brooklyn, Philadelphia, Atlanta—all over the lot. When she was needed at home this was especially disturbing, and she wrote him, *"Don't dare* talk of singing in opera next year. It is an impossible life, and I long for something very different."

In April she sang the alto part in Beethoven's Ninth Symphony, with a fine new soprano, Frieda Hempel. This was Arturo Toscanini's first appearance as a symphony conductor with the Metropolitan Orchestra, and the performance was called "transcendent." But she was distracted now, and trying to find some way out of a situation that had become untenable. "I will be glad when the season is over," she wrote him. "I only hope we are doing right in trying to stick it out. God is leading us, I am sure, my darling. And we mustn't worry and try to think things out for ourselves, for I *know* he will show us the way *plainly.*"

But there was no easy way, for she had now a good many responsibilities. The oldest daughter was in boarding school; in West Chester her mother needed very special care. Quite a few were dependent for their livelihood on her singing—and in any case, did she really want to stop? They settled, finally, on a compromise solution—a concert tour in the fall, a half-season of opera in the spring, and during the winter some free time at home with her family. It wasn't an ideal compromise, since the concert tours meant long separations. But concerts and the Victor were more profitable than opera, while at the same time engagements at the Metropolitan contributed to a singer's reputation as a concert artist and with the Victor Company. It was all relentlessly intertwined, and it was all very demanding.

In the summer they went to Lake George, and rented a house next door to the Paxtons'—a typically Victorian lakefront home, with porches and jutting bays. And after the hectic winter, her nature, as sensitive as a flower to changes in the environment, responded instinctively to the slower tempo, old friends nearby, the children flat on their stomachs on the dock, fishing with worms, and the early-rising sun etching with layers of light the islands, the mountains and the placid waters of the lake.

Sidney had his studio in the woods, and was setting to music, she wrote her mother, "passages from the works of John Masefield, an English poet we have recently discovered." He had

chosen for his songs dark, impassioned protests depicting the
evils of a too-complacent age, one a passage from "The Widow in
the Bye Street," another from "The Everlasting Mercy." She included both new songs in her concert programs that year.

In the fall Sidney returned to Kerhonkson for a few weeks
of that restorative regime, while she settled the children in West
Chester with his sister Georgie, a resourceful and well loved
member of the family. Then she took off on a tour of the West
that began in Columbus, Ohio, where she was introduced to the
audience by Governor Cox (who would later run for president
against Warren Harding). Here the press reported "thousands
turned away, five hundred spectators seated on the stage." But
on these tours all the crowds were big. In Northampton, when
she sang at John M. Greene Hall, it was said that "afterwards
she was so mobbed by the Smith College girls that to escape she
had to jump into a strange automobile and ask the driver to take
her to the home of the professor where she was staying"; while
in New Haven they wrote that "the pictures of her dark glowing
beauty aren't safe in Woolsey Hall, so fast are they taken away
by the admiring undergraduates." And at Mount Holyoke, when
she discovered that the youngest students had been turned away,
she gave a second, clandestine performance, the girls passing the
word around, then assembling in secret for an informal hour that
had its own kind of magic. "I wish you could have seen their
faces," she wrote him afterward.

After the fall tour there was supposed to be an interval of
rest and quiet in West Chester. But it seemed Gatti hadn't been
properly sold on the half-season of opera, and phoned so often,
asking, as a "personal favor," just one performance, that finally
they ran away altogether and sailed for Europe. This was the
rarest kind of adventure—just the two of them, off together—
sight-seeing in London, bobsledding in Switzerland, exploring
Venice and Rome, Naples and Pompeii. And though they didn't
realize it at the time, they were seeing Europe at a twilight hour
of history, a deceptively placid continent, just before the start
of a great war.

They moved the family back to New York for the last half
of the opera season, which was extended this year to include

most of April, and she sang all the familiar operas—*Götter-dämmerung, Die Walküre, Tristan, Boris Godunov, Lohengrin, Aida*, as well as several luminous performances of *Orfeo e Euridice*. They planned a similar schedule for the next year—a long concert tour in the fall, and a short season of opera in the spring. But when all the arrangements had been made, and the contracts signed, they discovered that another baby would be born in March. However, this was not something to be bruited about, and without telling any of the managers involved she took off on the fall tour anyhow, traveling far and wide, to areas as distant as Texas and Oklahoma.

Her shyness about these intimate family matters stemmed in part from the too zealous, even fatuous probing of the reporters. Again and again, while on tour, she was asked in interviews about her family, and especially whether it was desirable to have children and also a career in opera. And when she would reply in the affirmative the reporters would turn to some other singer, and receive, quite often, a divergent opinion. In this way she had been made, most unwillingly, the center of a controversy that was being debated, at this time, all over the country. The arguments were heated (the burning issue, a home and children versus a career), and the reporters did their best to fan the flames. First they would interview the celebrated soprano Olive Fremstad, and when she told them flatly that an opera singer's children would be sadly neglected, and she should be content with the companionship of dogs, they would rush back to the contralto and demand her reaction to these views. She didn't like the badgering, and during one Western tour wrote her mother, "Don't believe all those things they're writing about me and Olive Fremstad." But the public was fascinated and the debate continued. When Geraldine Farrar was questioned, she also believed, sincerely, that dogs were more suitable as companions, since an opera singer's life was so "harried" and demanding. And Emmy Destinn, with whom Louise shared an interview in Atlanta, advanced, with genuine eloquence, some unusually modern views about the importance of education and equality for women. Meanwhile, in the magazines, there were feature stories—big spreads with pictures of Ethel Barrymore and her infant son, beside photographs of Louise Homer with her twin daughters, to prove that even in the world of the theater there could be domestic scenes.

They had rented a house in Rye for the winter, quite a country place, with lawns and gardens, "ideal for a spring baby," he had written her. But there was still the matter of the contracts, and from Chicago she wrote him hopefully, "Will you see Gatti and break the news before I get home? I wish you would! And I certainly won't be there when you do!" It had always been his role to confide these personal matters to the managers, and since they didn't like to entrust anything so intimate to a letter or written form, he would do it in person or on the phone. So now he "broke the news" to Gatti, and the understanding manager wrote a tactfully vague reply, simply noting that "Louise Homer is unable to fulfill her contract with the Metropolitan for the 1914–15 season for reasons that have been explained to me verbally."

The press reports were also discreet, one attributing her "temporary retirement from the Metropolitan" to "a visit from the stork," and another reporting, somewhat mysteriously, that "a week ago Mr. and Mrs. Sidney Homer made a friendly call on Mr. Gatti-Casazza in his office, and there received the managerial blessing. Madame Homer looked the picture of health, and Mr. Homer was beaming. They have been all season in Rye, New York, enjoying life 'forty-five minutes from Broadway.' "

All this time her mother had been seriously ill with a third stroke and no hope of recovery. So her death, late in February, was almost a dispensation. Louise went to West Chester for the services; all her brothers and sisters were there, and for the assembled children the sorrow was lightened by their mother's enduring faith. Vicariously they had shared her patient longing for that never-to-be-doubted "reunion in the Promised Land." And at this time of loss there was, for Louise, that dramatic juxtaposition—the promise of birth, the finality of death, all the mysteries caught up together like a prism, a double exposure, the focus not blurred, but curiously merged.

Late in March Dr. Brodhead, the obstetrician, came out to Rye, and it seemed to the children rather strange to be having

A family photograph taken at Rye in 1914, when she was in "temporary retirement" before the birth of the youngest child.

breakfast with him in the morning. But then they were spirited away, to visit a friend at a distance, and when they returned, very late, in the dark, with stars in the sky, they heard a strange cry from a remote part of the house, and were told that they had a little sister. The baby girl was born March 28th and named Helen Joy—Helen for Louise's friend Helen Paxton, Joy because it was the title of a song Sidney had recently composed. And there was something unique about this event, for it was the first time in nineteen years, since the first little girl was born, that she hadn't had to plunge back into opera. She was now almost forty-four years old. And because she hadn't expected to have more children, this new baby in the family was regarded with unusual joy and tenderness, the ritual of the bath, the bottles, the airings in a carriage as adventurous and as beguiling as any role she had ever played.

During that leisurely spring in Rye their friends often took

them motoring in the afternoon, for the automobile was still
considered more a diversion than a means of transportation. On
tour she was often treated to "motor trips," and from Asheville
had written him, "These long country drives *satisfy* me in a way
no other distraction does." He felt as she did. They both welcomed the unique atmosphere of privacy, as well as the panorama of unfolding countryside. So now they undertook the
adventure of looking for an automobile to buy, and settled finally
on a Stevens-Duryea, with a canvas top that could be put up in
case of rain. For protection, while they rushed along, at thirty,
or even forty miles an hour, through the exhilarating winds,
she bought an array of veils to tie about her hats. And in June,
when they went to Lake George for the summer, they sent the
children on ahead with the maids and nurses, and motored up
themselves, stopping overnight on the way, and also, occasionally, by the roadside, so the chauffeur could change a flattened
tire.

But though it was an ideal summer, she had to pay a penalty,
for in the fall she found it very hard to leave the new baby girl
at home when she went on the long Western tour. She had cared
for the infant so constantly that she now felt indispensable, and
more than normally distrustful of nurses. She had never planned,
or even foreseen, these long separations from the children; they
had simply come about, since for an opera singer the solo concert tour was an indispensable source of income. No other type
of performance was nearly as profitable, and now, more than
ever, they needed the money. So late in September she packed
the big bags with the concert gowns, the spangled veils, the furs
and, of course, the case of music. And while she was away
Sidney sent her a telegram every day, describing in detail the
baby's weight, the number of ounces gained, the ounces of
bottle consumed and other items of importance.

She urgently needed these messages, for she was off on a
marathon tour—forty concerts from October through January,
the travel strenuous, the weather tempestuous and in each city
something new to cope with—a too artificial setting, perhaps,
and occasionally one that was dirty and dilapidated. In Chicago
she sang a joint recital with the great cellist Pablo Casals—an

exclusive subscription affair, held in the Congress Hotel. This should have been a rewarding occasion, for the cello-like tones of the contralto made a perfect foil for the marvelous strains of the cello. But the setting was all wrong, and for both artists the mood, the spirit, was alien to something inherent in their natures.

Casals was forty at this time, slight, dark-eyed, partly bald. As a fellow artist he was unassuming, so considerate and so sensitive that one might not have guessed that his American debut had been a sensation, and with his cello he had already captivated the world. Of his experiences as a concert artist Pablo Casals would write in later years, "To see people gathered in a music hall came to have a symbolic significance for me. When I looked into their faces, and when we shared the beauty of music, I knew that we were brothers and sisters, all members of the same family." And Louise had echoed this view in letters describing her concerts. "I am content," she had written, "when I can look into their faces, and see the intense earnestness and joy and intelligence of my hearers."

But during the musicale at the Congress Hotel there was an overlay of social amenities, a peacock atmosphere, society preening itself against a background of incidental music. Wrote a reporter, "The boxes were filled with grand opera stars and members of society . . . and the beautiful singer looked simply regal in a shimmering white hat and gown, and received a huge bouquet of roses from Madame Gadski." It was also noted that "seldom have stars received such a welcome as was given Louise Homer and Pablo Casals." But she found the luxurious atmosphere oppressive. "There was a carpet on the floor," she wrote Sidney, "and poor acoustics, and it was too social, not like a real concert at all."

However, performances could also be too drab, and in Topeka, Kansas, she might have welcomed some of that glossy polish. "Even the hotel was filthy," she wrote him, "and filthy theatre, damp, foggy night, pouring rain and mud everywhere. And dressing with hard, cold water to wash and poor lights and over-hot rooms—I can't imagine why anyone wanted a concert!" In Ames, Iowa, the huge gymnasium where she sang for the faculty and students of the University was not easily endowed with an

"When she walked out onto the concert stage to face her audience . . ."

aura of illusion; in Canton, Ohio, five hundred seats were packed onto a too-small stage; while in Peoria, Illinois, the concert took place in the midst of a tremendous blizzard. "To have the great Temple filled," wrote a reviewer the next day, "with a brilliant gathering from floor to roof, with the worst blizzard of the season in full blast, the streets choked with water, and the sleet and rain coming down in torrents, was a tribute so extraordinary that Louise Homer may well count it the greatest triumph of her career."

The response to these solo concerts was almost as varied as the conditions she encountered, and it seemed to derive, at least in part, from the personality of the critic. In Birmingham a lady reviewer was most impressed with her poise and appearance. "In stage presence," she wrote, "no other singer, not even Nordica, quite attains the magnetic effect Homer has on her audience. When she sings she appears tall as a queen, with a figure that for straightness and litheness is rarely seen. She dresses divinely, her back when she leaves is simply glorious, and she walks with an ease and grace that is inimitable." But in Pittsburgh the music critic Charles Henry Meltzer found most appealing a certain inherent integrity. "Some artists," he wrote, "are of themselves living harmonies, and Louise Homer is one of them. She is a woman who has rivals but no enemies. You cannot look at her without feeling the benign influence of her serenity, and this has almost as much to do with the success of her career as the rich fullness of her voice, the unusual loveliness of her face, and the sincerity of her art." However, a reviewer in Brooklyn was more susceptible to the brilliance and the drama. "Last night," he wrote, "Louise Homer blazed upon the sight of Brooklyn in a costume of rose satin and silver moyenage that shimmered about her form like the jewelled robe of Salome. . . . And when she sang *Mon Coeur* from *Dalila*, and threw out her arms to an invisible Samson, an audience of people with umbrellas stood up shouting from their chairs."

Chapter XXIV

The war in Europe had been in progress for a year and a half when she returned to the Metropolitan in February, 1916, and found an opera company that in her absence had been mysteriously diminished. The year before, when she'd been "in temporary retirement" in Rye, absorbed in such a different role, something had happened, but no one knew just what. If there had been drama, dissension, conflict, it was so muffled by discretion that for years afterward there would be speculation—just why did Arturo Toscanini leave the Metropolitan?

The only fact known with certainty was that after a routine performance of *Iris*, on April 14, 1915, that had taken place apparently without incident, the great conductor had simply stopped conducting. He had refused to return again to the podium, and when it was announced that he was too ill to appear, he had embarrassed the authorities by dining in public while someone else was conducting in his place. Meanwhile there were rumors. It was said that Toscanini was at odds with the management over matters of economy, substitutions in his casts, too-limited rehearsals and other sensitive areas in the routine of an opera company. But none of this was confirmed, and the final announcement was uncomfortably ambiguous, the directors simply stating that the conductor was so troubled by the war raging in Europe that he felt unable to continue. Toscanini's only son was serving with the Italian army, and undoubtedly this added to the stress. But it didn't account for the abruptness of his departure, and soon afterward, at the end of the season, Arturo Toscanini sailed for Europe, never to return to the Metropolitan.

Inevitably this meant changes in the repertoire, and when she was in Colorado Sidney had written her, "I learned yesterday that there will be no *Orfeo* this season. They think it will cause comment without Toscanini." Because the great conductor was indelibly associated with their revival, and the management didn't want to invite comparisons, *Orfeo e Euridice* was withdrawn from the stage. For her this meant a loss, both professional and personal, a source of regret, a diminishing, the marvelous poetic settings and the sublime experience of the music and the drama now relegated to memories.

This year when she returned to the Metropolitan, she plunged at once into Wagner—*Lohengrin, Die Walküre, Tristan, Götterdämmerung*. And for all these performances a new conductor was on the podium, a figure of some elegance—tall, thin, dynamic, intense. Artur Bodanzky, a Viennese musician, had made his debut at the start of the season, and Aldrich of the *Times* had called him "a conductor of exceptional and interesting qualities . . . a cause for rejoicing," while Krehbiel had commented that Gatti, faced with the loss of Toscanini, had been fortunate indeed to have had, already on his rolls for the coming season, such a gifted and resourceful leader.

But Gatti had other strings to his bow, as well, including a brilliant roster of singers—and chief among these was the greatest of them all, Enrico Caruso. Caruso's voice was now at its zenith, and had come to be regarded as a kind of national treasure. It was believed irreplaceable, which invited apprehension, and every year there were rumors. Again and again it was reported that the great tenor had "lost his voice," and Caruso himself lived in constant fear that he would discover, one day, that his so vulnerable instrument had suddenly vanished. But meanwhile he expended his great gift almost too lavishly, singing many, many performances, pouring out the liquid tones and appearing, night after night, in a great number of roles.

As a performer on the stage, in the theatrical sense, Caruso didn't have the unique artistry of Jean de Reszke, or the subtlety of Antonio Scotti, who was a very fine actor indeed. But he had, as compensation, a kind of ingenuous involvement, a directness, a sincerity, a personal commitment that endowed, with vitality and a most moving conviction, the parts he sang. Canio in *Pagliacci* was one of his most enduring roles, and then the soaring, sobbing, laughing tones as they poured forth from the forsaken clown conveyed a searing anguish of betrayal.

He made an effective and courageous Radames, an eloquent Manrico. And in the operas they sang together, *Aida, Il Trovatore, La Gioconda, Rigoletto*, their voices had a blending, an interplay of light and dark, a contrast and a texture that was ravishing. The "Ai Nostri Monti" in *Il Trovatore* was a tender, brooding tapestry of sorrow; and when the two voices soared in the "Gia i Sacerdoti" of *Aida* there was a molten braid of music that spiraled, like a magic flame, throughout the opera house.

This year they sang together, for the first time, a French opera that had been revived at the start of the season—Saint-Saëns' *Samson et Dalila*. Caruso made a wonderful Samson—heroic in the early scenes, tragically helpless in the later ones—chained to a mill wheel, blinded, reviled and finally, in the Temple of Dagon, rising to heights of eloquence as he plunged the entire stage into rubble. Louise hadn't sung Dalila since Angers, though she had wanted to, for the mezzo-soprano role was ideally suited to her voice. She had been singing the music year after year, in concerts, and she had already discovered that Dalila could be fashioned into a complex and magnetic character, seductive, beguiling, an enchantress on fire with religious ardor, sacrificing herself for the salvation of her people.

In *Samson et Dalila* Saint-Saëns has contrived, with his music, a striking tapestry of contrasts, for Dalila's truly beautiful arias, "Amour! viens aider ma faiblesse" and "Mon coeur s'ouvre à ta voix," are imposed against a counterpoint of the vivid and the dark—the austere and melancholy Hebrew chants, the sensuous rhythms of the pagan Philistines. The action throughout is somewhat static, too much a series of set pieces, with chorus and ballet. But this inherent flaw can be redeemed with the color, the pageantry and the music. She loved to sing Dalila, and after their first performance, on March 10, 1916, Max Smith accorded "the honors of the evening to the beloved American contralto. . . . What woman's voice heard at the Metropolitan recently," he wrote, "blends so well with Caruso's? Listening to those two great singers as they melted one into the other was in itself a sheer delight."

As usual she was trying to interweave the various aspects of her life. But a few days later, when she took the twins to a matinee performance of *Samson et Dalila*, there was another of those disconcerting moments, for when they saw Caruso clad in dismal rags, chained to a mill wheel, and then, in the final scene, the whole great temple collapse into a pile of rubble, with their mother among those obliterated on the stage, the eight-year-old twins burst into wild, wailing sobs. And since they were sitting in the front of a Grand Tier box, creating, with their rosy smocked dresses, an interesting double image within the prisms of the lorgnettes, this distraction didn't go unnoticed. ("Homer twins weep at opera," said a headline in the *Press* the next day.) And then, a few weeks later, when she was to sing *Aida* in Brooklyn, and before the performance took the baby girl, in the elevator, upstairs for her bottle, there was an unforeseen dilemma when the elevator got stuck, and that performance of *Aida*, with Caruso, Marie Rappold and Pasquale Amato in the cast, had to be suspended, like the elevator, for over an hour, while an announcement was made from the stage, and Billy Guard, the Metropolitan's talented press agent, issued bulletins to the press.

The elevator was a small gilt-and-mirror affair in their Riverside Drive house. For the children it was an indispensable prop in a game they'd invented, and since the game required a lot of button pushing and dashing up and down stairs, they had, perhaps, strained the machinery. So now, while the Otis Elevator people worked frantically in the cellar, and the audience waited unhappily in the Academy of Music, Louise sat on the small square of carpeted floor and sang to the baby girl—lovely, crooning, soothing songs, that floated upward throughout the house, until finally, unexpectedly, the small gilt box also floated upward and she could be released, and rushed, in a limousine, to the opera. There she was greeted with a fervent ovation, and the next day it was said that "her voice was more superb than ever, her concept more brilliant, her beauty more radiant. And her difficult solo in the first scene of the fourth act was an unrivalled masterpiece."

The war in Europe had now become an ever-recurring theme. This winter, when she sang a program of Sidney's songs at the Musicians Club, one reviewer noted that "if a few Zeppelin bombs had dropped in among the sky-scrapers of Forty-Fifth Street last night, half the musical stars would be missing today." "Members turned out hundreds strong," it was reported, "to hear member Sidney Homer's songs. And Louise Homer, beautiful in the simplest of Empress gowns, filled the packed rooms with something more than art in *Sheep and Lambs, Dearest,* and *The Battle of Blenheim,* a song strangely apropos to war undreamed of by the poet Southey."

Nostalgia, and the lengthening shadows of war, seemed to make her audiences especially susceptible to some quality in her singing. In the spring, when she went to Shadyside for a "Golden Jubilee" in honor of her father, it was said that "the audience was spellbound, and many were in tears. . . ." During the past fifty years, since he'd first been made the pastor of a church with twenty-nine members, Will Beatty had become a legendary figure in Shadyside. Now, with her sisters and her oldest daughter, she took part in a memorial service in his honor. Allie played the organ and they sang his favorite hymns—as solos, duets or trios, sometimes with the congregation joining in. And when she sang "Come Thou Almighty King," and let her voice drop down, down, down, in those great descending arpeggios, it was like a mysterious journey backward, into those early childhood days.

In the summer they again lived in a rented house at Lake George. But the annual upheaval of moving vans, trunks and packing boxes had become a great effort and expense, and this year they looked for a place to buy. The land they chose was too inaccessible to be practical for a singer who had to make many trips away—a wooded point, primitive and quite wild, that could be reached only by means of a narrow corduroy road.

At Lake George the year they started looking for a house.

But once they'd seen it nothing else would do, for this was land so beautiful and so varied that the children could roam about for months, or even years, and still find something new—a windy point, perhaps, with a peculiar tumble of strange-shaped rocks, or a gloomy swamp, filled with gorse and reeds, that opened unexpectedly into a sunlit cove. The land was too remote and too isolated for the life they planned to lead, but it had the one quality they most desired—more than any place they'd ever seen, it was romantic.

For years Louise had been dreaming up ideas for the house she would some day have. And all her plans had to do with a way of life she wanted for her family in which much of the time they would live outdoors—sleep outdoors, eat outdoors, play outdoors—all with a blithe informality that would extend also to the interior of the house, which must be made cozy and companionable. To this end she envisioned sleeping porches for everyone, a dining porch and a play porch, a terrace and a back porch, open fireplaces in the bedrooms as well as the other rooms and an array of window seats and interesting nooks and corners.

All this was meant to fulfill some vague yearning she had for a place that would be lively, yet serene and homelike. But the arrangements had to be made in haphazard fashion, many of them by mail, for in the fall she started the concerts, and in October toured throughout the West in *Il Trovatore*, with the Ellis Opera Company. The other offering on this opera tour was *Carmen*, with Geraldine Farrar, and wherever they went they were received with the wildest acclaim. Meanwhile Sidney was writing her that he had decided to have "the cellar dug" before the ground froze over, and was going to use "the new concrete" because it was "cheaper than stone."

But though his plan was meant to be farsighted, when the bids came in from the contractors they were twice what they were supposed to be. So then they had to start all over again with another architect, who would try to devise, on a large rambling cellar, stranded in the midst of some very dense woods, this vision she had of porches and sunlit rooms and a homelike atmosphere.

This year she sang the first half of the season at the Metropolitan—performances of *Tristan*, *Aida*, *Il Trovatore*, several of *Samson et Dalila* with Caruso. And for the first time she sang the Witch in *Hänsel und Gretel* at a Christmas matinee. Always before she had managed to avoid such a confusion of events. But now that most of the children were old enough, she could fit the tuneful little drama into the festivities at home—first the excitement of the stockings, the tree, the presents, then everyone off to the opera.

Before the performance they were carefully briefed—shown the soft plump mattress just inside the glowering oven where the Witch would land when she was pushed, and allowed to play with the cardboard "witch on a broomstick" that would suddenly appear at the end. Nevertheless it gave them a most peculiar feeling when they saw the bent old hag hobbling about on the stage, and heard the familiar tones of their mother's voice merged with the evil cackling. The whole thing was perhaps too vivid and too strange, and afterward it was a great relief when they could run behind the scenes to her dressing room and find her there, in that oddly unreal setting—the big mirrors, the white lights, the costumes hanging about—not changed at all, but looking just the same, as smiling, as familiar, and so radiant that the transformation would seem to them more than ever queer and most unlikely, the evil chin and nose there on the dressing table as confusing as the candy children suddenly come alive.

Ever since that first performance, in 1905, when she'd created the role of the Witch under the guidance of Engelbert Humperdinck, more than ten years ago, *Hänsel und Gretel* had been a favorite at the Metropolitan. Season after season it had been included in the repertoire. But after this Christmas matinee it wouldn't be heard again for a very long time, for the endearing little fantasy had one fatal flaw—it was sung in German. And now, with the imminence of war, and the rising tide of patriotism, there was, as a counterpart, a rising tide of hatred of anything Germanic. On April 13th, when Johanna Gadski sang Isolde in *Tristan*, that performance would prove to be not only Gadski's last appearance at the Metropolitan, but also the last opera sung in German for more than three years.

Even in concerts the German songs had to be eliminated, and doing without the Lieder was a great loss to the singers. It seemed that nothing could take the place of the Brahms, the Schumann, the Schubert, and during an interview in Ohio Louise told a reporter that some of the songs "were going to be translated" so that she could "include them in her program next year."

The United States entered the Great War on April 6, 1917, in a mood that was oddly euphoric. The country was unprepared, the soldiers training with wooden guns, the submarines a menace in the Atlantic. But this was a war sustained by symbols; perhaps, in a sense, an immature war, fought to "save the world for Democracy"—the "slacker" condemned, the enemy reviled and the "uniform" all but worshipped, the neat puttees, the gleaming brown belt, in time the "overseas cap." There were other symbols—medals, the flag, the National Anthem, and all this helped to cradle, and even camouflage, the ugliness and the suffering—the mud-filled trenches, the blight of shell shock and the lengthening casualty lists.

At the very outset Louise was caught up in this wartime panorama, and that meant trappings that weren't always easy to contend with—hastily raised platforms, confused officials,

high winds to blow away the voice, huge crowds stretching almost out of sight and a great array of flags, streamers, balloons,
horns, claxons, anything to create noise, color and participation. In May, Marshal Joffre and Premier Viviani came to New
York to raise funds for the French war orphans, and then the
city became almost hysterical with joy. A galaxy of events was
planned, and the first was the unveiling of a statue of Lafayette
that, by a happy coincidence, had just been completed in Prospect
Park in Brooklyn. "There was a high wind blowing," it was said
of this brilliant patriotic day, "and the flags could not have blown
straighter, but it was cold weather for the thousands of little
school girls who wore white frocks, and red, white and blue
bandeaux around their heads." In the *Press* it was reported that
"Marshal Joffre's first greeting, as he came from his automobile,
was from Louise Homer. She wore a flowing purple cape, and as
the two stood at the base of the monument, speaking together
in French, it might have been a bit of pageantry representing
Columbia greeting the French."

There were no shadowy areas in this conflict, no doubts,
above all, no inhibitions. And at the unveiling ceremony it was
said that "when Louise Homer lifted the American flag, while
Joffre and Viviani stood facing her, stiffly saluting, a hush fell
over the great gathering. Then, rich and clear, her voice rose in
the National Anthem, and it was like a match to straw. Those
who heard her were lifted out of themselves. Men and women
by the score cried openly, and not a sound came from all that
vast crowd to disturb the song—not a sound except low sobs."

The next day Joffre took part in a motorcade through the city.
To those who gathered to see the great war hero, he seemed
wonderfully benign, with his rosy complexion, his creamy
moustache, his monumental calm. In appearance he was a grandfather figure, a kind of jolly Santa Claus, and to a people plunged
suddenly into war, this unwarlike impression was immensely
reassuring.

The final event of his visit was a mammoth gala at the Metropolitan Opera House, billed as "A tribute from the citizens of
New York," in which almost all the great of the theatrical world
took part. Maude Adams portrayed Joan of Arc, Jacques Co-

peau, the celebrated French actor, gave a recitation and a striking series of tableaux was presented, representing all the Allied Nations (Herbert Witherspoon was King Albert of Belgium). Governor Whitman of New York introduced the guests of honor, among them a former governor, Charles Evans Hughes.

The opera house was crowded to suffocation for the farewell tribute, and when Joffre entered and took his place in a center box there was a storm of applause, followed by a stirring "Marseillaise," and an emotional "Star-Spangled Banner." Said *Musical America* afterward, "It was one of the most inspired scenes the Metropolitan has ever witnessed when Louise Homer, after singing the first verse of the National Anthem, stepped to the front of the stage, waved the flag, and the tremendous audience joined in."

The trappings for these great gatherings were dramatic, imaginative, sentimental and sometimes frivolous. On May 12th, the Actors Fund gave a gala benefit at the Grand Central Palace in New York, also to raise money for the French war orphans. As a curtain raiser for this colorful event President Woodrow Wilson, sitting in his study in the White House, pressed an electric button that instantly, as if by magic, "set bells ringing, buzzers and klaxons sounding, and unfurled the flags of all the Allied Nations, while the huge crowd cheered, gongs rattled, horns tooted, and every Boy Scout banged his drum."

The crowd at the Grand Central Palace was so immense that "twice police had to close the doors to prevent a riot." But finally "a sudden silence fell and all eyes turned to a rose-decorated balcony. Then Daniel Frohman, president of the Actors Fund, led forward Louise Homer, and she sang "The Star-Spangled Banner" in ringing tones that carried to every corner of the hall below. . . . As soon as she had finished pandemonium again broke loose, and with it seven hundred actresses, armed with flowers, cigarettes, muffs, collie dogs, knitting bags, hats and potatoes, began their drive upon pocket books."

Rationing was begun, "victory gardens" were springing up in thousands of back yards, and in the summer Louise had a large area dug out of the woods behind their half-finished house and began an ardent battle with mosquitos and rocks and roots.

Every effort must be made to send food to the embattled Allies, and this seemed to her a more direct and more appealing contribution. But there was now a tremendous drive to sell War Bonds; and in October she took part in a "Festival of Songs and Flags" in Philadelphia that was almost an apotheosis of the great patriotic gatherings.

At this time the Russian front was weakening and the Italians had suffered a disastrous defeat at Caporetto. But these reverses seemed only to heighten the exalted mood, and two hundred thousand people came to the huge bond rally, which was appropriately dedicated to "the boys in khaki." Ten thousand flags were distributed, and many wore pinned to their coats a white card with the name of the soldier they were honoring. Wrote a reporter for the *Ledger*:

> It was an inspiring sight—ten thousand American flags held aloft, waving in the breeze. Early in the afternoon a captive balloon rose to a great height and carried over the singers a blue and white banner on which was printed "Buy a Bond." At three the Presidential salute of twenty-one guns was fired from a battery of concealed mortars, the bombs bursting overhead in white puffs of smoke. . . . Madame Homer again mounted the platform and sang an aria from *Samson et Dalila.* The "Marseillaise" followed, and in the lowering sunlight, as the singer sent the thrill of the famous battle song into the very soul of the throng, the spirit of the festival was revealed. An American flag was put into her hands and the great throng stood almost spechless, watching the singer. Her left hand gripped the staff, her right hand was placed across her breast. As far as the throng extended the red, white and blue flags were waving. While she sang an anti-aircraft gun punctuated, with cannon shots, the rhythm of the hymn, and two seaplanes circled above her head and dropped upon the upturned faces, six thousand tiny American flags.

The next day there were headlines: "Contralto stirs populace," "Outburst of patriotism aroused as Homer sings National Anthem" and, in an adjoining column of the *Press,* another story about the war: "In Flanders the heavy rain which stopped Field Marshal Haig's drive yesterday was continuing today, increasing the depth of the sticky mud through which the British have been struggling in their advances."

This year there was such a heavy schedule of concerts that she sang only intermittently at the Metropolitan—performances of *Boris Godunov, Aida* and, on Christmas Eve, *Samson et Dalila.* Of this holiday performance Max Smith wrote that "to judge from the size of the audience domestic duties of this time of year did not affect the demand for operatic entertainment, though it must be admitted that Gatti was offering an attraction hard to resist, with Louise Homer and Enrico Caruso in the cast. . . . The opera house was crowded as it rarely is on Christmas Eve." However, he made no mention of Dalila's own "domestic duties," all the stockings at home to be filled, and for the children, in the middle of that opera night, the soft, electrifying whisper of tissue paper, in a kind of gentle cloud at the foot of the bed.

But it had all become increasingly complex—the whole matter of juggling the concerts, the opera and the responsibilities of family life. In the fall Sidney had been ill, with rheumatism and other troubles, and their lives had become so complicated that they'd sent the twins to a small family boarding school on Lake George. Sidney Jr. was also in boarding school, and the other three were home, while Louise was making frequent trips away.

Her season was to end with a long concert tour in Texas, starting early in April. But as the day approached when she would have to leave, his anxieties seemed suddenly overwhelming. He found he couldn't let her go—the tension and the depressions were too oppressive. And she, in turn, found she couldn't leave him. So she canceled the Texas tour (which meant reimbursing the managers for all their expenses—the promotion, the publicity, the rental of the halls), and instead of the long tour they drove away together, leaving behind the whole world of opera and concerts.

They went up into the hills, to a small sanitarium in the Berkshires, and there she settled down with him to a routine that they were told would restore his health and banish the anxieties. In the main this meant a careful regime of diet, rest and exercise,

and for her it meant a kind of suspension, all the activities suddenly at a standstill, the responsibilities poised uncertainly in a
vacuum. Three of the children were in boarding school and three
were in New York, where his sister Georgie and the oldest
daughter, now twenty-two, were entrusted with the care of the
two little girls. And up at Lake George the new house, though
finally finished, and even partly furnished, stood empty.

From a distance she tried to weave together these various
strands. She wrote the decorators and the contractors, and selected wallpaper from samples. And since one of the occupations
at the sanitarium was handiwork, she wove, for the new house,
an array of table covers and small rugs with fringe, in pretty
shades of blue and green and apricot. In this new haven they
had recreation, relaxation and companionship, but she missed
the children, especially the baby girl, and wrote endless letters to
the ones in boarding school and the ones at home, and hushed,
with the music of her love, the demons of his anxiety. And for
him the tension was somewhat eased, for this was a refuge he
truly needed. But as the weeks passed he clung to the quiet,
ordered routine, unable, now, to imagine any other.

In June he was still unable to leave, so it was arranged that
she would drive up to the twins' Commencement exercises, in
their school at Lake George, to reassure them (for they would
have to stay on at the school), and see the dances and entertainment. But when the time came for her to leave on this brief trip
away, she had become so indispensable that he found he simply
couldn't let her go. So finally, with great reluctance, they tele-
phoned the two little girls to tell them that her visit would have
to be postponed.

Patiently they explained over the phone that she would come
later, in a few days, or perhaps a few weeks. But children cannot measure time in such an indefinite way, and the ten-year-
old twins, while looking forward to their mother's visit, had
been wildly and painfully happy. They had made plans, and
since she was to share their own big room, they had filled it
with vases of flowers. They had even created what they thought
of as an altar—a small table with a lace cloth, two pieces of
wood nailed laboriously into a cross, a picture of Jesus praying

in a garden and a small bowl with narcissus bulbs in bloom. They had come to regard this homemade concoction as a kind of talisman, and all the time, when they were rehearsing their dances, they were saying to each other, "Tomorrow! Tomorrow!"

Now, too suddenly, they were being told that she would have to come some other time. And because they knew no valid way of expressing their desolation, they wailed, "But you won't see us dance! You won't see us dance!" though they didn't really care about the dances (one in which the whole school waved garlands back and forth while they ran in a pattern through a wooded grove, the other a peasant dance in which they put their hands on their hips and stamped their feet). It wasn't that they cared so much about the dances, but they had no other way of conveying their total despair.

That night he couldn't sleep for remembering those choked and weeping voices on the phone. It might seem a small matter, the Commencement exercises and the usual pallid ritual of entertainment. But the sound of those lonely, pleading voices, wailing about the dances at the school, had stirred up for him a forgotten reservoir of communication. He found he couldn't endure the thought of so much childhood misery, and the next day decided, on impulse, to go, himself, with her to the school. They would drive up together, reassure the children and stay just for the afternoon.

So that he wouldn't have to sustain such a strenuous undertaking for more than a few hours, they planned to return to the sanitarium the same day. But for the twins it was such a blissful turnaround that they all but forgot the forlorn arrangement that had them staying on afterward at the school, and began again the ecstatic counting of hours and minutes.

However, they had to contend with a tantalizing delay, for on the way to the school he decided that they must stop and look at the new house. Many of the plans had been made by mail, and he wanted to see how they'd turned out. But in part the impulse came from a certain holiday mood, the effect of a sudden excursion in the midst of the subtle bondage of a quiet, careful routine.

So they made a detour across the marsh, and continued on a

rutty, makeshift road. But when they rounded a curve and saw
the house, there it stood, in all its pristine newness, in the midst
of a hacked-out piece of woods. All about were huge piles of
debris, and the effect was oddly disappointing. He'd never realized
before how important it was to have landscaping—a lawn, grading and shrubbery—to soften the look of a new house. And he
decided he would have to return that night, so that he could
speak to a contractor in the morning and do something about
cleaning up the mess.

Meanwhile the twins, at their school, were anxiously watching
the road. But this ardent sentinel duty was unrewarded, and
finally they had to be routed from their posts to take part in the
first dance. This was a graceful skipping step, with all the girls in
the school waving their garlands back and forth, and weaving,
like wood nymphs, in and out among the trees, to the rhythm of
a piano played on the porch. Because they were the smallest,
they led the whole school in this dance, and they were almost at
the foot of the hill when, in the distance, they heard the family
tune, tooted over and over on the family car, and behind them
one of the bigger girls warning tensely, "Don't run away! Don't
run away!" an admonition that transfixed them into a turmoil
of indecision. But then, irresistibly, it flashed into view—the
familiar car, with the top down, and the usual profusion of coats
and wraps, and their mother smiling, and their father waving
his cane—and like wood nymphs suddenly in heaven, they broke
ranks and ran, letting the dance go on without them.

But there was an uneasy ambivalence to this occasion, and
after the exuberant reunion, and the peasant dance and the rest
of the program, they began to wonder—how long was it going to
last? As always happened when their parents were around, there
had been a shift in the tempo, and now the whole school was
basking in this aura they carried around with them, of kindliness
and exhilaration. One of the girls had sung for them, and asked
their advice about teachers; someone else had showed them a
prospectus. Everything about the school had suddenly become
more interesting and more animated, but how long would it last?
And then they discovered that their father and mother were
going to spend the night in the new house, and began a cam-

paign of begging to "come too," so ardent and relentless that finally their mother said they could. So then they got in the car with their mother and father, and drove to the new house to spend the night.

The contractors came early the next morning, but there were so many decisions to make, about grading and fill and other complex matters, that they had to stay another day, and then another and then on and on and on. Meanwhile their mother was busy arranging things in closets and cupboards, and their father was pondering, long and earnestly, the fate of every tree. Almost always it was the big gray towering beech trees that would be saved. And in the evening after supper they would all four walk down through the woods to watch the sun set over the marsh. This marsh was covered with a short, dark green bush that much of the time seemed tough and stark and rather forbidding. But in the spring the green bush bloomed with thousands and thousands of pink flowers, and sometimes in the evening there would be a radiant interval when the slanting rays of the sun set all the flowers on fire. And that was what they came to see—the dark mystery of the marsh, floating beneath a shimmering sea of flaming flowers.

But for the twins all this was tinged with a certain uneasiness, for the future was still uncertain. They had imagined they would only stay overnight, and instead here they still were, exploring the shore and the woods, day after blissful day. But they kept wondering how long it was going to last, and it was a great relief when finally the rest of the family started to arrive, along with the vans and trunks and boxes that meant they were really moving in.

However, for Sidney, during this suspended interval, the future was still uncertain, for he had never really left the sanitarium— officially he was still there. And so, while one seductive summer day slipped into another, he was haunted by a feeling of impermanence. He lingered because he was urgently needed, and the grading and seeding and planting couldn't wait. But in a sense he was neither here nor there, a kind of wayward truant. Finally, when he felt he could delay no longer, they returned together to the Berkshires for what he imagined would be an indefinite stay. But his doctor found him so much better that he sent him home that very day. And since he would never again have to seek either a retreat or a source of strength outside his home, this was, for him, a lifetime of relief.

Almost a million Americans were fighting in France now, and with this in mind he wrote the words and music of a war song called "Homeland." The Sunday *New York Times* published his song in full, the music as well as the words; Harold Flammer published it as sheet music. And before long, though they weren't quite sure how it came about, they had begun calling their new house by that same name, Homeland.

Meanwhile Louise was involved in the "homefront" war. With her oldest daughter she took lessons in war cookery, and learned how to make "war bread" from various sawdust-like ingredients, and meat substitutes out of beans and bran that tasted like beans and bran. And almost every morning, early, she worked in her "victory garden," wearing the usual "farmerette" costume—a shapeless brown coverall and a brown bandanna. Earnestly she hoed the long lines of beans and peas and corn. But there were compensations, for she'd always had a special feeling for the early morning hours—the sunlit quiet, the birds waking, the dew still on the grass. And the way she felt now was not unlike that eventful feeling, all those years ago, when she'd stood behind the parsonage, her arms filled with lilacs, and watched the sun reach for the top of the church spire.

Everywhere young men were rushing into uniform, and almost every week fledgling officers from the training camp in Platts-burgh would come to see the oldest daughter. Often they would make the trip in their sporty new roadsters, which meant that when there was an overflow the running boards would serve as daring transport, and then the trim uniforms, the glossy puttees, the polished gear—all this would make a dashing show as they rounded the curve of the new gravel driveway.

The "hymn sings" that summer were started by chance because President Wilson had requested "gasolineless Sundays" as a means of conserving fuel. Louise had intended a few family hymns in the evening, as a substitute because they couldn't go to church. But soon friends started coming from a distance, using ingenious means of transport—buggies or carryalls, electric boats or cars. Some came on horseback, others walked or rode bicycles, and there were those who rowed or paddled out into the lake on Sunday evening to hear the music as it floated across the water.

The atmosphere at the hymn sings was informal, the children and young people (many of them in uniform) sitting about on the floor. But the emotional tension because of the war, the unusual blending of the voices, all this conspired to weave a kind of spell. And when they sang the great religious music, the Bach, the Handel, the Mozart, as solos, duets or resounding choruses, they would often have an exquisite violin accompaniment.

The young violinists who came to the hymn sings were pupils of Professsor Leopold Auer, who had his studio, this summer, in Lake George village. Professor Auer had come to America in February, fleeing the Russian Revolution. He was a small and gentle man, with a bristle of white whiskers and dark melancholy eyes. At the Music Conservatory in St. Petersburg he had first discovered and then trained many of the greatest violinists in the world. He had the rare gift of communicating technique, and was a musician of such immense authority that he was revered by all those who studied with him. In America he had found a refuge from the upheaval in Russia, and was still giving occasional concerts, while devoting most of his time to teaching.

One of Professor Auer's most distinguished former pupils, Efrem Zimbalist, also had a vacation home near Lake George. Zimbalist was married to the lyric soprano Alma Gluck, the singer who had been such an ideal Happy Shade in *Orfeo e Euridice,* and throughout the summer there were occasional visits back and forth. During the past several years she and Louise had made many duets together for the Victor Company, records that sold by the thousands, perhaps because of some special affinity in the blending of the voices, a certain tenderness, a unique quality of accord. Some of their recordings were well-known hymns, "Abide with Me," "Jesus, Lover of My Soul," "I Waited for the Lord"; others were familiar lyrics like "Whispering Hope."

Efrem Zimbalist was something of an oddity as a violinist, for he seemed to have escaped altogether the tension and egotism so often associated with the instrumentalist. As a human being he was modest, friendly, most often buoyant. And he had an engaging air of spontaneity and good will that was almost irresistible. The Zimbalists made a sparkling couple. In New York, when she came to the house to rehearse, Alma Gluck would seem to the children beguilingly modern and stylish, in the new accordion-pleated skirts and satin blouses, her brown hair wound in braids about her head. But in the summers when they stopped by for a visit, they might find the pretty singer on her knees in her "victory garden," weeding the beans and wearing, of course, the familiar "farmerette" outfit, the shapeless brown coverall and brown bandanna. She lent even to that mundane costume a certain air of sophistication, and she might then abandon the weeds to show off the new baby boy, Efrem Zimbalist, Jr., a brown and sturdy infant, kicking exuberantly in a carriage under the trees.

General Pershing's Expeditionary Force was now engaged in combat in many sectors of the Western Front, and the casualty lists were growing longer. But the patriotic mood was keeping pace, and on her tour that fall Louise opened her concerts with "The Star-Spangled Banner," to a response that was often electrifying. By this time she had evolved for the familiar assignment an eloquent tapestry of pantomime, participation and soaring, velvety crescendos. First, resolutely, she would take the flag from its standard, and that in itself could become a breathless moment. Then, when she had sung one verse, and had her audience poised in a moment of supreme vulnerability, she would command them to sing, too, and while her own far-flung, ringing tones led the way, there would be a spontaneous outpouring of emotion. Wrote a Springfield, Ohio, reviewer, "The audience rose with the first note, and when the beautiful singer flung wide her arms, eight thousand people joined in the singing." "With audience and musicians standing," noted a reviewer in Cincinnati, "she pealed out the Anthem with clarion notes like bugle calls, until, with the highly-wrought emotion of her singing, and her erect, heroic carriage, she seemed to embody the very spirit of the country." "Her program," said a reviewer in Worcester, Massachusetts, "opened on a note of patriotism that fairly swept the audience off its feet."

This winter she was singing the first half of the year at the Metropolitan, and would open the season in *Samson et Dalila,* an opera considered by one critic most appropriate, since "few lyric dramas represent in as splendid a manner the nation to which we are bound by the closest ties." The date, November 11, 1918, was appropriate as well, for by chance they were able to present a double bill—the opening of the Metropolitan and the winning of the war.

No opening night she had ever sung was more historic, and throughout the evening a victory mood shimmered up and down the rising tiers of red and gold. At the end of the first act the elated singers staged a "victory pageant" for an emotional audience—the curtain parting unexpectedly to reveal the entire company massed on the stage. In her Dalila costume Louise stood in the center, just behind the footlights, holding a large American flag. Ananian was on her right with the British flag, Caruso on her left with the Italian, Rothier held the French flag, Reschiglian the Serbian, and behind them all the members of the chorus each had a flag to wave. A huge American flag had been hung at the back of the stage, and in this colorful array they sang the national anthems in stirring succession—"The Star-Spangled Banner," the "Marseillaise," the Italian "Hymn of Mamelli," "God Save the King." The audience then clamored for more, savoring the joyful intimacy of the opera house, the mood so jubilant and unrestrained that the drama in the auditorium all but overwhelmed the drama on the stage.

Chapter XXV

In February they all watched, from a hillside in Central Park, the famous Rainbow Division march down Fifth Avenue to Washington Square, where a beautiful spangled Victory Arch had been created, as well as a plaster replica of the Arc de Triomphe. But perhaps it was, after all, a plaster triumph, for within a few months many of the returning soldiers had joined the ranks of the unemployed and were sitting about on park benches, in bits and pieces of their discarded uniforms; while over in Versailles the victorious statesmen were laying the groundwork for an even more devastating World War. However, Sidney could not foresee this dismal aftermath, and he had such a longing for peace and justice that he imagined an idealism corresponding to his own, and wrote her, while she was on tour, "Never in the history of the world has there been such a yearning for the true way. Thousands, even millions of minds, are struggling with the problem. The true solution must mean the salvation of the *entire* race, and the world is seeking this for the *first* time in *history*."

However, the German language was still banned from the stage of the Metropolitan. And that meant no Ortrud, this season, no Brangäne or Magdalena, no perilous rides in Erda's rickety dumbwaiter, no treacherous journeys in Fricka's little goat cart (though, in fact, Gatti had eliminated that miserable mode of transport some time ago; now Fricka strode forth on her own feet, to cast the bleak shadow of her morality over the world of the gods). But she did have a new role this year, Fidès in *Le Prophète,* which she sang with Caruso as the prophet, John of Leyden.

This is an uneven music drama, with some scenes that are magnificent, and others less effective, for the libretto is too complex and too political. But within this excess of pageantry Meyerbeer has created in *Le Prophète* the first dramatic mother and son impasse in opera. His Fidès is a forerunner of Azucena, a powerful role throughout, and there are mezzo-soprano arias of great beauty: "Ah! Mon fils!" a masterpiece of consoling motherhood; the scornful, passionate "O prêtres de Baal"; "Donnez, donnez," a tremulous and most affecting expression of sorrow. Louise sang *Le Prophète* first on November 23, 1918, and afterward Pitts Sanborn wrote in the *Sun* that "her singing of *Ah! Mon fils!*—one of the pearls of Meyerbeer's genius—was superbly eloquent. Thanks to her skill and that of Caruso, the scene in the inn and the scene in the cathedral were two of the most engrossing and finished episodes one is likely to witness in this or any other season." In the *Times* the reviewer noted that "the American contralto sang magnificently, spanning with apparent ease the abnormal range of the part."

But though the outcome was reassuring, it was still a demanding role, especially the perils of that "abnormal range." And it seemed, in a way, symbolic, like the closing of a circle, a kind of lyric frame, that what was most likely the last big new role she would learn had also been the first, Fidèle Koenig's "showpiece," the one in which she had found herself, and discovered, so unpredictably, the control, the suppleness, the flights of song that would make possible what came after—the auditions for Monsieur Bussac and Maurice Grau, the contracts and the career.

Late in January she left home on a tour of the West, and as usual took a number of books with her to read on the trains and in the hotels. This had long been a habit, and as a rule the books were novels—the words of A. S. M. Hutchinson, John Galsworthy and other favorites. But recently she had discovered a

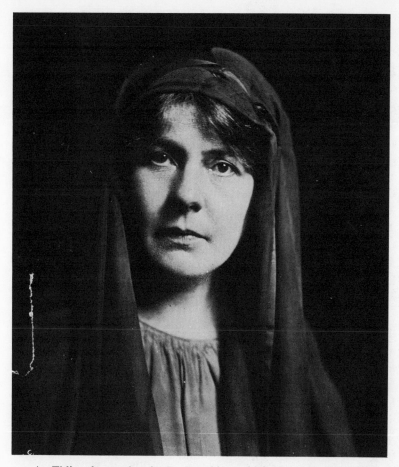

As Fidès, the mother in *Le Prophète,* which she sang in 1918, with Caruso as John of Leyden.

new preoccupation and had begun taking with her, while on tour, a number of books on the subject of philosophy and religious thought. She approached these with the zest of a detective-story addict, comparing views and ideas, searching for clues and trying, perhaps unconsciously, to reconcile the teachings of her childhood with the insight derived from experience and maturity. It was an ardent quest, and a demanding one, for as she probed deeper the whole subject of religious philosophy became increasingly complex. From Chicago she wrote him, "I *love* my new books. They're *just* what I need. I have finished the first: *The Bible in the Making.* Now I am reading *How We Got Our*

Bible, and I'm sorry I did not bring the others. Could you please send me to Boston *The Old Documents and the New Bible* PDQ so it will be there Monday waiting for me?! Please don't forget, my darling. I have two whole days, and am *so* interested!"

She pursued her new avocation in church, and often took down in shorthand, during the sermon, any thoughts or passages that appealed to her. As a rule the ministers became family friends, Dr. Jowett of the Fifth Avenue Church in New York, and Dr. Kelman, both distinguished theologians, and others from other denominations, among them Harry Emerson Fosdick. And at times, in the midst of a stimulating debate, she would startle her minister friend with her forthrightness, dismissing airily some long-established precept and setting forth, with beguiling earnestness, the gradual evolution of her philosophy.

There is a psychologist, Dr. David Gutmann, who has defined three stages of adulthood—a progression he considers as fateful and essential as the more obvious stages of childhood and adolescence. In his view the first stage, in young adulthood, is concerned with the external world, and means, for the individual, founding a career, a home and family, achieving success and a measure of approval. But when this has been accomplished he perceives, for the middle years, an essential second stage that turns inward to some more profound or personal fulfillment, and encompasses, perhaps, a change of direction, some new preoccupation, a more demanding effort, a new and deepening perspective. For the end of life Dr. Gutmann defines a third and final stage that once again turns outward, but this time to more altruistic and social endeavors, the drive of young adulthood and the inner strivings of the middle years at least in part fulfilled.

Just as there can be trouble for the adolescent trapped in childhood, or the adult still adolescent in his views, Dr. Gutmann believes that many traumas of the later years occur because of some fixated situation that leaves the individual stranded in the early adult stage, and therefore facing, in his middle years, monotony and disenchantment. As examples he cites the woman whose children have grown, the businessman who has achieved his goal—in both cases a confrontation that becomes in time too static, with, in effect, a diminishing return. And he might have included the opera singer who has scaled certain heights, often with immense effort, only to discover an uneasy plateau, with, in the future, to enchant the spirit, repetition and perhaps memories.

She had, of course, no knowledge of all these theories, and very little consciousness of self. But with the new philosophical studies, she had slipped instinctively into that so essential second stage. The quest for a deepening of understanding was a progression that had evolved from within her nature, just as thirty years before, after high school, while deciding airily but firmly that she was going to earn her living and become independent, she had plunged heedlessly, yet irresistibly, into maturity, and paved the way for whatever was to come. Now it was a less dramatic crossroads, in a sense an adventure of the spirit. But for her it was as challenging, and in its way as exhilarating, as that walk across Philadelphia, all those years ago, to ask Mr. Bonar about a choir position.

Unwittingly this added dimension in her life had the effect of outwitting the years, since the signs of age and maturity were touched now with a serenity, an intelligence, an affirmation that created a most affecting image on the stage. Again and again the reviewers were writing, these days, of "the silver strands," or "the gray in her hair," only to add that "it enhances her beauty" or "gives an added touch to her charm." Wrote a reviewer in Scranton, Pennsylvania, "Chiefly the audience studied the beautiful face of the singer, whose portraits never do her justice. The color came and went in her cheeks. Her eyes shone, and her hair, touched with silver, lay in soft thick waves, fastened in a low knot. She has the rarest poise, and every attitude is one of beauty."

When she returned home, now, after the long tours, the props would all be right there for the kind of home she'd always wanted to create. Though the children seldom remembered to use them, there were the separate lockers in the back hall, collecting a random supply of fishing gear and rubbers; and there were the sleeping porches, small cubicles with brick-red canvas on the floor, and sky-blue ceilings. In the serene, inviting living room there was a deep, inviting sofa, covered with purple chintz and amply proportioned—big enough for half a dozen children, and so sturdy that they could make a game of plunging, all in a row, backward into its enfolding depths, and the littlest ones could bounce about and turn it into a ship.

She had learned a piquant recipe for salad dressing, and at noon, when they had their lunch on the dining porch, which extended out onto the lawn, she would gather the ingredients around her, and stir and measure until she was satisfied with her creation. But often there would be a dramatic interruption, for already they had started what would become a tradition, and when the *Mohican,* one of the steamers on the lake, passed the house, they would all leave the table and dash out onto the terrace, their wildly waving napkins an exuberant salute, while the genial captain of the ship tooted over and over a joyous reply.

This broad brick terrace that they had, overlooking the lake, rivaled, in its setting, many of the rare beauty spots of the world, for Lake George is a glacial lake, long and narrow, with mountains rising steeply, islands floating serenely and a unique quality of light and temperament, so that the conformations, the points of land, the islands and bays, are forever changing. Their house was situated on a slight rise, and directly across from the most eloquent of the mountains. Intervening was a two-mile expanse of water, sometimes placid, sometimes stormy, and a span of sky and atmosphere so crystal clear that it would often seem that Buck Mountain was floating in the air, soaring, reaching, though at the same time safely moored, imponderable and timeless. This mountain had already become a part of their lives, for it greeted them, in its different guises, all day long—in the early morning decked with clouds, or golden with light, in the evening dark and calm and inexorably there.

They had a great many visitors at Homeland, friends and relatives who came and went all summer long. Sometimes they stayed for weeks at a time—her sister, Allie, who was widowed now; Bess and Daisy and their children; his sister, Georgie, and many others. But at the same time there were nooks and corners, isolated points of land and in time a playhouse and studios, so that anyone who wanted it could have solitude. This made a kind of pattern, a comfortable merging of activity and apart-

Homeland from the lake—this view shows the terrace and the dining porch.

Homeland on the driveway side.

ness, for there were hobbies, there were pets, there were games of all kinds—outdoor games and charades and guessing games and card games, and a lively parade of people coming and going, but anyone who wanted to could be peacefully alone.

Some years before, several members of the Peabody family had built baronial mansions on Lake George, palatial estates with an almost foreign air. One of these Peabody homes had recently been bought by Adolph Ochs, publisher of *The New York Times,* and when the children went there to visit they would admire the broad expanse of parquet floor and the marble statuary in the hall. They were invited often, for Adolph Ochs was a kind of Pied Piper to the children, with lively stories to relate, and a great fund of jokes, comical poems and puzzles. He had a complex nature, sensitive and very human—an idealism, a compassion that sometimes made burdensome his role in world affairs—and such an affinity for children that often at the family gatherings he would desert the older guests to join in the fun and foolishness of the younger ones. Farther up the lake, a few miles to the north, Charles Evans Hughes lived, in the summer, with his wife and daughters—the youngest, Elizabeth, a playmate for the twins. Two years before, Hughes had lost the presidency to Woodrow Wilson by the narrowest of margins. But though he was now temporarily retired from public life, there was no aura of disappointment, for Mr. and Mrs. Hughes, a quietly devoted couple, had, at all times, a rare dignity and an almost austere serenity. And to the south their nearest neighbors, Maurice and Polly Hoopes, could walk over from their place on the shore, to spend a leisurely hour on the terrace or join in the evening games in the living room. Mr. Hoopes was an old friend from West Chester, and he had a Quaker shyness and reserve that made him something of an observer, but a sympathetic and often fascinated observer of their uninhibited activities—the dressing up, the mysterious whispering in corners, the heated arguments when they played charades, and especially the laughter that was most often sparked by the familiar floating octaves of that irrepressible contralto.

Meanwhile there was the matter of a contract with the Metropolitan, and in the spring, after some debate, she decided not to sign for the coming season. By this time she had been nineteen years with the opera company (interrupted only once, by the birth of the youngest child), so this break would mean a new precedent, a turning point in her career. And though the concerts were more profitable, she was influenced most of all in her decision by the limitations of the opera repertoire. Too many of the roles she had sung over and over, with different sopranos and tenors and conductors, but always the same music. All that repetition could be tedious, and she decided this year to devote herself entirely to the concert tours—where the demand as well as the fees seemed to be increasing every year, and where she could build her own programs and interpret the music she most wanted to sing—the arias, the Gluck, the Mozart, Sidney's songs, the beautiful Lieder.

But she wasn't alone in this decision, for when there was an important step to take, it was almost always his view that prevailed. His was the major role in these matters, and he approached each aspect of her career with a complex blend of idealism and caution, weighing the practical and the needful against something that he considered even more essential—the inner life and evolution of the artist.

At times he was too visionary, for he had a whole tapestry of theories evolving about the hidden core of creativity, the "divine spark" in every man, and more than once his buoyant faith had sent some friend or acquaintance off in ardent pursuit of that elusive rainbow. But in his handling of her affairs he was most often astute and realistic, undertaking the responsibility in part because he believed that artists were too often the victims of exploitation. In his view the very nature of their work made the musician and the singer vulnerable to the strategies of those who hoped to profit from their art—to manipulation, flattery, even outright deception. Therefore it was his task to steer a passage through these dangerous shoals, and for her this careful collaboration was much more than a comfort—in its way it was indispensable.

But the decisions were never easy, for their overriding concern all these years had been the preservation of the home. A career in singing and a tranquil life—that had been their unlikely goal, and for a long time a contract with the Metropolitan had seemed the safest course. That way they could at least have a permanent home, and over the years, when she had received offers from Covent Garden and other European opera houses, glowing prospects of extended tours in Australia or the Orient, engagements that might have enhanced her reputation and furthered her career, she had refused, not wanting to disturb their life at home and perhaps diminish the stability and contentment they had managed to achieve.

Now they were still trying to reconcile those two divergent goals, and when he planned her concert tours he spaced them so that she wouldn't have to be away too long at a time. This upset the managers and made their work more difficult. But it meant that they could have more often those intermittent reunions when some of the children would go with the chauffeur to Fort Edward to meet the frost-encrusted train and bring her triumphantly back again. Wrapped in furs, laden with bags and packages, she would make the long trip home, and almost at once it would seem as though she had never been away.

In all her concerts she included a group of his songs, an arrangement that was facilitated because his lyrics had, in themselves, an unusual diversity. The quaint humor of "The House that Jack Built" would make a striking contrast to the bitter tragedy of "The Widow in the Bye Street," and when, from her place behind the footlights, she would see in the faces of her audience the enchanted smiles, the surprise and delight, turn, a moment later, to expressions of sorrow or pity, she would know that the chemistry was at work—that elusive alchemy that is the true measure of a concert. But it didn't always happen that way. Sometimes the rewarding moments were only occasional, and at other times the faces might be noncommittal, or only politely interested. Then, after a perfunctory round of applause, she would collect her fee, go on to the next city and walk out onto another stage, never entirely sure how it would be this time. And often, in that first vulnerable moment when she faced her audience, she would know.

This year she was sharing several of her recitals with her oldest daughter, an arrangement that had come about more or less by

chance, though for several years they had been singing duets
together at the hymn sings and for family and friends. Young
Louise had been musical ever since those long-ago days in Paris,
when, as a toddler, she had delighted her mother by picking up
a music roll and pretending she was "going to her lesson." She
had a lyric soprano voice with an unusual purity of tone, and for
some years had taken lessons with their old friend the bass singer
Herbert Witherspoon.

She had made her solo debut in 1917 at the Twentieth Century Club in Pittsburgh, then appeared, a few weeks later, at the
Academy of Music in Philadelphia. And that time they had gone
secretly to hear her, hiding clandestine fashion in the balcony,
so as not to disturb the precarious poise of an inexperienced
singer. But they had found that she was quite assured on the
stage—brown-eyed, serious, a quietly self-contained young artist.
The next year, when they'd gone again to hear her, in a concert
at the Globe Theatre, there'd been an impromptu finale that was
quite revealing. Noted a reviewer, "There came a moment at the
end of the regular numbers, when Miss Homer was recalled and
recalled, and finally bowed to the demand for her father's famous
Banjo Song. Then who should appear with her but that most
popular of American artists, Louise Homer, herself. It was beautiful. Without any sign—spontaneously—the huge audience
jumped to its feet to greet the Metropolitan artist." The first
duet stirred up such a storm that they had to sing several more.
Wrote the reviewer, "I heard the debut of Galli-Curci, and that
of Heifetz, but there was never such applause! And all went away
feeling that they had been present at an event."

This impromptu occasion interested the managers, who seemed
to feel that the presence of both mother and daughter on the
stage had an unusual appeal. They already had a repertoire of
duets, and would alternate the solo groups; contracts were signed
and they gave several recitals the first year, a few more the next.
Then, in the spring of 1921, they gave a joint concert at Carnegie Hall, with all the critics present, which made it, in effect,
the young singer's official debut. The next day *The New York
Times* reported that "Miss Homer's voice is a soprano of pleas-
ingly light and buoyant quality. . . . Her singing has intelligence,

With Louise Jr. when they were singing concerts together.

sincerity and musical feeling," while in the *Tribune* it was noted
that "she has a voice of light timbre but plenty of power."

In addition to the concerts they made a number of Victor
records together—one of them the *Stabat Mater* they had sung
together at the hymn sings, another Sidney's "Sheep and Lambs,"
a religious song that is still being sung today by choirs and
choral groups. This seemingly timeless spiritual lyric has, in the
opening passages, a light translucent quality, and throughout a
mood of comfort and quiet that rises, toward the end, to an
eloquent crescendo, when the sopranos soar brilliantly while
the altos maintain a yearning peace.

The hymn sings had, by this time, outgrown the Homeland

living room, and were being held in the country club, where hundreds came on Sunday evenings, filling the big rooms and spilling over onto the terrace, to share what had been intended as a most informal family pastime. But Louise had many to help her at the hymn sings—violinists, pianists, singers—for Lake George attracted musicians, just as it repelled painters. This might seem a paradox, since the surroundings were so uniquely beautiful. But it was a kind of beauty that quickly defeated the visual artist, who would find his talents dwarfed and dwindling and turn instead for his inspiration to the more intimate qualities of a Vermont landscape or a Cape Cod village.

Just as the lofty eloquence of the Swiss Alps rarely attracts artists, here at Lake George there was a distillation of beauty that resisted control, and when transferred to canvas became artificial, taking on the look of a picture postcard panorama. The ever-changing effects, the dramatic contours of the mountains, the deep blues and greens, the brilliant massing of clouds, the calm of an evening, the shafts of light and shade—all this could be a torment to the painter who found himself unable to translate onto canvas something that he lived with every day.

But though the painters stayed away, the most talented of musicians were attracted to this area. And one day when they were at lunch, at least a dozen of them in the Homeland dining room with the old refectory table from some monastery, the mantelpiece and woodwork painted a deep blue, she heard, from the hall, a voice, a phrase from *Lucia*, sung with a lilting modulation. And the delicate, ravishing tones, wafted eerily from the past, were so unexpected that for a moment she looked utterly astonished, then hurried to greet an old friend from the early days of opera—Marcella Sembrich.

Madame Sembrich had come to Lake George to establish a summer home and give her singing lessons in a charming studio, a few miles to the north. This reunion was to be a renewal of old friendships, and the gifted coloratura who had made her debut with the Metropolitan the year it opened was just as she had always been—the dark-brown eyes lively with intelligence, the personality a subtle blend of vivacity, warmth and rare dignity.

It was almost fifteen years ago that Sembrich had left the

stage with such a touching "farewell performance" at the Metropolitan. Since that time she had become an accomplished singing teacher, and now, in the summers, her pupils followed her to Lake George. That meant that during the season there would be enchanting musicales at the Sembrich studio, impeccable affairs, endowed with a certain continental air. And Marcella Sembrich, their hostess on these occasions, would be, as always, petite and elegant, the attire and the decor—the jeweled velvet chokers, the mass of auburn curls, perfectly coiffeured, the silk gloves and damask gowns—reminiscent of an earlier age, yet ideally suited to the style and the inimitable poise of one of the truly great of the musical world.

Chapter XXVI

Friends and relatives were always coming to visit at Homeland, and one who was there year after year was Louise's youngest sister, Daisy. Like Allie and Ella, Daisy had remained in West Chester and moved only a few blocks when she was married, from her mother's comfortable home to another on a similar tree-lined street. She had married a young doctor, Roy Barber, whose father had long been a doctor in town, and their comfortable brick-and-frame house had a wing to serve as Roy's office, and a waiting room for his patients. It seemed an ideal arrangement, but there had been a disappointment early in their marriage, for the first baby boy, born in the spring of 1908, had died at birth—a perfect infant, endowed with everything but the breath of life. ("It is planned," her mother had written sadly, "that Roy will take Daisy to Atlantic City to help her forget her sorrow.") Two years later, in 1910, another baby boy was born, this one blessed with perfect health—an unusually handsome child, strong, lively and intelligent. He was named for his grandfather, Samuel Osborne Barber, and his father planned that in time he would follow in the family footsteps and become a doctor.

It seemed to his parents a kind of dividend that young Sam Barber was musically gifted, and Daisy would write proudly that when he was barely two Sammy was making up tunes on

the piano, at six he was playing the cello, at seven he was conducting an "orchestra" of youngsters his own age, and at eight
he had begun writing down his own compositions. But once he
had started school the father became anxious about this preoccupation with music, for it kept the little boy too much at
the piano, instead of outdoors playing games with his classmates.
In West Chester music was regarded mainly as a diversion, and
a rather odd one at that. It wasn't considered a serious occupation, and so the parents worried and tried to make rules, until
one day the mother found a letter on her dressing table that was
meant to explain, once and for all, just how it was. "To begin
with," her little boy had written, "I wasn't meant to be an athelet.
I was meant to be a composer, and I will be, I am sure. Don't
ask me to forget this and go and play football. *Please*. Sometimes
I worry so much about this that it makes me mad! (not very)."

Although the plea had been softened at the end with a characteristic touch of self-mockery, what young Sam Barber was trying to convey was very real. In school, at home, wherever he
went in West Chester, there was a certain attitude toward music,
a belittlement, as though it had no valid place in the scheme of
things. But when he came to Homeland in the summer he would
find all that turned right around, with music center stage, and
all those other occupations relegated to the wings. For a youngster who was often in a vacuum at home this was profoundly
reassuring. And almost always, when he came, Sam would bring
some compositions.

The first one, called "Sadness," was composed when he was
nine years old. Each year there were others, and he would show
them to his Uncle Sidney in the studio by the lake. There, after
reviewing his work, they might study together a Bach *Invention*,
or some other classical work, mutually absorbed in what seemed
to both of them a kind of unfolding miracle. And so this composer uncle became, for young Samuel Barber, the one he could
turn to, the one who understood. When he was twelve years old,
and about to enter high school, he wrote a letter enclosing several compositions, and asking two important questions. He felt
that he had reached a crossroads; if he was to devote his life
to music he must begin now planning his future. So he asked:

Do you think from these works of mine that I can become a composer? And if so, what should I do to further my musical education?

For Sidney this youthful request for guidance posed certain problems, for he didn't want to go over the heads of the parents, who planned for their only son such a different future. But at the same time he recognized the urgency, for in music the training must start young. So he tried, in his reply, to steer a middle course, with a letter that was moderate in tone—feasible, explicit and geared most carefully to the understanding of a twelve-year-old.[15]

His letter was too precise and too persuasive to be overlooked in West Chester, and there it precipitated a crisis. The errant talent that had flowered so relentlessly must now be dealt with; the little boy who had ignored the bracing sunlit hours and preferred the piano to football was growing up. And so there were many anxious discussions, and finally a compromise was worked out. According to this arrangement, the young music student would go to Philadelphia every Friday for lessons in piano and composition at the Curtis Institute in the morning, and symphony or chamber music concerts in the afternoon. The weekly absence from school was easily managed, since Dr. Barber was chairman of the School Board, and could make a ruling that any student who was a composer could take Fridays off. For the father this was only a truce, and he still planned, for his only son, a proper and profitable profession. But meanwhile there were those weekly trips to Philadelphia, a timely shuttle back and forth, so that young Samuel Barber could study the works of the great masters, learn the intricacies of harmony and counterpoint and fashion for himself a future.

All summer long people came and went at Homeland, but in the fall there weren't many visitors, and then the cool, crisp, shining days closed in around them with a humming cadence of solitude and self-sufficiency. Sidney found this time of year irresistible—the brilliant windy weather, the gradual gold and gray of the hills, the open fires and lively comforts inside the house—and was tempted to stay on and on and on, later each year in the fall, to return earlier each year in the spring. That meant that the children popped in and out of their schools more or less at random, and were always behind in their studies. But he had always mistrusted schools in any case. He considered them a form of "petty tyranny," disliked what he called the "regimentation" and finally, as a kind of compromise, engaged young college girls as tutors, a system that was only mildly effective, for it wasn't easy to lure those reluctant students out of the woods. But that aspect of their education he scarcely noticed, for he was persuaded that they were better off doing as they pleased, one of them with paints and easel, for she was planning to become an artist, another with her mother's type-writer, for she wanted to become a writer, and all of them with the many pianos, the mysterious woodland and the big attic playroom that had, as part of its endowment, a huge trunk filled with opera costumes—velvets and crowns and trains and jewels—contributed by the chief costumer at the Metropolitan.

At night they slept in a playhouse on the lake, and warmly bundled, with a lantern to guide them, would coast down the hill to bed. But inevitably their lives had a kind of spectrum quality, the colors paling and brightening with the effect of a stage set, because their mother was so often either coming home or going away. This made a continuing drama of reunions and separations, a kind of seesaw of contentment and vague loss, yet when she was home it would seem, almost at once, as though she had never been away. There would be her voice, singing some message up the stairs, vague wisps of familiar radiance floating about the hall. There would be her typewriter, in a small office off the living room so that she would have a sociable set-ting when she rattled off the many letters, her fingers flying over the keys with a rhythm that they found astonishing, for they knew only vaguely about the Lingle College for lady typewriters. And there would be the continuing games with the youngest little girl, the ritual at bathtime, the special tunes and favorite books, the parrot that followed her about the house and rode to dinner on her shoulder, the walks through the woods, around the points, that she made somehow eventful, stopping to point out on the way a cluster of ferns, a vista or an especially pretty tree.

Sometimes they would hang around and watch while she packed the big bag (that had pasted inside the cover a long list of the things she must take), beginning, already, to feel a little forlorn, though there she still was, folding the crystal and glitter of the concert gowns into long strips of tissue paper. But she was always smiling when she said good-bye, as though everything was just as it was supposed to be, and that would make a safe bridge into that other, plainer spectrum where they lived when she was gone.

They were tempted to save the most interesting events until she had returned—a sleigh ride, for instance, with two horses and their sleds tied on behind, or a skating party on a pond they'd discovered a few miles to the north, the ice like glass, though the big lake was not yet frozen over. And when it was almost Christmas they would decorate the house with ground pine, and stars pasted onto strips of colored paper, until finally the double suspense of preparing for Christmas and waiting for her to come home would build into a pyramid of longing. But she would be making preparations, too, and would write him from Cleveland, "Don't open *any* of the packages when they come. I want everything to be a surprise!"

On that concert tour she had a bit of bad luck, for following the last concert in Springfield, Massachusetts, she had lost the fee she was given—$1,800 in cash. She had put the money in her pocketbook, and given it to her sister Bess to hold, while she greeted friends and well-wishers and signed autographs. In all the confusion Bess had somehow mislaid the pocketbook, and no one had been able to find it.

However, this didn't seem to affect the homecoming, and soon the children were able to persuade her that there was nothing she so much wanted as an afternoon of skating on a small pond with ice as smooth as glass. Vividly they described the joys ahead; ardently they begged her to join them in this most entrancing pastime. And finally they all went, two carloads of them, to the small pond some miles away, scarcely noticing the snow clouds overhead.

She was wearing her heavy beaver coat for this outing, and the beaver fur cap, for it was very cold. And at first she was

Anne at the time of the accident on the ice.

very careful on the ice, and let him hold both hands crossed, while they skated slowly, like figures in a painting, and all the others careened about, showing off. But after a while she became braver, for she had learned to skate all those years ago, in the water-main ditches in Minneapolis, she had skated many times since and she was sure she could do it alone. So then they all skated gaily here and there, until suddenly they looked around and there was all the beaver fur, in a motionless heap on the ice.

No one had seen her fall, and when they lifted her up there was no color at all in her face. She was waxen pale, which frightened the children, for they had never seen her like that, and she didn't know where she was. "Where am I?" she asked, in a child's voice. And she didn't know who they were, either.

They took her home in a sudden, driving snow that became, very quickly, a blizzard, almost obscuring the road. But the doctor was able to come, and he said he thought she had a concussion, possibly severe, and a sprained wrist, and had fallen so heavily on her face that perhaps only the thickness of the fur cap had saved her life. But what was a concussion? And was it, in fact, only a concussion? In the midst of all the Christmas decorations, and the wildly whirling snow, and their mother mysteriously stricken, this homecoming day had become, for the children, like a sudden swoop down a steep hill into nothing.

Even the house was strange, a numbed and shaken place. And it seemed to everyone like a kind of clown's joke when suddenly there was good news—a phone call from Springfield that her pocketbook had been found. Sidney went to her at once, and said, very gently, "They have found your pocketbook." But she didn't understand, and only murmured something incoherent, the words slurred together, weak and confused.

As abruptly as it had started, the storm stopped, and a brilliant moon soared over Buck Mountain. The twins were used to these dramatic changes in the weather, and to escape all the unanswered questions in the house, they walked for a long time along the silvered shore. Vaguely they understood that hovering above them now, obscuring, like a dark wind, the dazzling promise of Christmas, was a disaster so profound that they mustn't even touch it. So instead they walked at night in a brilliant silver world, feeling curiously remote, cold and contained, as though they were floating about in space, deprived of any feeling.

But finally, with reluctance, they left their fragile silver landscape to return to the beleaguered house, and there they discovered that in their absence something had happened, for when he had gone a second time to tell her about her pocketbook, she had exclaimed at once, in her own strong, beautiful voice, "You must call Bess right away. She'll be so happy and relieved!"

This dizzy swooping about gave a kind of drama to that Christmas, for though it was all familiar, even a certain way she had of sharing with each child a hushed and breathless moment when he was finally the one to open a present, this time, in the midst of the carols around the tree, and the presents from Cleveland, they would think of how vulnerable they were. But she didn't seem aware of it herself, and almost before they knew it she was off again, on another winter tour. And these were quite likely to be adventurous, especially during the blizzard season, for she had experienced, many times, unwelcome dramas or dismal episodes—trains stranded in deep snow, missed connections, ghostly waits in eerie stations.

Sometimes, when the timing was very close, there would be a madcap trip in a taxi, directly after a performance, a perilous ride that would deposit her, without ceremony, in an unfamiliar railroad station. And then, while she was plunging hurriedly into an alien world of travelers and porters, she might catch a glimpse of herself in a mirror, the makeup half on and half off, the hat somewhat awry, the shimmering velvet gown scarcely suitable, and for a moment would be richly, though fleetingly amused, for it would seem to her a comical situation, an odd counterpoint to the elegance of the performance, this impetuous and somewhat disheveled dash, with the train about to leave and not a moment to spare.

It was the manager's province to provide the itinerary—make the reservations, buy the tickets, arrange for hotel rooms. But now and then mistakes were made, and when she arrived in Minneapolis that winter she discovered that a hundred school children had waited at the railroad station, each with a flower to give her and a song they planned to sing. They had meant to welcome her to the Washington School, where she had gone when she was eleven, but though they waited a long time she never appeared, for someone in the manager's office had mixed up the dates. This forlorn conclusion she felt must somehow be righted, so the next morning, although it was snowing ("We may still get our blizzard," she wrote him), she went to the school and sang for the children. Then they sang for her, and showed her the room she had had in the seventh grade.

The contracts were usually signed in the spring, and while the tours were being plotted by her manager and their good friend Pop Adams of the Wolfsohn Music Bureau, Sidney would begin to worry about the finality of the commitments, and especially about the separations that would start all over again in the fall. These concert tours made for a strenuous life, as well as a lonely one, and increasingly he was beginning to wonder when she should retire.

He had theories about opera singers retiring, just as he had

On tour in 1923.

theories about their musical education—convictions that were idealistic and often persuasive, for he valued most of all a sense of personal fulfillment. But the decision wasn't easy, for no rules had ever been evolved for this aspect of an opera singer's life. Over the years there had been some, like Emma Eames, who had ended their careers in mid-flight, at the height of their powers, never to sing again. And there were many who continued far too long, trying to compensate, with the glamour of a world-wide reputation, and certain arts and airs, for a voice that was almost gone.

What he wanted for her was a reassuring middle ground, so that she could stop when she pleased, without fanfare or pressure. But that wasn't easy to achieve with a family still in the midst of growing up. Only one was married, Louise Jr., who now had a home and a baby daughter of her own (but since she lived near them, both summer and winter, and sang in occasional joint concerts, there had never been any real separation). Sidney Jr. was now in college, at Harvard, and the twins had finally been uprooted from their carefree life and sent off to boarding school for a formal education. The younger ones would soon follow, and all this had to be supported—the tuitions, the vacations, the home in New York and the home at Lake George.

However, she didn't really want to stop, though in the fall, when she was trying to coax her voice back into condition, she might think ruefully at times of those concert artists who could carry their instruments about with them in separate cases, a violin, perhaps, or a cello, and have always at their disposal a glowing tone, undiminished, perhaps even improved by age. These fortunate musicians could even replace their vibrant in- struments with others more satisfactory. But a voice could never be exchanged, and the mechanism was immensely delicate, the vocal chords becoming, in time, not quite so elastic, the timbre, the resonance, the power all variously affected by the passing of the years.

She had always thought of her voice as somehow apart—an unsought gift that had, through some mystery of fate or chance, been entrusted to her care. And now that so familiar responsibil- ity had taken a new turn and become a matter of trying to keep

Sidney Homer, Jr., when a
student at Harvard.

intact, for a while longer, the instrument she had had all her
life. Mainly this meant hard work, more practicing of scales
and arpeggios and breathing exercises, more subtlety with the
phrasing and interpretation. But though she was working harder
now, the tempo of her life hadn't changed, and when she was
on tour there was still a lively pace—a heavy schedule of concerts, and inevitably of interviews, with now and then a voluntary
appearance in, perhaps, a hospital, a prison or a school, and at
times a colorful patriotic occasion, like the ceremony in Missouri for General Pershing and Marshal Foch, where it was said
that after she had sung the "Marseillaise," the great French war
hero "saluted her three times, and thrust into her arms a huge
bouquet of flowers that had been given him by the children."

In 1922 there was still another challenge, an engagement as
"guest artist" with the new Chicago Civic Opera—an arrangement that would entail occasional performances as Azucena, or
Dalila or perhaps Fidès, at her usual concert fee. But she was
somewhat troubled by this commitment, for she wasn't sure she
could sing opera in such an intermittent fashion—with an unfamiliar conductor, a newly assembled company and almost no
time to rehearse.

The dedicated sponsor of the new Civic Opera Company was
one of Chicago's leading citizens—the utility magnate and art

patron Samuel Insull. Other prominent leaders were also involved; they had high hopes for the venture, and had engaged a number of distinguished artists, among them Galli-Curci, Feodor Chaliapin, Tito Schipa and Rosa Raisa.

But her worries about the rehearsals were not unjustified, for when she arrived in Chicago for a performance of *Il Trovatore* she had to go directly from the station to rehearse with a conductor, Georgio Polacco, who had his own ideas about tempi (which were later called by some "buoyant" and by others "willful"), and take part simultaneously in a lively family reunion, one reporter noting that "when the contralto stepped from the train she was met by her three brothers living in Chicago, and with her numerous nieces, nephews and friends, went directly to the theatre to begin rehearsals. There she found that she had been given the same dressing room she had had when she appeared here with the Metropolitan Opera Company more than ten years ago. The three brothers of the opera singer, William T. Beatty, Howard Beatty, and Samuel Fulton Beatty, are all business men with offices at 400 Michigan Avenue."

Will was now president of the same Austin company that he'd gone to work for as a stock boy the year they left Minneapolis. And after she had changed to the drab costume of the tragic gypsy mother, he watched with the others, from the darkened auditorium, the somewhat disorganized rehearsal. Then, the next night, they all went to hear her in *Il Trovatore*, a quite exhilarated family group, and by chance had a part in a wild demonstration that started, without warning, at the end of Azucena's recital of vengeance and woe—the "Stride La Vampa" aria, that bitter outpouring of rage and grief.

There is, in any case, an explosive quality to opera applause, a dynamic, torrential effect that is not quite like any other. Perhaps, in part, this is because the audience must be transfixed for so long, listening in controlled silence to the music, while the tensions build and the emotions become more inward and more involved, until, like coiled springs, they must erupt, when it is over, into wild outbursts and sweeping torrents of applause. And it was that way this time—a long moment of silence, and then the whole opera house exploding into turmoil, shouts of "Brava!" and cascades of excitement so uncontrolled that one critic was reminded of "a bomb bursting, that rocked the galleries and shook the floor with the stamping of thousands of feet." The ovation that followed seemed endless, the curtain rising and falling, the startled singer appearing again and again from the wings, to bow to such an avalanche of applause that the critics "lost track of the number of curtain calls," and finally the conductor, Polacco, aware that his performance was dissolving into pandemonium, tried to stem the furor by starting the music for the next scene. Rarely had Chicago experienced such a demonstration, and the next day there were headlines: "Wild acclaim" —"Sensational appearance"—"Homer wins triumph." "Never in this generation has there been such a marvel of a voice!" exclaimed the critic for the *Chicago Tribune*. "In private life she may admit to being a grandmother, but on the stage she is in the first flush of early maturity. And her voice today is young, fresh, beautiful of tone, wide of range, and with the same dramatic thrill." While another wrote that she was "as radiant, youthful and astonishingly brilliant" as when she had made her debut "almost twenty-five years ago."

For several seasons she continued her guest appearances with the Chicago Opera, singing Dalila and Amneris, as well as other roles, and the following winter, after a performance of *Le Prophète*, she wrote him, "I am all enthused about this company. Chorus wonderful, also ballet! I spoke of this to Insull and I think he was much pleased. . . . Chaliapin is *great*, but he *talks* much of his music, and doesn't *sing* enough for me." Meanwhile another challenge had come along (though at first it seemed more in the nature of a stunt or game), to shift the values and alter the patterns of the musical world.

For her it started in 1921, when Westinghouse experimented with a "radio-telephone" during a concert in Springfield, Massachusetts. Some wires were strung from a small gadget installed on the stage, and this novelty proved a welcome diversion when an interviewer asked her if she had a "message for the people," for then she could counter the uncomfortable question by asking, in turn, "What about this wonderful radio-telephone—can you tell me, will it really be possible for my children at a distance to hear me sing?"

The next day, in the *Springfield Union*, it was reported that "the Auditorium concert of last night was made a 'listening feature' of the big annual Police Ball in Buffalo, New York, through the agency of the modest little 'transmitter' which was placed in the middle of the front of the platform." It was also noted that after the performance Louise Homer exclaimed, "It is indeed hard to believe that they could all actually hear me sing!"

And, indeed, they actually couldn't, if one meant by that the quality of tone—the contralto voice heard as it was sung. But what the police, during this "listening feature" of their ball, could marvel at was the sheer wonder of it—the fact that any sound at all could travel so far. For most people it was this matter of distance that seemed such a tantalizing mystery, for there had been limited communication through the air for some time—"ham-operators" transmitting their usually garbled messages within a radius of a few miles. But now the range was being extended, and the next year there was an even more ambitious experiment, when, during a performance of *Il Trovatore* in Chicago, a transmitter was installed in the stage with a "hook-up" by means of telephone wires, that extended all the way to New York. "Did you listen to my Azucena on the radio?" she wrote him. "Could you hear anything at all?"

No way had yet been found to meet the expenses of these public broadcasts, and when she went to California in 1926 to sing with the San Francisco Symphony Orchestra, the city was in the midst of a fund-raising campaign. The *San Francisco Examiner* was sponsoring the project, and time was a factor, for if twenty-five thousand dollars was "subscribed" in time, the symphony concerts could be broadcast to the public. "The next two days will tell the outcome," the newspaper exhorted its readers, "but so far only a small fraction of those who have sets in the area have contributed. . . . Whereas, much of the money has come from persons who do not own radios, but who wish to assist the campaign for better music—invalids, the blind, and other unfortunates have done their share. . . ."

This appeal had its effect, the money was subscribed, and a little later a music columnist was able to write that he had "tuned in on Louise Homer's concert last week . . . and every nuance, word, inflection, even the softest tones of this superb American contralto, sung nearly five hundred miles away, came through with a clarity that was a wonderfully fine demonstration of the possibilities of radio."

But the business of trying to collect donations was soon abandoned, for the promoters had begun to recognize the advertising values of the medium. In various cities programs were being arranged within the soundproof booth of a studio. And that same year, in 1926, she sang over WEAF in New York for the "Atwater Kent Sunday Evening Radio Hour."

Atwater Kent was a pioneer in radio broadcasting, and one of the first to introduce serious and classical music over the air. A noted electrical inventor, he had recently begun manufacturing "radio receiver sets." Through annual competitions, he awarded musical scholarships to talented young singers, and he engaged for his Sunday evening broadcasts many of the most noted artists.

The "Atwater Kent Hour" was her first radio concert in a studio, and the tension was not unlike those early sessions with the Victor Company, for once again a delicate mechanism had to be evaluated in relation to the unusual timbre, resonance and power of her voice. The medium had its limitations, and some of the qualities most valued in a singer, especially the vibrant power, could be, if not properly handled, a serious drawback in a radio studio. And so she had to experiment—stand back for the full high tones, closer for the low ones, modulate, control —and there was considerable anxiety, for this time, if a mistake was made, there would be no second chance. She couldn't "remake" her recording; the audience (those mysterious listeners, not easy to imagine, and therefore so formidable when you stood in front of a microphone) would hear her the first time.

She was introduced over the air by Graham McNamee, a radio announcer already becoming famous for his informal, chatty ways. And for the artists his talents were a valuable asset, since he had an engaging personality and an ease of manner designed to allay anxiety. But the miracle was in the response, for continually, during that Sunday evening broadcast, phone calls and telegrams were pouring in from distant cities to WEAF. "Thanks for your angel voice, which is coming to me over the air," was the message from a listener in Cincinnati. And this so direct response seemed to her the very essence of communication, exhilarating, rewarding, yet somehow still unreal—all those unseen radios and homes and family living rooms, out there, somewhere, beyond the microphone.

The Victor Company profited from the radio, and introduced "electrical recording" in place of the old acoustic method. This technique, using a microphone instead of a horn, was a great improvement, for now the orchestra could be properly grouped, and the singers could project their voices with greater ease and assurance. Using the new "orthophonic" method, and with the fine musician Rosario Bourdon as conductor, Louise made eighteen Victor records in 1926 and 1927. Several were remakes of old recordings, and two were duets from *Il Trovatore* with Giovanni Martinelli, an old friend and a very fine operatic tenor, who had been with the Metropolitan since 1913. But there would be no more duets with Enrico Caruso, for that wonderful voice had been lost to the world in 1921, when the great tenor had died, so prematurely, in Naples.

Meanwhile, during those long crisscross tours about the country, she was continuing her religious studies. In Knoxville, Tennessee, a young reporter, turning up unexpectedly for an interview, listed the books he'd found on her piano: *Literature and Dogma, Prophets of Yesterday, The Character of Jesus.* Already one small sitting room in Homeland had its shelves filled with these philosophical texts. But she kept trying to probe deeper, hoping that each new thinker would illuminate some part of the mysterious whole. And in the summer she often went for a week or so to the Northfield Religious Conference, to hear the great theologians, Dr. Hutton, perhaps, or Dr. Buttrick.

She was attracted to the Northfield conferences in part because they were so free from any pattern of ritual or dogma, and had, inherently, a sparkling, irreverent atmosphere that may well have been an echo of Dwight Moody's own spirited view of religion. Under the guidance of Will Moody, son of the great evangelist, the conferences were never formal or ponderous affairs, but instead would take on something of the expansive air of an intellectual house party. The visiting lecturers were enter-

With the two youngest. Joy is on the left, and Hester (who
would later be called Happy) is on the right.

tained in the Moody home, where Will Moody's wife, May, and
his four daughters would provide a stimulating background of
afternoon teas, hearty fare and a nice leavening of comic relief.
For her this robust approach to religion was irresistible. One
year she taught a class herself to some of the delegates. Now and
then she would sing, at an evening service held on a hillside,
some familiar hymn. And those quiet songs, fading into the
evening, would be as eloquent as any she had ever sung.

Once more Sidney had begun going with her on her tours,
and in 1926, since distance was no longer a factor, she traveled
as before to the West Coast ("After all these years, her debut in
Portland!" exclaimed a reviewer). In California she sang a number of opera performances in San Francisco and Los Angeles,
under the fine conductor Richard Hageman. There was also a
series of concerts up and down the coast and, on Armistice Day,
a ceremony to lay the cornerstone for the new San Francisco
Opera House. Since she had been present at the destruction of
the old one, this was a strangely appropriate occasion, and after

the governor had dug a hole with a beribboned spade, she sang "Ring Out Wild Bells" and "The Battle Hymn of the Republic" to fifty thousand people massed about the square, including "thousands of soldiers in uniform."

She felt more natural when he was there, for she couldn't easily accept the schism of both a public and a private life, and tried whenever possible to combine the two. She sang his songs on all her programs; she sang recitals with her oldest daughter; and then, by chance, she thought of still another way of mixing up these various aspects of her life, for it occurred to her that one of the twins might be able to play her accompaniments.

In all these years she'd had just four accompanists, and they'd all become close friends—Evadna Lapham, Florence McMillan, who later founded the Parnassus Club for music students, Eleanor (Buckie) Scheib and Ruth Emerson. They had all been experienced troupers, which was essential, for they must be able to handle efficiently the complex travel arrangements, and they had all been fine musicians, which was also most essential, for when she walked out onto the stage to face her audience, the only support she had was the alert, professional woman who came out with her, to sit, poised and confident, at the piano. Now, since Ruth Emerson was going to be married, she would have to look for someone else, and it occurred to her, on impulse (for she was still, much of the time, blithely impulsive), that she might ask one of the twins to fill that important role.

After boarding school the twins had gone their separate ways—Anne on to college, at Smith, Kay to New York to study music. But though she had become a fine pianist, Kay was still an amateur. She'd had no experience on the stage, no background as a performer, and she was only nineteen years old. However, this mother wasn't too disturbed by the mercurial nature of the teenager, and in the spring Kay played the accompaniments for a few concerts near home—the first in West Chester, where young Samuel Barber (who would soon graduate from high school) played an organ accompaniment for his own song "Lullaby for a Madonna."

Then, during the summer, they rehearsed her program, and in

Katharine Homer when she was playing the accompaniment for her mother.

the fall took off together on a coast-to-coast tour, crisscrossing the country, traveling over fifteen thousand miles. And wherever they went—Wisconsin, Oregon, Colorado, California, Illinois— the youthful accompanist took charge: inspecting auditoriums, consulting with managers, warding off the press and handling the travel arrangements. Although she had plunged so suddenly into public life, it seemed that almost overnight she had become a poised, very protective teen-ager. And on the stage, when she played the accompaniments, her touch on the piano was angelic —rounded, melodious, the tempo and dynamics so perfectly attuned that quite soon it became apparent that she had a talent and a touch ideally suited to the nature of this task.

For the audiences it added a certain interest—the novelty of such a very young daughter at the piano—and the critics were favorably impressed. "Her support of her mother was well-nigh flawless," wrote one, while another noted that the young accompanist was "a penetrating artist whose beauty of rendition is matched only by her engaging personality," and still another found her "rarely beautiful and talented."

This was, perhaps unconsciously, Louise's way of resolving the isolation of the vocal artist. And when Louise Jr. joined them in Akron, Ohio, and other cities, for joint recitals, the effect on the audience was unique, for inevitably the two dark-haired young daughters at her side made doubly plain, for all to see, the passing of the years. And in its way this lack of artifice was quite touching—the hair allowed to silver yet still so pretty, arranged often with a flower or two tucked in to complement a complexion still flawless without paint, the beauty of character in her face, the grace and poise and still that subtle magic, the vitality and radiance they remembered.

When a singer has been a long time in public life, there is often a touch of nostalgia, a certain melancholy. And in fact, because she had had a career spanning so many historic events in opera, and had sung with so many of the great voices long since gone, it seemed to many that she must have been more than a quarter century behind the footlights. So when she shared the stage with her two daughters the effect was not so much a refutation as something much simpler—an affirmation, an eloquent acceptance of the years.

Chapter XXVII

For some time Gatti had been trying to persuade her to return to the Metropolitan as a guest artist, and from the critics there had been complaints about her absence. Taking note of the triumphs in Chicago and San Francisco, they would equate these with the loss to opera in New York and wonder, in print, when she would appear again. So there had been pressure and persuasion, and in 1927 she did return for a few performances—the first in *Aida*, on December 14th, with Giovanni Martinelli, Ezio Pinza and Grete Stückgold.

Tullio Serafin was their conductor, and in his music column the reviewer for the *New York World* described her welcome at the opera house. "Even the call boys could talk of little else," he wrote. " 'Louise Homer is back!' It trickled through the wilderness back stage. It swept the vast orchestra, up through the staid boxes into the family circle. 'Louise Homer is back!' ran the word. . . ." And for her it was reassuring to find so many old friends still in their accustomed roles—Billy Guard, the Metropolitan's ebullient press agent, the costumers, the seamstresses, the stagehands. In one way or another they were telling her that it was good to be home again. And when finally, costumed as Amneris, she made her entrance on the stage, arm raised in greeting to Radames, there was another welcome. Before she could sing a note it rippled down from the galleries, and surged up from the orchestra—an expanding crescendo of applause.

It seemed they had been waiting for her, poised each one to initiate a demonstration that drowned out the music and brought the performance so fervently to a halt that Serafin, with a gesture of understanding, laid down his baton and signaled the orchestra to stop playing. But to the children, watching from a box, the sudden upheaval, sounding like thunder, was unexpected, and for Anne, who had come down from Smith and hadn't seen her mother for many months, it was in the nature of a shock. She hadn't been prepared for the great roar of welcome, the cheers and shouts, the hoarse cries of "Homer!" "Homer!" the storm of applause swirling about her mother, motionless there on the stage in the velvets and brilliants of Amneris, the crown, the long dark curls, still turned away, a noble princess, serene, unmoved. The strangeness of it, and her own vague homesickness, made her especially vulnerable to this tumult of emotion, and she found to her surprise that the tears were streaming down her cheeks, and she felt shivery and very strange.

For a singer, applause in the middle of a scene can pose a delicate problem if, as an artist, she is unwilling to disturb the pattern of her role, and throughout the long ovation she remained motionless on the stage, turned away, in profile, though finally, without relaxing the regal poise of the Egyptian princess, she raised both arms, as though in greeting to the Sun God, Ra, painted on the scenery. This imperious gesture inspired another thunderous outburst, but since it was plain there would be no further acknowledgment, the ovation quieted finally, Serafin picked up his baton, the orchestra resumed playing. And when she began to sing there was an almost audible sigh of satisfaction, for it was apparent at once that all the original qualities were still there—the contralto velvet of the middle register, the distinctive low tones and the brilliant high ones that many who were listening remembered.

The next day, in his review of the opera, one critic wrote of this occasion:

Louise Homer sang the role at her Metropolitan debut twenty-seven years ago. And she sang it in memorable circumstances the first night of the Gatti-Casazza regime in

November, 1908. . . . Yesterday her voice was in particularly brilliant estate. Its substance and richness were a delight, as were the poise and sweep of her phrasing, and the searching authority of her musical interpretation. Her entrance in the opening tableau was the signal for the representation to stop while the huge audience greeted her long and vociferously. And there were further ovations later on. This was altogether natural, for the Amneris who, gorgeously apparelled, trod the Metropolitan boards yesterday, looked a veritable daughter of the Pharaohs, a proud refulgent princess of many-dynastied Egypt.

A little later there was another familiar role, that of the faithless Laura in *La Gioconda*, which she sang with two of the brightest stars now appearing at the Metropolitan—Beniamino Gigli, a fine Italian tenor, as Enzo, and as Gioconda, Rosa Ponselle. Ponselle had created operatic history when she'd gone, with her sister, Carmela, straight from the vaudeville stage to the stage of the Metropolitan. Now both sisters were in opera, and Rosa Ponselle, a striking brunette, with a rich and colorful voice, had become a great favorite. Especially she captivated her audiences with her flair for drama, and as Gioconda, in the final scene with Titta Ruffo as Barnaba, soared to lyric heights of sacrificial suicide, while Laura and Enzo were escaping mysteriously into the night.

In between the opera performances, they gave the children a lively vacation, and then, after an Atwater Kent broadcast and various other recitals, they made their own escape, sailing early in February on a cruise of the Mediterranean. Never before had she ended a season so soon, and at first such airy freedom was, as she noted in her diary, "impossible to believe!" "No telephone! No letters! No practicing!" she exclaimed, a state of affairs that she found "intoxicating!" Especially it was a relief to be free of the practicing, and since she had the gift of living with awareness, moment by moment, she could renew each day the dizzy contrast, while they settled down to a life of rest and travel.

In the diary she recorded a variety of experiences—the pathetic poverty in Algiers, the stony paths and tunnels in Gibraltar, the lively welcome in Dubrovnik from "the new little country, Jugoslavia," where "the military band was playing gaily, and everything was clean and lovely, everyone happy and smiling." Then there was "the grandeur of silence" at the Acropolis in Athens, the cold and snow in Constantinople, the biblical lands in Palestine, the pyramids in Egypt.

She didn't altogether approve the tour aspect of the trip ("We all line up like sheep to go ashore," she wrote), but they had adventures, made new friends and weren't too concerned that along the way Sidney had picked up a chronic cough. In part this was because there was such an orchestra of hollow coughs on board that the passengers had taken to calling them "cathedral coughs," believing they had acquired them as a result of the gloomy chill in the many churches they had visited.

Throughout the last days of the cruise there was a good deal of lighthearted banter on the subject of these "cathedral coughs," and they scarcely noticed that he still had his when, early in April, they went to Paris and settled down for a stay in the Hotel d'Iona. But though he was exhilarated to be once more in this city of memories, he seemed to tire too quickly, one day they discovered that he had a fever, and then the diary that had recorded so blithely the various travel notes—the "Tomb of Kings in Luxor . . . the Bazaars in Cairo . . . Sorrento so beautiful!"—became, instead, a medical report: "Temp, 9 A.M. 100, 5 P.M. 101.8, 7 P.M. 103.8 Trouble breathing."

She wasn't entirely alone, for Kay was in Paris this winter, studying music, and there were also cousins living nearby to recommend a Dr. Perrot, who initiated a variety of treatments: "Inhalation, cold compresses, fruit juice. . . ." But none of the treatments were effective and the fever soared: "Temp, 104.8, pulse 100, resp. 28, night nurse arrived 9 P.M."

The illness was double pneumonia, complicated by acute pleurisy as well as severe lung abscesses. There were, at this time, no antibiotics to stem the tide of infection, and he was sixty-three, an age when, more often than not, the victims succumbed to this dread disease. But stubbornly he refused to relinquish the quiet wonder of waking in the morning. Over the years he had written several songs dedicated to her on the theme of death: "Dearest, when I am gone, make one last song for me . . ." "Under the wide and starry sky, dig the grave and let me lie . . ." In theory, poetically, he had contemplated often that last long separation, but now he fought a stubborn battle to stay alive.

However, it was a long and weary one. The battleground moved after a time to the American Hospital in Neuilly, where she had a room adjoining his, and there was oxygen when it seemed he might strangle, and morphine, and consultations with specialists. ("My love is so weak he only whispers," she wrote, "and seldom even that.")

As the weeks turned into months he became increasingly frail, skeleton-thin and so ravaged, so altered in appearance, that the children, coming late in June to Paris, were shocked (and there was Anne, again, the tears streaming down her cheeks, for she had never seen anyone so ill). But he still lived, the voice, reed-thin, still spoke. And when finally the strength began to return (very gradually, with setbacks that had to be weathered month after month, even year after year), something profoundly central to his nature had been changed for all time. Something deep inside had relaxed, or meshed, or found a home, and many of the anxieties that had bothered him for so long, the forebodings, the tensions, had faded right away.

In August, when the doctors decided he should leave the hospital and go to Switzerland for a change of air, he traveled through the stations in a wheelchair, suit scarecrow-loose on his emaciated frame, tweed cap with visor at a jaunty angle, cane firmly in hand, moustache neatly trimmed. And when they had settled into a hotel in Gstaad, he was so stimulated by the continental atmosphere that he dressed for dinner, played host to his family, ordered wine and liqueurs and the next day was "weak and coughing," with another doctor in attendance. But nothing, now, could disturb the new contentment, an awareness, a tolerance, that he tried at times to communicate to the children. But of course they were too indestructible to respond to these intimations, and much too young, caught up irresistibly in the bright and brittle ways of their own generation—the new tight skirts and boyish bobs, the jazz, the Charleston, the cigarettes in fancy holders—become, indeed, impervious, and therefore easily beguiled by the facile modern views of the professors at college, who preached atheism as though they had invented it, and psychology as though that alone could pigeonhole the world.

They sailed for home early in September, and though the weather was stormy he sat for hours on deck, drawn irresistibly to the gray, restless sea. And when, finally, he was home again, to see the peacocks strutting proudly on the wallpaper in the hall, the open fires, the terrace, especially the mountains, and try to cope with still another setback, another heavy cold and cough, another doctor, a nurse, even another wheelchair, he was elated, for he hadn't been sure he'd ever see this home again.

But though he had survived, his illness had made them both more vulnerable to the demands of public life. The separations, the contracts, the practicing, the programs, the repertoire—all this had become an increasingly heavy burden, and they tried to cope with it by limiting the engagements and telling her managers, as she noted in her diary, "not to close anything between December 15th and March 15th."

For the winter months she took him to Florida, where they had gone often in the winter, and where the climate seemed ideal for his frail health. But in the spring she had to leave him there (with a nurse in attendance to care for him), and come north for more of the singing—a tour of concerts, a performance of *Trovatore*, another Atwater Kent broadcast. And this was in the nature of an occasion, the studio filled afterward with exhilarated friends and well-wishers on hand to pay tribute, among them the explorer Donald MacMillan, who had come to tell her that he had "named a stretch of mountainous terrain in the North Louise Homer Land" in honor of his "favorite opera singer." She was introduced over the air that spring by Will Rogers, a comedian whose wry humor and homespun philosophy had made him a beloved personality in homes all over America. "One day," Will Rogers drawled, "in the midst of the smoke of Pittsburgh, a little bird could be heard singing . . ."

He was too discreet to say how long ago it was—that first bird song in the smoky air of Pittsburgh—and instead included in his introduction a lively panorama of operatic events. But it did seem now as though a good many years had passed since those first songs—the little solos, with Miss Earnest at the piano, in the small Shadyside school behind the church, and later the ringing choruses in the bigger East Liberty school, two hundred voices singing in unison, that could have such an electrifying effect on a little girl of eight, cascading her, right there in school, onto a plane of shivery excitement not unlike that experienced at the opera when the mighty chorus in *Aida* celebrates the triumphant return of the Egyptian army.

Since then, more times than she could count, she had relived on the stage those stirring moments, the martial music and marching feet of the East Liberty school becoming, in time, the crescendo of Wagner, the grandeur of Verdi; so if it is, indeed, the secret of life to transfer into maturity the magic of childhood, she had had her share. But recently there had been a certain shifting about, the prism settling gradually into another pattern. By this time, with the two older children married, she had, already, four grandchildren, and she was as susceptible to that role as she had been, in the past, to all the others, as beguiled by each new solemn, sleeping infant given her to hold, as fascinated by the older ones, and so involved that at Homeland there were almost always playpens and baby carriages scattered about, toddlers at the table, an aura of cuddling and confusion, and for each one a special tenderness.

Meanwhile there was the opera, and when she sang Azucena on Thanksgiving afternoon, 1929, *The New York Times* had a headline: "Three Generations of Singer's Kin Witness Her Return in *Trovatore*." Wrote the reviewer:

> A memorable event took place at the opera house on Thursday when Louise Homer, famous American contralto, returned to the scene of her triumphs of bygone years, while three generations of her family sat in one of the boxes, among them her granddaughter and namesake, little Louise Homer. . . . This was an unusual occasion, for seldom, if ever, has an artist at the Metropolitan sung before three generations of her family, with her singing and acting as artistic and effective as ever.

As it happened, this was the last opera she would sing. She didn't realize it at the time, and for another year or so Gatti would keep her on his rolls as a guest artist. But for one reason or another she wouldn't appear, so this was the last performance at the Metropolitan—the end of the repertoire, the costuming, the rehearsals, the call boy, the waiting in the wings and the gold curtain that she'd helped initiate rippling so mysteriously apart.

A few months later they "dissolved" her contract with her concert managers, a decision that she celebrated by noting in her diary that they now felt "free as birds!!!" It wasn't quite the end of the singing; there would be a few more radio appearances, a few more concerts. But it was the end of the contracts, the long tours, the separations. And the life they had found in Florida was perfectly suited to this buoyant transition, for to occupy the newfound leisure there were new friendships, as well as a lively round of social events.

Year after year, when she was singing in opera, she'd had to refuse most invitations, for she'd believed she shouldn't go out the night before a performance. There had been a few notable occasions—a tea at Sherry's for Sarah Bernhardt at which she had "poured," a dinner at the Savoy-Plaza with Mark Twain among the celebrities. But most of the lighthearted fun had had to be curtailed, which added a certain cadence to the present situation, for now, when she was finally free of the familiar responsibilities, they found themselves caught up in a quite varied social life. Palm Beach at this time was like a luxurious small town, and all season long there were dinners, large and small, at the palatial homes along the shore, given by the Stotesburys, the Dillmans, the Seligmans, the Dobynes and a host of others. They had been made honorary members of the Bath and Tennis Club, and the hymn sings were held now in the Everglades Club, in a romantic setting of palm trees and Spanish patios.

And so their life at Palm Beach was an interesting confection of religious studies, hymn sings and colorful entertainment. There were many new friends—the Alfred Kays, the Seward Webbs, Captain and Mrs. Hugh Gibbons and, among the younger ones, the Arthur Somers Roches; John Charles Thomas, the singer; Eleanor Chace, a gifted novelist, and her architect husband, Maurice Fatio. It was a lively community, and the activities were varied—outdoor boxing matches, motor trips, excursions, unusual parties at Addison Mizner's, evenings at Mayor Shepherd's, a series of elaborate musicales when the New York String Quartet came to town, teas and moonlight dances at the Everglades. And best of all there was time to stroll about, play bridge in the evenings, go to tea or lunch and visit with friends.

"In Palm Beach there was time to stroll about . . .
go to tea or lunch and visit with friends."

The long sunny days were ideal for his health, and after a time
he began to gain some weight. He had always been rail-thin,
and they believed his sturdier build was due to the returning
health. But it may have been in part because of that so subtle
inward reconciliation during those long days and nights near
death in Paris. That intangible new dimension had never left
him. So now, while he sat out on the beach, experiencing so
much that was good—the steady roll and music of the sea, congenial friends about, the days a succession of vivid quietness—
he decided to write a book about their lives together. He would
tell something about his student years in Germany, describe their
adventures in Paris and London and include a good deal of his
philosophy in the realm of music and musicians, humanity and
kindness. He would call his book *My Wife and I*, and in its way
it would be a celebration of his survival.

Chapter XXVIII

In the spring, when they returned to Homeland, they would find themselves caught up in a succession of family events—weddings, christenings and graduations. Week after week the big house would be filled with young ones of all ages. But there were always the studios for work and solitude, and throughout the summer months a sparkling serenity, for here Buck Mountain was still a brooding guardian of their lives, the terrace still a tranquil solace, gathering them in.

One of those who came in the summer to visit was young Samuel Barber, and often he would bring with him his friend from the Curtis Institute of Music, Gian Carlo Menotti. At Homeland the two young composers would find a beguiling blend of their two such different backgrounds—the leisure and beauty of Lake Lugano and the sturdy heritage of West Chester. Here the contrasting elements were so artfully mixed together that at once they would both feel comfortably at home.

Gian Carlo Menotti had been just sixteen when he'd first come to America to study music, and since all his relatives were either in Italy or South America, he had spent many of his vacations with Samuel Barber in West Chester. That quiet Quaker town had been the lonely, displaced young foreigner's first introduction to family life in America, and it had made a lasting impression. Viewed from his own continental, more col-

orful and much livelier experience, the muted atmosphere and
the intense quiet had been something to ponder. The sense of
isolation in the big, aging houses, the retiring character of the
lives—all this had seemed to Gian Carlo a kind of phenomenon.
And he'd been so intrigued by the odd insular qualities, so fascinated by the inhibited yet kindly traditions, that these youthful
impressions would become the inspiration for his enchanting
little opera, *The Old Maid and the Thief*.

Meanwhile, during the summers, Sam would visit Gian Carlo
in his home at Cadogliano, on the shores of Lake Lugano, and
there he had found a quality of life that was, in its way, as
insular as West Chester, but very different. "Cadogliano seems
to me," he had written his mother, "the first spot in Europe
where I can claim a foothold, and which I truly love. Hidden
away in mountains of extreme natural beauty, and over-looking
a magnificent valley with parts of three lakes, there is this little
settlement of quaint villas, of all styles, of diverse degrees of
luxury, and almost all of them owned and inhabited by members of Gian Carlo's family." To the young music student, just
nineteen, impressionable and long accustomed to the subdued
and regulated routine of West Chester, there was a softness and
a vividness about life in Cadogliano, a patina of color and
romance that was like nothing he'd ever experienced. And he'd
been so moved by the quality of timelessness, so affected by
the patrician air of family interaction and allegiance, the graciousness, the repose, the elegance of the tensions, that this would
become the inspiration for his first opera at the Metropolitan,
Vanessa.

At Homeland, when they played charades, the two young
composers made sparkling competitors, for Samuel Barber,
product of a small town and fascinated by people, had a wry
and witty response to the vagaries of human nature, while
Gian Carlo Menotti would contribute a more sophisticated
humor—droll, unpredictable, entirely his own. But there would
be a quieter side to these visits, for always when he came to
Homeland Sam would spend some hours with his composer
uncle in the studio by the lake. There he might listen, perhaps,
to the new violin sonata Sidney was working on, debate musical

theories, share the creative life. And already there had begun that subtle shifting about of roles, young Samuel Barber, winner of the Prix de Rome and the Pulitzer Prize, listening as well as seeking, become now a loyal partisan, a source of strength, a comfort.

Meanwhile at Homeland, every year or so, usually in June, they would have one of those traditional upheavals, which meant, inevitably, weeks of feverish activity, preparation and planning. But she tried to keep it all as relaxed as possible, with the neighbors dropping in to arrange the flowers, the wedding on the lawn in an impromptu setting of greenery and potted plants, the wedding table on the porch, the reception strung casually along the terrace. Quite often, the morning of the wedding, the youngest grandchild would be christened, also on the terrace, with Louise Jr.'s husband, Ernest Stires, performing the service. Since he was both a minister and a most buoyant member of the family, he would preside at both events, first the christening, then the wedding. And so the long summer day would unwind with somewhat the continuity of a music drama, the backdrop a luminous expanse of lake and mountains, the several scenes played within a single set of greenery and flowers and, as a chorus, the assembled relatives and friends. In this mood the libretto, with its blend of various emotions, would seem a kind of lyric happening, perhaps in part because she had no talent for the formal, the ponderous or the solemn. Always she had been heedless of the conventions, and so, when the brides were married and the infants christened, there would be, in spite of the satin gowns and trailing veils, a lightness and a casualness that was her way.

And this was true, as well, of another June ritual—the honorary degree—and another traditional formality—the academic procession. Almost every spring she was awarded at least one, sometimes two, of these degrees, and would return home after the ceremonies with a colorful array of complimentary hoods, as well as scrolls proclaiming her a Doctor of Philosophy, of Art, of Music. She viewed all this with a certain lighthearted disbelief, since her formal education had ended with the Lingle College for lady typewriters. Nevertheless, when she walked in

"At Homeland there were almost always playpens and baby carriages scattered about. . . ."

the academic processions, the years of commitment and study were apparent in her face—all the languages she had learned, all the operatic roles, the oratorios, the songs, the hours of concentrated work. Throughout her life there had been a spirited acceptance of responsibility, and this discipline and intelligence were touchingly apparent when she rose, in cap and gown, to receive the diplomas.

In all the awards the interaction of character and career played a part, the college presidents dwelling, in their citations, on her "nobility of character . . . brilliance in artistry . . . richness in life and achievement." At Smith, President William Allan Neilson called it "the resolute maintenance of the lofty standards of her art." And at Tufts College there was a kind of summing up. "We pay tribute," they noted, "to the idealism that has marked your private as well as your public life. You have held the great gift that nature gave you as a sacred trust. . . . By the beauty of your voice you have enriched many lives. You are beloved not merely for what you have given, but for what you are."

Emily Dickinson once wrote of bestowing the laurel leaf "on one too intrinsic for renown," and in a sense it was this they were defining in their dual tributes. Although there had been the accident of fame, the intrinsic nature had been unaffected. But the responsibilities remained, and when the voice she believed had been "entrusted to her care" seemed in danger of exploitation, it became hers to protect, to respect and, finally, hers to relinquish.

She didn't make a formal announcement when she retired, or give any "farewell performances." But she refused all the offers that were still pouring in, some with big price tags (tours abroad, various opera companies, many concerts), and after a while she started teaching—a few singing pupils, at first, then a few more—at Lake George in the summer and Palm Beach in the winter. This might not have been necessary if they'd saved more when she was earning so much. But in one way or another they'd managed to spend most of it—building Homeland, creating that sweep of lawn, hiring all those governesses, educating the children. Then, too, when the money was so available they'd

given away a good deal—to relatives, friends, total strangers.
They'd educated other youngsters besides their own, helped
many who were in trouble, and forgotten to worry about the
future. Now, though their savings were quite limited, there was
still the youngest child just starting college, the weddings, the
visiting grandchildren, life in full swing. So to supplement their
income she undertook the teaching, and taught her pupils that
"the supreme effort is to appear effortless. . . . The voice is a
stringed instrument, bowed by the breath."

The mechanics of the teaching were made more difficult because Sidney had to have a warm climate. The doctors warned
that his weakened lungs had made the Northern winters dangerous. And that meant that she couldn't, like her friend Marcella Sembrich, enjoy the advantages of an established school
of music in New York or Philadelphia—the prestige and all the
facilities, the language courses, the practice rooms, the varied
curriculum. Such an association would have been much simpler,
if they hadn't had to outwit the cold and the snow. But there
were compensations, for the teaching soon became a family
project. Sidney gave courses in harmony and music appreciation, and helped, now and then, with the coaching. Friends
offered scholarships, and auditions were held, with hundreds of
young people applying. When they were ready the pupils gave
informal musicales for friends and neighbors. They took part
in the hymn sings, and had their lessons in one of the studios by
the lake. "Only a small stream of breath produces the vibrations
of a well-balanced tone," she wrote in her notes. "The open-
throat resonance of the O and U must be kept in the I E and
A. . . ."

In December, 1934, he had his seventieth birthday. "There
were just us two for dinner, no guests," she wrote the children
from Palm Beach, "and when I carried in the gorgeous cake,
lighted with many red, white and blue candles, it *was* beautiful.
I sang *Happy Birthday*, and we stood, and he said, 'Now you
must sing something!' Of course I filled up, as I always do when
moved, and said I couldn't. He said, 'Oh yes, you can! A hymn
—anything; *Silent Night*, anything.' So we started *Silent Night*
and croaked it through one verse—tears in eyes and smiles on

lips! It *was* funny and wonderful. . . ." After the birthday dinner, she wrote, some dear friends, Dr. and Mrs. McCarthy, came for the evening. Then at 8:30 all the pupils came unexpectedly in the back door, singing "Happy Birthday" and bringing gifts and refreshments and a play they'd written to perform in his honor. Then they all "played charades with great gusto" and funny word games, and so ended "a Great Day!" "Lately," she wrote them, "I have been working on my Harmony with my new professor, Sidney Homer. And if I am not being very brilliant, at least I am getting good training, and I *love* to study and be taught. I always have! Also we are reading Dewey's *Common Faith* out loud together. . . ."

If there is something of Robert Browning in all this—"Grow old along with me! . . . The last of life, for which the first was made . . ."—it was true there was now reflected, when they were together, in their faces, in their voices—in the glance, the smile, the gesture—that so touching imprint of a life that has been shared.

Meanwhile the gray hair was turning white. But for both of them it was a vivid fading, soft and bright for her, thick and rugged for him, illuminating, for her, the grace, the poise and the delicate tones of that still almost satin-smooth complexion; and for him, since he was so tall, when he wore white suits, as he often did, the effect of the leonine head, the unusual height, the drooping moustache, the fine dark eyes, the thick mane of white hair, was of an aging with distinction—a growing old in which character becomes a kind of definition.

They had a way of celebrating the milestones and the next year, in January, 1935, it was the fortieth wedding anniversary. To commemorate this a picture was taken informally, in their garden, a photograph so faithfully composed, so filled with sunlight, confidence and trust, that later, when it was used in his book, one critic would find it more revealing than the printed word. The caption in the newspaper, "One of the Community's Most Beloved Couples," defined a status that had been evolving over the years, for in Palm Beach there was a devoted circle of friends, and in the summer at Lake George it was the same—friendships that spanned the years, and in 1937 a dinner and evening in their honor, with gifts, scrolls, speeches and other tributes to the passing of the years.

Some of the children now had their own cottages at Lake George. But Homeland was still a magnet—the big sofa beginning, finally, to sag a little, since each grandchild had discovered, in turn, its capacious buoyancy, and the peacocks still strutting proudly on the wallpaper in the hall. Kay's twin daughters, a beguiling duplication of the past, explored the big costume trunk in the attic, and when Anne brought her little Jonathan to Homeland he would become a three-year-old magically attached to wings, that race for the lake the instant he arrived, down the broad expanse of lawn, short legs flying, arms turning like windmills, the exuberance of memory that cannot yet express itself in any other way.

They still streamed from the dining porch at noon to salute, with wildly waving napkins, the jubilant toots of the *Mohican*. And they still lingered on the terrace while the light changed on the big quiet mountain they had lived with for so long. Hour by hour the colors shifted—from gray to gold, from rose to gray. Starlight, moonlight—wait long enough and it all happened right there.

Chapter XXIX

"Very peaceful and quiet," she wrote in her diary. "The moss and ferns and mossy rocks, how I love them all!" In the fall, when there was an interval of quiet at Homeland, she would become especially susceptible to the quality of the now, the present—the snow clouds not yet, the open fires, the woodland a solitary place, for as ever she was listening to the music of the moment, and this was a time of transition. Soon they must hurry south, and so each day was weighted as well as buoyed by the mere fact of so much that was good. "Such peace and quiet and bliss," she wrote. "Walk every day through the woods, and yesterday we brought back to our rock garden ferns and moss and a wee lovely tree." "Having a heavenly time, what blissful days! Words are inadequate to express my outbursting feelings. . . ."

In 1938, because the growing class of pupils had made living arrangements, studios and other practical matters difficult in Palm Beach, they went instead to St. Augustine, believing that in that quiet resort town they might find an environment better suited to the teaching. "The streets are narrow and some of the houses are *very* old and have over-hanging balconies," she wrote the children. "The bays and the Mantazas River are romantic, the live oaks and oleanders beautiful. It is quaint and restful and I think we will love it here."

But though they had come intending to settle quietly into a

quiet community, they soon sparked, themselves, a good deal of activity. Almost at once their new friends formed a "Scholarship Foundation," to seek out local talent and provide funds for the most promising young singers. And in January, when auditions were held, telegrams poured in from all over the state of Florida, each urging the selection of a favorite candidate.

Almost unwittingly, it seemed, they had once again become involved in the life of a community. And when there was another milestone—the forty-fourth wedding anniversary—their new friends arranged an evening at the Ponce de Leon Hotel. Included in the festivities was a program of his compositions, and during that gala evening a sextet of school children sang his "Mother Goose," two fine musicians played his new violin sonata, others sang selections of his songs as solos, duets, ensembles. Many of the guests had written poems in honor of the anniversary, and there were flowers and toasts and tributes. But though the mood was lighthearted, there was another aspect, too, delicate as silence, fragile as sunlight on a misty day, for it seemed a long time ago, now, that bewitching moment when they had stepped from a train to greet the astonished proprietor of the Baldpate Inn.

A month later, in February, 1938, his book, *My Wife and I*, was published by the Macmillan Company, thus bringing to a satisfying conclusion that most subtle and difficult of compatabilities—the divergent views of publisher and author. He had intended his book as a memoir that would include a good deal of his philosophy in the realm of music and musicians, the artistic life, humanity, his hopes for the future, and at the outset had described his own childhood, those early years in a house of silence that had, nevertheless, been so vibrant with color. "My mother," he had written, "by example and precept, taught me that the world was a fascinating place in which to live, that love played a great part in it, that humanity could be trusted, that a physical handicap need not be discouraging. . . . She was one of those magnetic, dynamic souls that make life interesting, not only for themselves, but for others. I sometimes think that humanity is made up of suns and planets, radiating personalities and grateful satellites. . . . There have been no disillusion-

ments, and I feel that her instincts and her judgement were in-
fallible. . . ."

He had written at length, in his book, of those student days
in Germany, and described vividly the rather unconventional
start of his own musical career, and later their adventures in
Paris and the opera seasons in Vichy, Angers, London, Brussels.
But being in a nostalgic mood, identifying, from the vantage
point of maturity, with the patina of youthful dreams, he had
ended with her debut and first season at the Metropolitan, believing that this would make the most satisfying conclusion, since
"descriptions of past performances are something like descriptions of lost pictures; they are never quite adequate, and they
make one wistful."

However, his publishers hadn't been content with just one
season at the Metropolitan. They had wanted the book brought
up to date, and so he'd had to start all over again, writing of the
opera tours, the family, the Victor, the concerts, the founding of
ASCAP, in which he had had a part, and including, inevitably, a
good deal about his intense interest in opportunities for young
musicians and his passionate faith in the ultimate triumph of
justice for all. Meanwhile his sponsoring editor had vanished,
sailing, it seemed, for England. Another publisher had to be
found, and this one, too, had wanted changes and revisions—the
book cut, shaped up, made to conform.

But in spite of the many vicissitudes, it was still his book,
and the publication day, in February, was a great occasion. To
launch the book a luncheon was given at the Ponce de Leon
Hotel for over a hundred and fifty guests. As entertainment
there was a program of his songs, the novelist James Branch
Cabell presided, Louise contributed a lighthearted "post-script"
called *We*, a representative from Macmillan gave a "preface."

My Wife and I was reviewed by both the literary and the
music critics, who called it "warm . . . human . . . unpretentious . . . inspiring." In *The New York Times* it was noted:

Sidney Homer sees music as Albert Schweitzer sees it. For
him the artist is . . . an idealist serving with almost self-
less devotion. What matters is not the applause that rocks
the opera house but the beauty that is created there. . . .
There is nothing solemn or pretentious about Sidney

Homer's book; it has drama and humor . . . and every sentence is informed by a man's devotion to a great singer who is also his wife.

It was the critic for *The Argonaut* who found most revealing the photograph taken in the garden. He wrote:

Somewhere in every book there is a page that sums up and illuminates the whole. In *My Wife and I* that page is the frontispiece, a picture of Louise Homer and her noted composer husband, taken on their fortieth wedding anniversary. There, in her smiling, upturned face, is reflected the spiritual force, the artistry and the practical energy that could take her from a small Pennsylvania town to New York's Metropolitan. Just as clearly Sidney Homer's face mirrors the deep, human sympathy, the dramatic power, the unquenchable idealism that could enrich American music with songs such as *How's My Boy?*, *The Pauper's Drive*, *The Song of the Shirt*, and the beloved *Requiem*.

Because it was such a personal book, letters started coming in from all over the world, a communication that he found deeply rewarding. And in the early spring his book was made a feature of the Rollins College "Animated Magazine." The crowd that came for this breezy and quite imaginative occasion was big and varied, more than five thousand "subscribers," it was reported, "from every state in the union and many foreign countries." The college president, Hamilton Holt, presided, and the "contributors" included Arthur Hays Sulzberger, publisher of the *Times*, long an old friend; Mary Margaret McBride of the radio and Irving Bacheller, the novelist. It was noted that while they were speaking "a rather strong breeze rustled the palms and oaks . . . and afterwards the 'subscribers' bought the book, *My Wife and I*, and crowded to the platform to secure the autographs of Author Sidney Homer and his wife. . . ."

He would soon be seventy-five, and it was now more than ten years ago, that interval in Paris when life had seemed to be quietly slipping away. Since then, with the new awareness he'd discovered, the added days and years had seemed a kind of dividend. And now there was the youthful glow and fanfare of a first book published, the letters, the reviews, the literary occasions and the academic honors. Later that season Rollins College awarded him an honorary doctorate, and in 1941 he was awarded the degree of Doctor of Music by the Curtis Institute of Music in Philadelphia.

For several years Hamilton Holt had been trying to persuade them to move to Winter Park and become "honorary advisors" to the Rollins College music department. But they had been reluctant, believing they preferred the sea and the shore. However, in 1940 they did settle in Winter Park, and found there a community they could identify with in a most satisfying way. "Winter Park is a mixture of varied interests and thinking people," he wrote the children soon after they'd arrived. And it was this that most appealed to them. Because it was a college town, the atmosphere was youthful, and there were lectures, concerts and distinguished visitors to lend a certain cosmopolitan air. But essentially Winter Park was a small town, without the restlessness of the coastal resorts, with, instead, a certain quietness, an air of permanence, and the new friendships, too, had that enduring quality.

They were soon taking part in the artistic life of the town, and in February several of her pupils sang ensemble arrangements of his songs with Alexander Bloch's symphony orchestra. "It seemed a bold thing to do," she wrote the children, "to have seven girls sing at a dignified symphony concert, and I have to admit that I never expected the success we had. The girls looked simply beautiful, and when they opened up with the *Requiem*, the volume was astonishing and grand."

One of the critics referred to this climax as "beautiful beyond words," while another described the "ovation" when a "student-usher carried the presentation bouquet down the aisle to Madame Louise Homer. . . . The former opera star," she wrote, "was magnificently beautiful, charming and gracious in responding to the acclamation. Mr. Sidney Homer beamed and bowed in all directions. It was a memorable moment."

Although there was a reference to "the former opera star," nostalgia played only a small part in these "memorable moments." Much more it was the quality of the "now." And for the young people who were so often about, the pupils, the students, the youngish members of the faculty already becoming friends, it was disarming to discover that in spite of all those anniversaries, the present could still so brightly dim the past.

She liked to walk about Winter Park discovering the town—the houses, unpretentious but pretty, the small bright stores, the live oaks hung with moss, the bevies of young people from the college. More than half a century had vanished since those days, long ago, when she had first explored West Chester, braids bouncing merrily, and been so impressed with the subdued, solemn nature of their new hometown—all the big old houses, seeming almost empty, hardly any children about, and so many "old people" in somber cloaks and bonnets. She had been susceptible, then, to the hushed, careful tempo, and now, in reverse fashion, it was the same, for when she walked about Winter Park, the walk still light and airy, it was blithely reassuring to feel so in tune with the nature of her surroundings.

In Winter Park his violin sonata was performed, as well as his Quintet for Strings. And in 1942 Samuel Barber initiated two tributes to his composer uncle. One was an "all-Homer" radio program, and the other a special edition of his *Collected Songs*, published by Schirmer's. "It is," she wrote the children, "the first collection ever made of the works of a *living* composer." For this Sam selected the songs, some long since forgotten, from over a hundred that had been published, arranged them and wrote a preface. In his introduction he noted, "In those days when Homer songs were sung by Bispham, de Gogorza, Gluck, Gadski and Onegin, there was perhaps less need for an album such as this; but now it is to be hoped that the present collection may find enthusiastic support from a generation of singers to whom these songs are scarcely known. By furthering them, singers will be helping to build a tradition of higher standards and greater possibilities."

By this time Samuel Barber had himself achieved notable recognition as a composer. His songs, including the "Dover Beach," first interpreted by Rose Bampton, were being widely sung. His Symphony Opus 1 had been introduced by Artur Rodzinski in both Cleveland and New York, and his Adagio for Strings commissioned and then performed by Arturo Toscanini. His ensemble and orchestral works were appearing on many programs, and all this they had been sharing throughout the

Samuel Barber. "His ensemble and orchestral works were appearing on many programs . . ."

years, the disappointments and frustrations as well as the fulfill-
ments. Meanwhile the pendulum had swung full circle, the young
composer become now an ardent partisan of the one who had
grown old.

Although they saw the children only rarely in Winter Park,
they were always in close touch, and this year the youngest, Joy,
had written a book about her experiences in Asia, *Dawn Watch
in China*, and was lecturing to audiences all over the country;
Anne, too, had become a writer for the magazines. "Everyone
here is reading Joy's book," she wrote the children, "I hear words
of praise wherever I go, and of course I devour the reviews! . . .
Yesterday I was having my hair done, and as I started to sit under
the heater I thought, 'Wouldn't it be too good to be true if I could
find a story by my Anne!' So I looked, and there it was in the
American, and another in the *Journal*, so for once I had a wonderful time having my hair dried!" But though this was a rewarding accompaniment to their lives, it was just that, an accompaniment, a kind of background music, for they had their own work,

their own adventures, their own friends. "We love it here more than we ever did," she wrote from Winter Park. "We feel so happy here, and so at home."

But the next year there was a setback when Sidney began to have trouble with his eyes. The doctors told him the trouble was progressive, there was no cure or treatment, and quite suddenly he found that many of his favorite resources had vanished —the daily newspapers, the books, the bridge, the absorbing games of solitaire, the reading and writing of music. "He won't go anywhere," she wrote the children, soon after his eyesight began to fail. "He seems to just want to stay home. And it takes time to decide what to do with the hours he used to fill so easily."

He stayed home because he was timid about going out in a world that had become too shadowy. "He *can* see the trees," she wrote them, "and stars even, and birds; he cannot see to recognize people at any distance at all!" He found it unpredictable and unnerving, the formless faces and crowded rooms, and felt safer at home. But finally he did begin going about, the first time to a dress rehearsal of Bach's *St. Matthew Passion*, which made it a notable milestone. After that he became more confident, and in Winter Park a kind of pattern evolved. There were, she wrote the children, two "chess pals" who came every week to play with him, and a young man from Rollins College who came twice a week to read to him. Sallie Crane was another loyal friend who came often to read to him, and every Sunday at eleven, Helen Moore, a talented young pianist, would take him to her home nearby and play Beethoven for him. "He calls it Beethoven with wings," she wrote the children.

In recent years his hearing had also been gradually diminishing, which made more treacherous the failing eyesight. But once he had weathered that bleak transition, he accepted these formidable handicaps with exceptional calm and serenity. All his life he had been apprehensive about even minor ailments, but now that he was faced with blindness, as well as the gradual loss of his hearing, he was courageous and uncomplaining—grateful for the radio, still intensely interested in world affairs, still wholly involved, caught up, irresistibly, in the strong current of communication that had always been so much a part of his life.

For several years Homeland had been up for sale—the school

taxes and rising costs became now too heavy a burden. But in
the meantime they were making the most of it, and in 1941 had
a family reunion, twenty-eight of them, the youngest, Kay's little
Sally, only a few weeks old. "We must make a *great time* of it,"
he had written them, while they were planning this event, "for it
may be our last summer all together in that story wonder-
land. . . ." And about that he was quite right, for a few months
later the Japanese attacked Pearl Harbor and many in the family
began to scatter to distant places around the world, from North
Africa to India, each caught up, variously, in the global conflict.

In this war she couldn't sing to great throngs of people while
leaflets were dropped from the sky. But she could comply with the
food rationing and the gas rationing and other wartime rulings,
and accept without complaint the many complexities. Because of
the difficulties of travel, the next year they remained in Florida
and didn't come north at all. The summer after that they left
their car behind and stayed at a small inn on Lake George, an
attractive, friendly place, not far from Homeland. And perhaps
that was fortunate, for in August, Homeland was sold—the house,
most of the furniture, some of the land and one of the studios.

Anne happened to be the only one around to help with this
formidable move, and for a week they all three drove back and
forth, took sandwiches and pots of coffee, wandered about, sorted
things in trunks and cupboards and had a series of picnics on the
terrace that made the whole complicated process seem a kind of
holiday. Anne, at the time, didn't notice this somewhat topsy-
turvy effect, for it didn't occur to her that it was supposed to be
a melancholy occasion when a couple in their seventies, her father, indeed, almost eighty, were moving out of a home they had
built and loved for many years. Since her parents had always
been like that, she took for granted the gaiety, the serenity, the
warm, contented mood as they wandered about the house saying,
"We must keep this, it came from my father's house in Boston—
and of course this picture Kay painted—and the stereopticon—
and the set of Tolstoy . . ."

It didn't occur to her to wonder why there was no sadness at
this time, no strain, no artificial efforts to "keep up the spirits,"
why, indeed, it was such a happy interlude, going day after day
to Homeland, to wander about reliving the past. Her mother's

Anne, the year they moved out of Homeland.

voice called up and down the stairs, as it had for so long, as lilting and musical as ever—What shall we do with this, or that?—and, as it turned out, a great many things had to be saved and moved temporarily to the studio by the lake. Often they stopped to rest on the terrace, to enjoy the sweep of lawn, the vistas, the shimmering pattern of sunlight on the water. And since they had always gathered here on the terrace, that was when the memories took form, a parade of them, trailing back through the years, to be relived and remembered, not with nostalgia, but with something much lighter and brighter, more akin, indeed, to that placid noonday sparkle that they'd lived with for so long.

Chapter XXX

They were still celebrating the milestones, and in January, 1945, when they had their Golden Wedding Anniversary, it seemed that the whole of Winter Park turned out to honor the occasion. The festivities began with an evening reception at Hamilton Holt's, and continued the next day with a program of Sidney's music at the Annie Russell Theatre, where it was said that they "received an ovation when they made their dramatic entrance. . . ."

They lent to both these tributes a certain mixture of drama and humor, for they were susceptible to the symbols, but not to the nostalgia. In the press it was reported that he wore for the reception "two leaves of gold in his lapel," while she wore "a dress of creamy white silk, with accents of gold, reminiscent of her costume in *Orfeo e Euridice*—in her hair a wreath of gold leaves, in her hand a gold ostrich-plume fan." They had had no reception after the simple wedding a half century ago. But now, it seemed, they were to have one, for Hamilton Holt's gracious home had been transformed for the occasion into a bower of gold and white, with "hundreds of flowers—roses, gladioli and chrysanthemums —all white and gold." There was a sparkling four-tier wedding cake "trimmed with fifty gold candles"; and gifts that included "exquisitely-wrought antique French decanters of crystal and gold." A "special greeting," composed by Samuel Barber and Gian Carlo Menotti, was sung by "fourteen girls from the Rollins

Conservatory"; and telegrams were read from "friends all over the world—Arturo Toscanini, Dr. and Mrs. Walter Damrosch, Edward Johnson, manager of the Metropolitan, Mme. Geraldine Farrar . . ."

In a letter to Anne he described this occasion. "You would have loved it," he wrote, "so many things happened! With a big crowd lined up to meet us, the lights went out for twenty minutes! We all felt suddenly young in the dark. A maid with a candle looking for more candles started a fire in a curtain. Howard Bailey, our professor of dramatics, put it out. . . . Dr. Holt gave a wonderful address and read letters and telegrams. It was a marvelous night!"

That summer, while they were staying at the inn at Lake George, a bomb was dropped that sent a shiver of dread right around the world. The twins happened to be with them at the time, and a few days later they celebrated together the armistice, V-J Day, peace at last. Bottles of wine were opened, and soft drinks provided for the young ones. It was a balmy night, and the children, sensing the elation of the grown-ups, raced around in the dark. And though the setting wasn't as stirring as it had been almost thirty years ago, with the whole of the Metropolitan Opera joining her in the National Anthem, while she held aloft the American flag, still the mood was as exhilarating, as brilliant with relief. Once again Sidney talked confidently of what he called "a true brotherhood of man." He imagined that the time had now come to end forever poverty, inequality and injustice, and began to put his faith in the newly founded United Nations.

But the next year there was the first rift in the family, for in the fall of 1946, Joy, their youngest daughter, died suddenly in a hospital in New York. She'd been ill for some months, and they'd been living near her, in a house in Connecticut, but her death was unexpected. This was a shock and a great sorrow. But though they wept, they didn't shut themselves away. They didn't let their grief create a barrier, and it didn't affect the warm and generous communication they'd always had with the other children. With Anne, when she came to join them, her mother was especially comforting and reassuring, perhaps because Anne, too, had been ill and was expecting a baby. Although there were tears in her eyes, she held Anne's hand firmly during the simple home service they had, and was smiling and comforting and the same as always, and Anne would have that to remember in later years.

At the entrance to the road leading to Homeland there is a small country graveyard, a quiet, sunny place, ringed by tall trees, that they'd passed year after year, coming and going, and it was here that Joy was buried. Then they took up their lives again, in the usual way, and to their friends in the South she seemed much the same—still walking about Winter Park in that young and buoyant way she had, still teaching, still with the same warmth and serenity. But she had become more vulnerable and wrote Anne, "Often you remind me of my mother—it is in your glance, and a certain way you have of listening. . . ." In many letters there was some reference to her mother, as though the death of the daughter had somehow made more poignant that earlier loss.

In January, Kay came to visit them in Winter Park, and afterward Louise wrote the children, "Yesterday Kay left, and do we miss her! While she was here she made a beautiful recording of the violin sonata with Mr. Carlo. She also brought a book of my old records, and my pupils can hear me for the first time. . . . Anne has a story in the *Journal* this month, but I wish I knew when her *great date* is! . . ." With this duplicate she enclosed another letter to Anne. "When is your date, darling?" she asked. Perhaps because of all that had happened, she was apprehensive about this birth. "Your afghan will go to you in a day or two," she wrote. "The wool is so beautiful, I love to handle it. . . . *When* is your date, darling? Have you a fine specialist doctor? I love you so much—*what* is your date?"

A telegram came unexpectedly, early in February, and they were so vulnerable, so close at this time to birth and death, that the effect was overwhelming. Anne had had twins—a boy and a girl. "When the telegram came," she wrote the children, "we hugged each other, and longed to be with you all to rejoice. We even wanted to open a bottle of champagne a friend had given us. But we couldn't drink a whole bottle, just us two!" And in a note to Anne at the hospital she wrote, "Oh, dear God, how many wonderful blessings we have had!" Was this an expression of pain as well as joy?

The Fortieth Anniversary photograph.

The next day she wrote again: "We long to hear more and have been sort of waiting for further news." But there was no "further news," for up in the hospital in Vermont the premature baby girl wasn't expected to live, and Anne, perhaps mistakenly, was afraid of alarming her parents, and so, for a while, told them nothing. Meanwhile they worried and wondered. "I can't stand this separation at such a time!" she wrote the children. And later, in a duplicate, she described those days of uneasiness and suspense. "Each time the telephone or doorbell rang," she wrote, "we would jump and look at each other. Neither of us would *acknowledge* to the other that we were worried. But each knew the other was. We called Western Union often, telling them we were sure they had a telegram for us. We searched the papers every day, for an announcement of the twins' birth. But we found nothing, and that seemed very strange."

"On Friday," she wrote them, "we wired Anne again. On Saturday morning I ran to the telephone several times, but it was not a telegram. And then finally it *was* a telegram. And *such* good news: 'After slow start, both babies are fine. . . .' Of course we remember vividly," she wrote, "as though it was yesterday, how we worried about our own Anne, who was so tiny when she was born. The boy is named William Beatty, for my father. I am very proud and pleased, and I love the name 'Billy' too. I wonder what nickname Jono will give wee Anne?" On and on this letter went, for now she was unburdening herself after those days of unacknowledged dread, and reliving, as well, memories of the past.

It was February, not too early to start planning their summer, and now she knew what she wanted to do. They would rent a house in Vermont, near Anne, have Joy's baby daughter to stay with them, Kay and her family might rent a house nearby, the others would be close enough for family reunions . . . and all this revolved about the newborn twins, whose coming had somehow lighted up the past and created a future. "I love children, but I seem to adore babies," she wrote Anne, remembering, perhaps, that season at the Metropolitan that had been so mixed in with the unfolding drama at home. Or she may have been recalling that hectic year when she had written him at the sanitarium, "I

drew the twinnies a pig with my eyes closed and they were convulsed! It makes me sad that I can be with them so seldom. . . ."
It seemed, indeed, that there had never been quite time enough
when she was singing, and now her letters were full of plans.
"How I would love to help you with the babies," she wrote Anne.
"There is no bigger job in the world, I do believe. Did Jono get
the two baby books I sent? It is his clerical and loving duty to
keep their reports. Isn't it fun to think of us having a house *near*
you! Oh, I am determined to see a lot of those twinnies!"

But she never did see the twins.

It was late in March that the illness started—a heart attack,
though not a major one, and at first it was believed that a few
weeks of rest would effect a recovery. Meanwhile the letters from
Winter Park stopped coming—the summer plans, left stranded
in midair, taking on the distant shimmer of a mirage. They had
a doctor they were devoted to—a slender, capable, sensitive
young woman who for years had come quickly, at all hours of the
day or night, whenever they called her. Sidney was quite old,
now, eighty-three, frail, at times apprehensive, and she understood this, and knew how to reassure him. But this time there
could be no reassurance, for it seemed that something inexorable
had taken over, and the strong heart, which had been beating so
steadily for so long, was weakening with astonishing rapidity.

Before she became ill they had been looking for a home to
buy in Winter Park, and had found one they liked on Welbourne
Avenue—a small house, near enough so she could walk to town,
since she so loved walking, and all on one floor, which they both
preferred. They'd been especially happy with the comfortable
front porch and all the flowering bushes in the yard, and now
he made the decision, bought the house and took her there in an
ambulance. In this new and final home they settled her in her
room, with a hospital bed, day and night nurses and an oxygen
tank.

A heart specialist came, and then another. And the children
came, two or three at a time, until they were all there in the
unfamiliar room. They'd been told that if they all came at once
to Winter Park it might alarm their mother, but she was already
too far away on that mysterious journey to be alarmed by any-

thing. At first, almost inaudibly, she whispered their names. But during the night that followed, and the next day and the next night, she moved further and further away. She was in an oxygen tent, sleeping quietly—behind the filmy curtains she seemed remote, and no words could ever describe how beautiful she looked. Seldom is there such serenity in any face—such a look of spiritual calm, such peaceful, almost radiant quietness. Years before they had said of her father, "So quiet was his passage through death that they who watched thought him dead when sleeping, and sleeping when he died." And this time it was that way, too.

When they told him she was dead he wept, but really he was very strong. Within a day or two he was talking to the children about their mother, and even playing her records on the Victrola. It can be heartbreaking to hear the voice of someone who has died, but he listened to her singing the songs he had written, relived the memories and didn't turn away from her death or his grief. In 1916 he had written a song to words by Robert Bridges: "When death to either shall come, I pray it be first to me . . ." And now, when they told him she was dead, he wept, and exclaimed over and over, "I never dreamed she would go first!"

They had a simple service at home, and a memorial service at the Rollins College chapel. There many of her favorite hymns were sung—"Oh, Rest in the Lord," "A Mighty Fortress Is Our God," his "Sheep and Lambs" and "Requiem." She died on May 6, 1947, and afterward many editorials were written about her. In *The New York Times* they said that she had been "a shining figure in the Golden Age of Opera," and that her "Metropolitan career was the longest of any woman in the history of the theatre." They said that she was "a glowing personality and a great artist," that she was "one of the most beloved singers of her generation," and many wrote of experiencing "a great sense of personal loss." In the summer, when she was buried in the cemetery near Homeland, it was the kind of Lake George day she'd always loved, with sunlit clouds racing across the sky, and on the mountains shifting patterns of light and shade.

For several months that summer he lived with Kay, and during that interval he talked about the past. Over and over he described the events they had shared and the decisions they had made, recalling, especially, the small details—the dresses she had worn, the open fires in the rue de Lubeck, the evening strolls in the Trocadero Park. Then there was the gown she had worn for the audition with Lady de Grey . . . her first Paris gown, very chic, with, of course, a rose pinned in the glossy dark hair, and the voice startling everyone, so radiant, so artless, and how casual, how offhand she had been, saying blithely that she could sing in German and Italian, when, in fact, she never had. . . . And how the people in Angers had loved her! . . . On and on it went, this recreation of the past, and though Kay had a house full of children, she and her psychologist husband, Douglas Fryer, would drop everything to listen to an outpouring of memories that might, in time, knit the past with the present, and so achieve that subtle inward orientation so essential for the one who is grieving. He had other allies, too, in this fight against overwhelming loss—an unusual generosity of spirit that made him hesitate to sadden others, and an abiding interest in many aspects of life and living.

However, there was still the matter of a way of life, for he believed he must spend most of the year in the South. The favorable climate there had made him fearful of the northern winters, and more than ever susceptible to the snow and cold, so in the fall he returned to Winter Park. There the maid they'd had for many years came every day to cook and clean, but for someone who was so old and nearly blind, that wasn't enough. He needed protection at night, someone to be there most of the time, and finally, with the help of his devoted doctor, a way was found.

It seemed that during that final illness there'd been a nurse, Miss Julia Sullivan, who had come day after day for many weeks, and when she was not on duty, during that last long sleep, had knelt beside the bed in silent prayer. Miss Sullivan was a very gentle lady, quiet, kind, intuitive. Recently she had retired from nursing, and took only occasional cases to meet her small expenses. So now it was arranged that she would come to live in the house on Welbourne Avenue, and be there, an experienced trained nurse, to watch over his welfare and his precarious health.

Meanwhile he was trying to evolve a routine, and wrote Anne,

"Most of my mornings are taken up—Sallie Crane, reading, Tuesdays and Fridays, Helen Moore, piano, eleven to one Wednesdays and Sundays, Manley Duckworth, piano, Mondays. . . . I have many calls from friends nearly my age, and from young singers in the teen age, and I get along beautifully with both groups, one so wise, and the other so joyously unwise! . . ." He had begun going about, and in November attended a "first night" performance at the Annie Russell Theatre. And afterward, for the children, it seemed strange to see his picture in the paper, taken during an intermission, with Hamilton Holt and one or two friends—standing there in the glare of the flashbulbs, tall, white-haired, nearly blind, and now no hand tucked confidently under his arm, no radiant smiling wife at his side.

But his letters reflected a valiant spirit. "I have just heard a late quartet of Beethoven over the air," he wrote Anne, "and I am sure he lived in a world of continuous surprises, self-created, always expecting the unexpected. A world of inexhaustible riches. . . . Do you remember a letter you wrote Mother and me, years ago when you were in college, in which you described your sudden conviction of a future life? You will be surprised to know how much it helps me now. At regular intervals it comes back to me. It would help many people could they hear it. . . ."

There were new friends as well as old ones in Winter Park. Young singers came to him for advice; musicians came for help with their interpretations and their programs. He was frail and had to grope his way about the house. But his voice was strong, his handwriting firm, his interest unfailing. And when they came he talked to them about "the inexhaustible riches of the world."

In the summers he made the trip north to visit the children. "Tell those heavenly twins," he wrote, "that I think of them just as they were when I saw them, and will continue to do so until I see them again, and then won't I be surprised!" In 1949, when he was staying with Sidney Jr. in New York, a friend brought Albert Schweitzer to see him. And for more than two hours they sat together, in a bay window overlooking Gramercy Park, engaged in an island of conversation. There was a community of interest between these two, and a certain resemblance, as well, something about the sensitive contours of the forehead, the plain

ruggedness of the features, the heavy mane of hair. And to the
others in the room, since their voices had to be raised because
of his hearing, that conversation made an absorbing counterpoint
of music and justice.

But the increasing deafness was gradually depriving him of
one of the great consolations of his life. "I don't listen to music
critically any more," he wrote Sam Barber, "as I miss so many
notes! In familiar compositions I often have to supply the high
notes carrying the melody." However, in 1951, after a radio
performance of Sam's latest symphony, he wrote, "I have been
through a wringer! I am still hearing that tremendous downward
final passage, enough to break your heart; and asking myself:
Who am I? I wonder if I will ever know this work of yours inti-
mately, so I can grasp all the subtleties. . . ."

Finally he became too frail to make the trip north, and the
children came often to Winter Park to visit. Miss Sullivan was
still there, as companion and protector, and many friends were
living nearby. Samuel Barber also came to Winter Park, and
after one of these trips he wrote Sam, "We are still in the halo
of your visit. If it meant as much to you as it did to me you must
come often. Remember me to Toscanini, and tell him eighty-
seven is even better than eighty-five!" In this letter he also discussed what he called "a magnificent conception"—Truman's
Point Four Program. "A brave new world, what I call a 'giving
world' is opening up," he wrote. "I wish I could live another
fifty years and see the beauty that is going to unfold."

In the fall of 1952, when he was almost eighty-seven, he began
the task of revising all his music, working with the fine pianist
and musicologist Phyllis Sias. Twelve years before, when they
had first moved to St. Augustine, Phyllis had come to them as an
accompanist for the teaching. She had moved with them to Winter Park, and there, after a time, had married and raised a family.
But she had remained a close friend, and now she arranged to
help him revise his music. Particularly he was concerned about
the scoring of the dynamics and the tempi, for while working
with the singing pupils he had come to realize that the Italian
markings—*Andante, Allegro, Lento* and others—were open to
too many interpretations. The results were often unpredictable,

increasingly this troubled him, and he had decided, finally, that metronome markings would be more reliable.

But the substitution of metronome markings was a formidable task, for no changes could be made until each song or composition had been studied with the most meticulous precision. Phyllis came to work with him two days a week—on Tuesdays and Fridays—and together they reviewed all the songs, the dynamics, the rests and phrasing, the tempi, then made the necessary corrections and revisions. The process required subtlety and concentration, on his part and hers, too, for the melodies had to be translated reflectively, into the medium of the voice, and when they studied the quartet Phyllis had to improvise on the piano a quartet score in three clefs, while he, listening intently, heard, as well, the vibrant tones of the violins and the cello.

The technique was so exacting that the corrections took a long time. All through the winter and spring they worked, and into the summer. But finally, one day early in July, their task was completed. Every song and every composition had been played many times, analyzed and corrected. As Phyllis was leaving that day he said to her, as usual, "I'll see you on Tuesday!" And as usual she replied, "Yes, indeed, Dr. Homer!" But to herself she thought, "What will we do on Tuesday? Our work is finished!"

Everything was now in order, all his work was done, and before Tuesday came he had died in his sleep.

In a sense, then, it was over, the libretto played to the end, the music stilled, the footlights dimmed, the curtain finally down. Quietly they had left the stage, but for the audience, plunging back into the streets, there were still echoes of that contralto voice. And in his autobiography the manager, Gatti-Casazza, would write with a certain wonder of Louise Homer in *Orfeo e Euridice*—the sets "exquisite and full of poetry," the opera "a succession of miracles . . . a production that no one who saw or heard it can ever forget."

Notes

1. A *Biographical Sketch* of Will Beatty, published in 1882, notes the following:

"William Trimble Beatty was born June 1, 1834, near Rushville, in Fairfield County, Ohio, his parents being American born, of Scotch-Irish extraction. In 1851, while he was a student, at the age of 17, in the Mt. Pleasant Academy, in Kingston, Ohio, he united with the Presbyterian Church at the close of a series of revival meetings. At this date his preference was to enter the profession of law, and with this in mind he completed the classical course, and graduated at the Miami University, Ohio. But he soon came to feel it to be his duty to enter the ministry, and in pursuance of this conviction he studied theology one year at Danville, Kentucky, under Rev. Dr. Robert J. Breckenridge. He then taught school for nearly a year in Rushville, Ohio, and after that spent some time in active business in Missouri, dealing in Real Estate and Land Grants. While thus engaged his unusual ability as speaker, writer and thinker came to the attention of a leading clergyman, who persuaded Mr. Beatty to resume his theological studies, and in the year 1858 he went to Allegheny, Pa., where he completed his theological course in that city. In April 1859 he was ordained as a minister of the Presbyterian church at Zanesville, Ohio. He then supplied the pulpit of the Fourth Presbyterian Church, in Pittsburgh, Penn., for several months during the illness of the pastor, the Rev. Samuel Fulton, and in December, 1860, was called to the pastorate of the church at Greencastle, Penn., where he served for several years. In 1863 he received a very urgent call to the First Presbyterian Church at New Brunswick, New Jersey. In

June 1867 he was invited to become pastor of the Shadyside Presbyterian Church at Pittsburgh. While there he received the degree of doctor of divinity from the Western University at Pittsburgh, and took the very highest rank among clergymen of his denomination."

2. In the first *Historical Sketch* of the Shadyside church it is reported that in 1869, when he'd been their pastor just two years, Will Beatty, who "believed fervently" in educational opportunities for women, "initiated some informal agitation," and a meeting was held at the home of David Aiken on February 23rd. As a result of this, "the pastor was authorized to promise $20,000. towards the purchase of ground and the erection of a building suitable for such a purpose. This offer was promptly responded to by others, and such efforts put forth as to have resulted in the founding of the Pennsylvania Female College."

Unlike many women's colleges which began as seminaries, Pennsylvania Female College was from the first a full-fledged college, offering a varied curriculum with emphasis on classical training. In 1890 the name was changed to Pennsylvania College for Women, and in 1955 to Chatham College. Today Chatham College has an enrollment of over six hundred, and more than forty buildings (one of them Beatty Hall).

3. Auntie Fulton was the daughter of Elisha Macurdy, a missionary to the Indians and a noted preacher who had traveled throughout the East, holding revival meetings. She had been christened Sarah Colwell Macurdy, and when she married the young Presbyterian minister Samuel Fulton she was carrying on a family tradition, for in the immediate family, on both sides, among Colwells, Fultons and Macurdys, there were as many as twenty Presbyterian ministers.

Sarah and Samuel Fulton had no children of their own. But when Samuel Fulton's brother and his wife died in an epidemic, leaving five young children, they had taken four of them into their home —Robert, Elisha, Samuel and Sarah. (Elizabeth had gone to live with another uncle, John Irvine, who had steel mills in Pittsburgh.)

Samuel Fulton had been for many years pastor of the Fourth Presbyterian Church in Pittsburgh. But when his health had begun to fail, and the demands of a big city church had been too taxing, he'd moved to the country and become pastor of the Chester Valley Presbyterian Church. It was while he was in Pittsburgh that young Will Beatty had come from Ohio to supply the pulpit, met his niece, Sarah Fulton, then not quite twenty, and married her.

4. While he was in Europe Will Beatty tried to trace his family ancestry, and described his discoveries in a letter to a cousin. His mother was a Trimble, and in Scotland he'd been given an explanation of the name. "It seems," he wrote, "that the name of Turnbull from which Trimble originates, was given to one William Rule, who in 1296, saved the life of King Bruce by a gallant exploit. While hunting, the king was attacked and unhorsed by a wild bull, but was saved from death by this William Rule, who threw himself between the King and wild animal, seized it by the horns, overturned and killed it. Ever afterwards he was known as 'William Turnbull.'

"In north Ireland," he wrote, "I found the country full of Beattys, and was introduced to a clergyman by name of John Beatty, who is convinced that our grandfathers were either brothers or cousins. The old house and farm are in the parish of Anahilt, three miles from Hillsborough. . . . The Beatty tribe is worth finding out in the old country. They are all very decent people."

5. From a *Memorial of Rev. William T. Beatty, D.D.*, published by Johnson, Smith & Harrison, Minneapolis, Minnesota, in 1882.

6. In a recent history of the Shadyside church it is noted that "underground seepage of water from springs in the hillside to the South had caused serious damage to the fabric so that some of the walls and the tower had become unsafe. On April 8th, 1888, those who came to worship found the church closed. On the door they read: '*Notice,* Services in the Chapel. This building *unsafe.*' "

7. Mr. Grau and the Southern Pacific Company compiled a little booklet about the "Grand Opera Tour," complete with map, repertoire, itinerary, scenic pictures and an impressive photograph of the manager himself.

Here the train is described as "A Special Pullman Palace Car Train, with Dining Car, which makes the entire journey, New York to San Francisco and return . . . producing Grand Opera at enormous expense.

"Equipment of *Special Train*
Five Standard Pullman Sleeping Cars.
One Private Car 'Grasmere.'
One Dining Car.
Two Pullman Tourist Cars.
Eight Baggage Cars, containing complete scenery, costumes, properties, armor, electrical effects, and other paraphernalia, as used at the Metropolitan Opera House."

In the small brochure it is noted that "Mr. Maurice Grau has devoted many months, carefully selecting in Europe all the most famous artists that could be secured . . . and it is simple justice to say that never before in the history of Opera in the United States have so many of the world's greatest singers figured in one company."

It is also noted that "such an enormous operatic enterprise has never before been undertaken in America, and it is easy to believe that nowhere else has there been an impresario so bold and courageous as to gather together an aggregation of this size and expense. It is the very apotheosis of the star system."

8. From *Such Sweet Compulsion, The Autobiography of Geraldine Farrar,* published by Greystone Press in 1938.

9. Heinrich Conried died just a year later in the Austrian Tyrol, on April 27, 1909. Louise Homer was one of those who sang at his impressive funeral, which was held on the stage of the Metropolitan in an almost Wagnerian setting, with a catafalque seven feet high, tall, tapered candles and thousands of yards of black crepe draping the proscenium arch.

10. From *Some Memories and Reflections* by Emma Eames, published by D. Appleton and Company in 1927.

11. A portrait in this Orpheus costume, painted by Leopold Seiffert, is hanging now in the reception rooms of the Metropolitan Opera House.

12. From *Too Strong for Fantasy* by Marcia Davenport, published by Charles Scribner's Sons in 1967.

13. The great baritone Charles Gilibert died of a brain tumor at the start of the 1910–11 season, just three days after arriving from London to join the Metropolitan. On January 25, 1911, the Metropolitan artists gave a memorial concert in his honor, and raised almost twenty thousand dollars for the benefit of Gilibert's family. This concert precipitated a fashion dilemma, for in Paris, the previous spring, Louise and Emmy Destinn had both patronized the famous couturier Agnes, who had unwittingly, or at least most carelessly, sold them identical evening gowns. So when Emmy Destinn arrived at the opera house to sing an aria from *Tosca* at the Gilibert concert, she was dismayed to find Louise Homer already on the stage, singing

"Mon Coeur" from *Dalila* and wearing an identical creation of satin and lace and Parisienne elegance—a concert gown that was an exact duplicate of her own. She was so upset by this mischance that she sent her maid hurriedly back to her suite at the Ansonia Hotel for another costume, and later told the reporters that she'd had just time to make a quick change before her turn on the program.

14. One of these performances of *Orfeo e Euridice* was followed by a *Ballet Divertissement,* starring the great ballerina Anna Pavlova.

15. In his letter to his twelve-year-old nephew, Sidney wrote: "Dear Sam—I am returning the *Gypsy Dance* and the *Mother Goose* which you sent me. There is no doubt but that you have the making of a composer in you. There are touches all through this work which prove it. Therefore, I think it would be fully worth your while to take an intensive course of study with the best man in Philadelphia."

He then went on to outline "three things you must aim for definitely." The first was to develop a taste for the best in music that would "amount to a passion." "The way to do this," he wrote, "is to look ahead and see what programs are to be given in Philadelphia. You can't attend all the concerts, therefore you pick the best. Suppose, for instance, the Flonzaley Quartet is going to play a Beethoven Quartet. You get your ticket and buy a copy of the Quartet and study it beforehand. You then learn more in an hour at the performance than you could possibly learn any other way in a year." The second was "a good teacher in composition." "One fairly long lesson a week would be sufficient," he wrote. "If you will write to Mr. Stokowski, himself, and use my name, I am sure he will recommend someone to you." The third was to "master a practical instrument." "I should say," he wrote, "either the piano or the violin, or, better still, both. That is what Mozart and Beethoven did. If you can't do all three of these things, I should take up the first and third. You must not think that you can fool with music and get anywhere. Sooner or later you will have to do hard work, and you will make much more rapid progress now than when you are older. You can get good books on Harmony and Musical Notation, and they will interest you. For instance, in your last Mother Goose song, *I Love Little Pussy,* you divide the right hand part into groups of 3/8 notes, which give the appearance of 6/8 time, but the piece is in 3/4 time. At the beginning of the third measure, you write B natural, whereas it is really C flat. Little mistakes like these sometimes spoil the looks of really good music. Affectionately yours, Sidney Homer."

Acknowledgments and Bibliography

The essential source material for this biography was preserved for many years by my twin sister, Katharine Homer Fryer. She studied, analyzed and collated a treasure of memorabilia—letters, scrapbooks, diaries, hundreds of clippings and mementos. Without her care and devotion the book never could have been written.

I am also grateful for the ambiance in which I worked, and would like to acknowledge especially that most sustaining of commitments—the generous, spirited acceptance of my involvement by my husband and children. Approval, warmhearted but without interference, can be a boon to a writer who, while toiling at the typewriter, may leave her household chores more or less in limbo, and I want to thank them all—Bill, Jono, Kathie, Billy, Anne and Tom. There were others, too, both family and friends, who encouraged me in this undertaking, and because their interest was benignly uninsistent, without any elements of pressure, the work was made much easier.

The unique scope and quality of the primary source material for this book might almost be considered a biographer's dream. Included are all the milestones and all the highlights, as well as a panorama of those casual incidentals that can bring the past so eloquently to life. Most important are almost a hundred pages of reminiscences that my mother wrote, addressed to my father, when he was working on his book, *My Wife and I*. These memories, extending from her childhood years in Shadyside to the first season at Covent Garden, were written many years later in a blithe, haphazard fashion, and such random thoughts are never too precise. But they provided a fabric to serve as a background for the great wealth of memorabilia—the diaries, letters, telegrams, notebooks, account books, press clippings, contracts, scores, programs, documents. Even the smallest scrap of paper was preserved if it had significance—the hasty note from Mr. Jones, the calling card from Mr. Bliss; the letter from Mr. Bonar about the first job, the letter from Mr. Gatti-Casazza about the last one. Rarely does a biographer have such a spectrum of material, without any gaps, any empty places, no need to imagine, no cause to wonder.

During the writing two reference books were indispensable. *Metro-*

politan Opera Annals, published in association with the Metropolitan Opera Guild, is a compilation of every season at the Metropolitan from 1883 to 1947. In this valuable guide the personnel is listed for each season, and every performance is recorded, with conductor and cast. Contemporary reviews of significant debuts and premiere performances are included. *Opera Caravan,* also sponsored by the Opera Guild, contains a compilation of all Metropolitan performances outside of New York City, while the company was on tour, and during the season, in Brooklyn, Philadelphia and other nearby cities, from 1883 to 1956.

Because the background and supplemental reading was too extensive to list in its entirety, a partial selection is included.

Selected Bibliography

Aldrich, Richard, *Concert Life in New York 1902–1923.* New York: Alfred A. Knopf, 1928.

Belfour, Stanton, *Centennial History of the Shadyside Presbyterian Church.* Pittsburgh, Pa., 1966.

Brockway, Wallace, and Weinstock, Herbert, *The World of Opera.* New York: Random House, 1941.

Caruso, Dorothy, *Enrico Caruso: His Life and Death.* New York: Simon and Schuster, 1945.

Casals, Pablo, and Kahn, Albert E., *Joys and Sorrows: Reflections by Pablo Casals* as told to Albert E. Kahn. New York: Simon and Schuster, 1970.

Dysart, Laberta, *Chatham College: The First Ninety Years.* Pittsburgh, Pa.: Chatham College, 1959.

Eames, Emma, *Some Memories and Reflections.* New York: D. Appleton and Company, 1927.

Eaton, Quaintance, *Opera Caravan: Adventures of the Metropolitan on Tour, 1883–1956.* Sponsored by the Metropolitan Opera Guild. New York: Farrar, Straus and Cudahy, 1957.

————, *The Miracle of the Met.* New York: Meredith Press, 1968.

Editors of *Opera News, The Golden Horseshoe, The Life and Times of the Metropolitan Opera House.* New York: The Viking Press, Inc., 1965.

Farrar, Geraldine, *Such Sweet Compulsion: The Autobiography of Geraldine Farrar.* New York: The Greystone Press, 1938.

Garden, Mary, and Biancolli, Louis, *Mary Garden's Story.* New York: Simon and Schuster, 1951.

Gatti-Casazza, Giulio, *Memories of the Opera*. New York: Scribner's, 1941.

Heinsheimer, Hans W., *Best Regards to Aida*. New York: Alfred A. Knopf, 1968.

Homer, Sidney, *My Wife and I: The Story of Louise and Sidney Homer*. New York: The Macmillan Company, 1939.

Krehbiel, Henry Edward, *Chapters of Opera*. New York: Henry Holt and Company, 1908.

——, *More Chapters of Opera*. New York: Henry Holt and Company, 1919.

——, *A Book of Operas*. New York: The Macmillan Company, 1919.

Moorhead, Elizabeth, *These Two Were Here: Louise Homer and Willa Cather*. Pittsburgh, Pa.: University of Pittsburgh Press, 1950.

Newman, Ernest, *Stories of the Great Operas and Their Composers*. New York: Alfred A. Knopf, 1928.

Ordway, Edith B., *The Opera Book*. New York: Sully and Kleinteich, 1915.

Peltz, Mary Ellis, and Lawrence, Robert, *The Metropolitan Opera Guide*. New York: The Modern Library, 1939.

Seltsam, William H., *Metropolitan Opera Annals: A Chronicle of Artists and Performances*. New York: The H. W. Wilson Company, in association with The Metropolitan Opera Guild, Inc., 1947.

Stokowski, Olga Samaroff, *An American Musician's Story*. New York: W. W. Norton and Company, 1939.

Taubman, Howard, *The Maestro—The Life of Arturo Toscanini*. New York: Simon and Schuster, 1951.

Tharp, Louise Hall, *Saint-Gaudens and the Gilded Era*. Boston: Little, Brown and Company, 1969.

Thomas, Gordon, and Witts, Max Morgan, *The San Francisco Earthquake*. New York: Stein and Day, 1971.

Victor Talking Machine Co., *The Victor Book of the Opera*. Camden, N.J., 1912.

——, *The Victor Book of the Opera,* thirteenth edition, revised by Henry W. Simon. New York: Simon and Schuster, 1968.

Wechsberg, Joseph, *Red Plush and Black Velvet: The Story of Melba and Her Times*. Boston: Little, Brown and Company, 1961.

Index